NEW DESIRES, NEW SELVES

New Desires, New Selves

Sex, Love, and Piety among Turkish Youth

Gul Ozyegin

NEW YORK UNIVERSITY PRESS

New York and London

NEW YORK UNIVERSITY PRESS
New York and London
www.nyupress.org

References to Internet websites (URLs) were accurate at the time of writing. Neither the author nor New York University Press is responsible for URLs that may have expired or changed since the manuscript was prepared.

Library of Congress Cataloging-in-Publication Data
Ozyegin, Gul, 1955–
New desires, new selves : sex, love, and piety among Turkish youth / Gul Ozyegin.
pages cm   Includes bibliographical references and index.
ISBN 978-0-8147-6234-9 (cl : alk. paper) — ISBN 978-1-4798-5381-6 (pb : alk. paper)
1.Youth—Turkey—Social conditions. 2. Youth—Sexual behavior—Turkey.
3. Youth—Religious life—Turkey. I. Title.
HQ799.T9099   2015
305.23509561—dc23   2015007383

New York University Press books are printed on acid-free paper, and their binding materials are chosen for strength and durability. We strive to use environmentally responsible suppliers and materials to the greatest extent possible in publishing our books.

Manufactured in the United States of America

10 9 8 7 6 5 4 3 2 1

Also available as an ebook

To those brave parents in Turkey who lovingly embrace their offsprings' nonpatriarchal desires and struggles to enact new gender and sexual identities.

CONTENTS

ACKNOWLEDGMENTS

I most wish to acknowledge the anonymous subjects of this book, whose narratives, perspectives, conduct, and intimate experiences appear in these pages. Without them this book simply could not have been written. My profound thanks go to them for the trust, generous cooperation, and openness with which they accepted my inquiries. I tried to treat their stories with the utmost care and respect, as they deserve, but the retelling, with all the caveats that framing, selection, and interpretation entail, is mine.

I thank the Netherlands Institute for Advanced Studies in Humanities and Social Sciences for a fellowship during the academic year 2006–2007, which provided freedom to develop and work on the book. The research and the book were also supported by two research leaves from Arts and Sciences at the College of William and Mary. I wish to thank *Social Identities* and the *European Journal of Women's Studies* for their permission to publish in revised and expanded form portions of the articles "Reading the Closet through Connectivity" (*Social Identities* 8.2: 20–22) and "Virginal Façades: Sexual Freedom and Guilt among Young Turkish Women" (*European Journal of Women's Studies* 16.2: 103–23).

Many people in Istanbul, too numerous to name, contributed to the research for this book. Especially, I want to thank those colleagues and friends who often went beyond the call of friendship in supporting my work and providing such a stimulating environment in which to conduct research: Ferhunde Özbay and Nükhet Sirman and, above all, my research assistants—Cenk Özbay, Arzu Ünal, and Umut Sarı, who were of invaluable help in providing research assistance and reshaping the research design with their critical feedback. My former students Erin Caro and Laura Grandy at the College of William and Mary gave me research and editing assistance at different stages. My special thanks to them and to the following friends, mentors, and colleagues for reading the earlier drafts of the chapters and offering excellent, thoughtful suggestions for improvement: Kathy Davis, Helma Lutz on chapter 1, Sherri Grasmuck, Kay Jenkins, Magali Larson, Dee Royster and Ayşe Saktanber on chapter 3, and Pierrette Hondagneu-Sotelo on chapter 4. I am also grateful to Ilene Kalish, who offered unwavering support for this project from the beginning. My deep appreciation goes to Aslı Saktanber, the talented illustrator of the book cover, who has not read the book yet, but perfectly understood the gist of it to create a remarkable original artwork.

My close friends Nancy Gray and Sibel Zandi-Sayek, scholars in divergent fields, always engagingly listened to me and asked good questions throughout the process. I give thanks to them and to Ayşe Saktanber for lending passionate support and reminding me that what I was writing about was important and worthwhile. One friend and sister book writer in particular, Carla Freeman, came into my life thirty years ago and has been inspiring me ever since. Our deep friendship and intellectual companionship continues to delight me. Our intensive engagement with one another's work has created a less lonely context that has nurtured this book in important ways. With her discerning questions she helped me enormously to sharpen my ideas and pointed out what needed further elucidation. I am immeasurably grateful to Carla.

I have been writing this book, in one way or another, for a long time during which both the Turkish and American sides of my family grew. Thanks to the Weber clan, John, Joe, Kim, and Bobbi, I have four wonderful grandkids: Evelyn, Evan, Zack, and Kaleb. My nephews in Turkey—Paydaş, Yeliz, Mert, and Özge—gave me the gift of becoming a great-aunt to lovely Efe, Ada, and Bade. They all add great joy to my life. My family in Turkey has provided a central emotional underpinning to this project. I am grateful beyond measure for my sisters, Oya Özdağ, Yasemin Erbil, and Fatoş Mersin, for their example of female strength, connectivity, and compassion. I thank them for their unconditional love, endless nurturance and encouragement, and their pride in me. My brother, Murat Bozdemir, and my brothers-in-law, Celal Erbil and Selahattin Mersin, have been true loving supporters. I thank them and my nephews, Paydaş Mersin, Mert Özdağ, Ender Mersin, and Ulaş Bozdemir, for the optimism they inspire in me that women and girls in Turkey are not alone in their fight against patriarchy.

I owe special thanks to John Weber, who, besides sharing my love for my home country and its people, supported me in emotional and practical ways. He made frequent appearances in my home office to deliver caffeine intake and fruit plates and provided many other forms of infrastructural help that he called "butlering." I am glad that long hours in my "writing cave" in the pursuit of my passion provided ample distractions for him to pursue his own passion of golf more intensely.

Finally, this book would have been radically different without the meticulous editing of Elizabeth Ferris, my former student, who through her sensitive inquiries challenged me to make the book more readable. I deeply thank her for her brilliant and close intellectual companionship.

Introduction

During the last three decades, dramatic social and political changes in Turkey have introduced historical shifts in national, religious, and gender and sexual identities. The transformation from state-controlled capitalism to a privatized and liberalized market economy within the context of Islamization, neoliberal globalization, and Turkey's bid to join the European Union has altered the ways in which personal and collective identities are defined. These changes are perhaps most pronounced among young people. *New Desires, New Selves* examines the constitution of gender and sexual identities among upwardly mobile young adults born amid the societal changes of the 1980s. It links individual biographies with the "biography" of a nation, elaborating their interconnections in the creation of new selves in a country that has existed uneasily between West and East, modern and traditional, secular and Islamic.

At present, the driving force behind most projects of neoliberal globalization in virtually every country, including Europe and the United States, is the production of the presupposed neoliberal subject centered on the ideals of entrepreneurial freedom, self-invention, autonomy, and self-realization (Bourdieu 1998; Harvey 2005). The complex social, psychological, and material processes that collectively help form the neoliberal subject now occupy the research agendas of a growing number of scholars. In that framework, this book offers the voices of eighty-seven young Turks who represent diverse paths of social mobility and identity making. More than any prior generation in Turkish society, these educationally advantaged youth (between eighteen and twenty-four years old) see themselves as individuals with the ability to create and enact their own identities and relationships. They are not only intensely subjected to neoliberal images, ideologies, and institutions but also have the ability to appropriate, reject, or reshape the ethos of neoliberalism in many contexts. However, *New Desires, New Selves* also complicates the challenges of this theoretical moment. By shedding light on the intimate and complex—and at times contradictory—processes by which the neoliberal subject is produced, this book suggests that the apparent inevitability of neoliberal subjectivity, and indeed its global ubiquity, should not blind us to historicity and cultural specificity and its roots in social as well as gender and sexual relations.

Over the last two decades, virtually every debate on neoliberal globalization has centered on the same core question: Is neoliberal globalization, with its power to breach culturally specific sources of identity boundaries, securing global homogeneity or creating a world of hybridized/fused identities? The most recent literature on globalization has acknowledged and used rich empirical research to evidence how, in many different cultural contexts, globalization is actively constructed rather than passively received. As Carla Freeman (2010) has suggested, because "globalization itself is imbricated within cultural forms and meanings," we should examine how the global operates "in and through the stickiness and particularities of culture" rather than viewing globalization as a singular and homogenizing force that "operates outside the fabric of culture" (578). Conceptualizations such as Freeman's also invite us to historicize our studies of the local while paying attention to both the continuities of cultural ideas and the ruptures caused by globalization, urging us to see the deep structures of culture as capable of containing and exhibiting contradictions.

A pivotal cultural particularity in the production of the self in Turkey can be found in the notion of connectivity. Building on Suad Joseph's (1993, 1994, 1999) notion of connectivity—a model of selfhood rooted in fluidity that serves as an alternative to the (Western) model of the autonomous, bounded self—I argue that this cultural specificity assumes a special potency in Turkey. This setting supports the production of selves "who invite, require and initiate involvement with others in the shaping of the self" (Joseph 1993, 468). This paradigm of identity formation suggests that connective persons "[come] to see [themselves] as part of another" so concretely that their sense of completion and "security, identity, integrity, dignity, and self-worth . . . [are] tied to the actions of [that person]" (Joseph 1994, 55).

While connectivity does not exclude the possibility that individuals understand themselves through the language of autonomy, it is the connective self that is most desired. In societies such as Turkey, the key component of selfhood is a relational experience with members of one's family. How can we understand the formation of the neoliberal subject, who understands himself or herself on individual terms and as capable of and responsible for self-invention, in relation to this paradigm of the production of relational selves? Examination of this fundamental question through the critical lenses of gender and sexuality lies at the heart of *New Desires, New Selves*. I historicize my study of the national while paying attention to the specific social structural conditions and psychodynamic processes that continue to (re)cultivate connectivity, especially in view of the ruptures caused by Islamization and neoliberal globalization in Turkey. *New Desires, New Selves* thus invites unique readings of the production of neoliberal selves in a deeply patriarchal and paternalistic society.

At the center of this book lies an exploration of a "fractured desire." Young Turks on the path toward upward mobility embody and hold profound tension—a fractured desire. On the one hand, there is the desire to surrender to the seduction of sexual modernity, to renounce the normative model of selfless femininity and protective masculinity, and to reject power and authority located external to the individual. On the other hand, there is the longing to remain loyal and organically connected to social relations, identities, and histories that underwrite the construction of identity through connectivity. The young men and women of this book experience these contradictions in different ways, depending on gender- and class-based affiliations of privilege and vulnerability as well as provincial and urban origins. This book foregrounds this central tension in the particular biographies of young women and men with different class, religious, and sexual-orientation identifications. Through their narratives, I examine the specific ways this tension is expressed, escaped, problematized, and resolved.

Positioned within the backdrop of larger national and global transformations, the narratives of these young women and men constitute a uniquely rich site for complicating our theorization of the self and its relations to others and society. Narratives of romance and sex serve as the primary source for this book. I view this realm as a primary context within which new ideals of love and management of emotion, affect, and sexual desire are negotiated and tested. Young men and women making a place and identity for themselves participate in sexual communication and the market of "free emotions" (Luhmann 1986), where they orient, form, and manage their emotions, bodies, and desires and relate to others and themselves.

It is within the physical and discursive spaces of romance and sex that neoliberal subjectivity is actively cultivated, advanced, validated, or rejected. But it is not sexual selves alone that are in the process of being made, for the domain of romance and sexuality is also a space in which class aspirations are disciplined and regulated. These are the grounds upon which new gendered class aspirations operate, as a means of measuring, monitoring, and signaling one's social position to others and of differentiating and marking masculine and feminine identities. This domain and the relationships within it, often experienced as a realm of uncertainty and a source of anxiety, paradoxically offer a clear lens through which we can understand the forging of neoliberal selfhood and its intimate connections to gender, sexuality, and class. Within a societal context of rising neoliberal demands of self-regulation and realization, we see a shift in emphasis from external social controls to self-control.

I explore these theoretical questions empirically through the narratives of eighty-seven upwardly mobile young adults interviewed between 2002 and 2006 in Istanbul. Although they all share a strong sense of distinction through educational success, the young women and men in this book represent the most salient differences among this generation of upwardly mobile youth. They include those with provincial backgrounds who were raised in the sexually repressive rural communities of Anatolia as well as those who grew up in Istanbul and other metropolitan cities. They are also a diverse group along class lines. Class origin—along with religious devotion and sexual orientation—is a critical lens on gender and sexual transformation. In this book, I highlight both differences and commonality in order to escape the confines of a universalized understanding of neoliberal personhood.

I recruited my study's participants from Boğaziçi University in Istanbul. Established in 1863 as an American college, Boğaziçi University is one of the most prestigious public universities in Turkey, with the most rigorous admissions requirements. An elite institution, it offers its students an avenue for upward social and economic mobility but also brings together students with vastly different biographies. In addition to in-depth interviews, three other sources of field data—a representative survey, participant observation, and focus group research—form the empirical foundation of this study. Between September 2002 and June 2003, I surveyed a representative sample of 360 students and conducted five focus group discussions.

This book is about multiple façades in the pursuit of new desires, the way façades enter the process of self-making at crucial moments of liminality, and the moments of their creation and assembly. The concept of façades suggests convergences: they can be a form of deception, a barrier, a form of protection, and a liberating means by which to claim a new/different self/identity. The conjuncture of façades occurs in different domains: when secular young women forsake virgin identities but put on ambiguous identities; when pious women are compelled to enter the university with secular appearances, masquerading as secularly Muslim; when gay men's same-sex desires become "open secrets" but they remain "secret subjects"; and when young heterosexual men carry the outward signs of escape from patriarchal constructions of masculinity as controlling and dominant while exercising gender domination. One of the key arguments of this book is that investing in façades is a collaborative and collective act; not only the subjects of this book but also previous generations and institutions are invested in it. As a theoretical construct, the façade's capacity to elucidate lies in its illumination of the lived contradictions at the intersections/breaches that are opened between long-term cultural legacies and demands and individual desires in a complex and increasingly pluralistic society. This conception of façades is thus a common thread across the different chapters. In each chapter, façade articulates the challenges of constructing new selves. Façades provide resistance, and repudiation, and can offer access to feelings, identities, and experiences whose pursuits give individuals agency. They also permit enactments of rituals of conformity, connectivity, and continuity. Through façades, denied and prohibited desires are brought within the realm of the knowable and may be realized. Individuals are allowed to find pleasures even as the collective fiction of a prohibitive gender and sexual order is preserved, and the boundaries of permitted and prohibited are reiterated while simultaneously redrawn in the creation of a new gender and sexual order.

The four subgroups (heterosexually identified women, heterosexually identified men, pious women, and gay-identified men) who are subjects of the substantive chapters are embedded in a range of personal and familial histories and are located in—and speak from—different and overlapping experiences, each bringing different analytical dimensions to the book as well as serving as interacting frames. I should note that two other important subgroups are not covered in this book: pious young men (who refused to be interviewed due to my topic) and lesbians, except Alev, whose story forms one of the vignettes. (I interviewed six lesbians, but my interview tapes with four of them were damaged beyond repair while going through airport security.) A unique feature of *New Desires, New Selves* is the presentation of four vignettes offering biographical particularities, accompanying and enhancing the four chapters of the book. These short sections feature a young lesbian feminist who voices her self-transformation from an adolescent self "carrying a man's soul stranded in a woman's body" to a lesbian self as well as a key shift in her object of same-sex desire from a figure of the flamboyant femme to a figure of androgyny; a young man from a rural background who expresses an underrepresented class subjectivity by rejecting the exclusivity of urban middle-classness; a pious woman who possesses double cultural capital through her Islamic and secular education and contests the sanctioned boundary between private religion and public secularism; and a group interview with three gay men who transgress both the mainstream and the Western ways of imagining homosexual identity. In presenting these biographies, my aim is to reemphasize the emergence of a plurality of assertive self-definitions and their contradictory meanings and effects in a Muslim country as it continues to struggle to recraft its national identity.

Transformations: Turkish Identity in Question

Modern Turkish national identity has always been characterized by an uneasy in-betweenness of West and East, modern and traditional, secular and Islamic. But over the last twenty years, Turkey has reached a critical crossroads, and as Kasaba and Bozdogan (2000) succinctly note, "it is no longer possible to detect a consensus regarding modern Turkish identity" (12). A convergence of several forces has given rise to major transformations in Turkish society: the declining power of the paternalistic Turkish state and its institutions in organizing and regulating economic and cultural life; the growing power of Islamic politics in defining the Turkish Republic and the increasing Islamization of the public sphere; the country's relatively late but growing and intense participation in the neoglobal economic order that has created a vastly liberalized economy and culture in Turkey; and Turkey's bid to join the European Union (EU). (Turkey became an EU candidate country in 1999, and the EU accession process involves bringing the country's legal, political, and economic structures into alignment with EU standards.)

Within this general context of transformations, important societal shifts have taken place. These multilayered social and economic changes have opened new paths of social differentiation and diversity in Turkish society. In the following pages I trace key societal changes that have brought about many uncertainties in social and political life and fractured Turkish society along secular and Muslim lines. There is an overwhelming sense that the ground has shifted. The historical background of dynamic destabilization during the formative years of the subjects of this book is crucial for understanding the contestation of the monolithic, secularly Muslim Turkish identity and, particularly, for understanding the specific conditions for, and operations of, self-making in Turkey today.

De-Islamization

Secularism was the most important component of the founding of the modern Turkish state in 1923, a process that strove to create a modern, Westernized nation-state in a predominantly Muslim, rural country. The early Republicans implemented a series of secularizing measures that went beyond mere separation of religion and the state with the aim of controlling and regulating religion in the private realm. These reforms were meant to undermine the basic Islamic way of life that formed the legal basis of the Ottoman state (Tekeli 1981). The new regime annulled the religious legal framework that was based on the Shariat (Islamic law), and all religious schools were closed. Religious institutions and Islamic education were linked to the state bureaucracy through a Directorate of Religious Affairs. Later, the state opened vocational schools, called "İmam-Hatip," in order to train religious personnel (*İmams*, prayer leaders). Thus, the state controlled the training of all religious officers and personnel, regulated the dissemination of religious norms, and controlled the production of theological knowledge. Religion was made subservient to the state.

Characterized by the state's active role in excluding religion from public areas and cultivating private religiosity, this form of secularism is referred to as "laicism" (national secularism) (White 2002) or "assertive secularism" (Kuru 2009). It is important to note that this form of radical secularism is quite different from the American form (Adrian 2006). Jefferson's "Wall of Separation between Church and State," which exemplifies "passive secularism" (Kuru 2009), was designed to protect the state from religious intrusion and to protect religion from government interference. In contrast, scholars note that Turkey's form of secularism is about "the sign of power and the authority" of the state (Yerginar 2000, 36) and "a particular production of religion that justifies the existence of secularism" (Cinar 2008, 896; also see Asad 2003). This concept of secularism in Turkey (and France) generates problems in the public expression of religiosity: it runs against state-sanctioned religious practice.

This understanding of the public sphere as secular and modern is critical to understanding the relationship between gender constructions and the nation-building process, allowing us to comprehend why the headscarves worn by university students are today considered a threat to Turkish notions of modernity and secularism. As a focus of the radical secularist and Westernist program, the new Turkish woman represented the ideals of the West and the rejection of an Ottoman past and Islam. It has been noted that in Turkey, "women's corporal visibility and citizenship rights constitute the political stakes around which the public sphere is defined" (Göle 1997a, 6). During the nation-building process in Turkey, the contours of the public sphere were drawn "in relation to norms of secularism and modernity by the forging and display of new gender identities, especially through regulations on clothing and the appearance of women" (Cinar 2008, 891). In particular, women participating in the public sphere by shedding their veils became symbolic of their liberation from the restrictive traditional religion and the backwardness of the private sphere. Public representations of new Turkish women as representing the nation-state's modernity as well as secular identities through their modern, Westernized attire achieved the overriding goal of obliterating Islamic visibility.

However, this radical secularization of the public sphere was complex because "women are included in public if only as a subordinate to the state's rationale" (Kandiyoti 1991, 430) in a country where the overwhelming majority of women were rural. Indeed, the sweeping reforms of the early twentieth century generated a public sphere marked by a hegemonic secular trajectory and identity. Turkish interpretations of Western modernity were produced by a binary opposition to Islamic practices, which were deemed uncivilized, backward, rural, uneducated, obstructionist, and indicative of the lower classes. The Western definition of modernity was officially disseminated through state, educational, political, and economic institutions. It materialized in new civil laws and the adaptation of modern marriages, Western time and metric measurements, Western clothing, and the Western alphabet. The modernist elites imposed a regimen that would ideally result in "civilization," defined as the emulation of Western (superior) practices and the elimination of their own "barbarians" (Muslims) (Göle 1997b). The infiltration of modernity superimposed a hierarchy in which European practices, like dancing, shaking hands, and writing left to right, were deemed superior to Turkish-Islamic practices.

Until the mid-1980s, the popular conception of the modern Turkish state as an authoritarian protector of the populace made this secularism and modernity a success. It also produced a form of religious identity among secularized Turks who defined themselves as sincere and good Muslims, even though they didn't adhere rigidly to the rituals of Islam. After the military coup of 1980 and the inauguration of neoliberal market liberalization and global integration starting in 1984, Turkey came to a new opening, creating an active space for renegotiating the relationship among Islam, secularism, and modernity.

Islamization

The 1980 military coup was aimed at stopping the increasing violence between the Left and Right and curtailing the growing leftist movement of the 1970s. Defining its main objective as the creation of a new national culture, the military regime (1980–1983) "utilized Islam not only as antidote to communist movements, but also a resource to mould a more obedient generation" (Yavuz and Esposito 2003, xxv; see also Atasoy 2005). For the first time in modern Turkish history, the military, the guardian of secularism in Turkey, actively encouraged religious education (Mardin 2006). The new 1982 constitution made religious courses compulsory in primary schools, middle-level high schools, and high schools (*lise*), except in military schools. A later law allowed graduates of religious high schools—the İmam-Hatip schools—to take the centralized university entrance examinations. This transformed vocational İmam-Hatip schools, originally established to train religious personnel, into alternative high schools and opened the path for their graduates to attend universities. Although the state continued to control the curriculum of these schools, their numbers increased tremendously. According to Atasoy (2005), "the ratio of İmam-Hatip school students to official general high school students increased from a ratio of one to 37 in the 1965–1966 academic year to one to ten in the 1985–1986 academic year" (144). This shift has resulted in an increased number of religiously educated students, often with rural and lower-class backgrounds, entering universities and studying to become professionals. Although there is no concept of female clergy in Islam, one-sixth of students in these schools were girls in that time period. The number of Koran Schools, another important source of Islamic education, also started mushrooming in the mid-1980s. The beginning of the expansion of Islamic activism and the resurfacing of Islam in public life also included the resurfacing of religious Sufi lodges and orders that had been outlawed during the early years of the Republic, some of which started financing the educations of underprivileged youngsters.

All of these developments in education, including the increased privatization of educational provisions at all levels, contributed centrally to the emergence of a new religiously conscious group within the professional middle classes (Arat 2001; Ozdalga 1998). The new educational system has changed class structures, particularly the trajectory of social mobility and the class reproduction of the religiously conscious segment of the population. During the 1990s, a strong Islamist movement among university students marked the political landscape, including female students protesting for the right to wear headcoverings. Sit-ins, demonstrations, and hunger strikes placed covered women in the spotlight (Keskin 2002).

The reconfiguration of "national culture" and the new 1982 constitution under the military dictatorship were followed by other transformations. Turkey started its integration with the global economy and began the mass privatization of the state-centered economy, education, and media. Although the new constitution restricted civil liberties, the vast liberalization of the economy within the context of globalization and European integration and the subsequent market-generated cultural forms increased freedom of expression. New and old identity-based groups and organizations, such as feminists, LGBT groups, ethnic rights groups (chief among them the Kurdish), and human rights groups emerged and diversified, constituting a vibrant civil society (Neyzi 2001; Seckinelgin 2006). Pro-Islamic parties were established and won elections, giving the force of legitimacy to Islamic lifestyles, although the secularist courts closed these parties several times. A variety of other complex social and political dynamics contributed to this expansion of Islamic visibility, including the mass migration of rural dwellers to major cities, where they became the targets of pro-Islamic grass-roots efforts. These efforts, in turn, "became the locus of the struggle between political Islam and secular Kemalism" (Kadioglu 1998, 13).

The Islamic media has greatly contributed to this increasing Islamization of the public sphere. The relaxation of controls on the media and publishing has permitted the proliferation of Islamic TV stations, newspapers, journals, and publishing houses. Extensive access to Islamic media has constituted the main public discursive framework within which women and men have identified their own Islamic identities. The amount of Islamic youth-oriented literature has vastly increased, helping to integrate and authenticate young people's religious identity. This, together with youth-oriented music and other forms of cultural expressions, has triggered the evolution of the modern Islamic youth: intellectual, well read, ambitious, and socially conscious, these young people are no longer burdened by an inferiority complex in relationship to the West and their secular peers (Saktanber 2002c).

In the late 1980s, the public sphere expanded to accommodate Islamic consumption and leisure and became a major locus of Islamic identities. Members of the rapidly growing Islamic middle class emerged as modern consumers, and an Islamic service sector emerged to cater specifically to them. For example, "Islamicized" leisure time is characterized by segregated beaches, nonalcoholic bars, and respect for prayer hours (Göle 2000). An Islamic fashion culture has flourished, and the wardrobes of urban Islamic women are now full of variety (Kilicbay and Mutlu 2002). Islamic firms manufacture clothing (Navaro-Yashin 2002; Gökarıksel and Secor 2010) on a continuum from the flamboyant styles adopted by well-to-do Islamic women, dubbed by some as "Islamic chic" (White 1999), to the restrained, simple (*sade*) styles adopted by pious women engaged in a critique of capitalist consumerism.

Consumer culture and class-based hierarchies among pious women have problematized Islamic self-expression as women manipulate their external appearance in their struggle with the paradox of being "new Muslim women." Access to communication, media, fashion, and technologies allows the new middle-class, pious Islamist woman to "circulate among different publics with ease" (Göle 2003, 822). By integrating two cultural codes—Islam and modernity—these women occupy a very conspicuous position in public life. Furthermore, these covered women's adoption of the symbols of modernity reduces the social distance between them and the secular elites (Göle 2003).

The increasing commodification of the Islamic way of life has given rise to a new Islamic individualism embodied by educated, headscarved women in the big cities. In contrast to the localized, confined, isolated Islamic identities of the 1970s and 1980s, this new Islamic individualism is blurring the distinction between religious/traditional and secular/modern. It breaks the headscarf's association with ignorance and tradition while signaling its own distance from Islamic fundamentalism and anticonsumerism. Some scholars conclude that "being modern in Turkey is no longer associated with being 'secular.'" And neither is it "restricted to the narrow definition of western" (Genel and Karaosmanoglu 2006, 478).

Post-Islamism?

Since the 1990s, Islamism in Turkey has proven to be divergent, multifaceted, and ever changing. Support for the establishment of an Islamic state in Turkey has declined. Indeed, it has been estimated that "the ratio of people who said they want an Islamic state decreased from around 20 percent throughout the 1990s to 9 percent in 2009" (Carkoglu and Toprak 2006, qtd. in Tugal 2009).

While scholarship produced on Islamic revivalism and visibility during the 1990s was marked by the term "Islamist" (*Islamcı*) to denote connection to political and revolutionary Islamic identities, the post-2000 literature has been devoid of such vocabulary. Instead, the term "post-Islamism" received significant scholarly and political attention. Cihan Tugal (2009) conceptualizes this transition from Islamism to post-Islamism in terms of Gramsci as a passive revolution "as a result of which erstwhile radicals and their followers are brought into the fold of neoliberalism, secularism, and Western domination" (4). Since they came to power with a landslide victory in the 2002 election and repeated similar victories in 2007 and 2011, the AKP (the Justice and Development Party, with links to a banned Islamist movement and political party) has pursued a liberal agenda with a pro–European Union and pro–human rights discourse. As the AKP consolidated its power, it drastically reduced the power of the military,[1] seen in Turkey as the champion and guardian of secularism against religious fundamentalism, and a bulwark against Kurdish separatism.

Turkey today has one of the fastest-growing economies in the world (with an annualized growth rate of 12 percent in the first quarter of 2010), even in the face of global financial crises, as well as a growing regional influence. The last two decades have seen a dramatic turn from a state-centered economy to a neoliberal order. The massive privatization of key sectors has changed class structure and mobility; created new forms of employment demanding less fixed, more mobile, and more adaptable work; created new sources of wealth; expanded suburbanization; and opened up new public spaces for leisure consumption. The discrepancies in access to the material benefits of neoliberal globalization have given rise to "unprecedented fragmentation and polarization within the middle classes" (Kandiyoti 2002, 7). This fragmentation has created a new poor among the salaried classes, while members of multinational firms, the private sector, and corporate elites have become increasingly affluent.

A recent edited volume (Dedeoğlu and Elveren 2012) presents an empirical assessment of the effects on women and gender relations of the intersections of neoliberal economic and social policies, the conservative agenda of political Islam, and the EU accession process. The emerging broader picture is bleak: the effects of the AKP's reform of the welfare system, social security, health insurance, and the pension system, which entailed a high degree of marketization and privatization, have created new vulnerabilities and disadvantages for women. The dismantling of the paternalistic welfare state theoretically results in the recognition of women as independent individuals and citizens, yet the patriarchal constructions of women as dependents are reproduced on the ground in complex ways with different implications for different classes of women.

Historically, the Turkish welfare system has been structured around a patriarchal male-breadwinner family norm in which women's dependence on male protection formed a vital source of security for them. For instance, most women benefited from social security on the basis of their dependent relationship with men, as fathers or husbands. This has traditionally created a system of social transfers positively discriminatory to women without male protection: widowed women had access to lifelong social security benefits through deceased husbands, and unmarried daughters had this access as orphans. Similarly, women were entitled to lifelong health benefits through their insured fathers and husbands. Such access structurally discourages women's formal labor force participation as well as reinforces traditional gender roles, particularly the valorization of motherhood and caregiving as women's central roles and identities in society. It is striking that today the vast majority (62.5 percent) of working-age women in Turkey do not have any personal income as opposed to only a minority (5.4 percent) of men (Dayıoğlu and Başlevent 2012).

The AKP's reform of the welfare system was instigated by gender-neutral neoliberal policies, with an emphasis on the privatization of the benefits systems. The reforms eliminated women's privileged access to social transfers. However, the care provision for children and the elderly has not been addressed, leaving care arrangements in the private sphere as women's responsibility. This dismantling is increasing women's vulnerability to economic and social risks precisely because there is another dynamic at play: women's decreasing participation in the formal sector of the labor force and their growing concentration in the informal sector, which more than ever is making women dependent on their fathers' or husbands' social security. Furthermore, neoliberal policies replaced state-based modes of social aid and services with Islamic traditions of charity (Buğra 2012), "making religious communities key actors at the grass-roots level in the provision of poverty relief and new forms of social solidarity" (Kandiyoti 2011; also see Buğra 2012).

The specific macroeconomic policies of neoliberalism in Turkey are characterized by economists as "growth without employment" and male predominance in new jobs. Between 1988 and 2007, "the number of people of working age increased by 19 million while the increase in employment remained at 5 million. Of this total figure, 4.5 million are males" (Toksöz 2012, 55). These figures alone powerfully testify to the gendered implications of the Turkish brand of neoliberalism and its inability (by design) to pull women into the formal labor market. Not only does a substantial sex gap remain between men's and women's labor force participation, but women's labor force participation has declined between 1988 and 2007 from 34.3 percent to 24.4 percent. Furthermore, the employment rate of women fell from 30.6 percent to 21.7 percent in the same period (Töksoz 2012, 55). While the number of women employed in manufacturing showed a meager increase, their employment in the rapidly growing service sector (wholesale and retail trade, restaurants and hotels) grew about threefold in the last two decades. Researchers point out a key structuring force in these trends: the absence of direct foreign capital investment in industry in Turkey, which has translated into limited demand for female labor in labor-intensive manufacturing.

In Turkey, rather than foreign capital being used in direct, new investments, a considerable part of foreign capital has gone to the purchase of newly privatized public enterprises and banks. This is accompanied by the government's mass construction projects aimed at creating and renovating the country's infrastructure and converting previously public land for the purpose of building shopping malls that sell international brand names. This injection of foreign capital into the economy has created job opportunities for the well-educated middle classes in finance and business services, product design, retail management, the professions, and creative industries. A growing service economy with less well-paid and less secure jobs supports this emerging well-paid middle class. Informal economic activities in Turkey, the lower echelons of which are dominated by women, have gained further importance as the public sector has withdrawn from the economy and subcontracting and outsourcing have become the norm in both public and private enterprises. Employment in the informal sector means work without social security and a lack of protective legislation for working conditions. Governmental support for the further feminization of the informal sector can be also found in the most recent plan for the 2007–2013 period, designed by the present AKP government. This plan aims to promote and encourage flexible forms of employment for women, including part-time and temporary work and female entrepreneurship, types of work accorded the least protection, remuneration, and stability, but supposedly also enabling women to attend to their duties as mothers and wives at home.

Turkish Feminism

After the collapse of the Ottoman Empire, Turkey was the first Islamic country to transition to a secular state and was one of the first countries in the world where the political rights of women as citizens were recognized. During the early years of the Republic, as I explained above, women represented the crux of modernity as a focus of the radical Westernist and secularizing program of reform. The most important social reforms centered on women, sexuality, and family (Göle 1997a; Kandiyoti 1987). The new ideal woman embodied gender in a dual manner: as an "enlightened" mother in the private sphere and as a "masculinized" public actor (Kandiyoti 1995). The envisioned modern woman was joined with traditional essentialist conceptualizations of womanhood to create a virtuous, asexual, nationalistic mother. Turkish modernization did not eliminate the transcription of traditional virtues onto female bodies; it merely transfigured these bodies as both modern and chaste—the paradoxical performance of modern yet modest, publicly visible yet virtuous. Patriarchy, strongly fused with state and individual forms of paternalism, helped to solidify this gender consensus, despite its many lived contradictions. The emerging strong feminist movement in the 1980s, however, when the country was under the military dictatorship, questioned this normative gender and sexual order.

Modern Turkish feminism is characterized by a complex and complicated engagement with state feminism. Until the 1980s, the Republican consensus that the reforms of the founding fathers had emancipated women and that there was no need for an independent women's movement remained uncontested. While attempting to carve out an independent political space vis-à-vis leftist political movements, the feminist activists of the 1980s based their politics on a rejection of the conceptualization of women as objects of paternalistic Republican reforms that "granted them their rights" and instead claimed subjecthood in their own lives (Sirman 1989; Arat 1997). The feminist movement initiated important changes in the civil and penal codes.

During the early 2000s, a strong feminist campaign within the context of the EU accession process resulted in gender-egalitarian legal and policy reforms that have granted women equal citizenship rights. The new civil code of 2001 equalized the status of husband and wife in the conjugal union by abolishing the concept of the head of family, establishing full equality with respect to rights over the family abode, marital property, divorce, child custody, and rights to work and travel. By dividing property acquired during marriage equally, the new divorce law now recognizes women's unpaid labor contributions at home. The new penal code of 2005 recognized a woman's right to be the sole controller of her body. It reclassifies sexual crimes like rape as crimes against the individual rather than crimes against "public morality" or "community order." And the discrimination between virgins and nonvirgins, married and unmarried women in sexual crimes was abolished. The new labor law of 2003 prohibited discriminatory practices based on a woman's marital status or family responsibilities, such as prohibiting dismissal on grounds of pregnancy, and included provisions prohibiting sexual harassment in the workplace. The equalization of retirement ages at sixty-five (implementation planned for 2048) was another policy aimed at gender equality. These feminist legal victories are based on a particular alignment of external and internal factors, chiefly EU conditions and women's groups. However, the disconnect between Turkey's progressive legislation and realities on the ground is glaringly enormous. Turkey ranked 124th among 135 countries in the Global Gender Gap index generated by the World Economic Forum in 2009. Only Saudi Arabia, Benin, Pakistan, Chad, and Yemen ranked lower.

In Turkey, feminists have opened women's shelters and established significant institutions such as women's research centers, introduced women's/gender studies into university curricula, and called for a quota system in Parliament. Building these institutions has allowed feminists to articulate and disseminate feminist discourses and enabled them to reach beyond their immediate circles. Issues such as virginity, honor killings, and domestic violence have been the main focus of feminist discourses and activism. In addition to mass demonstrations and public marches, the proliferation of feminist journals and magazines in the post-1980 period has not only ushered feminist issues, including women's sexuality, into the public realm and consciousness but has also helped to develop multiple feminist lenses through which to interpret and interrogate popular culture and divisions among feminists on Islam (Arat 2004). However, feminists also have separated along two sharply defined principles: the reconciliation of feminism with Islam to promote a civil society that strengthens liberal democracy and the defense of secularism against Islamists (Arat 2001), an issue that I will discuss in detail in chapter 4.

A New Twist

Turkey's profound transformation continues to unfold. The secularist section of Turkish society continues to be highly skeptical of the AKP's post-Islamism. They strongly believe that the AKP's hidden goal is the eradication of secularism and ultimately the imposition of Islamic law. Feminists meanwhile underscore the irony that post-Islamist men might have discarded the idea of creating an Islamic social order in Turkey but still have an undeclared Islamist agenda for women (Saktanber 2006). Given the AKP's current determination to overhaul the constitution and the deterioration of the desire for EU membership within the Turkish public,[2] the reconfiguration of Turkey will be affected by multiple forces.

Indeed, in recent years, with the power conferred by its electoral mandate, the AKP has begun a more concerted, aggressive program of Islamization. The AKP's decade-long, uncontested rule has cemented its control over state institutions and brought the infiltration of Islamist perspectives and personnel with religious identities into the state's actions and decision-making processes, as well as the expansion of the capital accumulation power of religious businessmen (Narlı 1999; Göle 1997b; Öniş 1997).

The AKP's radical revisioning of Turkey pivots around a central desire and mission expressed by Tayyip Erdoğan as "raising a pious generation." This vision centers unblinkingly on gender and sexuality: "I do not believe in equal opportunities. Men and women are different and complementary." As noted by Kandiyoti, Prime Minister Tayyip Erdoğan's view of the nature of gender expresses *fitrat*, "a tenet of Islam that attributes distinct and divinely ordained natures to men and women" (Kandiyoti 2011). Framed in distinctly gendered terms, the prime minister's key emphasis is on the significance of maternal roles for women and the strengthening of traditional family structures and roles. The specific policy aspirations highlighted in his speeches are pro-natalist policies and schemes: restricting abortion rights; stress on the importance of mothers breast-feeding their babies for one and a half years; and women giving birth to at least three children. The project of injecting piousness into the public sphere targets girls' and women's bodies and includes some recent legislative attempts such as changing the dress code in schools to replace school uniforms with individually chosen outfits, thus allowing religiously conservative families to send their daughters to school in conservative outfits, including head coverings.

The prime minister considers drinking alcohol to be the mark of a "sick society," and very recently the AKP government reregulated the distribution and sale of alcohol with the aim of limiting alcohol consumption in the public sphere. Regarded as a powerful leader with authoritarian tendencies by his foreign and local commentators,[3] Tayyip Erdoğan has been canonized as a hero of the Turkish conservative classes—his name has been given to a newly opened university and stadium. The liberal opposition, with its pluralistic vision of Turkey, has condemned particular instances of the AKP's policies of replacing the old "authoritarian" Republican order—which produced monolithic secular identities and suppressed (with force and integration) differences based on religious, linguistic, and ethnic identities—with another order, which is socially and culturally Islamic, economically neoliberal.

As I was engaged with the final revisions of this book at the end of May 2013, a massive resistance movement started. The initial protest was organized to save one of the last green areas in Istanbul, a public park, from demolishment to make space for yet another shopping mall complex modeled after Ottoman barracks. This protest quickly morphed into a country-wide protest against the AKP's rule and the ravages of neoliberal capitalism. What is unique about this political upheaval, which set in motion resistance and defiance amidst police brutality and violence, was the way it has been embraced by the different sectors of society: old and young, men and women, straight and LGBT, feminists, nationalists, staunch Kemalists, anticapitalist Muslims, trade and professional unions, and Kurdish groups—a unity of loosely defined purpose and action demanding a liberal democracy that has never been seen in Turkish history. Now responding to the immensely changing circumstances of their lives within the context of a rapidly Islamicized Turkey and economic neoliberalization, different sectors of society, it seems, will engage in struggle and contestation that will parallel the continuing reshaping of Turkey. This resistance movement features a creative combativeness amidst state violence and the unlawful detention of protesters and a commitment to intervene in any attempt to control their lives. The backlash against the neoliberal policies and the curtailment of individual liberties by the Islamic government provides the latest twist in the remaking of the nation.

Theoretical and Empirical Foundations: Key Concepts and Analytical Perspective

The young women and men in this book came of age in the midst of changes that are transforming notions of the self and collective identity. Not only are they subjects of these profound changes, but they are situated at this strategic crossroads as upwardly mobile members of the future elite classes who will inhabit positions of power. They articulate and give substance to the changing gender and sexual order of Turkish society and will shape and inhabit the new forms of gender identities and sexualities.

In focusing my study on young Turks, I am following the theoretical lead of researchers who emphasize the importance of one's formative years (youth) to the project of self-making. Karl Mannheim (1972) privileged the formative years in the development of a person's identity because he believed that individuals carry their identity with them as they grow older. Because of their potential to become "generative of the conditions of thinking and action of subsequent cohorts" (Turner 2002, 19), Turner also stresses the importance of studying young adults. Similarly, feminist sociologist Gerson (2009) emphasizes young adults' "fulcrum" role in forging social change, especially in an era of unprecedented social-economic transformations: "Poised between the dependency of childhood and the irrevocable investments of later adulthood, this life stage represents both a time of individual transition and a potential engine for social change" (737).

In order to analyze the new desires pursued and produced by the young Turks I studied, I draw upon concepts developed in several distinct theoretical analyses of gender, sexuality, love, social class, mobility, and self-making. In the narratives of these young Turks, a key expression of desire takes the form of an escape from the normative patriarchal conceptions of gender—the selfless feminine and protective masculine. The deep aspiration towards building individualized selves is related to another significant desire for sexual modernity and rejection of dominant virginity norms as traditional and backward. My investigation of the paradoxes and contradictions of these new desires particularly highlights several concepts within my analytical and interpretive frame. Below I juxtapose two broad models of self-making—autonomous self-formation and connective selving—and introduce a feminist psychoanalytical formulation of the intersubjective construction of gender and the intertwined relationship among love, recognition, and domination. I also elaborate my approach to class as a cultural practice rather than purely an economic designation.

Two Approaches to Self-Making
The Detraditionalized Self and "Choice Biographies"

Theorizing large-scale social and historical trends, a number of contemporary thinkers across different disciplines have highlighted self-making in reflexive modernity (or late modernity, postmodernity, the neoliberal age) as a key field for research to investigate its genealogy, constitution, and transformations.[4] Embodied in a host of investigations of subjectivity, self, the body, desire, and identity, such scholars indicate that our present ways of perceiving the formation of selfhood have moved from fixity to uncertainty and contingency, from habit to reflexivity across all domains of existence and experience as individuals have become increasingly disembedded from local, place-based orientations and released from traditional bonds and status relations that integrated them in groups, including family, class, and the nation. The pivotal concept for such a reflexive modernity is "the self as a project in the making" (McLeod 2002, 211). This project is identified and underscored as the detraditionalization of the self, the formation of the self as a reflexive and self-conscious biography (Beck 1992; Beck and Beck-Gernsheim 1995; Giddens 1991). Giddens, the most prominent sociologist of modernity and detraditionalization, for example, claims that "self-identity has to be created" rather than being "given" and "discovered" (1991, 186). Replacing once inherited and prescribed roles and futures, the "enterprising self" (Freeman 2014) or "choice biographies"—constructed, worked upon, and resulting from choices—increase self-monitoring, internal regulation, and reflexivity (Beck 1992, 135; Beck and Beck-Gernsheim 1995). Writing within the paradigm of neoliberal subject formation, Nikolas Rose (1991) suggests that an individual bears the burden of "render[ing] his or her life meaningful as if it were the outcome of individual choices made in furtherance of a biographical project of self-realization" (240).

How does this broad, universalizing theory of modernity and the self translate to the particular settings of upwardly mobile young Turks? Is detraditionalized selfhood culturally significant in a deeply patriarchal and paternalistic society at once modern and traditional and at once Western and non-Western? Do young Turks pursue detraditionalized pathways? In order to understand how young Turks negotiate relationships with others and themselves in an era marked by neoliberalism, we need to bring into focus another theory of self-making that more centrally integrates patriarchy into the analysis.

Connective Selving

Suad Joseph offers connectivity as an alternative to the (Western) model of the bounded self (i.e., the self who is completely autonomous and separate from others). Although Joseph theorizes connectivity as a non–culturally specific concept, writing about Arab families in Lebanon, she applies it directly to societies in which the key component of selfhood is not autonomy or individuality, as it is in many Western contexts, but rather a relational experience with members of one's family. Western models of selfhood traditionally emphasize the role of liberal, market-based economies in creating a subject whose preparedness for a career path has pushed him or her toward complete autonomy. In other words, according to Joseph, such models take the flexibility of the modern worker as the greatest factor influencing self-construction and perfect individuation as the most important component of that self. But Joseph suggests that this model fails to explain how people understand themselves in cultures in which the family is valued over society and the individual. In such contexts, she argues, individuals "are open to and require the involvement of others in shaping their emotions, desires, attitudes and identities" (Joseph 1993, 468). The actions and opinions of family members do not simply influence an individual's selfhood—they are instrumental to its completion. Their "security, identity, integrity, dignity, and self-worth . . . [are] tied to the actions of [that person]" (Joseph 1993, 467).

Joseph also challenges the Western-centeredness of feminist object relations theory on sexual difference—the idea that feminine personality is defined relationally and masculine personality is defined as a denial of relation. She expands the concept of object relations and connectivity beyond the strictly gendered, arguing that relationality is a masculine as well as a feminine prerogative. However, patriarchal structures prioritize the needs and desires of the men, producing different feminine and masculine experiences of connectivity. Joseph argues that the merging of connectivity with patriarchy shapes "relationality into a system of domination" (468). In Joseph's model, familial relationships become significant forces in socializing individuals and (re)producing patriarchal systems.

I suggest that Joseph's overall conceptualization of connectivity applies to the Turkish case, in which connectivity is produced and pursued in interrelated institutional, affective, and psychological domains. Connectivity also functions as an important site for constructions of sexual selves. I use this notion of connectivity to explore upwardly mobile young Turks' negotiations of tensions and ambivalences in gender dynamics and enactments of their sexual selves. The widespread Turkish recognition and reification of mother-daughter connectivity (and identification) is nowhere more strongly portrayed than in the proverb "anasına bak kızını al."[5] The English equivalent of this idiom, "like mother, like daughter," does not do justice to the deeper meaning attached to this proverb, which expresses the view that a young girl (or a bride) will eventually look and behave exactly like her mother. Mother-daughter connectivity in Turkey plays a crucial role in the formation of young women's sexual selves. Particularly, as we will see in the next chapter, deviance from the virginity norm is often experienced as a rupture and denial of connectivity with the mother. Connectivity also forms an important analytical category in elucidating the meanings and practices attached to coming out in the gay men's narratives.

In contemporary Turkey, patriarchal kinship continues to link sex and age groups in patterns of hierarchy and dependence, conferring particular statuses and identities. Kinship is thus deeply implicated in the process of self-production. Turkish legal institutions are key to maintaining patriarchal kinship networks. In addition to traditional marriage, which remains central to Turkish individuals' social identities (White 1994), kinship in Turkey also operates institutionally through a civil and penal code that is organized "to protect the social and familial order rather than the rights of the individual" (Sirman 2004, 51). It was only recently that the penal code was changed to prioritize the rights of victims as individuals in cases of rape and female abduction over the preservation of family honor and public decency. Despite amendments to the code brought about by feminist and human rights organizations and an effort by the Turkish government to align the code with EU standards, it continues to preserve the family "as the foundation of Turkish society" while defining marriage as an entity "based on equality between spouses" (WWHR 2005).

The domain of kinship also overlaps with the public sphere, where relationships and social interaction are couched in elaborate kinship language, morality, and imagery. As Joseph argues, connectivity is particularly enacted and crystallized through bodily and linguistic practices. As Joseph observed among the Arab families in Lebanon she studied, the use of idioms that merge body imagery with phrases of love and affection, such as "you are my heart," "you are my soul," and "you are my eyes" in kin and significant non-kin relations evidences how the imaginary continuity between individuals is also expressed through the symbolic realm of language. Enactment of kinship morality in the public sphere is achieved through deployment of kinship terms when unrelated men and women address each other as "aunt," "brother," "sister," and "uncle" (for example, in a store), thereby desexualizing the encounter.

Within middle-class and upwardly mobile households, connectivity and relatedness are also built through mothers' cultivation of their children's potential, particularly with regard to education. Because academic excellence facilitates individuals' successful placement in the nation's elite universities and provides social connections for their adult lives, education is seen as the most important vehicle to upper-middle-class status. Within Turkey's competitive educational system, mothers play a pivotal role in fostering their children's high performance by offering their children "a measure of emotional security and intimacy with which to survive these demands" (Allison 2000, 108). As mothers merge practices of monitoring and overseeing the educational regimens of their children with practices of maternal nurturance, indulgence, ego boosting, and love, a high degree of practical and emotional dependency is built in the construction of both masculinity and femininity. These long-term emotional and physical investments and sacrifices cultivate a strong sense of loyalty and emotional indebtedness to one's parents, producing significant psychological obstacles for the formation of sexually liberated selves.

Since the 1980s, the consolidation of neoliberal social and economic reforms and global consumer culture has brought about important changes in Turkish society and introduced new modes of social integration that have created alternative notions of self and new social ties. For example, the liberalized market economy and extensive access to the media and Internet have granted Turkish youth more freedom in self-expression, sociability, and sexual communication. Increased suburbanization has led to increased privatization of the nuclear family and ruptured some connective tissues embedded in the domain of extended family and kinship (Ayata 2002). Yet some of the traditional forms of connectivity have not been profoundly displaced. Moreover, because they frame individuals by their wider social networks, these new integrative social practices also have a collective orientation, albeit differently produced and realized. Maintenance of connectedness and sociability are clearly reflected, for example, in the modern summer vacationing patterns of the middle classes, in which nuclear families connected with one another own summer houses next to or near one another, creating fluid and permeable boundaries between households and each other's lives. Thus, despite large-scale changes to Turkey's cultural and political landscape, the middle-class families continue to promote personal enrichment and maturity through connection with members of different generations, kin and non-kin alike.

The generic story of the neoliberal subject centered on self-invention, autonomy, and self-realization under neoliberal globalization diminishes the importance of traditional frames of reference for identity development, thus missing this strong presence of connectedness. Further, autonomy or connectivity in self-making does not interpolate in all young Turks in the same way. Such orientations are mediated by class, gender differences, and religious identity. I make this point not to suggest that we ignore evidence of individualizing forces or ideologies of the autonomous self emerging in Turkey. Rather, I make it to refocus our attention on the negotiations and tensions between the desire for relatedness and the desire for untied autonomy.

The upwardly mobile young Turks I studied, whose new desires for autonomy in self-making and sexuality threaten familial identification, bring out the conundrums of emancipation from connective selving. Their rejection of selfless-femininity and protective-masculinity constructions imply a denial of connection, a decoupling of connectivity and patriarchy. In their eyes, the affirmation of connectivity can cost one the knowledge and appreciation of one's own desires. They would like to stop seeing themselves through the eyes of the other. Thus, they suggest that the focus of moral and sexual agency should be relocated to the individual and separated from the individual's roles and status as daughter and son—roles that cast their actions as representative of the respectability, reputation, and honor of the group, the family, and the nation.

However, for women and men inhabiting new sexual and gender terrains, attempting to escape from patriarchal masculinity and the constraints of normative femininity and exploring new sexual subjectivities are sources of both opportunity and anxiety and guilt. And in order to understand and analyze these inner struggles, we need additional conceptual tools to accompany Joseph's notion of connective selving. This entails making fuller use of Benjamin's psychoanalytical feminist perspective, which has long been concerned with the "unconscious structure of patriarchy."

Gender, the Bonds of Love, Recognition, and Domination

Although integration of psychoanalysis with feminist theory has been challenged on many fronts, feminist revisions of psychoanalytically informed theories remain a significant method and theory. As Madelon Sprengnether (1990) succinctly puts it, psychoanalysis "offers a means of comprehending the unconscious structure of patriarchy" (8). Joseph's deconstruction of the binary personality development of femininity and masculinity challenges the unilateral alignment of femininity with relationality and of masculinity with containment and individuality. Jessica Benjamin (1988) further advances our understanding of the patriarchal constructions of gender with her argument about the deep intertwining of love, recognition, and domination. She problematizes and revises the gendered division between sex = masculine and love = feminine. As this book will attempt to show, the desire for recognition is much more important than the desire for sex in some male narratives of romance and sex. Desire for recognition is a powerful formative force in structuring masculinities in a cultural context that steeps desire in a patriarchal tradition, a tradition of motherly devotion and of the privileging and adulation of sons' desires and needs. Benjamin's notion of recognition also becomes essential for understanding male domination, particularly from the perspective of those who attempt to escape the patriarchal construction of masculinity as dominant, controlling, and protective. Finally, Benjamin's construction of intersubjectivity is relevant to research on intimate relationships that highlight the dialogical construction of gender. I emphasize the intersubjective articulation of gender by the subjects of this book: young women are not passive recipients of masculine ideals, but coproducers and active participants in its construction, and, equally, young men emerge as significant cocreators of feminine ideals.

Although Benjamin agrees with Freud that patriarchal relations are supported by deep psychological mechanisms and that these mechanisms are shaped by anatomy, she denies the genital primacy for which Freud argued. Instead she suggests that because "the psychological integration of biological reality is largely the work of culture," the psychic roots of patriarchy and female submission are "social arrangements that we can change or direct" (1988, 90). For Benjamin, unwriting the patriarchal script requires uncovering the unconscious processes by which desire comes to ratify male power.

Benjamin suggests that to better understand the unconscious roots of female desire, or lack of desire, we should look not at the oedipal stage, as Freud does, but at preoedipal life. For Freud, the key to a young girl's sexual development was her realization that like her mother she lacked a penis and her subsequent identification with her father, the bearer of power she could only achieve vicariously. But in Benjamin's account, the father achieves his symbolic power "because he (with his phallus) represents freedom from dependency on the powerful mother of early infancy" (95). In this formulation, the penis becomes a symbol of separation not from maternal lack, but instead from an engulfing maternal presence. In Benjamin's estimation, this model of maternal power and paternal freedom is rooted in the different ways in which mothers and fathers interact with their children.

The problem of female desire, then, is rooted in the problem of paternal identification for the young girl. While little boys are able to be like the father, the symbol of the outside world, little girls can only wish to have him. Little girls' early attempts to identify with their fathers are often thwarted, either by his unwillingness to recognize her sameness to him or by her own perception of anatomical difference. Ultimately, it is this inability to fully identify with the outside that prevents women from making desire and agency their own and leads them into relationships of submission and passivity.

If the root of female submission is the girl's failed identification with her father, then any vision of female desire and agency must begin with the dismantling of the symbolic structures that join power and desire to fatherhood exclusively. For Benjamin, the key to disrupting the patriarchal script lies in the potential for intersubjectivity, the experience of one's selfhood as something that exists both within oneself and between that self and others. An intersubjective construction of selfhood would not only grant women desire and subjectivity, in Benjamin's account, but would also lead to a fuller experience of the erotic, one in which two subjects meet in mutual recognition and get pleasure both in and with the other. However, according to Benjamin, this mutual recognition can only be achieved when children of either sex receive full recognition from both parents and when mothers and fathers equally share as figures of independence and agency.

The narratives I collected call for a complex understanding of masculinity/femininity and power—one that would account, for example, for some young men's strong desire *not* to be dominant, controlling, and protective. Gender scholars often approach this question with various theoretical tools gleaned from Raewyn Connell (1987, 2002), particularly her concepts of hegemonic masculinity and emphasized femininity. But, as her critics point out (Demetriou 2001; Hearn 2004; Moller 2007; Coles 2009), her model encourages a kind of disciplinary tunnel vision that overdetermines and oversimplifies male behavior. Connell's paradigm directs us to see masculine power in domination, subordination, and oppression, but often to overlook the more mundane ways in which power and privilege are exercised and felt. Furthermore, she encourages us to see power as only domination and tells us to read every such practice as an attempt to increase male power. One of the central projects of Benjamin's *Bonds of Love* (1988) is to account for the way or ways in which "domination [is] anchored in the hearts of those who submit to it" (52). For Freud, all manifestations of domination were rooted in the child's initial dependency on his mother and his attempt to deny that dependency and differentiate himself as an independent subject. Benjamin suggests that the desire to dominate is born out of the infantile fantasy of omnipotence, the desire to be recognized as an individual subject but not to return that recognition—that is, the desire to assert one's selfhood without acknowledging the selfhood of others. Benjamin suggests that domination is configured as masculine because the original differentiation of the infant from the mother is more extreme for boys than it is for girls, who can retain some continuity with the mother because of their shared gender. However, because separation from the mother can never be complete, omnipotence never gained, and tension never relieved, "the repudiated maternal body persists as the object to be done to and violated" (77). Likewise, female submission can be traced to the unique relationship between girls and their mothers, which, according to Benjamin, "emphasiz[es] merging and continuity at the expense of individuality and independence" and thus "provides fertile ground for submission" (78–79). Ultimately, Benjamin argues that erotic domination, like other practices of love, should be understood primarily as the desire for recognition. Although this desire might manifest itself in relations of power, control, and submission, they are in their essence "desires for freedom and communion," the very desires from which, she concludes, "the bonds of love are forged" (84). Thus it is that love, romance, and courtship figure significantly in the crystallization of new masculine and feminine subjectivities.

Varieties of Love: Passion, Romantic Love, and Pure Love

In the last decade of the twentieth century, two influential books, *The Transformation of Intimacy* (1992) by Anthony Giddens and *Consuming the Romantic Utopia* (1997) by Eva Illouz, provoked new insights into conceptualizations of love, intimacy, and romance. Giddens's historical account of changes in intimate relationships forms a narrative that begins with a premodern understanding of love as passion, an all-encompassing sexual attraction for another regarded by premodern people as "disruptive" and "dangerous" due to its power in "generating a break with routine and duty" (38); moves through a modern conception in the second half of the twentieth century of the ideal of romantic love as a basis for heterosexual marriage; and concludes with a shift, in the latter half of the twentieth century, to a postmodern, gender-egalitarian confluent or pure love entered into for its own sake and defined by the ideal of intimacy—the sharing of emotional selves through mutual disclosure. Illouz's work explores the intimate link forged between romance and capitalism. Although like Giddens, Illouz emphasizes the potential of postmodern love in producing a genderless ideal, her analysis highlights the centrality of a romantic utopia enacted through practices of consumption and leisure.

Giddens's historical account identifies an important transformation in intimate sexual relationships, a shift from the ideal of "romantic" love to that of "pure" or "confluent" love. Under the ideal of romantic love, individuals who strive to embody the idealized qualities of their genders find another who "by being who he or she is, answers a lack which the individual does not even necessarily recognise" (45). Through romantic love, "the flawed individual is made whole" (45). Its accomplishment has been based on a projective identification; the desire for the other has been the desire for what one is missing (61). According to Giddens, this view of love generates a particular life trajectory for individuals by interconnecting mutual responsibilities and duties with desire—a lifelong heterosexual marriage and parenthood (41). Historically, romantic love and lifelong heterosexual marriage seeped into religious and moral traditions as well as legal and institutional spheres, powerfully constraining different and alternative life trajectories.

In the second half of the twentieth century, however, the romantic love ideal began to be displaced by what Giddens calls "pure" or "confluent" love. While in the past, kinship groups and communities had the capacity to ground intimate relationships—to provide the framework of moral obligation and trust—in the pure relationship contexts, the connection between romantic partners as two individuals takes precedence in the absence of a deep embeddedness of the relationship within familial structures. Giddens defines a "pure" relationship as one in which "a social relation is entered into for its own sake, for what can be derived by each person from a sustained association with another, and which is continued only insofar as it is thought by both parties to deliver enough satisfactions for each individual to stay within it" (58). Whereas romantic love relationships revolved around idealized visions of masculinity and femininity, the pure relationship is an effort to achieve, through constant communication, an intimate knowledge of the other's unique and authentic self. Intimacy is sought as a means to self-development; if the relationship loses its reason for being, it becomes subject to dissolution. An individual committed to a pure love relationship—even through marriage—is therefore committed only contingently. Confluent love "introduces the ars erotica into the core of the conjugal relationship" (629). In this model, "a person's sexuality is but one factor that has to be negotiated as part of a relationship" (63).

Giddens proposes that pure love relationships are more egalitarian because romantic love rested on essentialist conceptions about natural gender differences. Women's subscription to romantic love often was translated into obligations and dependencies and "domestic subjection" (62). Embedded in the values of autonomy and equality, pure relationships, Giddens believes, are fundamentally democratic. Therefore, a shift to a society full of pure relationships would represent nothing less than the democratization of private life. He also suggests a connection between the diffusion of pure love relationships and the solidification of democratic ideals in the larger society. For this reason, he suggests, "the transformation of intimacy might be a subversive influence upon modern institutions as a whole" (3).

Although Giddens's thesis of the detraditionalization of gender under the ideal of pure love is considered by many scholars to be optimistic, utopian, and overstated,[6] the narratives of young Turks, especially the young women's narratives of relationship and marriage ideals (both pious and secular) accentuate the desire for Giddens's confluent or pure love. Those narratives reflect these women's identities as high achievers whose aspirations for their futures are not centrally tied to marriage and motherhood. Their ideal of romantic love and marriage is not about longing for unity with a different person who "can make one's life . . . complete" (Giddens 1992, 61) but about relating to and melding together two autonomous and equal life projects, hers and his.

Giddens sees variations in the transformation of intimate spheres "according to context and differential socioeconomic position." Illouz (1997) explains this variation by examining the incorporation of romantic love into the culture of capitalism. Indeed, according to Illouz, "the inequalities constitutive of the market have been transferred to the romantic bond itself" (22). Illouz argues that love is a privileged site for the experience of utopia. With secularization in Western societies, "love began to be represented not only as a value in itself but as an important motive in the pursuit of happiness, now defined increasingly in individualistic and private terms" (29–30). For Illouz, "Utopias make us dream a better world, about alternative arrangements, and even if those dreams often degenerate into control and manipulation, we still must account for the hope and creativity they contain and often generate. Utopias inspire change" (197). These utopian meanings (and yearnings) are experienced through the "cyclical performance of rituals of consumption" (8) of such commodities as travel, dining out, the exchange of gifts, cultural events, and the use of special artifacts.

In Illouz's account, the merging of capitalism and romance registers at other levels as well. The promotion and dissemination of a "therapeutic discourse" about romance (especially in women's magazines), in which it is presented as an emotional sphere subject to analytical examination, description, and, ultimately, rational management, also registers romance as a product of work and calculation. Perhaps the most interesting aspect of Illouz's account concerns the relationship between gender and the ideal of intimacy. Pointing out a paradox, she argues that the romantic utopia "reproduces ideals of masculinity and femininity, yet is simultaneously a genderless ideal" (197). By drawing men inside the domain of private selves and emotions, "the sole repository of authenticity, meaning and commitment" (196), and by offering to "merge men and women in a genderless model of intimacy" (197), the romantic utopia "feminizes" men. In other words, the ideal of intimacy enjoins women and men to create selves that are similar. Illouz's argument about the relationship between men and romantic utopia both points to and is part of a new body of research addressing intimacy and the affective dimensions of masculinity. Romance is no longer anathema to masculine selfhood, but is increasingly becoming an important component of masculinity (Allen 2003; Korobov 2009; Maxwell 2007; Redman 2001).

Rituals of romance are much affected by socioeconomic class. The romantic utopia is more readily available to members of the privileged and upwardly mobile classes, because they possess the economic resources necessary for more frequent and varied access to its self-renewing liminal space. The effects of class on young Turks' aspirations and practices of romance and sex are complex and multiple. Illuminating the links among class, gender, romance, and sex is central to my interpretive frame, and these linkages require me to widen the framework of analysis beyond the relationship between consumption practices and romance.

Class, Habitus, and Upward Mobility

Both as an economic location and as an (embodied) identity of individuals, class figures as a prominent category of analysis in this book. My analysis demonstrates the processes by which class is experienced in and through gender and sexuality in complex and specific ways. As Bourdieu (1984) wrote in his oft-quoted passage, "sexual properties are as inseparable from class properties as the yellowness of a lemon from its acidity: a class is defined in an essential respect by the place and value it gives to the sexes and to their socially constituted dispositions" (107). I want to outline broadly what I see as Bourdieu's two main concerns relevant to the construction of my interpretive frame: his notion of habitus and its link to class structure, and his conceptualization of exclusion and inclusion as boundary making in the romantic and sexual landscape. A multidimensional approach to class enables us to take account of the contradictions and complexities in relation to other intersectional categories that tend to disappear in less nuanced accounts.

The complexity and ambivalences of class identification in contemporary Turkey reflect the way class-based distinctions are thought of in Turkish society. Multiple and layered distinctions—such as whether one is from Istanbul or Anatolia; whether one's income derives from trade, commerce, agriculture, or professions; what types of schooling (private or public) one receives; and whether one grows up in a modern or traditional patriarchal family—enter into people's calculations and inform the way they judge and are judged in class terms. Class distinctions and differences are always articulated with reference to the powerful binaries of rural-urban, modern-traditional, civilized-uncivilized. Historically, the process of urbanization, which since the early 1970s has been drawing the rural population into the big cities in massive waves, has underlined these intersections. These rural-to-urban migrants' integration and their aspirations for economic and social mobility have been important sources of anxiety about the threat of "mixing" among the established urban, educated, and modern middle classes (Öncü 2002; Ozyegin 2001). Even though some people with rural origins achieve economic mobility and become well-do-to over time, they are still not considered people "with class" (as in "he/she doesn't have class," referencing a lack of modern, middle-class dispositions and manners). In short, there is no easy and close correspondence between one's economic status and one's claim to middle-class status and identity.[7]

I suggest that the way people in Turkey—especially young Turks in between different class identifications—view and understand "class" can be conceptualized as a folk understanding using Bourdieu's notion of habitus. Bourdieu (1977) argues that "the structures constitutive of a particular type of environment (e.g.: the material conditions of existence characteristic of a class condition) produce habitus, i.e., a system of lasting transposable dispositions which, integrating past experiences, functions at every moment as a matrix of perceptions, appreciations, and actions and makes possible the achievement of infinitely diversified tasks" (83). That is, one's socioeconomic position determines one's tastes, predispositions, and values affiliated with that structural position. Thus Bourdieu's habitus defines a set of "structuring dispositions" that the individual brings to day-to-day life and that orient the individual to act and react in certain taken-for-granted ways. While an individual's habitus is not governed by strict rules, it nevertheless conforms to general social boundaries. Thus, individuals take for granted most dispositions and practices that they enact, despite the profound significance these strategies have for the way individuals acquire capital and position themselves within a given field.

By reconceptualizing "the socialized self" through his concept of habitus, Bourdieu positions the body at the center of the negotiation of structure and agency, the society and the individual. He claims that "to speak of habitus is to assert that the individual, even the person, the subjective, is social, collective. Habitus is socialized subjectivity" (Bourdieu and Wacquant 1992, 126). Bourdieu conceptualizes the key resources in this development of the "socialized self" in the social field as "capitals": economic, social, and cultural. A social field is a domain of social life, like gender or the family, in which individuals struggle over and are positioned according to their relative economic, social, and cultural capital. The child is socialized in the capital holdings of the family, which determine the child's initial capital holdings as his/her habitus is formed. For Bourdieu, the social in the habitus, the structured and structuring dispositions, frame bodily conduct, skills and competence, speech habits, vocabulary, accent, and so on. This implies that the means of emotional competencies, masculine or feminine, and their expressive displays are acquired and internalized through the techniques of the body learned in childhood in the context of communication and identification within class-specific family and either homosocial or mixed-gender communities.

Although some of Bourdieu's feminist critics point out a systematic exclusion of gender in his theory,[8] I think his concept of "structured" and "structuring dispositions" lends itself to a gendered analysis. Some feminist scholars are utilizing Bourdieu. To take one example, Beverley Skeggs's (1997) study of working-class women's experiences and negotiation of this intersection has powerfully illustrated performative gender and embodied notions of class. The women Skeggs studied lacked the economic and social capital to inhabit the norms of middle-class femininity, but they invested heavily in their bodies and consumption practices to create "respectful femininity" while simultaneously identifying and dis-identifying with their structural class position. Similarly, Tony Coles (2009) urges that studies of hegemonic masculinity should be informed by Bourdieu's theoretical models in order to illuminate "the more subtle interplay of masculinities that exists in men's lives" (30).

Bourdieu's theory is especially relevant for understanding class as an embodied identity and subjectivity, not just an economic location in a class hierarchy. This understanding is particularly trenchant in the stories of young Turks from nonurban family backgrounds who are in a dialogical relationship with both their parental class culture and their middle-class culture/class destination, who experience the dynamic interconnection between identification and distantiation. Using a Bourdeusian account to focus on the dispositions and emotional competencies that young Turks bring to their intimate and sexual relationships is essential in studying societies such as Turkey, where the practices of boundary making are accentuated by the threat of blurring class/urban-rural/Muslim-secular boundaries. Bourdieu's habitus comes sharply into view in considerations of how the young men and women in this book mobilized habitus-based qualities and dispositions in constructing the ideal, desirable femininity/masculinity.

As we will see in the chapters to come, habitus is embodied and exemplified partly through durable ways of standing, speaking, walking, and other other aspects of deportment, what Bourdieu calls "hexis." Taste in things and people plays a crucial signaling role in conveying either affinity or difference—the absence or presence of confidence and familiarity with class-based resources, relationships, and practices. Locating young Turks' constructions of desirable femininity and masculinity within the wider class habitus, configured as instances of boundary making, also helps to explain young Turks' contributions to and investments in the maintenance of existing class boundaries and other divisions. The notion of habitus is also pertinent for understanding the inclusion and exclusion that occur when people belonging to different habituses share the same social space, like the pious young woman in this book who carries her Muslim habitus to the secular public environment of the university.

The economics of class—"the haves and the have-nots"—are also present in the way romantic and sexual relationships are lived. Romance and sex are important sites for exercising class privileges and disadvantages. Glaring differences in young Turks' financial situations are reflected in their on-/off-campus housing patterns and consumption choices as well as their leisure and entertainment activities. Affluent students spend hundreds of dollars for a pair of designer shoes, while their poorer counterparts try to get by with the same amount of money for a month. In the absence of places of their own, those with class disadvantages experience intimate moments of sexual expression literally in public places. The street, parks, vacated, unlit campus offices and hallways, and other public places become vital sites for exploring sexual intimacy for those who have no personal space that is not controlled by parents and/or live in crowded single-sex dorm rooms, producing distinctions such as "clothed" and "naked" sex. Those with class advantages draw strong boundaries and evaluate their class-disadvantaged peers by referring to their sexual behavior on the basis of how they conduct themselves in intimate, sexual relations. As perceived by the privileged classes, the Anatolians (lower classes), because they come from repressive family backgrounds, are unable to exercise control over the new freedom and liberty at their disposal now. Therefore they transgress boundaries by engaging in "sex"/sexual behavior in public places, indulging in sexual displays (see also Erdur 2002).

For Bourdieu, the embodied dispositions formed during childhood as part of one's primary socialization are further developed throughout life. But as many critics point out, Bourdieu's "social actor" is overly social or overly determined: "lasting transposable dispositions" are obstinate and rigid (though he posits that "there exist dispositions to resist") and may be so intractable precisely because Bourdieu links habitus to the reproduction of class structure (81). How does one's habitus change as one subsequently moves across the "social field," as is the case for people who experience mobility? What happens when, in upward mobility, an individual becomes dislocated from his/her habitus's moorings that once carried his/her capital holdings? Does the movement from class origins to new class destinations mean complete escape from the original habitus?

Valerie Walkerdine (2003) suggests that upward mobility has to be analyzed in terms of the deep ambivalence and emotional turmoil produced by individuals' relationships to their upwardly mobile identities. Her central thesis is that upward mobility must be understood as invested with both desire and defense. Lived through a constant psychic and material reinvention, upward mobility becomes a site of fantasy and invested with desire. Yet this mobility also represents a threat—the threat of inevitable failure, but also the threat of losing all material and emotional connections to one's past or, conversely, of not being able to distance oneself enough from that past. For Walkerdine, the process of fully embodying a new class identity and "the complete displacement of what one was" (247), cutting all psychic and material ties with one's other self, can never be seamless. Rather, it necessarily becomes a site of contradiction, what Zygmunt Bauman calls "ambivalence"—as Walkerdine explains it, "the discursive place where there [is] a slipping or sliding, an ambiguity between classifications." Ultimately this ambivalence, according to Walkerdine, is "experienced as great pain and anxiety for the subject," a pain that is balanced by the promise of eventual pleasure from a self-realized identity that will never be achieved (247).

In considering how young Turks produce their upward mobility in the cultural context of connective selving, I find Walkerdine's notion of upward mobility as a site of ambivalence evocative precisely because of her attention to psychic struggles. As we shall see, one of the key benefits of drawing from Walkerdine's formulation is that it illuminates the tension and liminality between identification and dis-identification. Some young Turks negotiate discrepancies and dis-identification between the dispositions, values, and lifestyles rooted in their class and habitus origins and competing efforts to define themselves in relation to upward mobility. Their efforts foreground a complex terrain of intimate transformations predicated upon gender relations and sex.

Research Setting and Empirical Foundation

Established in 1863 as the oldest American college outside of the United States, Boğaziçi (Bosphorus) University became a public university in 1971 as a successor to the Robert College. Considered one of the most beautiful campuses in the world, the university is located on the

European side of the Bosphorus Strait in Istanbul with a view of the strait and the fortress Rumelihisarı, dating back to 1453. Boğaziçi is one of the most prestigious and coveted universities in Turkey. It requires the highest scores on the competitive centralized entrance examinations (taken by nearly 1.5 million students each year) and accepts students from among the top-ranking high school graduates (the upper 5 percent) (Baslanti and McCoach 2006). Because of its selectivity, students at the university have a strong sense of distinction as gifted and high achievers and identify themselves as a select crowd. The teaching medium throughout the university is English, and there is a vibrant cultural and intellectual student life. Extracurricular activities are organized around more than fifty different student clubs, ranging from dance and theater to mountain climbing and scuba diving to chess and engineering. There are several culturally well-defined cliques and groups as well as politically based student organizations. Student profiles exhibit social-class and regional diversity: children from affluent families, modestly salaried classes, and poor backgrounds are almost equally represented in the student body. The gender composition of the student body was 43 percent women and 55 percent men in 2001, when I surveyed the Boğaziçi students' experiences and ideologies of gender and sexuality.

I chose this university as my research setting because it reflects, articulates, and actively constructs the culture of globalization, urbanism, and modernity, countering regional, local, or rural specificity with the cosmopolitanism and sophistication of the city. As an elite institution, it offers its students one of the major avenues for upward social and economic mobility but also brings together students with vastly different biographies, shaped by family backgrounds and regional and urban-rural distinctions, thereby providing me with a rich site for developing culturally specific examples of gender, sexuality, and self-making among upwardly mobile young Turks. Three sources of field data—a survey, in-depth interviews, and focus group research—provide the foundation of this book.

Surveying Sexual and Gender Ideologies of Boğaziçi Women and Men

Boğaziçi students (n = 360) who responded to the written survey were likely to express general views on sexuality that reflected both sexually inhibitive mores and the effect of sexual modernity, and the conflict between old and new values was apparent in their responses. A sizable majority, 74 percent of women and 63 percent of men, disagreed with the statement that "premarital sexuality is not acceptable because it is against our traditions" (appendix 1, table 1.1), although roughly 45 percent of men and women claimed that they didn't express/experience their sexuality at all (table 1.2). The majority of both women and men endorsed the idea that "it is important to establish emotional intimacy before engaging in sex"—88 percent and 62 percent of women and men, respectively (table 1.2). Thirty percent of men and 7 percent of women responded that they didn't need intimacy in order to have sexual relations, while 60 percent of men and 18 percent of women—double the number in each case—said they would consider having sex with an attractive person despite a lack of an intimate relationship.

There was a gender divergence in the way these young Turks believed sexuality should be expressed by men and by women, as well as in the actual level of sexual activity they reported (table 1.1). Men showed a stronger preference for sexual purity than women, though they were essentially divided on its importance. Forty-two percent of men placed significant import on marrying a virgin, and 51 percent agreed with the statement, "I want to marry a virgin," while a third of men wanted a sexually experienced partner. Slightly more than half of the women wanted their future partner to have had some sexual experience but not to have had sexual intercourse (table 1.2). Only a small minority (15 percent) preferred a spouse who was a virgin. Women's and men's virginity status did not show a great divergence: 64 percent of women and 49 percent of men claimed that they were virgins.

Between 80 percent and 90 percent of all Boğaziçi students believed that young Turkish men were "sexually hungry" (table 1.2). This belief may be behind most respondents' assertion that masturbation is normal for men (83 percent of men and 74 percent of women). Only a very tiny minority of women disapproved of female masturbation, and this disapproval was higher in men's responses (11 percent).

Notable was the large number of Boğaziçi men and women who responded with "no opinion" to questions about specific sex acts (table 1.2). Nearly 25 percent of women claimed they had no opinion about whether or not women should masturbate or whether their future spouse should have sexual experience outside of intercourse. Nearly 34 percent of women responded "no opinion" on whether it was acceptable for them to perform or receive oral sex. On the same topics, roughly one in five men also had no opinion. Whether these topics are an afterthought to most students, are truly neutral, or are taboo to the point of causing survey respondents to withhold their true feelings is difficult to ascertain.

When asked about their relationships, eight in ten students reported having had a boyfriend or girlfriend, and roughly half were in a relationship at the time of the survey (table 1.3). About half of those students in relationships said that they were having intercourse with their current partner. The number of men reporting sex was slightly higher than the number of women, at 53 percent of male versus 47 percent of female respondents.

The survey also addressed the experience of "hookups," or casual encounters of a sexual nature, among students (table 1.4). Women and men reported similar rates of hook-ups, with 26 percent of women and 32 percent of men stating that they had had such an experience; those who had had hook-ups claimed roughly two experiences within the previous year. Just over a third of students said their hook-up partner was already a friend, and another third met their hook-up at a party, at a bar, or on the Internet. (Only men, and rather few, at 4 percent, met their hook-up partner on the Internet. Presumably, women met men on the Internet, but none of these were surveyed.) Eighteen percent of women and 34 percent of men said they met their hook-up partner in some other location, indicating a creative dating culture. Most were sober or relatively sober at the time of the experience.

After the basics of frequency and fact, men and women's accounts of hook-ups diverged wildly. Only 7 percent of women thought they had initiated the encounter, while 22 percent of men reported that the woman had initiated their hookups. Roughly half of each gender said it "just happened." Women mainly claimed that the experience extended only to sex above the waist (44 percent), while only 15 percent of men claimed such an encounter. Twice as many men as women (60 percent versus 30 percent) reported having had sexual intercourse. The survey did ask if birth control had been used, and roughly half of respondents reported that they had not used any method of birth control. Still, if half or more of the women did not engage in intercourse, then it seems the other half were taking some sort of precaution. Across the board, more men than women seemed to believe that birth control had been used. Twice as many men reported believing their partner was on hormonal birth control (6 percent) as women reported being on birth control (3 percent). Men were far more satisfied with their hook-ups, with two-thirds claiming sexual and/or emotional satisfaction. Only one-third of women expressed such satisfaction, and only one in five thought the event, which was ostensibly caused by sexual drive, was actually sexually satisfying.

Boğaziçi men and women expressed similar views on gender roles as they relate to career, children, and domestic duties, with most men and women leaning toward an egalitarian approach (table 1.5). Women were more inclined than men to support progressive roles for women in the home and workforce, but the college men surveyed were also overwhelmingly in favor of women having roles outside of the domestic sphere. In a full divergence from the domestic lives of their mothers, Boğaziçi men and women expected that men would contribute to the household maintenance and that women would contribute financially. Although twice as many men as women thought that being a housewife was as satisfying as having a career, only 16 percent of men and 8 percent of women expressed that view. When asked about the statement, "what women really want is a home and children," only 7 percent of women and 14 percent of men agreed. Three-quarters of the women and two-thirds of the men thought that men were able and willing to do household chores, and nearly all women and three-quarters of men agreed that a man could raise children as well as a woman could.

As upwardly mobile college students, the respondents were focused on their future careers. Nearly all women (97 percent) and 85 percent of men expected that the female partner in a marriage would contribute financially to the family income. Most women and over half of men agreed that a working woman could properly care for her children, but when presented with the question in another light ("preschool children can be negatively affected from a working mother"), women were half as confident, and about half of men and women agreed.

In-Depth Interviews

What lies behind all these figures and regularities showing both gender divergences and convergences? A survey based on a representative sample (for the sampling procedures, see appendix 2) provides a significant amount of reliable information about the people we study and is an efficient tool for discovering and accounting for certain patterns and trends, but it cannot account easily for the processes and feelings behind stated opinions, and, by imposing preconceived categories that may have no meaning to the individual, it disregards the individual's definition of a situation. For instance, the survey results indicated that the level of educational attainment of the respondents' mothers directly and consistently affected their sexual views (table 1.6). The more education a mother had, the more likely her child was to hold liberated ideas about his or her sexuality and sexual expectations. Sixty-one percent of students whose mothers had only an elementary-level education reported that they wanted to marry a virgin, while only 18 percent of those whose mothers had gone to college held such a preference. One in two children of lower-education mothers also claimed that premarital sex was unacceptable because it went against their traditions. Only 15 percent of respondents whose mothers had a high-school-level education or higher agreed with the same statement. Children of high school– and college-educated women were also more likely to act on these views, with roughly one in two reporting having had intercourse. Only about one in four students of lower-education mothers reported having had sex. How should we understand and theorize this seemingly intimate interaction and intersection between social class, indexed by mothers' education, and sexuality? Why is there such a connection? What happens to those who transgress the maternal boundaries of sexual prohibition? How is the virginity norm negotiated between men and women in intimate relationships? These and similar important questions and goals of the study required collecting intimate accounts of young Turks through in-depth interviews.

Although I employed a uniform interview guide, my interview design enabled me to do extensive probing on questions that revealed self-reflections on conflicts and contradictions: How do young Turks position themselves within dominant cultural norms (coexisting and contradictory) that guide them in their emotional and sexual lives? How do they negotiate competing global and local cultural constructions of their roles, identities, and sexual selves? How and in what manner do they perceive, evaluate, and import the various models of gender identities and relations into their biographies? How do they balance their own individuality against the interests of their families and social class? Moreover, my interview design allowed for the incorporation of participants' own understandings of these processes into the analysis. This strategy proved to be successful in bringing into focus their points of view and their active participation in constructing their worlds.

In the interviews, I asked these young women and men to tell me about their families and the values of the people around them (family, school, neighbors, friends) during their childhoods and in the present. I asked how their upbringing may have played out in their romantic and sexual lives—whether it was enabling or inhibiting. I asked them how their romantic and sexual lives developed over time and how each significant relationship they engaged in evolved and was experienced emotionally and sexually. There were also specific questions regarding virginity and what the social/collective investment in the hymen signifies to them. My questions about their parents elicited descriptions of the ways in which they are similar to and different from their mothers and fathers, as well as how they viewed their parents' marriages. I wanted to know how they saw their futures professionally and with regard to building marriages and families. I asked them to describe how they imagined the kinds of mothers and fathers they would become. Some specific questions also elicited their views of feminism and whether they were involved in feminist activism. In addition to these and similar general questions, the interviews diverged in accordance with the participants' unique biographies and identities. For instance, in the interviews with the gay men, I asked questions about coming out, and when I interviewed the pious women, there were questions about exploring religiosity in their families of origin as well as questions relating to how they conceptualized their identity and about the social distance and difference as well as closeness and interaction they felt in relation to secular Muslim peers and older generations.

The interpretation of in-depth narrative-based interviews involves a number of difficult methodological and epistemological questions. We cannot simply treat "the complex architecture of narration about oneself" (Passerini 1989, 196–97) as documenting facts and events. We must ask: What are the rules and "routines" governing their interpretation? "All autobiographic memory is true. It is up to the interpreter to discover in which sense, where, for which purpose," writes Luisa Passerini (1989, 197).

I aimed to understand the narratives I collected as "a way of selectively organizing experience to produce and explain one's self" (Scott 1996, xii), and in my interpretations, I sought to understand my participants' purposes for telling me their biographies and about their romantic and sexual lives, the dialogical conditions that generated or undermined particular narratives, and the narrative resources (cognitive and emotional) that guided their vocabulary. For instance, in relation to the interviews I conducted with the pious young women, I was very aware that some of the narrative resources and vocabularies informed by their Islamic knowledge were constrained because they, correctly, assumed that they were explaining themselves to someone who was not steeped in Islamic knowledge. In situations when these women appropriated a narrative resource or a quotation from an Islamic text, their vocabulary was restrained in that it involved a "secular translation" for me.

In "Lost in Translation" A. Ka Tat Tsang and P. Sik Ying Ho (2007) brilliantly examine how academic language and the "everyday language" of people "interact and affect" each other (624). Although the authors believe that academic language and theories can enrich our understanding of people's experiences and behaviors, they "caution against its unquestioned privileging" (640). They remind us that all narratives, those related directly in everyday language by the people who lived them and those related indirectly by academics, are mere representations (626). However, the authors are particularly critical of theoretical discourses that seek totality at the expense of "elements that might threaten their cohesiveness or unity" (629). People can provide more subtle or nuanced understandings of their own experiences than theoretical systems often admit because "fragmentation, incoherence, and even contradiction are better tolerated in everyday speech" than in theoretical discourses (638). In such instances, they write, referring to research about sexuality, the "ambivalent nature of desire" defies categorization (636). This, they suggest, helps everyday language remain "inclusive and embracing" while "professional discourse . . . seeks to define and defend its discrete territory" (638). Yet they are careful to clarify that everyday language by itself is neither a superior nor an entirely sufficient form of representation and that theoretical discourse has a place in unraveling and illuminating people's lived experiences.

Throughout the book, I attempt in different ways to render my interpretative lenses visible to the reader. In analyzing the narratives, I focus on the deeply felt tensions and disjunctures my respondents face between self and other, sex and love, societal responsibility and autonomy, and identification and dis-identification. Also central to my analytical strategy is to probe whether individual meanings attached to tensions and contradictions are internally consistent and whether they are shared by others. Equally important, I have tried to analyze the narratives with the goal of empowering the reader by making clear not only how the theoretical/analytical perspectives I adopted or developed actually relate to the words and vocabularies participants chose and mobilized themselves but also how my theoretical interpretations of their lives as a feminist social scientist relates to my subjects' personal understandings and assertions about their behaviors, experiences, and aspirations. I hope this method, as an attempt "to 'represent' the 'voices' of the participants and let them interact with the theoretical articulations of professional discourse" (Tsang and Ho 2007, 630), enables alternative readings of the narratives for the reader.

1

Virginal Façades

Sonay's mother raised her to believe that "sex is something men want and that good girls don't give."[1] Although Sonay thinks that in the past her sexual assertiveness was repressed, she no longer has difficulty defining or initiating what she wants sexually. Yet, she cannot get rid of her mother's views on virginity. A "technical" virgin, she has been in an exclusive relationship with a man for three and half years, but she hasn't had sexual intercourse:

> People would do it after such a long relationship, and they do. People around me are very comfortable in this regard. I am certainly not against it; I have many friends who are not virgins, and I never changed my mind about them because of it. I do think it is something to be experienced, but I cannot practice it myself. Directly, I think of my mother, as if staying virgin is my responsibility to her.

Charged with personal, societal, and legal significance, the hymen, a fold of flesh, has the power to rule the sexual selves of unmarried women in Turkey. The classification of women into two categories of "*kadın*" and "*kız*" on the basis of the status of their hymen is still pervasive in Turkish culture and clearly reflected in Turkish vernacular. When an unmarried woman is described or addressed, the word "*kız*" (girl, intact hymen) is used. The *kız* becomes a *kadın* (woman, nonvirgin) when she is married and her hymen is broken. Explicit in the notion of *kız* is not only sexual purity and innocence but also, particularly importantly, the desexualization of unmarried women and the normative expectation that the transition from girlhood/nonsexual to womanhood/sexual should occur within the institution of marriage. In short, a nonvirgin unmarried woman has no place in the societal classification.

It is important to emphasize here that it would be wrong to assume that virginity norms remained an unquestioned conundrum or were not violated—openly or clandestinely—by the earlier generations of women in Turkey. I examine the strategic responses the young, upwardly mobile women I studied have to the tensions and disjunctures they face when their quest for sexual autonomy and freedom conflicts with the expectations of significant others. In probing the significance of virginity as a charged site of control over women's sexuality, I aim to illuminate the violation or preservation of virginity norms within the context of the multilayered societal transformations of the recent two decades, marked by the emergence of public discursivity—the proliferation of the production of "knowledge" and "talk"—about and on women's sexuality and virginity. Indeed, in recent years, the term "*bayan*" ("Ms." or "lady" in English) has gained currency as a form of address for women in both professional and social contexts in Turkey, a reflection of the increasing presence of professional young women in the public sphere and business circles. Although American feminists claimed "Ms." in the early 1970s against the sexist terms "Miss" and "Mrs.," which identify and divide women in relation to men and their marital status, the adoption of the title "*bayan*" in the Turkish context is quite different. In fact, there has been an ongoing feminist campaign against "*bayan*." As Turkish feminists maintain, this polite term, devoid of any sexual connotation, is deployed to avoid using "woman" and is thus a form of societal refusal to recognize the existence of women who are sexual but unmarried.[2]

In considering the violation or preservation of virginity norms in the contemporary context, I draw upon the narratives of a particular group of young women who, more than any other group of women in Turkish society, are likely to denounce virginity norms and forsake virgin identities. They are the upwardly mobile young women[3] whose investment in an elite education and a professional identity stands in stark contrast with virginity norms dictating chastity throughout schooling, including postgraduate education (thus considerably extending "girlhood"). The study of these young women thus sheds light on the degree, effect, and meanings of women's challenges to the dominant norms of virginity and patriarchal constructions of women's sexuality in Turkey. In forsaking virgin identities, women reveal the capacity to destabilize the resilient societal classification of two distinct categories based on hymen status.

This chapter draws upon interview data from thirty-seven young women between the ages of nineteen and twenty-three born amid the social transformations of the 1980s. The young women whose narratives are the focus of this chapter are homogenous in terms of their identities as secular Turks and share a commonality in their general embracement of feminist ideas, although they vary in claiming or refuting the feminist label. Class is a major source of difference among this group of young women, which includes privileged young women who come from well-to-do families with a range of resources and cultural capital as well as disadvantaged women with limited parental economic and cultural resources. This diversity allows us to explore the role of class-based permissive and prohibitive family environments in the formation of sexual subjectivities.

Do these educationally advantaged women emerge as active violators of the virginity norm? What are some of contradictions and tensions they face when their sexual autonomy and freedom conflicts with the expectations of significant others, such as parents? To what extent is resistance or conformity to virginity codes shaped by other sources of identity, such as family class origins?

Conceptualizing the Hymen

How can we conceptualize the hymen sociologically, this fold of flesh that rules the sexual lives of unmarried women? What does this social/collective investment in the hymen signify? As Mary Douglas (1989) formulated and analyzed with great clarity, "what is carved in human flesh is the image of society." Douglas conceptualizes that what delineates the confines of the body, its surface and skin, is systematically used to signify the other boundaries informed by social taboos and anticipated transgression. Indeed, within her analysis, the boundaries of the body parallel the confines of the social world. From Douglas's perspective, the hymen as a part of the body becomes a medium for societal classification. The hymen represents the line that demarcates women (*kadın*) from girls (*kız*), dividing two social statuses. The law, which codifies the image of a society, exposes these demarcations. Notably, while an attack on the male body is conceptualized as a violation of individual rights, an attack on a female body constitutes a violation of the family order. The virgin or nonvirgin status of a woman, combined with her marital status, frequently defines the nature of crime and its punishment. In

Turkey, up until recent changes in the penal code, the preservation of the family's honor and public decency took precedence at the expense of the victim. For example, a rapist was not held accountable if he consented to marry the woman he raped. Also, a man who abducted an unmarried woman would receive only three years in prison, as opposed to seven if the woman was married. Virginity examinations performed on "political detainees, women suspected of prostitution, and on girls in state orphanages, dormitories, and high schools" (Parla 2001, 168) were state sanctioned in Turkey until 1999. Because of extensive campaigns by feminist and human rights organizations and in order to harmonize the Turkish civil and penal law with those of the European Union, Turkey reformed its civil and penal codes in 2001 and 2004, including the ones pertaining to sexuality and gender relations.

The cultural significance of virginity in societies like Turkey has been explained in terms of the Mediterranean honor and shame complex (Goddard 1987; Lindisfarne 1994). Preoccupation with women's chastity/sexual purity appears in the code of honor. In its classical conceptualization, the code of honor refers to the honor or moral purity of a group—that is, the group defined as family, lineage, caste, class, region, and nation—and this honor is determined by the behavior of its women-folk. Honor is lost as a result of female misconduct. Women thus carry the burden of safeguarding group identity and group honor. The female body symbolizes the social boundaries of cultural identities, and virginity ultimately represents the demarcation between in-group and out-group mores. Moroccan immigrants in the Netherlands, for example, attempt to strategically assert moral superiority by controlling female sexuality, actively enforcing the moral order of their own marginalized community in relation to the dominant majority group (Buitelaar 2002).

Feminist activism in Turkey today continues to pivot around the question of so-called honor crimes in southeastern Turkey—the murder by family or kin members of women suspected of having transgressed the limits of sexual behavior as imposed by traditions, for example, engaging in premarital relationships, flirting, or dressing "inappropriately." While many human-rights and feminist interventions depend on a misguided vision of a modern nation-state and polity composed of sovereign, ungendered, autonomous subjects conceived of as explicitly transcendent of kinship, linked by the shared values embedded in the honor code, new feminist scholarship refuses to frame these "honor crimes" within the singular and narrow paradigm of an honor code. Instead, scholars suggest that we must turn our focus from solely examining particular "cultures" or "traditions" to an examination of the institutional, juridical, and legislative practices of the state, arguing that "what are defined as honor crimes and the ways of dealing with them are produced in relation to these institutional practices and discourses" (Kocacioglu 2004, 119). Outlining how the concept of honor is crucial to "the power regime of the modern nation-state in Turkey," Sirman (2004) argues that delegating honor to the realm of tradition as simply a cultural relation is "to render invisible the modes through which it still regulates the identity and the life of all women" (53). Moreover, "the legal institution recognizes the key role played by kinship and the family in the political order and organizes the clauses of the Civil and Penal codes so as to protect the social and familial order rather than the rights of the individual" (51).

Similarly, Ayse Parla (2001) challenges the framing of virginity exams as an appalling and reactionary expression of lingering traditions constructed in diametrical opposition to the nationalist sacred policy of modernization in the making of the modern Turkish nation-state.[4] By locating virginity exams in a very specific historical and political context, Parla elucidates how they function as a disciplinary tool of the modern state, which continues to inscribe the paradoxical nationalist ideologies of both "traditional" virginity and new modernity onto female bodies (modest yet publicly visible yet virtuous). In the post-1980s period, when women began reclaiming identities not endorsed by official ideology, the state increased the implementation of virginity exams to correct and to discipline female bodies in the name of the nation. Legal ambiguity and systematic gender discrimination continue to enable the state's routinized intrusion into women's bodies. Furthermore, the police are literally entrusted with protecting honor and chastity. Anyone who violates "public morality and the rules of modesty" may be detained. Such ambiguity has allowed police to threaten or force women to undergo virginity examinations, particularly in state institutions like orphanages and prisons. The threat strategically produces disciplined desexualized citizens, while the exam, as a corrective penalty, differentiates, classifies, and punishes deviants. This systematic regulation of female bodies in the name of the nation is most visible in the treatment of political detainees and prostitutes because their sexual behavior is perceived as an act against the state.

The increasing demand for artificial, surgically reconstructed virginity sheds intriguing light on the relationship between virginity and women's own attempts to gain control over their sexualities as well as the powerful hold virginity retains in the social milieu. It is argued that this demand among unmarried women for fake virginity is a sign of the weakening of traditional patriarchal control over women's bodies (Cindoglu 1997; Mernissi 1982). Cindoruk calls artificial virginity in Turkey a survival strategy for women, arguing that "a woman's utilization of medicine for her own needs, that is, repairs, may be conceptualized as the manifestation of women's demands for control over their own bodies" (260). Hymen repair, on the one hand, might be a helpful intervention for women in a climate that still values virginity. But, on the other hand, it also reifies virginity itself.

Despite the unquestionable significance virginity holds for the control and regulation of women's sexuality in Turkey, the meanings girls and women attribute to virginity remains an understudied topic. During the early 1990s, the question of virginity acquired a prominent place in public discourses and became a focus of feminist activism. Extensive media attention around virginity in the 1990s emerged because of a tragic event: the suicide of two teenage girls. Suspected of having engaged in sexual misconduct, these girls were asked to undergo "virginity tests" to determine if their hymens were intact. The supposed "shame" of their "sexual misconduct," or perhaps merely being subjects of such suspicions, drove them to suicide. As a result of national and international feminist activism to make this practice illegal, in 1999 a decree passed making it illegal for state officials to initiate/request virginity tests without the consent of the woman/girl in question.

Feminist scholars studying specific interpretations of virginity in other cultural contexts have applied Bourdieu's notion of capital to virginity, conceptualizing virginity as a form of sexual capital that can be traded for social and economic advantage (Gonzalez-Lopez 2005). In the United States, Laura Carpenter (2002) discerned three distinct frames in her study of the experience of virginity lost: virginity as a gift to be reciprocated for love and commitment, as a shameful stigma to be gotten rid of, and as a process of gaining sexual experience and knowledge. The author found that the virginity-as-a-gift metaphor is used by and affects the sexual behavior of women, while the stigma metaphor is more commonly used by men. Although these studies raise important questions, my interest and approach to the study of virginity in Turkey requires me to deviate from a strict application of Bourdieu's notion of capital. My intervention in this chapter has relevance to the premise of Bourdieu's theory: whether virginity is regarded as a legitimate (perceived and recognized) form of symbolic capital to be capitalized upon.

"Virginity Is Not between the Legs; It Resides in the Brain": The Making of "Modern" Sexualities

In addition to the thirty-seven women whose narratives make up the exploration of virginity attitudes in this chapter, I spoke to twenty-two men about their experiences and attitudes on sexuality, which is the subject of the next chapter. The narratives I collected reveal an overall strong gender convergence on ideas of sexuality in general, and virginity in particular.

First, both the women and the men viewed societal insistence on female virginity as a mark of traditionalism. They strongly rejected the idealization of female chastity and the symbolic value of virginity, its equation with honor and female purity. The intact hymen is not seen as the property of "others," family, parents, nation, culture.

Second, the women and men shared a common narrative in rejecting what they called "societal sexual restraint and repression." They promoted heterosexual desire experienced in premarital relations as a positive force—something important to individual happiness and successful future marriages. They also emphasized that the greatest obstacles to the sexual liberation of young Turks are anachronistic notions of virginity and sexual honor.

Third, both the women and men subscribed to an emerging code of sexual ethics that promotes premarital sex within the context of emotionality (*duygusallık*) and love.

Fourth, a vocabulary of gender equality dominated both the women's and the men's narratives. Four of the men I interviewed agreed with a conservative single standard that supports the concept of virginity for both men and women; sixteen of the men embraced a liberal single standard of virginity for neither; and one man I interviewed supported a blatantly sexist double standard of virginity for only women. None of the women I interviewed supported the traditional norm of virginity until marriage.

Fifth, the lived experiences of the tension between embracing a liberal sexual ideology and one's actual sexual practices brought to light another important gender commonality. The representation of "technical virgins" (those who engage in various sexual activities but avoid penile-vaginal intercourse) as a large middle category (nine) between virgins (ten) and nonvirgins (eighteen) among the young women I interviewed highlights this tension.

Finally, but not surprisingly, the men and women both drew contrasts between their own values concerning virginity and sexuality and those of their parents' generation. This contrast is sharpest among those participants who were raised in sexually restrictive small towns where mixed-gender interaction among youth and dating practices were limited.

In short, the values held by this group of young Turks mark an important transition to what they consider sexual modernity. As tradition-free agents, they subscribe to the principle that losing or preserving one's virginity should be a personal matter or choice. The concept of personal responsibility and ownership of the hymen is the key to this shift from external to internal authority. Power located external to the individual (a mark of tradition) is rejected and restraint from within is emphasized (a mark of modernity) (Adam 1996, 138). The changing emphasis from the physical reality of virginity to the morality of virginity is central to this sexual modernity: "virginity is not between the legs; it resides in the brain" is the way this idea was expressed colloquially by some young women and men I interviewed.

Irrespective of their actual sexual experiences and privately held views, both the men and the women stated that expressing a desire for a virgin bride or wanting to be a virgin bride was no longer an acceptable public narrative. This ideological resistance to the preservation of virginity is a prerequisite to the making of modern femininities and masculinities among the educated young secular Turks I studied. For young men, it is neither entirely advantageous nor practical to desire a virgin, because the status of virgin by definition signals inaccessibility and un-availability, a situation that is at odds with new definitions of masculin-ity aligned with the values of sexual modernity. Engaging in premarital sex is not only a means of expressing modern, liberated masculinity but also a strategy of social distinction from other "traditional," sexually re-pressed men.[5] Similarly, for young women, a man who wants a virgin as his bride is seen as backward and therefore not a desirable partner.

It is important to note that these young men's and women's shifting notions of sexuality are couched in the language of the tradition/moder-nity opposition, revealing the centrality of this dualism to the constitu-tion of their subjectivities. The tradition/modernity opposition exercises a special potency in organizing experience and consciousness, giving rise to a self-reflexivity in which the conduct and feelings of the self are continuously assessed for their modernity or traditionality. I con-cur with those who argue for the abandonment of the tradition/mo-dernity opposition. However, I believe the centrality of this dualism in people's understanding poses a serious challenge to theoretical attempts to abandon it. Failure to acknowledge the tradition/modernity opposi-tion in interpretation risks a misconstruing of the terms most central to the self-understanding and worldview of its subjects. I preserve the language of my subjects while critically analyzing the binary with regard to virginal façades to explain the complexity of negotiations and resigni-fications attached to virginity and sexual honor.

In Search of a Self: Home Is Not Where the Heart Is

The overwhelming majority of both the women and the men in my study agreed with the idea that their parents' generation was defined by the ideals of selfless femininity and protective masculinity. Renouncing these gender ideals, they expressed a desire for individualized, liber-ated selves—for autonomy and self-realization in work, marriage, and leisure. The ideology of individualism, constructed against the selfless feminine and protective masculine of the parental generation, is pivotal in fashioning new gender and sexual identities for these young Turks. This includes claims for sexual freedom and autonomy and antipathy toward marriage and parenthood, forming a strong critique of the patri-archal construction of womanhood among their mothers' generation.

Because they believe exclusively maternal identities vacate a subjective experience of having an independent self, they all see the model of womanhood represented by their mothers as problematic.

The antagonism against marriage and the position of housewifery among these young women highlights the rejection of the selfless feminine embodied by their mothers. The following fragments from two interviews capture how these women's antimaternal narratives are constructed against the backdrop of their mothers' lives:

> I am so different from my mother. She has devoted herself to her children. I can say that she has no private life of her own. . . . She doesn't have any hobbies, nothing she does is for herself, she devoted her entire life to constructing a future for us. I don't think I would construct a life like hers, and I don't want her to do so either. I am warning her but with no avail. As a result, she is putting happiness aside and seeing herself only as a mother, and she has built her life on the basis of this duty. . . . I wouldn't design a life for myself over children. . . . Even my mother herself started saying that when she looks back now she didn't live a life. When I go back to look at my life in the future I don't want to say, "I didn't live a life." (Ekin, 21)

> This is what is never going to happen [to me]: my mother is university educated, an economist—she even has a master's degree . . . but since my father was required to go different places because of his job, he is a civil engineer, and in that same juncture my brother had problems in the daycare center, my mother quit her job. . . . I never imagine I would do such a thing, leaving aside all my labor for my education since I was seven years old—considering I have been receiving education since that age— for someone who enters my life later. I mean a husband here, and marriage and a child. Would I leave my job? . . . I hope I won't. (Canan, 23)

In Ekin's and Canan's narratives, we see that their adverse feelings toward mothering hinge on a construction of motherhood and the self as coterminous, with no permission for the mothers to develop any independent desires and self-interests outside of motherhood. These young women are equally negative about marriage and especially about the dangers of the "housewifely" role affiliated with it. Beril (21) and

Sena (21) below articulate this association and their objections to marriage and even cohabitation.

> I don't want to get married because I don't want to end up thinking, unconsciously, ok we got married, now it is going to be difficult to divorce. Living together in the same house and being married are really two different things. For example, now I spend a lot of time with Beymen [her boyfriend] at his place and I have my stuff at his place but we are lovers. I don't pay attention to cleaning etc. . . . but had this place been our home, that might have been an issue. Knowing that your partner can just walk away any moment I think may cause you to show better behavior. I can live together but I don't think I can manage marriage. This year one time for the first time I set the table and called him "let's eat" but then I felt like a housewife, and for two days I tried to convince myself that "it is normal, no big deal I just put a dish and forks in front of him, there is nothing to exaggerate and get worked up about." (Beril)

> I don't look at marriage warmly. . . . I prefer living alone; [my lover and I] might have different friends, and one of us sometimes wants to be alone. These things could be difficult when you are married or living with someone. You start intervening in each other's life too much, and in my opinion spending too much time with the same person alienates you from each other. Instead of living together, each one should have his/her own place and they should come together only when they desire. This sounds more logical to me. (Sena)

While there are no empirical studies of Turkish young women from a generational perspective, one recent study conducted by Ayca Alemdaroglu (2007) articulates the emergence of a shared common identity among young women who, despite their economic and educational differences, seek an escape from femininity and negotiate respectability on their own terms. However, the escape from traditional femininity and respectability to individual selfhood is fraught with tensions and contradictions because it occurs amidst a continued societal emphasis on virginity. This insistence on virginity forms and regulates the sexual behavior of young women and figures centrally in the ways in which they enter, experience, negotiate, or exit romantic and sexual relationships.

Rewriting Romance: Construction of the Desired Man and
Relationship Ideals

These young women's romantic energies and longings are not centered
on finding and securing a mate for making a good marriage. In seeking
relationships to expand and enrich their selves, they chart a new, nonpatriarchal romantic/intimate relationship trajectory. This relationship
ideal is expressed succinctly by Canan: "A relationship is about what
you add to each other. When a relationship is over, the important question is this: What did I gain from it? What did the relationship and he
add to myself?" This ideal of intimate relationships is also key to understanding how desirable masculinity is constructed by these women.
As Talbot and Quayle (2010) note, women are not "passive consumers
or recipients of masculinity." They are active participants in the construction and maintenance of (potentially counterfeminist) masculine
ideals, helping to "coproduce, normalize, and even fetishize masculinities" (256). Among my research participants, a trope of emancipation
from patriarchal romance—the merging or loss of the self in another—
organizes the imagery of the desired relationships and the desired man.
Particularly, female desire for masculine ideals is negotiated through
problematizing a patriarchal male identity predicated on conceptions
of dominance, control, and intrusion upon female identity. Rewriting
romance as a sphere of self-assertion and a site for the expression of
agency and autonomy rather than a sphere of self-sacrifice and female
subservience to accommodate men and their desires represents a very
significant shift in the construction of ideal masculinity.

The Ideal Man: Conformism and Transgression

The narratives of the ideal man in these women's accounts are marked
by a dominant storyline about escaping from the possessive, protection-
ist, and restrictive masculinity of patriarchal romance. However diverse
the representations of the desired man are—variously inflected, multiply
defined—they are notable for their emphasis on a repudiation of a model of
masculinity that is only experienced as restrictive and limiting by women.
Therefore, the figure of the ideal man emerges as a reaction or alternative
to patriarchal masculinity. To put it differently, patriarchal male identity

in Turkish society is subjected to extensive interrogation by these young women as a way of negotiating and then refiguring the ideal man.

The portrayal of the desired man is constructed around the dual demands of gender egalitarianism and possession of power, a highly specific blend of conformism and transgression. By "conformism" here, I refer to the young women's embracement of high ambition in men to become socially, culturally, and economically dominant—vital for upward mobility. By "transgression," I mean the dislodging of men's gender-based traditional privileges and their traditional superiority feelings and displays. Ayşe's narrative captures this dual desire:

> He should be extremely intelligent with ambitions and accumulation to achieve his goals. When I look at him, I should be able to see confidence and power in his personality. Of course I don't mean power over me or other women in his life. On the contrary, I cannot imagine myself being with a man who treats women as second-class citizens and tries to dominate them. (Ayşe, 22)

As Ayşe's description makes clear, desiring a man who holds gender-egalitarian views and is capable of acting on them does not mean that the dominating agency of men is rejected. These women's descriptions of the desired man do not articulate what is commonly referred to as "nonhegemonic masculinities" (emotionality, a desire to nurture, and rejection of power and dominance assigned to them by the dominant culture) (Talbot and Quayle 2010), nor do they celebrate the relinquishment of mastery and control in men. On the contrary, the pervasive emphasis is on the image of a powerful man as a source of admiration, attraction, and desire. However, there is a very significant underlying uniformity in the ways the desired man is made to relate to power: he should be able to possess and exude power, not simply because he is a male but by virtue of his earned power as a result of his accomplishments, cultural accumulations, and high-level aspirations for himself. As expressed by Yelda, "When I mean power, I mean power emanating from achieving something . . . only that kind of male power creates admiration and desire in me."

The construction of the desired man is imbricated with the imagery of an ambitious, self-directed man who has long-term goals for developing his potential to its maximum, who cares about improving himself, and who is interested in self-enrichment through participating in activities that provide intellectual stimulation and opportunities for unique and creative accomplishments. This desired man—who is invariably depicted in terms of his capacity to create intellectual and cultural stimulation and awakening—is multidimensional, possessing varying interests. Having intellectual, cultural, and artistic interests outside academic work is seen as reflective of a masculine desire for self-expansion. For these women, this multidimensionality offers the potential for engagement with a wider realm of social and cultural worlds with renewable sources of excitement. In other words, the idealized embodied masculinity is more expansive than middle-class cerebral masculinity that privileges intellect and academic success (McDowell 2003).

It is important to note that these women do not cherish ambition that is overpowering. Those men who are overly ambitious to achieve what they want are offered as examples of undesired men because they are inauthentic, egotistical, and deceitful. In the service of their ambitions, they develop false and insincere relationships, manipulating their environments and people to advance themselves. The women reject this trait because sensitivity toward others, male altruism (doing good for others even against one's own rational interests or desires), and social responsibility also form the contours of the desired man. Men who behave indifferently toward others do not appeal to these women. As Didem (22) observes, "every lover can make his lover feel special, but if he cannot approach a woman who is falling down in the street, this does not have any meaning for me."

In addition to well-regulated ambition, the image of the desired man is also grounded in the physical language of the body: modes of self-presentation, bodily habitus, and external appearance play a significant role in attraction and desirability. While the body features prominently, what is referred to as having potential attractiveness, seductiveness, or pleasure is not necessarily male beauty or handsomeness. Rather, the stress is on continuities between the body, the psyche, and internal selfhood—the body that represents the self. Hale's (22) description of this association between the body and internal selfhood is quite typical: "Inner qualities that appeal to me are reflected in physical characteristics—his walk, his posture, and his tone—self-confident or not. If he is not self-assured, weak, and doesn't know his own self-worth, this is reflected in his walk, his talk, his overall demeanor and gestures." In other words, the ideal man carries power in his body. Body language also embodies the tastes and norms of the urban middle-class habitus. In this regard, Feray (22) refers to eating habits: "I shouldn't be disturbed while watching him eat; he should know the rules about how to eat." Bourdieu's concept of habitus (1984) is very relevant here as he stresses that class-based dispositions are embodied and internalized in particular ways.

Not surprisingly, images of desirable masculinity are constituted in large part through the exclusion of men who are considered to be unsophisticated, one-dimensional, unambitious, overly cerebral and lifeless, and meek—men without any cultural accumulation, who carry themselves with signs of a certain helplessness. Additionally, men who enact macho stereotypes are regarded as vulgar, rude, sexist and overbearing, and dominating. In short, men who are actively devalued, rendered peripheral and marginal in the urban, middle-class social and cultural realms, are deemed undesirable by these women. It goes without saying that desiring particular men and not others is a class-based phenomenon and learned in one's class habitus (Bourdieu 1984). Reading enactments of different forms of masculinity through class, these women intimately connect differences in men with differences in class locations and urban/rural origins. As Iris Marion Young (1989) writes, boundaries are key to the construction of any identity category: "Any move to define an identity, a closed totality, always depends on excluding some elements, separating the pure from the impure. . . . The logic of identity seeks to keep those borders firmly drawn" (303). The construction of desired masculinity, then, is also about a policing of borders and serves to prohibit cross-class romantic and sexual relationships, while also actually serving to produce and consolidate class identities. Indeed, almost all the relationships these young women engage in carry class convergences in terms of similarity in family socioeconomic backgrounds, ethnicity, and family class cultures. In this regard, breakup narratives significantly revealed instances in which relationships that were otherwise going well were ended upon the discovery of the presence of pious religious identities or Kurdish ethnic origin in boyfriends' family biographies.

It is important to underscore that the young women who give form and content to the articulations of desired masculinity reflect their own high statuses. They are concerned that forming romantic liaisons with educationally low-status men will trigger male insecurity and resentfulness in their partners about being in a disadvantaged position due to their lesser human and cultural capital. They even find it difficult to contemplate romantically attaching with men outside elite universities like Boğaziçi, or even consider it out of the question to do so. This desire—finding men who are able to share their successes and not be threatened by them—serves to make class boundaries nonpermeable.

Indeed, in romantic relationships that reflect their own status as high achievers and their own cultural capital, they claim respect and recognition for their intellectual capabilities. Nonrecognition of what they consider "their value" by their romantic partners is one of the most important reasons for breakups. Selda (21) claimed that while her friends always valued the force of her ideas, conveying to her that "your ideas are very important for us because they orient us," her former boyfriend was making her feel "lacking" (*yetersiz*) and cultivating a sense of deficiency in her: "He was not valuing me, in fact he was valuing me, but not my thoughts and ideas. On the contrary, he would look at me by making funny faces: 'look at the things you know. You know everything blah blah'—kind of look."

In their study of young, upwardly mobile South African women's constructions of acceptable masculinity, sociologists Kirsten Talbot and Michael Quayle (2010) found that women's attitudes toward displays of hegemonic masculinity are heavily context dependent. As a rule, the researchers found that when discussing masculinities in social or work-based contexts, the women tended to appeal to "nice guy" traits coded traditionally as unmasculine, such as romantic passivity, emotionality, and a desire to nurture. On the other hand, when discussing masculinities in romantic or familial settings, the women used more traditional, hegemonic masculine traits such as being assertive, active, and protective, to describe ideal masculinities. In contrast, young Turkish women's constructions of the idealized embodied masculinity do not neatly divide masculinities by such contexts but rather emphasize merging of constitutive traits of conservative and transgressive. What appeals to the young women I studied is male versatility (as opposed to rigidity) in modulating conduct to practice imaginative engagement with contexts and women, articulated with the expression "knowing how to behave depending on the context/situation" (*duruma göre nasıl davranacağını bilmek*). Indeed, the deployment of flexibility in men's subjectivities is considered a core disposition of middle-classness and nonpatriarchalness.

Relationship Ideals: "Without Restricting Each Other's Freedom"

The powerful longing of young women for equal relationships in which their intellectual power is cherished is accompanied by another central longing: the creation and maintenance of autonomy and independence in a relationship such that there is no "merging or loss of the self in another." Among this group of young women, Ekin deployed highly conventionalized language that offered imagery of an ideal relationship based on a balance between sharing intimacy and maintaining independence:

> This idea of two people becoming one disturbs me; two different people in fact means two different lives. There should be an independence through which you can lead your own life to do things you want to do. But at the same time, along with this independence, sharing should also be at the maximum level.

Similarly, Meltem (21) noted that lovers "should have [their] own lives but those lives should merge with one life." Firmly couched in the expression of "a relationship without restricting each other's freedom" (*birbirlerinin özgürlüklerini kısıtlamadıkları*), this notion of autonomy and independence in a relationship means the ability to pursue one's own interests while respecting the ability of the other to do the same, as well as the ability not only to express one's own desires, interests, and thoughts in a relationship but also to act on them.

When my respondents refer to freedom concretely, they mean freedom to shape their existence and to determine their involvement outside intimate relationships. This notion of freedom is again constructed against patriarchal courtship/romance/marriage, where male actions infringe upon the independence of women, circumscribing their behaviors and identities. Autonomy serves as the crucial component of this nonpatriarchal relationship ideal because it allows for romantic partners to relate on an equal level and entails respecting the desires and personalities of one another, making possible mutual recognition—full comprehension, deep understanding of each other. My participants' definition of the ideal relationship is remarkably similar to what Giddens (1992) calls a "pure relationship" in which personal democracy allows for autonomy, and with autonomy comes the responsibility to respect one's partner's independence, to be reflective about one's own actions, and to hold one another accountable to maintaining a situation of equality.

For these young women, intimacy as an expression of love and relatedness helps lay the path for autonomy and independence. How do they define intimacy? In order to describe what they consider to be true intimacy, they reference the ability to completely and mutually self-disclose without any reservations and to elicit the total understanding of themselves and their value by their romantic others. Sonay, whose story opened this chapter, illustrates this perspective with a particular reference to the virginity issue. Sonay claimed that her boyfriend of three and a half years is comfortable with her decision not to have vaginal intercourse because "he knows well why I am not 'being together'" (a euphemism for coitus, the most complete expression of sexual intimacy):

I know occasionally he wants it and vocalizes, like "at this moment I really want it" but he never pressures me. In fact we talked about it the other day. I said, "What would you do if I said I wanted it?" His response was, "That was a desire in the moment when we were making love (being sexual without vaginal intercourse) and later you would regret it; I don't want you to be unhappy."

Later he reassured her that "it will not happen until you are absolutely sure." For Sonay, because there is a true love and intimacy between them, her boyfriend deeply understands her and her motivation (she defines it as "my consideration of my mother's feeling") to the extent that he even can anticipate the emotional and psychic consequences for her of potential transgression. Instead of competing with Sonay's mother's wishes regarding her sexuality, thus threatening Sonay's deep attachment to the mother, he recognizes the importance of mother-daughter connectivity in shaping Sonay's sexual self.

Sezen's (23) story describes her attempts to withstand and respond to the creation of a subjugated, merged self, illustrating young women's yearning to establish and negotiate relationships in which they can maintain their personal autonomy. Her story is instructive as it is an illustration from a fresh relationship. It also brings to the discussion a complex experience of contradictory desires of the body and the mind. Although she has never engaged in any sexual activity other than being kissed and touched by her very first boyfriend, whom she had started seeing just two weeks before her interview, 23-year-old virgin Sezen said, "I don't feel myself a woman or a girl, I see myself in between." In high school she "didn't think that relationships with men were wrong," but she "couldn't practice it [herself]." She explained, "Maybe I wasn't good at it, or maybe had my body concurred with my thoughts, I would have experienced things in high school." When Sezen arrived at college, she and most of her close friends lacked any sexual or romantic history, and she wasn't able to experience any romance until her last year in college, although she fell madly in love with a man at Boğaziçi who never noticed her.

She had been in love with her boyfriend for six or seven months before they got together, but she couldn't approach him. He was not aware that she was interested in him. She made him feel that he was the one who had feelings about her first—something that makes Sezen happy: "Men don't like girls being dominant—knowing more than boys." The central preoccupation animating Sezen's romantic and sexual experimentation with her very first boyfriend was avoiding self-subjugation—not allowing him to dictate what she should want.

Sezen admits that she is drawn to her boyfriend and sexually awakened by him because she loves the attention she gets from him—she has never had close attention from a man before—for example, his pushing back her hair when it falls forward on her temple. He is more experienced and knows she has no experience, so he is careful to behave cautiously, making sure that she does not show negative reactions to his sexual advances. Neither Sezen nor he has private space, so they are getting closer sexually (no kissing on the mouth yet) in parks and other similar places. Her love for him is sensual and arouses sexual desire. He makes her very sexually excited, even when she is only thinking about him. Indeed, Sezen's inexperienced status and sexual innocence made her the subject of a remark by her best friend, who, knowing that she had never gone out with a man before, told her, "You will have orgasm when you first hold a man's hand."

While Sezen discovered the thrill of sexual desire attached to a specific man, a consuming dilemma surfaced: "When we sit in a booth I don't sit across from him, but he tries to be face-to-face, trying to get close. In fact I like it, but my body behaves in a way that indicates it does not like it." Her body acting the part of the sexually timid female, responding to a model of sexual interaction in which female passivity is enacted, bothers her. And indeed, during our conversation, Sezen recounted how she was acutely aware of and uncomfortable with a passive and submissive role during the first act of intimacy with her boyfriend—touching hands. When they took a long stroll, she kept her hands in her pocket. He tried to get her hands out of her pockets, but she said to him, "I like to walk with my hands in my pockets." She added, "But I also wanted to hold hands with him." Reflecting on her inexperience, Sezen observed,

> I don't know how to hold hands—you are not supposed to hold his hand as if you are holding your mother's hand. Indeed, he changed the way I held his hand and I said, "you know I am a rookie"—that is we showed that he is the experienced one and I am the inexperienced one. . . . While holding hands he was constantly putting his thumb on mine. One time I took my thumb over his. This troubled him. He said, "Hmm you are trying to dominate, aren't you?" [Sezen replied,] "How much we are interested in satisfying the need for dominance, even a finger reveals this."

To say "I am in love" makes Sezen uncomfortable "because regardless of what the other side does, you feel you are being besieged and conquered. The feeling of imminent disempowerment, self-subjugation prevents me from feeling powerful." To explain this feeling of being besieged, she cited a particular incident. Like many men in Turkish society, her boyfriend is an ardent fan of a particular football team, and he wanted to convert her to his team. She said no. Although she could have easily converted, as she is not an ardent fan of any team, she saw this conversion as an important symbol of her besiegement and submission to his will. She read this demand as a demand for self-renunciation, her love culminating in a loss of identity. Sezen's attempt to withstand a submissive role extends beyond sexual interaction. As the relationship unfolds, she said she was continuing to discover many other issues emerging in the realm of domination and subordination, fostering in her a sense of unease and disappointment. In this regard, she also observed that her boyfriend is already feeling a lack because of her superior knowledge and taste in their common hobbies (films and jazz music).

Caught in between her sexual desire for her boyfriend and her desire not be subjugated in the relationship, Sezen feels ambivalent about whether she is ready to go "all the way" with him. Because love presents itself in the form of submission to his wishes and her surrender, if she does have sex with him and commit more fully to the relationship, she thinks it will involve renouncing her personality and her interests. Sezen is against marriage—seeing it as bringing unhealthy dependencies and many responsibilities: "The idea of sharing what I plan to do with another person scares me and having to make all of my decisions with that other person." For her, achieving an independent female identity— being a woman who possesses her own decision-making abilities—in a marriage is not within the realm of possibility. The ideal in her head is to have a "lonely world": she wants to live alone, but have a lover who occasionally visits her in a world in which neither restricts the other's freedom.

Another participant, Didem, commented on male ideals of the perfect woman by noting that "unfortunately, Turkish men like women who need them, the type of woman who is needy." Speaking in a male voice, she further elaborated the desired woman in the male narrative: "It would be nice if she is voiceless and if she does whatever I say to her." But Didem simultaneously complicated her own formulation with a counternarrative, stating that men are, in fact, attracted to unsubordinated, self-possessed, and self-trusting women like her because the idea of chasing after and getting such powerful girls strokes their pride and serves to increase their self-esteem, but they find relationships with these girls difficult, a topic that I examine in depth in the next chapter.

Given the noncomplicity these upwardly mobile, highly educated women demonstrated in maintaining traditional gender roles in romantic contexts, we should conclude that romantic ideals act as sites of contestation for patriarchal, hegemonic masculinity in Turkish society and are important sources of its dissolution. In the next chapter, we will see the complex challenges some men face in disowning the patriarchal construction of masculinity as protective, controlling, and dominant.

Virginal Façades

A virgin is an elite female among females, withheld, untouched, exclusive. (Ortner 1978, 32)

Among upwardly mobile, educated young Turks, a virgin is no longer an "elite" (valued) woman, but then neither is a self-proclaimed nonvirgin. It is within this dichotomy between the two undesirable states of the virgin and the nonvirgin that new constructions of young elite women are being built. In order to achieve the new expectations of desirability, the new elite woman must demonstrate a capacity for passion and sex, not just romance and marriage. She must not be sexually innocent or naïve, but neither should she exude excessive sexual experience. She must evoke sexual availability and accessibility and must be ready to disregard the spatial and moral boundaries of her family. Vis-à-vis her female peers, she must reveal a self that is in control, a capacity to negotiate and attract and reject men successfully. Vis-à-vis her parents, she must maintain a façade of being sexually untouched while also engaging in relationships with men.

In order to negotiate the contradictory expectations and normative definitions of how young women behave, feel, and relate sexually to men, the young women I studied attempted to create identities in relation to their state of virginhood that are purposefully ambiguous. I call these identities virginal façades to capture the dynamic nature of putting on appearances, pretensions, and creating or permitting silences that enable young women to accommodate their own desires and negotiate the often conflicting expectations of parents, men, and peers. The notion of virginal façades, ironically, also befits the façade embedded in the popular and official reference to unmarried women as "*kız*" (girl), which assumes that all unmarried women are virgins. Finally, the notion of façade helps to signify the importance of the "audience" in managing identities; the self must be properly presented and then evaluated by others. Peer-group and parental scrutiny and judgment of the sexual behavior of young women figure strongly in the construction of this virginal façade. First, I proceed by examining how peer judgments are articulated and experienced.

Motor Girl: A Cautionary Tale

Evaluations of the sexual behavior of women by their peers operate within what Skeggs (1997) terms a dialogic form of recognition: recognizing the recognitions of others. Recognitions are always deeply imbued with value judgments of others. The power of these judgments lies in their explicit or implicit expression through day-to-day peer conversations, romantic and sexual storytelling about others, and gossip. These all operate to differentiate, categorize, and label young women and their sexual behaviors and practices, distinguishing "respectable" girls and relationships from "bad" girls and undesirable relationships.

Those young women who engage repeatedly in uncommitted encounters involving acts of penetrative sex are judged and categorized as "promiscuous" and referred to as "motor girls" or "*bir gecelik kızlar*" (one-night girls). They are alternatively labeled as "*yırtık*" (torn) or "*bozulmuş*" (spoilt), explicit references to the broken hymen. It is not, however, the broken hymen alone that differentiates the motor girl from other girls, but also her refusal to seek sex within a setting of love. Most importantly, the motor girl signifies fear of unbridled sexuality and unrestrained sexual freedom. She is the personification of the notion that a young woman who loses her virginity loses control of her sexuality, because as a nonvirgin, she has to sleep with every man she has a relationship with.[6] This fear of "falling" is not only associated with the danger and stigmatization of multiple sexual encounters and sexual adventure, as personified by "motors," but is also linked to a host of other conducts and practices, ranging from having multiple brief affairs with or without sexual intimacy to changing boyfriends too often and even to falling in and out of love too frequently. All these practices are open to the potential interpretation of a manifestation of unbridled female sexuality. The nonvirgin women I interviewed explained that this was the reason some girls are reluctant to "go all the way." It is this anxiety about navigating the domain of complex and freer sexual choices when no longer a virgin that figures centrally in young women's choices to remain technical virgins. This unease is a sign of danger on the threshold of identity, an identity in-between, with its claims of innocence and sexual purity and its fears of dissolution and falling to impurity. It is in this context that losing virginity is considered such a transformative and enduring event.

Feray (22) talked about how her best friend responded harshly after she broke up with a young man whom she didn't even have sex with, telling her, "You finished it again, once more a relationship began quickly and ended quickly." For Feray, her friend's "reaction was very hurtful because it was like a reaction: 'let me tell you how many men you slept with.' This was very disturbing to me because it was as if she was saying 'it is not even clear how many men you have had so far.'"

The motor girl's opposite is not a virgin but a girl who is in control, who "doesn't let herself be used in a relationship," and who demonstrates internal restraint. Leyla (22) described the reaction of her dorm friends to her relationship with men by relating how her friends quizzed her motives, asking her questions that, in her view, emphasized their denial of her own desires and pleasure:

> "Why are you sleeping with every man who comes to your way? You shouldn't sleep with everyone. How long have you known that man? Do you love him? Did you really fall for him? . . . Why are you letting yourself be used?" As if I myself didn't want it; as if he used me and left me . . . they say, "don't be stupid, you deserve better," as if I need to get something in return: "will he see you again?"

The imperative to "not let yourself be used" dictates the most salient dimension of "respectable" expressions of a young woman's sexual behavior, the opposite of what a motor girl is imagined to practice. The language of self-control and self-respect contained in the vocabulary of "not letting yourself be used" strongly resonates with this particular group of women who are foremost defined by their high-achiever status. Yet because this imperative is relative—whether one is "letting herself be used" cannot be determined outside specific situational contexts—only those who experience sex with a steady boyfriend in a long-term relationship are able to change the meaning of it. Thus the virginal façade is not merely about displaying and narrating a self that cannot be recognized as "motor" by others but more importantly is about presenting relationships with men in such a way that compliance to the framework of the fusion of love and sex is clearly present.

In these new definitions of purity and impurity, a girl who loses her virginity in a long-term relationship, which is assumed to be connected to love, is still morally a virgin (pure), while a woman who loses her virginity during a casual encounter becomes impure. Because long-term relationships and sex within those relationships are privileged in this new code of sexual ethics, the young women I interviewed chose not to disclose their sexual histories and experiences even to close friends, with the exception of a few confidantes. They neither disclose their state of virginhood nor share any information regarding how far they go sexually. Instead, they adopt virginal façades.

Parental expectations form the strongest source of internalized pressure to remain a virgin before marriage, though this is not the only moral gauge. In the next section I turn to an examination of what parental expectations contribute to the construction of virginal façades.

Don't Ask, Don't Tell: Navigating Parental Expectations

While not the only moral gauge for these women, parental expectations form the strongest source of internalized pressure for them to stay virgins. Even though daughters' understanding of parental expectation concerning their sexuality involves the dictum that they should remain untouched until marriage, it would be quite wrong to assume that parental control manifests itself only in terms of inhibition. According to these young women's narratives, daughters are actively encouraged by their mothers to "find one" so that they can maintain a "respectable" relationship with a desirable young man who could potentially become a future husband. This parental expectation is especially present for lower-status families who are eager to marry their daughters upward. Even the most sexually conservative parents expect their daughters to use their chances to build romantic relationships that could lead to marriage with a higher-status spouse. Similarly, upper-middle-class families' downward-mobility concerns also motivate an interest in their daughters' intimate relationships.

Generally speaking, for the parents of Boğaziçi women, the relative sexual freedom of their daughters, the ease with which they interact with male peers, and the formation of deep cross-gender friendships are in fact symbolic of their modern, educated, and cultivated status. As high-achieving girls, they are also expected to have fun and engage in respectable courtship with men. Yet the parental definition of a respectable relationship promotes sexual modesty, restraint, and the preservation of virginity. How do daughters then manage such a tightrope of liberated modernity and sexual restraint?

By and large, young women remain silent about temporary boyfriends. Boyfriends are introduced to parents if the relationship is intended to last. Daughters also don't disclose boyfriends when they anticipate parental disapproval of a particular partner. Moreover, they do not talk about or introduce partners who fit the definition of a perfect future "groom" if they are ambivalent about them—this is to avoid the opposite problem: being pressured to maintain an unsatisfying relationship. However, the most important concern for a young woman as a high-achiever daughter is to avoid creating an image of herself as a serial dater, someone who struggles and constantly fails in her relationships and continually needs to move on to the next man, blemishing her high-achiever status. In response to my question why she was hiding her current relationship from her parents, Buket (21) related a very common experience:

> Why do I feel the need to keep it secret? . . . Because I already told [my parents] about the previous boyfriend and about the one before him. Both of them ended fairly quickly, we didn't get along. This time I decided not to tell them before I get certain things [in the relationship] on track. Because if it ends again quickly I don't want to face them once more to say, "it has finished again."

These silences also enhance daughters' freedom to navigate their clandestine lives without constantly lying. A virginal façade inevitably leads to a clandestine life. Those who live away from family and/or live on- or off-campus alone or with friends have ample opportunities for transgressions; therefore, they tend to disclose less to their parents, and their secret lives tend to be more extensive. In contrast, young women who live with their families in Istanbul have limited opportunities to transgress, and thus their secret lives tend to be hard to manage.

According to the young women I interviewed, all of their parents adopt a "don't ask, don't tell policy" concerning their daughters' virginity, including the most sexually liberal parents. This policy, freeing daughters from feigning compliance and shielding them from potential conflicts with their parents, saves the parents from the anxieties of knowing. Indeed, everyone is invested in the façade.

"A False Sense of Self": Guilt, Class, and Sexual Secrecy

Not surprisingly, sexual secrecy creates guilt, and guilt is steeped in social class. Indeed, the women who expressed the most guilt are those who come from modest class backgrounds with uneducated parents, typically with rural origins. Compared to savvy, highly educated, upper-middle-class parents, these parents' lack of knowledge about the daily lives of their daughters equip them poorly to understand the cultural milieu and relationships that their daughters have entered through their education in an elite environment in Istanbul, enabling their daughters to put on façades easily. Mehtap (22) had many short-term sexual relationships as well as a longer relationship with a boyfriend but was still a technical virgin. She comes from a modest family background with uneducated parents. Living at home made it especially hard for her to experience her sexual autonomy and required her to lie constantly, intensifying her guilt about posing as what she called "a false sense of self":

I am not who my parents think I am . . . in my parents' mind I am so far away from sexuality (being a sexual being). . . . I am such a little innocent girl. I have nothing to do with those kinds of things. . . . I feel like I have to behave the way they want me to behave, because they are the ones who give me everything. When I go home after a sexual experience and see them treat me as an innocent person [it] makes me feel guilty. I feel so bad about myself. . . . This weekend I told them I went to Ankara for a school trip, though I went to see a male friend [with whom she had a sexual encounter]. Everything was fine and beautiful there for a while, but it was still on my mind while I was having sex what my parents were thinking, that I am innocently taking tours in the university . . . it is so hard to feel this pressure. . . . It is so hard to live with this contradiction. I think it is engraved in my subconscious that sometimes I think that when something bad happens to me I feel I am being punished for posing a different self to my family and for doing things that I am not supposed to do. In the past, because premarital sexuality is sin and forbidden, I felt guilty also in front of God, but I overcame that. But I can't overcome this one.

Another technical virgin with a modest social-class background, Sonay, whom I quoted earlier, made the following comment in response to my question about whether she will tell her mother if she loses her virginity: "If I lose it of course I won't tell my mother, but then every time I see my mother I will remember it [losing my virginity] and will feel guilty, thinking 'how did I do such a thing? She doesn't feel anything right now but if she knew she would be feeling horrible and a huge disappointment in me.'" Acceptance to an elite university, such as Boğaziçi University, demands long-term investment by modest families in their children's education and many financial and emotional parental sacrifices. In turn, these daughters have a strong sense of emotional indebtedness to their parents that translates into an intense desire to protect their parents from potential disappointments and unhappiness. It is within this modest social-class context that we should consider young women's intense feelings of guilt. Yet, as will see in the following pages, there is a more complex explanation for the strong maternal voice in young women's sexual lives.

None of the upper-middle-class daughters' narratives contained expressions of guilt toward their mothers in relation to their secret sexual practices or virginity status. It seems they take parental sacrifices for granted because their class privileges and advantages assume familial investment in their elite education. Also, it seems their parents are those who most often "feign" ignorance about their daughters' virginal façades. Perhaps because these women recognize that their parents know the truth but feign otherwise, they are less likely to feel guilt.

The Turkish case reminds us that we cannot isolate sex and sexuality from questions of social class and its privileges as well as its injuries. Class is central to the formation of women's sexual subjectivities, especially in relation to young women's assertions of sexual autonomy and resistance against the regulation of their desires. Those young women who actively elude and resist the merging of sex with love are staging a clandestine and individualized sexual revolution. But some of these personal sexual revolutions have greater potential to be stalled than others because they carry with them the extra burden of social-class disadvantage, personally experienced as sexual guilt. Sexual guilt reveals its capacity to articulate class and sexuality, but it reveals much more as well. Mehtap, whom I quoted earlier, was plagued by guilt. Unlike her upper-middle-class peers, she did not plan to pursue postgraduate education, despite the fact that she was majoring in a prestigious field and was about to graduate with good grades. She wanted to get married (even if she did not fall in love) as soon as possible, the only way she thought she could end her masquerade as an "innocent" girl vis-à-vis her parents. Pushing her into early marriage and domesticity, guilt became the single most important feeling in the formation of her personal and professional identity. Unlike disadvantaged revolutionaries like Mehtap, upper-middle-class young women's class status shields them from the injuries of sexual guilt and shame when they transgress parental boundaries, because their class privilege does not construe an elite education as a source of parental indebtedness.

Formation of Sexual Subjectivities/Selves: Permitted versus Prohibited

The particular constellation of these young women's family backgrounds places them on different trajectories in their formation of sexual selves.[7] Maternal educational background (closely linked with social-class origins and urban or small-town upbringing) was the most influential dimension in the complex dynamics of the development and expression of sexual subjectivity among the young women I studied. Generally speaking, those young women, raised by stay-at-home mothers with limited formal education and lower-middle-class origins, acutely experience competing forces between family expectations for sexual purity and personal desires. In contrast, university-educated mothers place their daughters on a trajectory in which the daughters feel little to no tension between meeting familial expectations and fulfilling personal desires. While the daughters of highly educated parents received explicit messages about parental recognition of sexual feelings and the potential for sexual intimacy with boys during their adolescent years, those who grew up in conservative family circles faced complete parental silence on anything relating to sex and sexuality. Described by these daughters as "uncomfortable with sex and sexuality," this familial voice creates a negative/prohibited view of the sexual self and the world of sexual intimacy with men. Describing this kind of parental background, Sezen said the broader familial message in her teens was that sex did not exist: "Even when watching a documentary about animals, when it comes to the scene about animals copulating, the remote control was searched to change the channel. They pretended there is no such thing—sexuality." Concerns about maintaining the sexual purity of their daughters often prompted these parents to exert silence in order to withold recognition and devalue their sexual desires and feelings. Like Sezen, Sena observed that sexuality in her family was always a silenced topic, "something that cannot be experienced before marriage, and after marriage not for pleasure but for reproduction." She explained, "They don't think girls' sexuality is dangerous because they are sexually passive, but there is danger and that danger comes from men. Therefore they told me we trust you but we don't trust men."

In contrast to these women's experiences, the young women who came from urban, middle-class families with educated mothers described their parents as comfortable with the realm of sexuality, providing these women with a central orientation to foster self-trust in order to become self-regulating individuals. Beril observed that her father never interferes with and gives tremendous importance to her privacy, saying, "It is a matter of private life," while her mother encourages her to prolong the pleasures of youth and courtship. In fact, her mother remarked that "boyfriends are temporary; [pointing out the long duration of Beril's current relationship] this has been too long—aren't you considering splitting up?"

Young women like Beril have had more opportunities to begin courtship at an early age and acquire sexual and romantic experience earlier, thus building skills and capital in negotiating intimate and emotional relations and exploring their sexual desires and capabilities. They often feel no need to keep their romantic selves separate from their role as daughters and are able to share and integrate their romantic lives into their family lives. In dramatic contrast, the messages of prohibitive parents like Sezen's and Sena's continue to exert a powerful hold on these daughters, who keep their romantic and sexual lives clandestine. For these young women, family relations are seen as invariably antipathetic to their own romantic and sexual interest; it is, indeed, a realm that threatens these interests and is therefore a realm, in a few cases, of open contestation and, in most cases, of inner struggle.

The consequences of these class-based family differences in the development of sexual subjectivity for the young women I interviewed are long-lasting and have a multifaceted impact on them, their sense of femininity, and their relationships with men, as we will see in the following pages. However, it is important to note that like all abstractly constructed taxonomies, the divide between the permissive and prohibited family environments is also an artificial one, as some other important distinctions are obscured or lost by dividing young women's development of sexual subjectivities into two neat categories. For example, Feray developed her sexual subjectivity in a mismatched relational context; she grew up in a small town, yet a relatively liberal home environment. Her university-educated parents were open to her having boyfriends in high school. Particularly, she was seen by her father as capable of the emotional intimacy necessary for connecting with boys. Her father always told her, "You will live your life as you know it and I trust you. This is your life and you will make your own choices." Her mother's advice was, "Of course you will go out with men, but don't engage in behavior that would harm you." But she was surrounded by sexually conservative friends in her small town and it bothered her to have drastically opposing views from her friends'. Feray referred to the collective imagination of her girlhood friends in the small town where girls had no vocabulary, no permission, and no shared identity with which to describe their sexual feelings: "[For them] no sexual relationship was acceptable before marriage. There wasn't even talk with a sexual content, like to know your body, your sexual desires and passion—something like 'I like that boy and he excites me also sexually'—you couldn't even form such a sentence. It was like a closed box." It was indeed difficult for Feray's parents to provide her with a social and material environment that reflected their more permissive views.

Furthermore, mothers who deny and refuse to recognize their daughters' sexual subjectivities often soften their prohibitive stance as their daughters reach early adulthood without any romantic engagement—a disturbing issue and source of anxiety for these mothers. For example,

Sezen pointed out that her mother has changed her tune in her senior year. Leaving behind her usual cautionary voice, she has been increasingly encouraging Sezen to engage in a chaste courtship (but save sex for marriage) in order to find a suitable man for marriage before she graduates, although when it comes to specific situations her mother continues to verbalize her fears, frequently asking, "Is there anything [sexual] between you and that boy?" To put it differently, it might appear that Sezen's mother also acted as an agent of change/encouragement in the formation of Sezen's newly found relationship in her senior year. Indeed, these and similar contradictions we face in building classifications signal real complexities and ambiguities.

What sorts of conditions are necessary for effective personal transformation, pushing and transforming the limits of young women's negative/repressive/inhibiting sexual socialization? It seems this is accomplished only if reciprocal affective and communicative relations with other women are in place. Young women who fashion their own freedom despite their mother's strong voice tend to have real-life intimate role models that they find in their immediate circles, such as older sisters and cousins. For other young women, like Sena, who have no close role models, no blueprints as they try out new identities, personal transformation in the context of and as a response to sexual inhibition can be accomplished only if there are conceptual and normative resources, like feminism, for girls to draw upon in naming, understanding, criticizing, and ultimately overcoming norms, ideals, and experiences that reinforce sexual repression.

Sena's and Feray's stories illustrate this point. For Sena, it was the discovery of feminism in college that made the difference: in the past ashamed even of her womanhood, she now "reached the lightness of womanhood because of feminism." She said that for a period, she felt sorry that she lacked a penis and wished she were a man. She struggled with asking herself, "Why are men being rewarded for their penises and my vagina must be hidden?" and described the feeling as "an uncomfortableness of being yourself and wanting to become something else that is not possible." Now, she explains, "Feminism opens my mind and is a source of power because it keeps me wide awake, gives me consciousness." For Feray, the power of permission to inhabit the identity of the sexually independent woman came from a (sexually liberated) female cousin who was six years older than she: "She made me comfortable—[I thought,] she lived through it, why can't I? . . . there is the possibility I can too." It seems the power of permission comes from other women's voices and embodied experiences.

The Impossibility of Being Sexual and a "Good" Daughter

Despite many instances of achieving sexual transgression, in most cases, these young women still bear an uneasy relationship to the cautionary voices of their mothers, saturated with the language of struggle, guilt, and shame, inviting a need to self-enforce the virginal façade. Indeed, the fragile balance of young women's desires to be both "sexual" and "good daughters" was revealed in many narratives. For instance, even though her parents know that she has been in a relationship for three years, Sena's mother never revealed to her neighbors or friends that she has a boyfriend. "On the contrary," Sena revealed, "this is a source of shame for her." Reflecting on her virginity loss, she observed that "losing my virginity—the fear I inherited from my family—I carried that for a while when I came here; couldn't defeat it. In fact, since I cannot share it with my family, it means I still couldn't defeat it. The feeling that they'd know I am not virgin anymore disturbs me." Sonay said that if she loses her virginity she will protect her virginal façade. When she goes back home to her small town and occasionally finds herself part of female conversations about "bad girls in Istanbul, doing bad things," she finds peace that "I don't have such a problem; I am not one of those bad girls—I didn't do anything bad—bad from their perspective." Her mother doesn't ask about her experience, but if she did, Sonay would like to be able to say, "There is nothing sexual between us." Her dilemma of wanting to be both sexual and a "good daughter" is always present: she wanted the experience of "being together" (having penetrative sex) many times, "but because of my consideration of my mother's feelings I put it in the back of my mind . . . but on the other hand, I am thinking in the future I might regret that because of me, we had missed living certain things, but yet my family's side outweighs it [ailem ağır basıyor]." The deep feelings of right and wrong in sexual matters, which she got from her mother, motivate her more powerfully than her other desires and are resistant to change.

Even Feray is distinctive in the extent to which she still carries what she regards as her mother's fixation—"don't do anything to harm yourself"—even though there are no parental controls over her ("if they try, they know I would distance myself from them"). She feels defeated about changing her mother's perspective, and therefore, even though she continues introducing her boyfriends to her parents and having conversations with her mother about her boyfriends and about how her relationships are going, she only talks about the emotional aspects, not the sexual dimensions. The mother knows that she is possibly not a virgin but "she is afraid of learning/knowing it." More importantly, Feray explains, "We don't think alike on this issue," signaling an absence of identification with her mother. She feels sad knowing that her mother thinks, "'My daughter shouldn't hold these views.'" She explains, "The image of the purest girl in her white gown—that image carries a lot of meaning for her. . . . Because I know she gets sad talking about these issues, I don't talk."

The maternal voice forms the emotive center of the family in many narratives, and its deep affective strength is present as the daughters embark on their sexual and romantic encounters. In order to better comprehend the psychic struggles involved in managing the contradiction between being sexual and being a "good daughter," I will explore Sena's and Mehtap's stories in much greater detail below.

Sexual Guilt and Feeling Feminine: Sena's and Mehtap's Stories

The romantic and sexual histories of the young women who come from sexually prohibitive families hinge on the strongly felt contradiction or impossibility posed by being sexual and a "good daughter," between sexual selfhood and connective identification with their mothers. As they embark on sexual and romantic encounters and become sexually awakened, they claim to become more conscious of having been repressed sexually while continuing to grapple with a feeling of disloyalty carried over from girlhood and the question of how to be responsible with respect to virginity. The burden of managing this contradiction comes at considerable emotional cost for these women. However, this contradiction's impact on the women not only is limited to emotions of sexual guilt and shame, but profoundly shapes their sense of femininity in the relationships they engage in, even significantly affecting the domination-subordination dynamics of some relationships. Although they chose different paths in becoming sexual, Sena through open rebellion and Mehtap through having a secretive sexual life, Sena's and Mehtap's stories powerfully illustrate how this contradiction is managed through the production and enactment of forms of traditional femininity tied to mothers in their self-making.

Sena's story captures her almost simultaneous desires to meet the expectations of her family and to defy them. She is free and trapped in unexpected and tragic ways. As discussed before, Sena's sense of sexual subjectivity was shaped by her conservative family upbringing. But she identifies a quick change in her views once she came to Boğaziçi. In the past, she used to think, "If I am going to have a sexual relationship I have to love that person to death and feel a great deal of passion." When Sena's boyfriend, four years her senior, wanted to move quickly, she wondered "if he wants to take advantage of me—because I internalized that idea." They were exploring sexually in open-air places; one evening he took her t-shirt off, and she got angry because it triggered the message she received from her mother: "men only want sex." She said to him, "What are you doing? Who do you think I am?" He apologized later and said, "You are an innocent girl and I am dirtying you," affirming her mother's view.

Sena has been with this lover (her word) more than three years and has been living with him for two years. She calls her relationship oppressive, constricting, and intolerable and identifies it as akin to "living in a classical family dynamic." She acutely recognizes herself as oppressed, although her understanding of oppression is complicated and highly complex. As she narrated, living together for two years has turned her love/passion into mercifulness (şefkat): "I call him my son. When he gets sick, I panic; when his morale is low, I do everything to make him happy, and I hug him constantly." What has emerged is a relationship between a "mother" who supplies unreciprocated maternal care and a "son" who is needy and controlling. In Sena's narrative, this dynamic is not positive, but it still makes her happy. Acting out a maternal role is not an unwanted desire for Sena, as the helpless child (her boyfriend) depends for his very survival on powerful Sena, and to think him a small, needy child offers satisfaction. Yet she sees herself as sacrificing too much for him, as the parameters of her maternal role are quite broad. The corrosive effects of this dynamic are captured by her description of how much she subordinated her needs to his: "He took too much from me, I missed my exams to take care of him and his problems. I gave my energy to him. In the process of giving order to his life, I ignored my own studies. I lied to my family and got withdrawn from my friends, particularly male friends, because he doesn't want them to visit me."

One striking feature of Sena's narrative of oppression is that she tells herself/me that she is being oppressed, but believes that "from an emotional point of view, it is not really harmful"—perhaps because of the satisfaction she finds in responding to a needy "son" with her affection and care. What she finds really harmful/oppressive is being demoted by him as a submissive, subservient woman in front of others. Being consistently subjected to shaming behavior by him—he discloses to outsiders her obedience to his desires—brings her the shame of female subordination while bringing him pleasure: "He takes pleasure for belittling me in front of others." Sena's boyfriend constantly orders her around, telling her, for instance, "Bring me a glass of water, bring me that journal." Her usual response is, "Why don't you get it?" But then he declares to the interlocutors, "Don't mind her behavior now, in fact she obeys me normally," and she shuts up and complies. According to Sena, in these instances of being humiliated and ridiculed in front of others, when she sees a degraded image of herself, she behaves exactly like her mother because "I am concerned about what the others/audience think, and he uses this and can be very oppressive, because I don't want to fight in front of other people and I tend to go along and soften the situation." In these instances, the way her public (feminist) and private (submissive) behavior are at odds is displayed, and the way she is in private and the way she appears in public (dominated like her mother) converge. Sena places herself in a parallel relationship with her mother: she becomes what she likes least in her mother—"a carrier of patriarchy more than my father," and obsessed with patriarchal respectability—"what the neighbors think."

In the past, according to Sena, there was much romance and sharing of intellectuality between the lovers; they read and discussed poetry and listened to music together, which they now no longer do. Now she has intellectual conversations only with her friends, which her lover finds problematic and objects to, asking her, "What are you doing without me?" But from the very beginning the worst part of the relationship was sex:

> It was given in the beginning that I was the inexperienced one, he was the experienced; he knows, I don't know. It continued a while like this—like a game. Our sexual life has been terrible since the beginning. But he says relationships are like this, don't expect better than this, "what more do you need"—it is his way of covering his weaknesses. Expressing my desires verbally is unacceptable—in this sense the relationship I have is very limiting, constricting, and oppressive.

Sena remains silent about her own desires:

> For instance I don't say "I like this or that"—my saying so from his perspective is an indication of my openness to sex, and he thinks therefore I can be open to other men. My sexual desires shouldn't be expressed—whatever there is should be enough for me. He is so oppressive in this regard, because he is not happy with himself and because he knows I am not happy. He tries to keep minimizing it: [he is] mute on this topic. If there is talk it is a threat for him or he makes fun of what I want to shut me up.

Sena described her sexual appetite as having become blunt: "My sexual life independent of him—with another man—just out of question, including masturbation—it terrifies him." Sena has tried to convince herself that sex is not important, that "we are together and we love each other; that should be enough." But she added that "of course it does not work that way." She had a sexual relationship with another man that lasted a month. She confessed to her boyfriend, "Yes, I also loved that man and he excites me. I cannot lie to you." Not surprisingly, her boyfriend's reaction was very hostile: "You sold your soul and your freedom, what kind of a person are you?" Since her confession, he repeatedly asks her, "Are you a whore? How large are your sexual desires?"

When I asked Sena why she didn't leave her boyfriend, she told me that he says he will commit suicide. Yet she also cited another significant reason: Sena blames herself and calls herself a scapegoat: "I cheated on him without telling him; I made him so unhappy." I asked her if she is still in love with him and if this also contributed to her staying. She said no and elaborated: "It is mercifulness (*şefkat*), affection, like a relationship of a mother and child. It reached that point—a traditional relationship with a modern appearance" (modern because they live together unmarried). When I talked with Sena, her boyfriend was about to leave Istanbul for an internship, and his biggest fear was that she would sleep around in his absence. Sena said she doesn't have similar concerns about him; on the contrary, "If he will be happy with another person, he should, because I saw I can be happy with another person. I am unhappy with him. It is like I chose unhappiness."

Why did Sena choose unhappiness? Her resignation is truly tragic. How can we comprehend the density of meanings associated with Sena's construction of a maternal sense of self by positioning herself as a mother and dubbing her boyfriend her "son"? Why does she allow herself to miss out on academic and fun things in order to care for her "son"? Why can she not free herself from a form of femininity very much tied to her mother? Why can she not bring her choices into line with her feminist ideology? Why is she compelled to inhabit an oppressive relationship? What is not within Sena's power to change?

The most striking aspect of Sena's story is the irony of the disjunction between her embracement of a feminist identity, which for her means a commitment to a nonsubordinated self, and the self she is compelled to inhabit, which is disturbingly out of sync with that feminist identity. As she described it and as I quoted earlier, for her, coming to have a feminist consciousness is the experience of coming to see things about oneself and one's society that were previously hidden. For her, feminism means, for one thing, that one's very sense of self and personhood are seen as socially constructed: "In the past I always wished I had another family and I had another lover, now I understand why I have this family and this lover." Indeed, embracing a feminist vision of personal transformation has effected what she considers a radical change in her young life, from growing up in a sterile family environment in a small town to living independently in Istanbul. Sena is one of those rare young women from a modest class background who managed to achieve independent living in a studio apartment, shared with her boyfriend, with financial help from her parents, who know her boyfriend visits but do not know (or perhaps more accurately "pretend not to know") that he lives with her. Her separation from her family home was full of challenges, and she still feels tremendous parental control and pressure through phone calls. (Her parents constantly remind her that "[her boyfriend] should only come to [her] apartment with friends. If others see a single man coming in, it would be shameful.") Indeed, because they fear that financial independence would enable Sena to further separate from them, her parents pressure her not to have a job, although she wants one. She identifies her family as the greatest obstacle to her personal happiness: "Even though I separated my home from theirs physically and despite the fact that I live with my boyfriend—which is a radical act really—to be able to depart from that kind of understanding to reach this point, I haven't discarded them in my head."

What Sena hasn't been able to discard is a strong maternal voice, which invades her consciousness so pervasively, equating being sexual with being bad. Happiness is denied to Sena because she undertook action that is too self-regarding, independent, and sexual, putting respectful femininity in danger. It seems she cannot be autonomously sexual without in some sense compensating for that "lost" femininty. Being properly submissive to the decisions of her boyfirend and adopting a maternal, self-sacrificing role allows Sena to compensate for the femininity she has "lost" by being sexual and allows her to feel respectable. Although her sexuality threatens her femininity, Sena is able to "redeem" herself by enacting the traditional feminine virtues of devotion, self-sacrifice, patience, and compliance.The way out of Sena's predicament seems to be to abandon her lover, but to do so would mean abandoning the good, maternal, self-sacrificing self she has produced though the relationship. And she needs this self to feel she still belongs to the category of "good" because she retains a sense of identification with her mother and implied complicity and connectivity with her.

Consumed by extreme guilt, Mehtap, whom I quoted earlier, manages this contradiction between being sexual and being a good daughter by following the model of womanhood that her mother charted for her, with the exception of her secret sexual life. We find an expression of the complex interplay between femininity and sexuality in Mehtap's approach to sexual pleasure and her accommodation to her mother's desires. She clearly disassociates sexual pleasure from love: "The bottom line is I am enjoying this, getting pleasure out of this, and in order to experience [pleasure] you don't need to be in love." As a result, she avoids or drops lovers who want to have, as she puts it, a long-term "emotional relationship." However, she believes that every sexual engagement has its emotionality: "[Lovemaking] is not a mechanical thing that can be lived without emotionality. You have a moment of emotionality. If it doesn't exist, you don't have lovemaking [*sevişme*]. In fact, lovemaking is emotionality." Then she goes on to explain that even when there is no love, "You have to feel a moment of love if you are going to experience something together, and I love to do nice things to a man, to feel like a woman, feminine." Mehtap's way of feeling feminine involves an accommodation of her mother's model of womanhood.

> I took the model of womanhood that my mother created for me in her mind, the woman that my mother wanted me to become. My mother always wanted me to become educated and in possession of a profession— she never wanted me to be become a stay-at-home girl, but she didn't want me also to completely disengage from housework etc.—generally it is the case that when education is emphasized for girls, they distance themselves from housework etc. She didn't want me to become like that either. She gave me all the qualities associated with housewifery.

Using the housewifery skills that her mother instilled in her makes Mehtap feel feminine and perhaps allows her to reinstate and restore a sense of a true, good self "damaged" by her sexual explorations. Mehtap's narrative about her relationships with her lovers is full of examples in which she displays womanly qualities and skills that make her feel feminine. She strongly connects feeling one's gender identity with the performance of one's gender-related duties. The weekend spent in Ankara with the man mentioned in the quotation in the previous section is a good illustration of this interesting intersection:

> He was working that Friday, and I arrived Thursday night. He had to work until noon. I got there early in the morning to tidy up his place and cooked several wonderful dishes. And made dessert and then dressed up and put on makeup and started waiting for him. This is what I love most, to do things for a man. And then look your best to wait for him.

Mehtap's narrative powerfully articulates the contradictions between a desire to follow the model of womanhood that her mother charted for her and a desire for sexual pleasure without being in love. As mentioned before, Mehtap's secret sexual life contains many short-term sexual relationships, including a more long-lasting relationship with a boyfriend. But she is still technically a virgin who avoids penile-vaginal intercourse. By enacting and performing a housewifely femininity, Mehtap seeks to escape the contradictions of her opposing desires and to restore a sense of a true, good self, a self that she feels is being destroyed by her masquerade as a sexually "innocent" girl, while Sena's attempt to resolve the conflict amounts to splitting herself between a maternal femininity and a feminist self.

What connects Sena's and Mehtap's voices is their pasts—girlhood environments marked by the wider familial context of sexual inhibition—and how their inner struggle with their mothers' voices continues to shape their sense of femininity. The psychic struggles of these young women are also intricately related with the issue of upward mobility. They are the ones who feel the greatest distance and difference between their future selves, embodying a new class status and the invention of unsubordinated female selves, and their mothers. As Walkerdine (2003) theorizes, the threat of losing all material and emotional connections to the mother, or conversely of not being able to distance oneself enough from the mother (243), generates a complex bind in the construction of these young women's sexual and gendered selves. It seems impossible for these women to unlearn, to forget, the cautionary voice of their mothers, even when their acts of sexual freedom cannot obliterate the guilt-ridden maternal standard by which they have been raised. Indeed, we have seen how very present their mothers are in these women's most intimate sexual moments, and sexual guilt, it seems, never disappears because of the mother's intractable presence. For some, being different from their mothers will always feel like a betrayal.

Without Sexual Guilt: Feray's Story

For those women who feel torn between competing desires of being sexual and being a good daughter, we have seen that more than any other emotion, guilt determines the dynamics of sexual selfhood. Feray, who doesn't experience this powerful contradiction and thus is freer to explore her sexual desires and feelings, makes an interesting contrast with women like Mehtap and Sena. In many ways, Feray epitomizes the new generation of liberated Turkish women whose navigation of romantic and sexual relations is unconstrained by family concerns and the maternal voice. Raised within a small-town context, yet also encouraged by her parents (both university-educated professionals) to find her own voice in making decisions, Feray believes that sex, to feel sexual, is given, not to be deferred until marriage. Determined to integrate her sexuality more fully into her life, Feray believes in her right to sexual freedom and the self-knowledge she gains from her romantic and sexual explorations. For her, being in love is not a requirement to having sex:

> Before I go out with a man I don't need to be in love—only being affected by that person is enough. I don't exaggerate the importance of a good relationship that has ended and say since I won't have the same feelings, therefore I shouldn't go out with another guy. Instead, I think, "yes that was a good relationship, but I cannot wait for a similar man to emerge; he could appear in five or ten years or never, why should I wait?" I want to live life—there is no reason a relationship needs to last five years. Relationships that end in two or five months also can be successful.

Feray's true love was a man whom she said she "desired . . . in his totality." She was in love with both his mind and his emotional and sexual self, but he was in another long-term relationship. Her love was destructive. During that time she lost herself in the relationship: she withdrew from everyone and ignored her coursework, etc., and started living "alone." Learning that she was cheated on made her sad, because she believed "we lived a lie." Still, she does not regret the relationship, because she really loved him: "I don't hate him—I am glad I met him and experienced these things."

At the time of our discussion, Feray had just ended a relationship that had lasted for two and a half months and was in a new relationship. Her expectation from a relationship was not just to have fun, but to share intellectually: "We have to look at the world from the same point of view. Frame of thought is the most important quality—what can I learn from him and how in interacting with each other can we learn together?"

Her previous relationship ended, in part, because her boyfriend was insensitive to societal issues and very individualistic: "It is good to go out a couple of months, and then when you deepen the relationship, you realize 'I cannot be with such a man—a man with such views.'" When Feray and this boyfriend went out with friends, they had fun, but when they were alone they had nothing to talk about: "I remember listening to the conversations of the people sitting in the next booth." For the first month, the sexual relationship went well; sexually she was very eager. She felt a sexual attraction and desire for him before she felt love for him, and her desires were embodied—she constantly wanted to touch him and to be touched: "That is the reason it continued more than a month even though I felt we were not sharing emotionality." A key instance of this lack of emotionality was his inability to share his feelings. According to Feray, he wasn't revealing his interiority. Feray addressed this issue head on, and they talked about it. He said, "I cannot even tell my mom I love her. I have such a problem." Feray reflected that when he revealed this information, she tried to mobilize her sense of empathy, one of the traditional qualities of femininity: "I thought of myself, 'Feray you are so brutal. Try to understand him, try to enter in his interior self' . . . but I couldn't do it with the type of guy who couldn't express his feelings—you cannot be with such a man." Because he never shared anything with her, neither his anger nor his love, he was unfeeling; he drove her "crazy." At the end, she said, "I am disgusted by you." Feray observed that "when you are sexually close to someone, you seek out emotional closeness" and added, "If I cannot share emotional things, I cannot share sexuality either." When her emotions toward him started declining, she started trying to avoid him whenever she saw him. Describing this "very strange thing," she explained, "Even holding hands, kissing were making me uncomfortable—it should be over because I had started becoming uncomfortable from his physical touch."

Feray describes her new relationship as being filled with intellectual desire, but lacking sexual excitement: "I cannot say I sexually desire him. I concentrated on his brain, and his frame of thought excites me. I desire him, but this desire does not have a sexual content." Indeed, later (by the time we talked a second time), she told him that she did not desire him sexually at all. He was upset by her stance and accused her of not giving romance a chance—focusing only on sex. He said, "You put only my sexuality in desire . . . how come you didn't give it more time? You take an instant photo and only look at that photo and see no sexual desire and conclude it should be over."

Feray enjoys her freedom to find out what excites her sexually as well as intellectually, and the self-knowledge she gains from her explorations is valuable for her. Accepting sex as a natural extension of her life empowers her in negotiating her own identity and making decisions about whom she wants to attach with.

Conclusion

The norm of virginity in Turkey is fragile and subject to challenges from the new elite women whose parents' insistence that they remain untouched is profoundly contradicted by these parents' heavy investments in their daughters' education, which stretches between puberty and marriage. This contradiction opens up, both discursively and experientially, new paths of sexual freedom and autonomy for young women who forsake virginity and negotiate new identities as unmarried nonvirgins. In the process of negotiating often-contradictory expectations of their sexual behavior, they cultivate virginal façades to accommodate the old norms still grounded in virginity as well as the new rules of an emerging premarital-sex culture. The moralizing discourses of this new culture privilege the morality of virginity as a new norm by which it becomes acceptable for young women to lose their virginity as long as they do so within the context of love and emotional investment.

This chapter has illustrated how young women's sexual agency is linked to social class and gender in complex ways. Competing forces of familial expectations for sexual purity and personal desires are felt and managed in significantly class-based ways. While the young women with urban, middle-class backgrounds, who were raised in sexually less inhibited family environments, are able to dislodge patriarchal claims of the equivalency between being sexually pure and a good daughter in their self-making, those who were raised in sexually repressive family circles struggle a great deal with undoing this equivalency in their "transgressive" sexual explorations, in most cases compensating for their feelings of sexual guilt and shame by enacting traditional gender roles and by fashioning submissive selves in their relationship with men.

Although both groups of women share an important commonality in rewriting the patriarchal romance—desiring nonpatriarchal men and seeking relationships in which they can safeguard their autonomy and independence—the daughters from sexually prohibitive backgrounds, whose upward mobility also threatens to breach their maternal attachments, are less able to act upon on new relationship ideals defined by female autonomy and unsubmissiveness.

It is important to note that this premarital sex culture and its ideals for young women's sexuality are being formed in a cultural milieu of increasingly diversified moral values. Particularly, this new premarital culture is being formed in a complex field of tension with a new Islamic morality that tolerates male-female intimacies and socialization only within the accepted boundaries of Islam. The embrace of pious identities among other educationally advantaged young women and men, who are the subjects of chapter 4, has invited new challenges to sexual politics in Turkey. The top-down imposition of pious values and policies by the AKP government adds a new layer of complexity as desire, pleasure, and sexual entitlement for women as sexual subjects continues to be the most challenging issue confronting feminist politics in Turkey.

Addressing the question of whether virginal façades empower or disempower young women is difficult. Ambiguity, vagueness, and secrecy, in their various combinations, have the potential to empower young women because they allow them to enter their sexual lives to negotiate their sexuality. They enable young women to transgress parental boundaries by enlarging the parameters within which they can express desire, engage in sexual interaction, and increase their sexual knowledge.

Yet putting on "virginal façades" ultimately reinforces the privileging of virginity and diverts attention away from articulating a discourse of desire and pleasure as well as exploring the social and emotional risks of sexual intimacy (see Fine 1988). One of the young women I interviewed was vivid in describing a very close friend's virginal façade: "Every man she is with, she shows him as if he is the first man in her life. Her every kiss is as if it is her first kiss. Her every love-making is as if it is the first time." I asked her and others whether men believed such façades. Their response was reasonable: "Yes because they would like to believe." Virginal façades help young men cope with the tension between modern masculine renunciation of the importance of virginity and loss of the male prerogative of being the first man a woman has a sexual relationship with.

Protecting one's reputation with a virginal façade comes with a heavy price. Deborah Tolman identifies this cost as the price of losing an important source of empowerment: "authentic relationships with other girls and women" within which "collectively articulated critiques are carved out and voiced. Such knowledge of how a patriarchal society systematically keeps girls and women from their own desire can instigate demand and agency for social change" (Tolman 1994, 339–40). Indeed, some examples we encountered in this chapter reveal that effective transformation of the repressive and inhibiting sexual socialization of girls can be accomplished only if there are normative empowering resources like feminism and embodied experiences of close role models. It seems that only women can liberate other women to be sexual. The loss of empowerment among young Turkish women find its powerful expression in virginal façades as private enactments of hidden subversions—not as collective/public challenges.

Passive Resistance and Class in Lesbian Self-Making: Alev's Story

In her early twenties, lesbian feminist Alev talked about her self-transformation from an adolescent self "carrying a man's soul stranded [*sıkışmış*] in a woman's body" to a lesbian self: "I am a woman and I am happy to be a woman and I am a woman who loves women." Highlighted in her self-description was also a key shift in her object of same-sex desire from a figure of the flamboyant femme ("excessively feminine, thin, and petite") to a figure of androgyny ("childish/boyish masculine"). The story of this transformation is quite complex, involving the negotiation of Alev's identity and subjectivity within a network of many actors and discourses, among which the power of her mother's homophobic imagery, which constructed homosexuality as deviance and sickness, played a central role. Situated between open defiance and collusion with her mother's hostility, Alev managed to simultaneously accommodate these contradictory orientations in her self-making. She claimed to achieve a "harmony" (*denge*) by what she called her "passive resistance," allowing her to stay connected with her mother via the creation of façades and pretensions that enabled her to be seen as heterosexual, while simultaneously keeping her lesbianism in the forefront of her mother's consciousness. A significant element in Alev's narrative of self-transformation is her same-sex relationship with Pembe, a young woman of her educational level who belongs to a vastly different social class and gender habitus. This relationship of class unequals brought Alev into an intimate connection to the gender and class cultures of her lover's working-class family and community. Alev's story helps us locate the specificity of class differences in sexual identity formation and demonstrates how sexual desires and impulses and gender nonconformity manifest themselves in specific class-based communities that imbue them with specific meanings. Particularly, Alev's narrative and her lover's story as they appeared in her account reveal how lesbian identities are diversely realized as well as how enactment of lesbian sexualities is articulated and embraced or rejected in a complex and nuanced way in the context of class belonging, which polarizes and structures experiences of gender identity and sexuality. Defined by the constant need to negotiate differences in their class habitus, Alev and Pembe's relationship also brings the co-construction of gender and class into focus.

When Alev was growing up, she saw herself as different from other kids, both boys and girls, and had a very clear awareness of her difference. The words she used to describe her differentness were "strange" (*garip*) and "extraordinary" (*sıra dışı*). Alev did not experience her difference as an expression of gender nonconformity, and she did not conceive of her difference as based on sexual orientation until she felt desire for a girl at age fourteen. Instead, being more mature and intellectually oriented than other kids in her school were the important features of her difference. For even at a very young age, Alev was preoccupied with activities like reading encyclopedias and watching opera, ballet, and documentaries on TV, which seemed peculiar to her peers. Because her friends always found her extraordinary, Alev rarely had dialogues with her peers. She explained, "I didn't know their games, there is a language among kids, I was also foreigner to that language." Significant to observe here is the class identity of activities Alev engaged in, reflecting her socialization into upper-class taste in high culture. The isolation and loneliness of her early girlhood years partially ended in high school. As she put it, "I was loved more in high school." Yet her classmates in high school also supported this picture of her exclusion and differentness. She was in a class of thirty-four with twelve girls. When boys ranked the girls by level of prettiness, "the list stopped at eleven." She explained, "I wouldn't be placed even as twelve on that list. I was nonexistent; I couldn't be among girls or boys."

She experienced her first love—same-sex desire—within the peer context. In fact, her love and desire for girls first appeared to her as another site of her real authentic difference from her peers. She perceived it as an integral part or extension of her being strange. She fell in love again the next year, and the intense feelings of sexual desire motivated her to confess her love to her object of desire: "She asked if I am bisexual or lesbian. I said I don't know. She quizzed, 'how could you not know?' I said, 'the only thing I know is I love you.'" Her object of desire urged Alev to self-question to find out if she was lesbian. But Alev was afraid of asking and confronting that question. However, she started thinking that because she desired women, she must be a man: "Of course I wasn't thinking lesbianism. I didn't know what it was. I was thinking I am neither girl nor boy, a third kind. Maybe a bad copy of a man—a copy in a woman's body." It was very difficult to accept what her feelings meant—that is, that she had homosexual desire—because homosexuality was damned by her homophobic parents. Her guilt became an unbearable emotion: "Homosexuals are bad people, did I become one of them? If I am, my family will be ashamed of me." A year later when she was sixteen, she came out to her mother in a "funny way." She described the scene:

> I sat across from my mother and told her with a sobbing voice, "I have something important to tell you." I buried my face in a pillow, because I was feeling extreme shame, as if I was going to die from shame. She said, "what happened?" and started to name a couple of possibilities: "are you using drugs?"; "are you pregnant?"; "are you a terrorist?" The last possibility she listed was, "are you liking women?" When she raised that possibility, I felt so ashamed I further pressed my face into the pillow. I said, "I cannot tell you because I am shamed so much; it is alright if a close friend of mine would tell you." She said alright. I phoned my friend, who knew from the very beginning, a very close friend. She told my mother how I was in love with a woman, how I was constantly chasing her, and how I was writing her love letters, in addition to listing all my other secret "sins"—"she is also smoking, and she is an atheist." The moment my mother heard, she started crying violently and became very sad, as if I had cancer. She immediately called her gynecologist, sobbing on the phone, "My daughter claims she is a lesbian, what shall we do? Should I bring her to you?"

The gynecologist recommended a psychiatrist. Alev thinks that her mother called the gynecologist because her testosterone level was high and she attributed Alev's having "masculine feelings" to it. The recommended psychiatrist was a big name in Turkey, but after a couple of sessions she told Alev that they didn't connect and referred her to another one. Alev resented this psychiatrist's asking her "stupid questions" at the first session like, "'tell me about your fantasies." "I was so fearful and under great stress. How could I tell someone at my mother's age about my fantasies? Later she called my mother in and told her I was a lesbian, without asking my permission. The diagnosis further destroyed my mother."

Alev went through a very difficult period. Because the psychiatrist put her on antidepressants, she could no longer think straight and was constantly sleepy. There were lots of fights with her mother: "My mother destroyed all my posters of women artists and sports figures in my room. She bought me lots of skirts, and she insisted that I should put makeup on. Whenever I trained my gaze on a woman on TV, she gave me a jumbled and messed-up look and instantly changed the channel." Did Alev put on makeup and don skirts? "Makeup yes, but not skirts." The way Alev reflected on her reaction to her mother's efforts to make her feminine through proper gender display was telling about how she started managing contradictory demands of the self and others:

> I did not try to make her happy/pleased; I wasn't doing anything to please her, really. It was interesting: on the one hand I was feeling extremely guilty—how I was a bad child and why I am doing this horrible thing to my family. And, on the other hand, I was putting up a struggle to pursue my life the way I desired.

Alev's mother told her father, "Our daughter is in love with another girl." Responding in his typical "passive attitude toward anything relating to family matters," her father observed that it was a problem of adolescence and comforted her mother by saying that it was a passing phase and that they would take her to a doctor. He never confronted Alev—never asked any questions. On the contrary, according to Alev, he treated her as if she were sick: "He would gently slap me on the back and say 'you will become better.'" Her mother also told Alev's older sister. The sister's very loving and positive response and her expressed commitment to be on Alev's side caused "big fights" between the mother and the older daughter. Her mother declared openly, "If my daughter is a lesbian, I cannot live with her under the same roof; I cannot share this home with a deviant [sapık]." Because of her schooling (at that time she was attending a highly selective high school in Istanbul), Alev could not completely move in with her sister, who resided in another city. Thus her elite education kept her rooted in her family home. However, Alev started spending her every summer and every other school break with her sister, who on the day the school was out would fly to Istanbul to take Alev back to her home. Alev's mother's rejection of her as deviant was offset by her older sister's acceptance and support. Her sister also had her own history of family exclusion and rejection: after she became pregnant and had a child out of wedlock, she was thrown out of the family home at a relatively young age. Alev noted that for her mother, the most important thing in the world is family, and she gives great importance to the concept of honor. An honorable girl should not engage in sex until marriage: "If she does, [my mother] treats this as the biggest shame. For her, virginity loss before marriage and someone learning about this is the worst possible thing. She considers it as a stain on [parents'] honor."

The second psychiatrist Alev was sent to was very helpful and made her realize that openly defying her parents was perilous. She discontinued the antidepressant prescription and advised Alev to keep her family dialogue limited to her school life, to not share her private life or her friends with her family members until she finished high school. "I was screaming all the time and breaking things and threatening my mother that I was going to kill myself." The psychiatrist told her, "Don't do these things. You will damage yourself." Because the psychiatrist stopped the medicine and told Alev's mother that she did not need any therapy and that she was very intelligent and balanced, her mother believed that she was "cured." "Because my mother sees depression and homosexuality as illnesses, by definition they naturally emerge together: homosexuality is deviance engendering psychological problems. If the doctor is not giving medicine and discontinued therapy, [I] must have been cured." Alev acknowledged to her mother that she was cured but did not say, "I am not lesbian." What she acknowledged was that she no longer felt unhappy and depressed. According to Alev, her mother was satisfied with this partial acknowledgment simply because "she cannot believe a lesbian can be happy and balanced."

"Cured," Alev started putting on façades. At the university, she had a gay classmate who had similar issues with his own family. They made a pact to pass as a couple vis-à-vis their respective families. She changed her female lovers' names to male ones; when she received a gift from her girlfriend, she introduced it to her mother as a gift from her boyfriend; and when she went out to a dinner to celebrate the six-month anniversary of togetherness with her girlfriend, she marked it as a celebratory dinner with her boyfriend. Despite Alev's mother's tough stance with her older sister in relation to her daughter's interaction with men and virginity, her attitude with regard to Alev's boyfriends was relaxed and even very encouraging. For instance, Alev was allowed to take vacations with her "boyfriend," albeit in groups, and her mother even expressed that she was pleased that "he is always with you to protect you." According to Alev, the possibility of Alev sleeping with the "boyfriend" never crossed her mother's mind. Perhaps it is not that it didn't cross her mind, but that she was so desperate to see her daughter in a heterosexual relationship that she was willing to set aside her mores about virginity.

Despite the enactment of all these façades, Alev also simultaneously kept her lesbianism in the forefront of her mother's consciousness through her open displays of contact with other women. Negotiating the line between collusion and open opposition, Alev's passive resistance to her mother's desires can be said to constitute a silent rebellion against being a "secret subject"—a refusal, despite the façades, to allow her identity as a lesbian to be fully repressed, denied, or ignored by her family. For instance, one summer her lover (pretending to be a female friend) stayed with her in the family home. Because her parents were away vacationing, the house was empty. "Naturally we slept in the same bed. I don't know if innocently or politically, I told my mother that we slept in the same bed, despite the fact that there are plenty of other rooms. 'Why,' she asked; I said, 'because we wanted to.'" Alev also never refrained from showing and receiving physical affection from women around her mother, despite the fact that her mother always got very upset and uncomfortable when she saw Alev kissing and hugging girls and women.

Alev's first "lesbian"[8] relationship was with a close friend who, in Alev's terminology, was heterosexual—the same friend she came out to in her senior year of high school. One night when Alev stayed overnight with her, her friend got drunk and became obsessed with finding out whether Alev loved her. Alev said she loved her as a friend, but the friend insisted on knowing whether Alev also found her attractive. With the influence of alcohol, they made love and started seeing each other. Solely based on sex, the relationship was devoid of any claim making over each other. The lack of recognition of the relationship by outsiders ("Nobody knew. She even hid it from her best friends because she was heterosexual.") made this relationship the worst kind for Alev. It lasted for five months. The girlfriend started giving her the cold shoulder and called one day to say, "I don't love you anymore, and I see you as a friend and besides there is no future in these types of relationships." Alev observed that her reference to the relationship without naming it a homosexual relationship was particularly hurtful. Alev, who had developed a strong bond and loved this woman, was devastated: "I begged and cried and went after her but she didn't accept me." Recently they had run into each other. She had been with her boyfriend and introduced him in a way that screamed, "my lover is a man" and even said to Alev, "I see you haven't learned your lesson yet," meaning that Alev was still a lesbian.

When I talked with Alev, her relationship with Pembe was seven months old. Alev described Pembe as having been raised in a "proletarian family" in a squatter settlement neighborhood in one of the poorest out-skirts of Istanbul. Intertwining low-income and rural-migrant statuses, this neighborhood is inhabited by socially and economically marginal first- or second-generation migrants from rural or provincial areas. In stark contrast, Alev was raised upper-middle-class in Istanbul in a palatial home by high-powered professional parents who are "Westernized and modern and economically even more than upper-middle-class," and who spent some early childhood years in Europe. The vast disparities between the two women's class backgrounds made the relationship challenging, especially at the beginning, as they navigated class-divided social and ma-terial environments and friendship networks to find spaces where both were comfortable. Alev said Pembe felt oppressed but also made Alev ashamed of her class advantages. Whenever and wherever she tried to in-tegrate Pembe into her own circles, she resisted: "She didn't want to meet with my friends; she did not want to be in my circles. I became a source of shame for her." To me, it seemed that one of Alev's personal struggles was to avoid not translating the imbalance of their class-based material and symbolic resources into a power imbalance. Alev's narrative was full of illustrations of her "class equalizing/balancing work," the routine actions and strategies through which Alev maintained the relationship across the line of class, so that Pembe did not feel a subject of class domination. For instance, Alev always made sure that Pembe received gifts from her with high value in symbolism, not in materiality. She avoided taking her to middle-class leisure and consumption sites, and they spent from a com-mon purse by pooling together their funds. But more importantly, she protected Pembe from her mother's class-based prejudices against her by concealing her own emotions about the subject—hurt feelings and pain.

Alev claimed that they were eventually able to transcend these prob-lems, in large part because their "gender roles" were so compatible. In-deed, Pembe perfectly embodied Alev's desire for an androgynous lover.

According to Alev, Pembe is "neither totally a woman nor totally a man. She draws elements of femininity and masculinity. It is great that she captures this balance in our relationship. Otherwise, it is a problem among lesbians; who is active and who is passive, what are we going to do? Some want to see themselves as completely men." Alev described the relationship as "a romantic relationship, like a heterosexual marriage. We are together at every sphere of life and in school: we shop together, share a common budget with pooling our respective allowances together. Except for living together, it is a relationship of husband and wife." Romantic passion is embraced fully by Pembe. Images of Pembe's romantic acts include Pembe singing songs to Alev every morning on the ferry, writing poetic essays for her, preparing romantic animations on the computer, writing and playing songs for her, and arriving unexpectedly with huge bouquets of flowers. But the most romantic moment was when Pembe produced a set of rings on Alev's birthday on the exact minute she was born. When she presented the rings, Pembe declared, "I want to be with you for the rest of my life."

This rosy picture is frequently marred by Pembe's desire to remain in the closet and refusal to participate in and integrate into the lesbian community. Alev is embedded within a lesbian community and social and political networks that allow her to enact a lesbian identity, and she is heavily invested in political organizing. Indeed, she is a founding member of a university-based LGBT organization. Alev feels a sense of pleasure and belonging in political and friendship networks and in the spaces of lesbian establishments like cafes, bars, and clubs where she feels she and Pembe can feel recognized and be open in their affections. In contrast, for Pembe queer spaces are threatening in multiple ways, and she sees other lesbians as predators of Alev. Indeed, according to Alev, she only frequents lesbian spaces and events to control Alev's interaction with other lesbians. I inquired about why Pembe was not interested in participating in the lesbian community and political activities. She listed two main reasons. The first one relates to her biggest fear: that she will be found out by her family and outed in the university if she is seen in lesbian political circles and her picture and name appear in publications. The second reason, according to Alev, is that she simply finds it unnecessary to be political. Reciting Pembe's words, she says, "'I have a lover and I am happy; I am with the one I love' (from the very first day, she has been thinking it will be a lifelong relationship with me). 'My siblings know, my closest friends know. I am comfortable.'" Alev assessed that Pembe could not comprehend the issue of gaining rights via political struggle and public visibility.

Managing these contradictory orientations, Alev's seeking out and Pembe's active avoidance of the lesbian community constitutes one of the important tensions in their relationship. Alev confronts this tension at multiple levels: as Pembe's excessive jealousy, as an obstacle for her social and political activities, and as an obstacle for her own integration into the lesbian community. Pembe's excessive jealousy is also directed toward those outside the lesbian community. Pembe even prevents Alev from interacting with her close heterosexual friends: "I cannot stay overnight at their places anymore, and I cannot invite them. She is reviewing my phone bills to see whom I called and how long I talked. She even tried to break up with me once when I happened to say 'hi' to an ex in the street when we bumped into each other." Pembe blames Alev for her lack of trust. However, for Alev, the issue runs deeper than trust: it is about their divergent understandings of relationships. Pembe's understanding is that "'you are mine and I am yours.' It is constructing a relationship of dominance over each other." Pembe is consumed by jealousy because she prefers to conform to a masculine ethos of romantic love in which possessiveness and jealousy are valued elements, while Alev subscribes to androgyny and sexual equality. Also, sexually, Alev identified an important inequality in enacting and realizing their respective desires. Alev feels that Pembe acts on her own desires without taking hers into account: "Everything I desire to act out is to be limited, but I can permit her to do everything she desires." Particularly, Pembe builds sexual boundaries that prohibit certain sexual acts: "like things with enduring effects such as losing her virginity—she desires to preserve her virginity because of her family considerations, she says 'until I gain my economic freedom, I should stay as a virgin'—or things that would bring pain to her like anal sex." Because of the fundamental difference in how they define relationship ideals, Alev said she sometimes finds herself captured by a state of hopelessness, wondering whether there is a potential to change the relationship dynamics. Nevertheless, she once again deploys her passive resistance, meaning "to be seen as agreeable to Pembe's desires outwardly but influencing her choices and behaviors inwardly [içten *içe*]." As we will see later, what Alev wants to see changed about Pembe and the relationship is entangled with Pembe's enactment of working-class gender identity. Indeed, while the realms of gender and romance enabled the couple to deemphasize the significance of class differences, it did not render them trivial.

Establishing intimacy in the context of class inequality added another layer of class challenge for Alev, who has a seemingly impossible quest: to have her mother like and show affection toward Pembe. When Alev introduced Pembe to her mother as a close friend from school, a friend she likes a lot, her mother behaved nicely toward her, yet she was very formal and cold and had an elitist stance. In fact, her mother reacted at the mere sight of her girlfriend and told Alev that "she looks like the daughter of a doorkeeper." On another occasion, after Alev's mother happened to talk with Pembe's mother on the phone, she remarked that "she sounds like the woman who cleans our house." Alev named her mother as a class elitist, who is full of class-based prejudices and holds the view that lower-classness constitutes an irremediable difference. Alev's efforts to integrate her girlfriend into her family life as a regular friend are on a fragile path, because she is so afraid that Pembe will detect her mother's class prejudices (as they apply to her) and have her dignity and pride wounded. In stark contrast to Alev's mother's class-based hostility, Pembe's family is extremely embracing of Alev; they adore and love her. Pembe's parents tell her, "You are like our daughter." And "they pay attention to everything about me more than my own parents. Her father even occasionally asks me if I need allowance/pocket money." The differences between her experience with Pembe's family and Pembe's almost nonexistent relationship with her own family is a great source of pain for Alev: "I am experiencing this as oppression. I always wish my own family could also reciprocate and show the same kind of love to Pembe that I receive from her family."

However, Alev's integration into Pembe's family is not without any threats. First of all, Pembe's four siblings, who all know Pembe's sexuality, sometimes allude to the true nature of the relationship in front of her father and her mother. Pembe is more fearful of the involuntary outing of her relationship with Alev as a same-sex relation than she is of her parents learning she is a lesbian. Yet the more intriguing dimension of this threatening dynamic relates to one of Pembe's brothers. According to Alev, this brother makes advances and behaves as if he has a crush on Alev, a behavior she attributed to his jealousy of Pembe having a girl-friend. Incidents such as his publicly recounting a dream in which he saw himself making love with Alev make Alev very uncomfortable and also cause friction between sister and brother—Pembe did not talk with her brother for a while (küs kaldılar) over the "dream" episode. In order to discern fully why Alev understands the brother's behavior as an ex-pression of sibling jealousy, we need to understand how Pembe's gender identity is perceived in the family.

Excelling in soccer and the masculine ways of fighting and swearing (enactments of rough, working-class, boy masculinity) when growing up, Pembe is treated and proudly loved as if she were a son by her par-ents and extended kin (Alev said, "Her mother even calls her 'my son' when affectionately addressing her."). Pembe also receives support and encouragement for her masculine gender displays, for instance, for how she wears her hair: "She gets a very short masculine haircut and comes home, her family members say 'good but we wish you got it cut even shorter.'" Pembe's parents were also very vocal in expressing their wish that Pembe were actually a man so that she could marry their beloved Alev. Pembe's recognition as a son shocks Alev. Erotically, Pembe is also assigned a heterosexual male role by her family. To wit, Alev referenced a couple of family scenes she witnessed with astonishment. For instance, on one occasion, Pembe came home and told her aunt that "there were beautiful girls on the bus today." In response, the aunt said, "You should have groped/felt up them [dandik atmak]" (being groped by men in crowded buses is a common experience of girls and women in Turkey). Or in her parents' company, Pembe would raucously shout at a pass-erby woman in the street something like "you are a girl to be taken" (götürmelik kız). It is not only her family members who assigned Pembe male sexual agency but also the neighborhood girls. According to Alev, before Pembe and Alev became lovers, Pembe could find a lot of girls, es-pecially in her neighborhood, to "satisfy her sexual needs"—Pembe pos-sessed the power of seduction as she was seen and accepted as a man. It was very surprising and shocking for Alev to learn that "she would call a neighbor's daughter, even headscarved ones, just to sleep with her, like 'come to our place now there is no one home right now,' with ease. They both knew what they were doing."

Alev marked her alienness from these same-sex casual sexual intimacies practiced by Pembe with a mobilizing vocabulary including the
words "strange," "astonishing," "baffled," and "unintelligible" when recounting Pembe's experiences and described such events as an outside
observer. Pembe's gender nonconformity, which not only escaped the
negative response of being deemed unnatural or forbidden but also was
given encouragement by her family members, runs counter to Alev's
own experience. She also finds Pembe's spontaneous same-sex practices
peculiar because they disrupt her understanding of lesbian identity, an
understanding closely connected with middle-classness. She articulated
the class connotations this way: "I always thought that if you were a lesbian, you would be at a bar or on the computer chatting with another
lesbian, but a headscarved neighborhood girl in a squatter settlement
can sleep with a neighbor's daughter . . . ?" Alev's power of imagination
only permits a scenario for same-sex desire that is similar to her experiences, in which "two young girls fall in love before they discover themselves." She can, in her words, "imagine this more romantic scenario but
not this [referring to Pembe's experience with her neighborhood girls]."
For Alev, one's coming out to herself consolidates and stabilizes desire
into the attitude of sexual orientation and the person of the lesbian. An
expression of same-sex desire or spontaneous homosexual activity that
does not channel the person into a particular identity contradicts Alev's
understanding of same-sex desire as the basis for identity. On yet another level, Alev's descriptions of her relationship dynamics revealed how
these desires and identities are governed by class norms that are worked
out through concrete interactions. Proper and improper, respectful and
disrespectful class and gender expressions and actions are intertwined
and made inseparable in her narrative.

Alev's description of an experience she and Pembe had in a high-end
lesbian bar encapsulated these inseparable dimensions of class, gender,
and sexuality. That night Pembe got very drunk and started giving ag-
gressively sexual hugs to every woman in the bar. She also lay on the floor
and behaved in other inappropriate ways that prompted an intervention
from the security guards. In her telling of this incident, Alev was careful
to clarify to me that she was ashamed of the situation and not of Pembe,
because she loves her. Pembe was acting out like a lower-class macho
man, and her disruptive and crass behavior intersected with sexual ag-

gression. She was putting forward a compromised identity as a deviation from the androgynous and romantic self that Alev desires her to be. Less drastic but nonetheless apparent, additional signaling and routine marking of Pembe's working-class upbringing was explicitly articulated when Alev mentioned Pembe's deportment, mannerisms, and bodily gestures—how in public Pembe laughs too loudly and constantly swears: "I couldn't ascribe these things to her identity [yakıştıramıyorum]. Yes her family is not educated but still it is a self-educated family." Simultaneously tied and untied to her class habitus and upbringing, Pembe troubles the paradigm of gentle, boyish masculine figure of androgyny, Alev's object of desire and her middle-class sense of balance.

I think it would not be incorrect to infer from Alev's narrative about Pembe that Pembe's assimilation into the lesbian community may mean suppressing or fracturing parts of her self—the parts loved and cherished by her family—and conforming to a particular gender and sexual identity by transgressing class boundaries, which she might experience as a kind of class dominance. By refusing to join Alev's lesbian circles and community, Pembe is denying herself a new community of affirmation but also refusing to be a subject of class domination. Also, it seems that openly claiming to be a lesbian might not bring an experience of liberation for Pembe, whose family connectivity is important in the way (positively self-affirming) it is not for Alev. In contrast, on the surface it seems that for Alev self-affirmation is about the work of building and maintaining a lesbian identity that is disclosed, monogamously coupled, and visible. However, Alev's self-making is not completely disassociated from her family and its attending class attachments and affective affirmations or denials.

Strongly signaled within the story of the bar episode was Alev's own behavior: she explained how in trying to control Pembe's disrespectful class and sexual conduct, she found herself transformed into a macho persona (maçholaşabiliyorum) by becoming rough and coarse. Thus, Pembe's public behaviors have the countereffect of making Alev display a macho identity. Alev's own androgynous identity can be compromised by association with Pembe. Yet any exploration of the ways in which Pembe's lower-classness threatens to undo Alev's own self-making would be incomplete if we neglect to take into account Alev's yearnings for recognition from her mother as a kind of inscription of her lesbian identity onto the affective family order. Nor should we minimize the importance of her desire to integrate Pembe into her family as a shared affiliation and attachment across class. Indeed, what we see here is the imbrication of these two desires—how they are intertwined and simultaneously pursued in Alev's self-making. Part of Alev's passive resistance is motivated by the desire to keep her sexuality from being totally invisible to her mother. It is a rebellion against the powers of invisibility, of silencing oneself, of remaining unspoken, and of submitting to heteronormative demands. Yet, despite her mother's rejections and her own establishment of affirmative networks outside the family, Alev's self-making cannot be entirely complete without some recognition from her mother. In this way, Pembe's lower-classness adds an extra layer of difficulty in making Alev's lesbianism visible to her mother and thus legitimizing and manifesting her lesbian identity completely. Alev's identity in fact takes shape through the evolution of this relationship of submission and rebellion and is also forged through her struggle to make class boundaries permeable. Alev's refusal to accept a lesbian identity and life dissociated from her family biography and her desire to give same-sex love access to legitimate family expression bespeak the power of and desire for connective selving in the construction of new selves in Turkish society.

At the end of the interview, I asked Alev if she had anything to add. This is what she said:

> I was always told homosexuality equals unhappiness, but this is not true. I also believed this secretly for so many years until I met Pembe. There is no such thing as unhappiness. We are as happy as a heterosexual couple. I hope other gays and lesbians discover this because they are approaching their identities with this fear. Even my sister thought I was going to be unhappy. Why should we unhappy?

Indeed, she has proved her mother wrong.

2

Making a New Man

Recognition, Romance, Sex, and Neoliberal Masculinity

My girlfriend and I were having dinner at a restaurant. I noticed that my former girlfriend and a bunch of common friends we used to hang around had also arrived and were seated in an adjoining dining room. I stood up and told my girlfriend that I would like to go to their table to say hi. While I was chatting, my girlfriend approached me from behind and turned me around to land a passionate kiss with eyes screaming to say, "he is mine; he belongs to me." I was so stunned that I reached the point of ecstasy. That moment was the greatest moment: I felt like I lost my consciousness and felt great about myself. (Alp, 23)

By recounting this cherished memory, Alp conveyed the most thrilling experience of his life. The dynamic evoked by this seemingly straightforward episode encompasses a range of issues that are central to understanding and analyzing the complicated relationships among romance, sex, and the desire for recognition in the self-making of young men. Alp's account helps construct a new narrative of male desire, one in which the pleasurable embodiment of masculinity is deeply tied to being publicly recognized as an object of female desire. But it also signals that being recognized as a desired man depends on the girlfriend's public sexual expression.

This chapter identifies heterosexual romance as a significant site of masculinity in which desire for recognition and connectivity are cultivated. I argue that the realms of romance and courtship figure significantly in the crystallization of neoliberal masculine subjectivity centered around ideals of "entrepreneurship of the self" (Freeman 2014) and masculine self-expansion, which is attained in relation to the gendered other and has multiple authors: the making of the neoliberal masculine self is intertwined with the identity making of young women.

By emphasizing the importance of romance for the new constructions of masculinity, I hope to complicate dominant formulations of the relationship between gender and sexuality that define the realm of romance as feminine and the realm of sex as masculine. Dominant discourses of heterosexuality contain some powerful polarities that neatly and monolithically divide and distribute the desire for love/romance/ intimacy and the desire for sex by gender. Summed up by the cliché "women want love, while men want sex," these discourses position women as sexual gatekeepers who are vulnerable to falling in love and who value the emotional aspects of intimacy over sexual desire. Men, by contrast, are understood as always ready for sexual activity, as the "driving" sexual partners who are emotionally detached, and male sexuality is understood to be easily satisfied. I suggest that longings for love and sex are not independent of, but rather are complicated by, another significant longing: the longing for recognition, a longing that itself often leads to masculine domination and control.

Although romance—with its connotations of femininity and emotionality—has traditionally been read as anathema to masculine selfhood, romance is increasingly being imagined as an acceptable and even important component of masculinity. Indeed, recent research in different geographies has signaled both the "resistance" to dominant discourses of heterosexuality and the emergence of "alternative" narratives (Allen 2003; Korobov 2009; Maxwell 2007; Redman 2001). However, these narratives have "remained tenuous and unstable" (Maxwell 2007, 555) and do not represent a significant disruption of hegemonic masculinity as much as they represent "an example of the way in which hegemonic masculinity has appropriated and reconfigured a previously subordinated romantic masculinity" (Allen 2003, 148–49). In this light, Allen notes that to ensure its success, hegemonic masculinity must remain flexible and "[adjust] to the demands of a particular cultural/historical context" (149), such as the rise of the feminist movement and its influence on what women demand from their partners. Situating relationally constructed masculinities explicitly in class and race constructions, Peter Redman (2001) draws attention to the ways young men use heterosexual romance narratives to construct their masculinities according to codes of middle-class, professional, and implicitly white identities in Britain. More adult, romance-based relationships become part of a process of individuation in the competition for cultural and economic capital, differentiating their actors from other heterosexual masculine identities "characterized by [their] sexual objectification of women, commitment to homosociability and homophobia, and oppositional and casual attitude to school" (195). In this way, romance narratives become disciplinary practices themselves, "policing class, gender, and sexual relations" and granting young men symbolic access to "agency, authority, sexual probity, maturity, masculinity [and] cultural capital" (198).

My analysis offers a valuable point of departure for understanding why some Turkish young men desire romance over sex, as well as an exploration of how they attempt to integrate their sexual and romantic desires. The relationship between the desire for recognition and masculine selfhood has been conspicuously overlooked in the study of neoliberal masculinity, and as a consequence, the dimensions arguably of the most relevance to complicating our understanding of the formation of the neoliberal subject defined by self-invention, autonomy, and self-realization, the concepts of relationality and dependency, and the intersubjective formulation of masculinity and feminity have gone largely undocumented in the literature on the subject.

In order to introduce the reader to the desires produced and pursued by these young men, I first trace a significant shift in the normative construction of masculinity in the context of a burgeoning neoliberal capitalism from a narrowly defined protective paternalism embodied by the previous generation to an emergent desire for masculine self-expansion and enrichment. This new model of masculinity is based on rejecting the self-denials of the father and creating selves that are layered and protean. The way this self-construction is articulated, shaped, animated, and inhabited, as well as what its ramifications are, is intimately and organically linked to a new vision of femininity in intimate relationships. This new ideal of femininity in male narratives is marked by dualities of, on the one hand, ambitious, charismatic, and "selfish" girls[1] who privilege their own desires, and, on the other hand, the repudiated maternally selfless, "positive girls" who are capable of giving energy to intimate masculine others. I provide an account of these men's sexual and romantic stories in order to explore the centrality of desire in this dialectic between selfish and positive girls. Arguing that the enactment and achievement of ideal masculine selves needs both at once (selfish, autonomous girls provide selves suitable to meet the male desire for recognition, while positive girls nurture and discipline connectedness), I suggest that the new ideal of femininity reflects and actively constructs connective selving in the construction of masculine subjectivity to support the new masculine desire for expanded selfhood. It is this dependency of masculinity on both selfish and selfless female selves that aligns the structures of connective selving with neoliberal selfhood.

Although this chapter is based on the narratives I collected of twenty-two young men, the stories and themes I draw upon in this chapter bring some young men more than others into the foreground in ways that help make concrete theoretical points about what interrupts or changes the patriarchal construction of masculinity as dominant and protective in Turkish society as well as the nuances that lie between complete rejection and complete embracing of patriarchal masculinity that are articulated in the men's narratives. It is crucial at the outset to explain that in my interpretive frame, I avoid adopting labels for categories of masculinity that are available in the literature, such as "egalitarian," "macho," "sensitive," and "complicit." Placing the young men I interviewed neatly into a system of rigid categorization—attaching adjectives to a more or less identifiable mode of masculinity—has the danger of giving a false sense of coherence and fixity when forms of self-making are not simple, one-dimensional, or clear-cut.[2] Indeed, in practice young adults' masculine ideals may shift in one direction or another, and young men may hold contradictory identities simultaneously. In part because of my commitment to placing and understanding self-making within the generational processes of change and continuity, I employ a semantic strategy that draws attention to a central orientation in the young men's narratives: rejecting/embracing patriarchal masculinity. As a liminal category, my concept of vulnerable masculinity highlights or provides leverage on these two polar orientations and allows for the interrogation of tensions and contradictions in the men's narratives. My hope is that this semantic strategy draws attention to the ways in which masculinity and masculine self-making are entangled with other formative forces.

These two broad orientations, the rejection or embracing of patriarchal masculinity, cannot be explained in purely class terms but are the products of continuous interaction with class origins, locality, upbringing, connective selving, and neoliberal aspirations. Analyzing individual narratives within broad orientations can indicate the direction and flow of collective identities, especially when the naming of such orientations adopts the labels/self-definitions of the social actors themselves, such as a few young men in this chapter who define themselves as holders (*tutucu*) of their parental patriarchal gender and sexual values. Those who define themselves as upholders of these values desire to embrace dominant masculinity in their self-making. But in their attempts to protect, reinforce, and channel familiar values, rather than challenge them, they also become vulnerable in the area of attracting women and negotiating romance. Because of their patriarchal attitudes and displays, they earn widespread disapproval from desirable young women, and they often experience conflict in expectations between themselves and the young women with whom they wish to form relationships.

In numerical and sociological terms, the overwhelming majority of the men in this chapter manifest a great awareness and need to renounce the oppressive, protective dimensions of masculinity. The biographical context common to these men, who lay claim to nonpatriarchal masculinity, egalitarian attitudes in gender relations, and sexual modernity, is marked by urban upbringings where emotional and sexual subjectivities are developed in cross-gender relational contexts (peer and adult cultures). These young men receive parental recognition and approval for their maturity for learning to negotiate emotional and sexual intimacy through romantic engagements. They were raised by highly educated mothers who receive recognition as subjects in their own right due to their professional status. In a sense, they have been more prepared than the minority of other men I interviewed to confront the challenges of turning away from the dominant patriarchal culture that constructs masculinity as protective. In seeking new identities that contest the traditional sexual codes of the older generation, they are privileged in having access to the class-based emotional, normative, and material resources necessary to be recognized as desirable.

In contrast, a small group of men in this study (like Ali, whose story I detail in the next chapter) experience significant disadvantage not routinely experienced by the majority in seeking to distance or differentiate themselves from the oppressive, protective dimensions of masculinity and to be recognized as desirable, and thus they negotiate their masculine identities in admittedly often demanding contexts. These are the young men whose homosocial socialization into masculinity and sexually conservative upbringings render them vulnerable with regard to negotiating emotional and sexual intimacy. Furthermore, their lack of dependency on affirming, reliable others, most signicantly parents, makes heterosexual intimate relationships particularly crucial for this group of men. This small group commands our attention because the greatest dislocation occurs among these men, who, in attempting to move away from the traditional and rigid patriarchal upbringings in their personal histories, confront the growing discrepancies between their families' ideals and expectations about gender relations and sexuality and their own new ideal selves. The issue of how to be different without deserting one's connective tissues confronts these young men even more sharply, and a chasm of communication and information between them and their parents constitutes a sign of rapid and deep cultural change.

The patriarchal upbringing of these young Turks continues to convey for men that loving and protecting women entails controlling them, and for women that loving men means submitting to them (Joseph 1994). The weight of this tradition makes it difficult for young men to relate to young women who now claim autonomy and sexual independence and who refuse subordinate positions in their personal lives. To recall Benjamin's theory of domination from the introduction, domination hinges on the infantile desire to be recognized as a subject without returning that recognition, to deny the other's independent subjectivity and autonomy. For Benjamin, it is through intersubjective recognition—reciprocal, mutually influencing interaction between two subjects that fosters the "two-way street" of subjecthood—that patriarchal domination can be transcended and the "bonds of love" truly be fostered. In the following narratives, we will see the struggles faced by young men to reconcile tensions between opposing models of masculininity and femininity, as well as their own efforts to forge new paths for themselves and new subjectivities in relation to their parents, their new peer groups, and their intimate others (desired and/or realized).

The twenty-two men in this chapter ranged in age from eighteen to twenty-three years. In terms of their family class origins, the sons of the middle and upper-middle strata were better represented than the very well-to-do or the poor. About half of them (thirteen) identified their family class background as middle-class (nine) or lower-middle-class (four), while seven identified their backgrounds as upper-middle-class and two as upper-class. Twelve of them came from families in which mothers were homemakers with marginal to modest educational backgrounds; the rest of the mothers were professionals.

Rejecting Patriarchal Masculinity

For the fathers of the young men in this chapter, who started their careers in the mid-1970s as upwardly mobile university graduates, or in some cases as uneducated manual laborers, government employment was more attractive than employment in private sectors or trade. The government bureaucracy, with its career ladder and clearly defined goals, was both collectively and individually perceived as a more glamorous and secure career path leading to more status and power than were available in the private sector. The state was a mobilizing agent for development in Turkey and a symbol of collective aspirations. Engineers of the fathers' generation especially were celebrated as the designers of a developing industrial society. Educated young men of that era tended to identify with the state and its ethos, rather than with the unglamorous capitalistic free enterprises, and they regarded the state as a vehicle for their social ambitions. Their sons, in contrast, see the state as an inhibiting structure, one that produces a passive stance toward the world and is therefore an important obstacle to the creation of authentic, individualized selves. They see the global neoliberal economic order,[3] alternatively, as introducing individuals to the possibility of shaping their own future. As Harvey (2005) theorizes, the processes of neoliberalism entail creative destructions "not only of prior institutional frameworks and powers but also of divisions of labor, social relations, welfare provisions, technological mixes, ways of life and thought, reproductive activities, attachments to land and habits of the heart" (3). Indeed, the young men's view of the state as an inhibiting force reflects the destruction of the social contract between the state (which was vital for the earlier generation's class formation) and the middle class under Turkey's neoliberalization (Rutz and Balkan 2009).

Contemporary changes in Turkey, especially with respect to widespread privatization, have produced two larger social movements associated with the entrepreneurial impulse of the male youth culture centered on the ideals of entrepreneurial freedom, self-invention, autonomy, and self-realization: the end of lifelong careers and the movement away fom state-sector jobs. The link between job stability and manhood was crucial to the patriarchal familial order in which manliness was defined as responsible providerhood, and men were driven by the desire to protect their dependents. While this patriarchal order, based on gender privilege, helped to shore up men's position at home, it also caused their lives to be characterized by inertia and risk aversion. Indeed, the end of lifelong state careers in Turkey both expresses and legitimates the profoundly "anti-*memur*" ethos of the young men I studied. "*Memur kafası*" (mind of the government employee) is a Turkish expression without an equivalent in English. It is used to describe people who are order takers, who have no power to initiate things, who deliver results, but with obedience to the rules and conformity, and who never question authority. Over the course of the last three decades, the shift away from salaried state-sector jobs and the end of lifelong careers have undermined the old touchstone of middle-class masculinity.

As the meaning of masculinity changed from provider/protector in the context of a burgeoning neoliberal capitalism, youths' desire to broaden the parameters of normative masculinity, to bring together discrepant realms of experience—the desire to, in other words, create total life experiences—has grown. These young men desire not just to be economic providers but to participate in a full range of enjoyable activities, to pursue careers that are both profitable and fun, and to fully take advantage of life by developing creative pursuits (in music, cinema, caricature, theater, dance, poetry). The young men I studied frame competent manhood in terms of the production of desire, self-actualization or self-expression, and the ability to take risks in the process of achieving personal growth and professional achievement.

The career aspirations of these young men registered this shift powerfully: not one respondent expressed any desire to have a job in the state sector. Instead, they hoped to set up their own businesses, even in occupational areas outside the expertise of their educational training. Neither working under a boss nor working in what they consider uncreative and "square" occupations appealed to them. Wanting to be equally at home in all dimensions of their professional and cultural experiences, they aspired to assume leadership roles or at least a sustained cultivation not only in areas of their respective future expertise but also in other areas of life.

The neoliberal turn orients these men to aspirations, occupational and otherwise, that constitute radical departures from those of their fathers. The renunciation of protective masculinity is a powerful motivating force in the formation of new identities among the educated classes. A core component of this identity making is the desire to create and become a part of a world beyond the confines of rigidly separated work/family experiences in order to widen the range of expressive possibilities for men. The providing, protective father as a model of manhood is seen as problematic by these men because taking care of the needs of others can cost one the knowledge and appreciation of his own needs, interests, and hobbies. Sons' narratives about their fathers reflect their rapid transition from a culture in which a central index of manhood was breadwinning to one in which self-actualization or self-expression is paramount. At the center of this notion of self-actualization lies selfishness and self-indulgence in the service of creative subjectivities and a richer life. The way these young men negotiate the tensions of desires impinged on selfishness is one of the important questions of this chapter.

Overall, young men's narratives about their fathers paint a picture of masculinity based on sameness and uniformity. The young men I spoke with believed that their fathers' lives followed a predetermined teleological course imbricated in a patriarchal history. Their lives were marked by the conformity of protective paternalism. This attitude affected how they related to women and how they constructed their subjectivities as men. The fathers described by these young men never crossed the boundaries of normative desires and the conventions of respectable fatherhood and husbandhood. The young men frequently employed the tropes of "inert person" (*kendi halinde*) and "*memur kafalı*" when describing their fathers, invoking passivity, the dutiful following of orders, and risk aversion. They suggested that their fathers' pursuit of security denied them authentic voices.

Anıl (22), who believed that a rich life could only be developed in tandem with risk taking and entrepreneurship, provides us with an example of the paternal aversion to risk taking: "Compared to my father, I am the kind of person who takes risks. He doesn't like risks, even though he is a lawyer—potentially an independent professional within the realm of free enterprise. And indeed, by taking risks, he could have practiced in a free enterprise situation, but what he does is closer to being a government employee." Similarly, Oktay (23) emphasized that his father is not innovative because "he believes deeply in the things he believes in, he never questions." Gencay (20) spoke of his father being absorbed into a good-provider role, assimilated into the practice of *memur kafası* with no desire to mark himself and his individuality. By contrast, Gencay describes himself as "more inconstant, flighty [*maymun iştahlı*—completely lacking in 'stick-to-it-iveness']. I have ambitions to see the world—and my father hasn't seen the world. Had he wanted to, he could have easily." Wanting to become the type of individual whose actions have a decisive and significant effect on the world in which he lived, Gencay identified a lack of motivation in his father:

I see things around me like inequalities or things that shouldn't exist. I ask myself how I can influence big masses . . . let's say, if I am able to change a school book in the national curriculum program, I could influence a whole generation. That is how I think differently than my father and I have these kinds of thoughts: how I can realize my ideals; my father does not have the motivation as to how to spread the ideas in his mind.

In these men's view, their fathers' lives were structured by a patriarchal order that devalued male passion and creative interests outside work and did not permit men passion or an authentic voice. Within this framework, the father is understood as a controlling ideal and a site of inertia.

Working to reject this type of masculinity, these young men position themselves as desiring, active individuals pursuing lives geared toward self-actualization. Fathers who achieved success through self-denial are therefore offered as negative examples by these men. Bora (21) addressed this issue:

I am more individualistic—that is, selfish. I aim to live my own life. My father lives through compromising himself to make his family happy. If I could add this [individualism] on top of my father's qualities, I would reach a nice place. He is also a bit materialistic; what he considers unnecessary spending may be very important for me, for instance going on vacations, taking lessons. I tell him "money is not important—think about the contributions of what I spent on myself, what they will add to myself."

For Bora, like other young men, fathers' identities are intimately linked to delayed gratifications and self-sacrifice. Similarly, Altan (22) posits that whether a man is selfish or generous indicates whether or not he is motivated by his own ambitions:

> My father is a well-intentioned, altruistic person. He can reveal his interior easily (not a calculating person). If he learns something new and thinks it's useful to other people, he shares it widely. I won't share. I am more selfish. I would rather think that "this knowledge should stay with me. I should be the only one who benefits from this." . . . I can say that my father doesn't have ambition. He wants things to happen naturally. He is very content with his predicament; he is a government employee, his salary is low but he is pleased. He has no desire to do extra work or to have a second job. Making more money doesn't interest him. . . . I am more ambitious; my father is not . . . and I can express my feelings more comfortably.

Emin (23) provided a somewhat exaggerated comparative description of his father and himself in order to emphasize how his father always plays it safe, even in mundane moments:

> My father is like a father; he leaves home with an umbrella even though it is not raining outside. . . . He gets up at 5 a.m. to go to work, and comes back home with three kilograms of tomatoes. If he needs to go to bed early to be able to get up early, he goes to bed early. If a job takes five hours to complete, he takes ten hours. . . . I leave home five minutes before my bus leaves and run to catch it. I never miss my bus. My father leaves home two hours before the bus's arrival and sits there waiting for his bus. He is so responsible, so orderly—should I say so monotonous.

Determined not to be "like a father," Emin desires to live for himself: "I am not going to take every action for my children. I will orient my life according to my own desires."

While it was their fathers' passivity and aversion to risk, as well as their lack of ambition outside the professional realm, that my participants most explicitly and frequently constructed negatively, they also referenced the problematic nature of the provider role. Cansın (18) described in detail the gender expectations and behaviors associated with this role:

> My father is this type of man: he can't leave or end a meeting saying "my wife is calling." I would never be such a person. That meeting is only my job, but my wife has a special place in my life, and if she needs to reach me at that moment, I can break the meeting. My father is an executive—it is not like he is a subordinate who cannot leave a meeting. Or let's say, he is away on business traveling. He never tells us, "I will come back on this day, at this time." He might say, "I might be back such and such a day." We would wait but he wouldn't show up, leaving us without making any plans for ourselves. . . . This doesn't mean that he doesn't value us, but he could not show the value he gives to my mother and his family. . . . Plus, I have never even once heard my dad saying to my mom "I love you" or seen him kissing her in front of us. I wouldn't be that kind of person. I will give you another example: recently, it was their wedding anniversary. He was away, but sent flowers. I am glad he remembered, but there was only the card of the flower shop attached to the flowers. Nothing like a special note. Why can't he show any emotion? There is no emotionality to my father. He is passive and devoid of emotions.

For Cansın, his father's identity as a breadwinner signals a narrow subjectivity, not competent manhood, because this provider role lacks emotionality. His father has little consideration for his family's emotional needs, putting his job and breadwinner role above everything else. Fathers like Cansın's do not provide a relatable legacy for their sons. To the sons, their fathers' priorities seem a one-dimensional masculinity that positions the emotional and affectional dimensions of fatherhood and husbandhood as unimportant. Indeed, a recent study among different groups of men in Turkey (Sancar 2011) confirms the absence of paternal emotionality and affection in sons' lives as a highly shared experience among young men.

At the heart of the young men's view of their parents' gender relations is a deeply critical view of marriage, particularly of what the men define as a disconnect between the wife and husband within the home. From their perspective, child-rearing duties, including pressures to cultivate and finance (via savings) their children's upward mobility, competed with desire, companionate connection, and acts of self-indulgence in their parents' marriages. Moreover, because traditional marriage rests on rigidly segregated gender roles that cast husbands as breadwinners and wives as caregivers and homemakers, their parents structurally lacked opportunities to develop common interests and pleasurable pursuits. What they see in their parents' marriage is not marital conflict so much as detachment and a lack of emotional and communicative engagement.

These narratives mobilize the father as both a symbolic figure and a specific person, who, for these young men, serves as an example of an undesirable outcome, and they envision alternatives for themselves. It is also critical to note that, at times, fathers emerged in their sons' accounts as figures to be admired for their "iron wills," discipline as altruistic protectors, cool-headedness, and ability to deal with major problems. Even as they criticized their fathers' adherence to the paternal model, some young men attributed their own ability to reject this model to the fact that their fathers did not put limitations on their desires or tell them to be like "this or that person."[4]

Although the impact of fathers is complex and dynamic, what remains consistent across the young men's narratives is a sense that adhering to the patriarchal association between masculinity and protection provided their fathers with narrow ranges of identity. By contrast, these young men's identity making involves self-expansion through the invention of new forms of subjectivities, pleasures, and relationships. They use the paternal model as an example from which to differentiate themselves.

As upwardly mobile high achievers, these young men see themselves as uniquely positioned to transform the content, form, and process of becoming different types of men. They perceive themselves as closely linked to a new lifestyle predicated on self-discovery via extracurricular activities, travel, and romantic and sexual exploration, allowing them to map desires that are more open ended and ambitious than those of their fathers. Young men's narratives about their explorations of the meanings of love and sex, and particularly the construction of a new ideal of femininity, help us understand the ways in which they negotiate and test the allure and threat of these new desires.

Dialectic between Selfish and Positive Girls

Tensions arising from the dangers of fulfilling their desires for intimacy, love, sex, and recognition pervaded young men's narratives about girls. These narratives capture the contradictory qualities and forms of femininity young men seek in romantic and sexual partners. These men uneasily straddle the divide between a desire to partner with emancipated "selfish girls," who claim autonomy and independent sexuality, and who embody the desire for autonomy and self-reliance, and a desire to be with "positive girls," who are capable of giving them energy.

With the expression "selfish girls," I wish to convey unsubmissive, autonomous, and self-possessed femininity. As a theoretical construct, "selfish girls" implies both egotism and self-centeredness, as well as distraction from another, the opposite of altruism and selflessness. The expression "positive girls" indicates more than active, cheerful girls. It is also a metaphor for nurturing connectedness and relationality. These men's choices of romantic partners, and the reasons why they choose, maintain, or reject certain relationships, also make visible the ways constructions of masculinity are differentiated by class and upbringing. The competing desire for selfish or positive girls illuminates the way in which love, sex, recognition, and domination entangle in the production of an emerging neoliberal masculinity.

The creation and legitimization of male self-expansion could not be achieved without gendered coauthors. Male self-expansion inevitably requires the transmission and reception of female energy through which men sustain, pursue, and even realize the dream of their idealized selves. These are not traditional stories about men acting and women reacting. Women do not disappear as actors. On the contrary, the realization of ideal selfhood for these men requires recognition, and that recognition can only come from the "selfish," autonomous woman who gives equal importance to her own desires. That is, only recognition from modern, liberated women validates these men, giving meaning to their new neoliberal masculine selves.

Selfish, Charismatic Girls

Although class-based differences inflect masculine tastes in different ways, the men's discussions of their ideal girls shared common language, symbols, metaphors, and structures of emotion. The range of qualities that most men described in their ideal partner was quite broad, but they coalesced around a specific notion of the ideal woman. She should possess charisma characterized by independence, high intelligence, brightness, cultivation, risk tolerance, and self-confidence in speech and style. These men repeatedly acknowledged that they find it very difficult to tolerate girls who are considered empty, stupid, pretentious, etc.— "those who like to appear to know all but know nothing," as Demirhan (20) puts it.

Although the men cited the importance of mutual identification through common interests at the beginning of a relationship, what they really cherished was having different interests. They saw creating "wonder" as central to making their relationships vibrant and keeping their desires alive and thought that different interests could cultivate these feelings. Their ideal girl, as Tayfun (19) described her, was "the type of girl you think you know, but who surprises you, complicating herself, not only in a new social setting or when seen through another interlocutor's perspective, but in ordinary situations."

The need to be constantly intrigued by one's lover was considered a main component of maintaining desire. For these young men, sameness carried the risk of desire dissolving into indifference or normalization. The challenge they saw was to integrate those differences into an authentic "we." Underlying the importance of maintaining excitement in a relationship, Gencay spoke to the importance of ambiguity in creating wonder or, as he phrased it, "indeterminacy/uncertainty": "If certain things in a relationship are undefined, or the other person's qualities are undefined or ambiguous, then the desire continues. For instance, you think she will definitely behave this way when I do this, or she would never like this. Indeed she likes it; she behaves so differently than expected. Then the excitement continues."

This significant concern about maintaining thrill and desire was also an important source of anxiety for these young men, especially with regard to the duration of relationships, and it had paradoxical dimensions. They expected that a long-term relationship would maximize emotional closeness, require less concentration to build and maintain the relationship, secure a regular sexual life, and minimize the impact of the external world on the relationship. Isolated long-term relationships that courted certain forms of domesticity were considered undesirable simply because they approximated the daily routines of a marriage, like those of their parents. Consistent with their desire for self-expansion, these men saw long-term relationships as a retreat to the realm of self-containment, limiting their abilities to engage in what might be other enriching experiences. Paradoxically, however, short-term relationships often signified immaturity—the inability to build and maintain a long-term relationship—as Menderes (22) put it, "acting like a high school boy changing girlfriends every other day."

Physical appearance played a salient role in the way this emblematic "charismatic partner" was constructed, although conventional beauty (looking "like a model," as my participants put it) was not necessarily the key to making a girl really beautiful. Rather, these men read dispositions, individuality, and inner essences in girls' external appearances. Generally speaking, physical appearances that signaled self-confidence were perceived to be beautiful. For example, they cited excessive make-up as signaling a lack of self-assuredness and therefore not attractive. Their idealizations of a refined self-presentation were situated between flashy and simple or ordinary. Physical appearance was considered a form of self-definition and a reflection of one's worldview. Onur (20) elaborated, "If someone is dressed too conservatively, I would think that that person is also covered/close in other realms of life. If she avoids people, it means that she lacks self-confidence and does not take risks in saying what she thinks." They also read women's sexual statuses through their clothing choices, although, as Oktay explained, there were no clear or fast rules in this regard—it was all about what kind of "air" a girl created and transmitted: "You can have a mini-skirt on but could still appear very lady-like. On the other hand, you might have a long skirt on but you create an air of motor."

The description of ideal femininity in these men's narratives provides a good example of the way gender, class, and desirability are configured as instances of boundary making. As Bourdieu (1984) famously theorized, "taste classifies, and it classifies the classifer" (6). Whether or not girls were deemed interesting or desirable was generally dependent on whether they possessed certain class-related cultural resources and dispositions. As Onur noted, compatibility "doesn't mean that we should have the same thoughts when we look at a painting, but she should look at a painting."

The expression "between equals" (*dengi dengine*) spoke to that long-standing cultural ideal that what one individual brings to an intimate relationship in terms of resources and class background should be matched by the other. These men see connecting oneself intimately with someone from a different social class as problematic, an invitation to conflict and unresolvable issues arising from feelings of superiority or inferiority. This guiding principle of "between equals" extends to sexual desirability. As Gencay pointed out, girls who evoked desire in other men were considered desirable: "If I have a potential to impress and thrill another girl, and the girl I am interested in has also potential to thrill other men, then I see it balanced, and I like this."

A girl's taste in music, film, people, and personal style and her relationship to certain practices signified either social difference and distance or affinity and closeness, thus circumscribing the possibility of romantic connection. The men relied on taste in hobbies and chosen social groups as key class-based navigational tools, transmitting important social knowledge about girls' identities and the values they held. For them, taste in music unambiguously identified where one belonged, situating and fixing girls' identities and linking them to existing subgroups on campus. In this way, the men participated in relatively closed, homogeneous social groupings. Within the romantic market, they collectively contributed to the social reproduction of classes by choosing and defining girls according to class-related markers.

The images of desirable girls were also constructed with more explicit references to undoing gender by some young men I interviewed. For example, Cansın, like many others, employed the language of equality when emphasizing the significance of self-confidence and ambition in girls:

A really successful businesswoman, one who elicits everyone's respect and who is very capable. . . . Someone who takes the leadership position in groups. In contrast to those who stay silently in a corner, in a moment of group indecisiveness, the one who says "let's go here" appeals to me, leads the whole group, motivates the whole group. To be able to defend gender equality in all realms of life, that is the most important. She shouldn't let any man oppress her in any sphere. If a man tries to block her, because of her sex, in her work, she should not accept that under any condition.

While Cansın referenced girls who learned to trust their own judgment and gained the confidence to silence those who dared silence them, Anıl avoided girls who adopted traditional norms of feminine behavior, including risk aversion: imitating a traditional girl, he said, "Oh . . . I can't do this or that, I can't go out at night." Anıl, who highly valued his resistance to rigid and polarized gender codes, preferred girls who distanced themselves from traditional gender conventions. As he explained, he liked people who deconstructed the emotional and experiential dimensions of gender differences:

> Because I believe that men also can think and feel like women and women can think and feel like men . . . I like a woman like that. That is, in Turkish vernacular, a little bit like a manly girl, but this is not a macho discourse because I am at the same time a bit of a girly man with respect to being an emotional individual. . . . I believe there should be no distinction between a man and a woman, except for extreme things. . . . I would have been very happy with someone who did not assign different roles and attitudes to women and men.

Most significantly, charismatic girls were defined by an absence of maternal selflessness. They were selfish girls who could "put forward their own desires," instead of merely responding to the desires of others. Indeed, the qualities the men used to define desirable partners for themselves contrasted strongly with a vision of femininity organized largely around notions of maternal selflessness. These men desired women whose self-conceptions were not organized around others but around the pursuit of individual self-interest, autonomy, and self-reliance. Yet even as these men view selflessness as an essentially conventional subordinated (maternal) female role, as we will see in the next section, they express a dependency on "energy-giving girls," whom they construct as precious, valuable, and vital to fostering dispositions of discipline.

"Men Like Positive Girls"[5]

The expression "girls who give energy" and its corollary, "positive girls," resonate with such commanding authority alongside selfish, charismatic girls in the male vernacular that nearly every narrative referenced this notion as a staple feature of both the ideal and the real. What is the exact nature of the identification of "giving energy" and "being positive" with regard to desired girls in male narratives? Is this identification only a trope of the patriarchal construction of girls' identities, or does it shed light on deeper processes of self and other?

The expression "positive girls" has the common features of affirming, cooperative, noncompetitive, nondemanding, altruistic femininity. This embodied capacity to give energy to another person requires a combination of caring about another's interests, emanating warmth, and possessing the capacity to adapt successfully to the capricious moods of another person in order to invoke and support the masculine desire for expanded selfhood. However, giving energy is far from rigid and monolithic. Plastic, local, and divergent, it combines both cooperative and competitive aspects. It is, in fact, the idiosyncrasies of giving energy that put it in circulation in the male vernacular.

The concept of positive girls is dramatized by Gencay, who sees himself as constantly innovating his selfhood. (As he puts it, "I am not the same Gencay I was a year ago.") He noted that his ideal partner

> should make me feel special, show understanding, satisfy my ego. . . . A positive, brave, forward-looking girl who encourages me, because encouragement is a very important concept for me. I initiate certain things, if I am not encouraged I fail, but if I have encouragement, I believe I can reach the highest point—develop my potential to its maximum point.

Gencay's view represents one of the more extreme formulations of positive girls, because during his interview he was mourning the end of his two-year relationship. Speaking in the context of what he considered the emptiness of his life, he said,

> Right now my life has no colors, I am black and white. I want color TV— this is what is missing. I am an emotionally centered person. For this

reason, it is very important that someone support and motivate me . . . motivation from someone whom I love has meaningful significance for me because it affects me deeply. . . . I am dispossessed from this influence. . . . There is no beauty in my life, there is an incompleteness, lack, and void in my life right now.

Like others, Onur deployed the concept of giving energy as a primary quality in a partner. When asked to elaborate, he gave the example of his former girlfriend: "She was promising and actually delivering that need (giving energy); she never had a concern to be the top person; she didn't have a concern for competition; she was merciful, cooperative when you needed; not forceful—a girl without too many demands, a girl who satisfies you tremendously."

As Emin's account makes clear, the construction of positive girls is tied to female attentiveness to the male ego: "Showing care to me, attention to every single word that comes out of my mouth are very important for me, and the warmth that creates makes me feel good about myself." Baykal (20) used the idiom of positive girls to describe a flexible girl who could accommodate a capricious self. He articulated the meaning he attached to positive girls through his expectations of his current girlfriend: "Sometimes when I am immersed on the computer for hours I don't want her to disturb me with her demands like come to bed or let's go out, but other times I want her to extract me from that self-centered world to force me to socialize and motivate me to do other things."

This identification of "giving energy" reflects, articulates, and actively constructs connective, transitive selving in the creation of masculine subjectivity. The meanings articulated by men with regard to this identification endorse connectedness and transitivity and promote dependency. It is this idea of dependency in the construction of masculinity that aligns the structures of connective selving with neoliberal selfhood. Although there are variations in emphasis throughout the sample, in effect what is being articulated is the familiar lure of dependency on selfless femininity.

Given the importance that self-enrichment plays in defining the identity of this group of men, the dependence on positive girls and selfless femininity should not be overlooked. When young women reproduce the patriarchal order of maternal selflessness—as Emin puts it, "showing care to me, attention to every single word that comes out of my mouth"—they foster what Benjamin (1988) describes as "self-obliteration," becoming a surrogate for the "permissive parent who cannot face [that making a perfect world for her child in which all wants are fulfilled] does not bring happiness to the child who gets everything he demands." In this way, dependency on energy-giving girls can actually threaten the young men's agency. As Benjamin writes, when the "parent has ceased to function as an other who sets a boundary to the child's will, and the child experiences this as abandonment" and the parent "co-opts all the child's intentions," she "push[es] him back into an illusory oneness where he has no agency of his own. . . . *The painful result of success in the battle for omnipotence is that to win is to win nothing: the result is negation, emptiness, isolation*" (35, italics added). As we will see in the next section, the dangers—the threat of obliteration—posed by the self-sacrificing mothers is constructed as a force of oppression in the development of new masculinities by men in relationships with selfless girls.

"Selfless" Women Oppress the New Masculinity

Within relationships, men felt oppressed by "selfless" girls. The qualities men used to define desirable partners strongly contrasted with a type of femininity organized largely around notions of maternal selflessness. Women whose self-conceptions are not organized around others (especially, parental boundaries) but around the pursuit of self-interest and who are motivated by the desire for self-reliance are the most desirable. However, their narratives are marked by real relationships with selfless girls. Altan yearns for a girlfriend who "can put forward her own desires," whom he "can seriously respect." He illustrated this in explaining why his current girlfriend is not "the one":

> For instance, there are two pieces of cake. She says, "I don't want it, really. Please you have them both." I eat it, but then afterwards I learn that she likes cakes. I don't want to be oppressed under such circumstances. This type of moment is constantly repeated. [I want] someone who really knows what she wants, is seriously able to express what she wants to do, her expectations from me and this relationship.

Altan put a premium on maintaining individuality in his relationships, and described his current relationship as oppressive because of its (to him traditional) emphasis on total togetherness: "To do things for the sake and well-being of others, I see this as traditional. In a modern relationship, you are in a relationship as individuals. There is a 'we,' and this 'we' emerges out of jointly created and shared commonality. There is no sacred a priori 'we.'" Similarly, for Sermet (21), selflessness and the absence of self-confidence signaled behavioral conformity, which he associated with a lack of character, less autonomy and independence, and submission to male agency:

> There is this issue; as I mentioned before, she isn't grounded. Right now, I am her greatest source of trust; I am even more important to her than her parents from her perspective. And this is what happens: because she wants a source of trust from outside of herself, she wants to model herself after those who provide sources of grounding for her. That is why she gets to know me first and starts thinking like me, and she becomes like me. In my opinion, if she wants to be like me, it means she doesn't have a certain character—"whoever gives me power/support/trust I will take his/her shape." Like dough.

Another significant way Sermet's girlfriend signaled her lack of agency (and therefore her inadequacy) was through her unquestioning submission to his point of view:

> If I say I am like this or that, she will conform to that. There is nothing like, "why are you like this? You shouldn't be like this," only, "if you are like this, it must be right." There is always acceptance of and conformity to what I say. I don't want to have this kind of relationship. I want to have a relationship with someone who can stand on her own two feet.

This masculine search for romantic partners who can "put forward [their] own desires," was closely related to the ways in which girls manage their intimate sexual lives vis-à-vis parental control. In the men's accounts of their relationships, we see how such intimate negotiations over the desires and needs of girls are carried out in the face of parental control.

To come back to the main point of the previous chapter, managing virginal façades demands lies. Particularly, girls who live with their families face significant constraints on their mobility, and the more families actually know of or suspect a daughter's romantic attachment, the more constraints proliferate and the more elaborate lies and pretensions become. Though various strategies of virginal façades offer a kind of freedom to these daughters, relieving them from close parental supervision in order to explore intimacy and sex, they also expose their lack of autonomy.

Maintaining the virginal façades requires complicity on behalf of boyfriends. For some men, like Oktay, this complicity is complicated: "I don't like to lie. I can lie to my own parents, but I don't want my girlfriend to lie to her parents because of me." Oktay finds his girlfriend's lies dishonorable because they threaten his sense of honor. Emotional disputes and conflicts over this issue had become a significant part of his relationship. More importantly, girls who sacrifice their own pleasures for the sake of their parents' wishes are seen by their boyfriends as analogous to the self-sacrificing mother. In families that carefully controlled daughters' movements, the boundaries of the self and others is a vexing issue. Bora described the frustration of maintaining a three-year relationship with a young woman whose movements are carefully controlled by her parents: "For instance, [her parents] tell her 'you are not going to come home late, you will not go here and there, you will not stay there. Why do you need to go there? Stay at home. Why are you going to movies at night? Go during the day.'" Dubbing this predicament his "biggest life struggle," Bora claimed that although he and his girlfriend "took leaps," he has "struggled with this issue so much":

> I constantly warn her, "Look, this is wrong. You will regret it when you look back. It is in your hands to change this. Why should it be this way? Why should your dad dictate to you? Why should he become happy while you are unhappy?" This type of talk takes ten thousand pages with her. The situation right now is not very hopeful, but compared to three years ago, we have progressed a lot.

Because his girlfriend's parents are aware of their relationship, Bora said he understands that his girlfriend faces a difficult dilemma, "because what I desire contradicts what her family desires." She can either make her family unhappy or him; she is caught between them. As he put it, "She is destined to be a prisoner in the middle." Yet he told her, "This is a bit your fault, so you can change it." Change demands risking the loss of parental financial and emotional support, but, according to Bora, "overall in the end, she would be happy. When she is thirty years old, she could look back and say 'yes my finances were cut off, but I lived a good life.'" Bora attributed his girlfriend's passive attitude and aversion to risk to the way she was raised: "She cannot express her ideas; she accepts them from others—she only says 'okay.' This needs to be changed; hopefully it will with time. Because of this, without wanting to be, I am more dominant."

Wanting to escape from a perceived dominant position in a relationship had a different dimension for Gencay. He identified a lack of intellectual compatibility in his three-year relationship, signaled by the absence of critical and satisfying conversations with his girlfriend. He has a passion for the fellowship of intellectual life—the debates, the shared jovial challenges and enrichments. Because his ambitions and intellectual preoccupations are not recognized and shared by his girlfriend, he feels ambivalent about his desire for her: "Sometimes I feel passionate to see her. Other times I find myself feeling disinterested." What continues to attach him to her is sexual intimacy and what he warmly receives from her: "a hard-to-find kind of love and care."

For Gencay, intellectual companionship is a marker of real romance, and his girlfriend disappoints him in this regard. As exciting as sex with her is, he wants some indication that there would eventually be more intellectual compatibility in their relationship. Indeed, he actively plotted to initiate and fuel his girlfriend's interest in things he enjoyed. He even bought her books with the anticipation that they would discuss them together, but she never read them. His longing for her to become his intellectual companion was not fulfilled. His desire intensified as he realized that there were others girls who would satisfy his longing for intellectual companionship. They were girls who would understand his references; girls with voices who would talk back, argue, and debate; girls who would recognize his intellectual attainments and challenge him.

Interrelated with Gencay's strong sense of intellectual distance is the issue of his girlfriend's passivity. Gencay was bothered by his girlfriend's reputation for being silent in their circle of friends: "She doesn't express what she thinks and my friends have started making fun of her, which disturbs me." Although he described encouraging her to develop her voice (telling her, for instance, "this is not working, try to develop self-confidence"), he said that he could not bring himself to be more straightforward with her. He explained, "How can you tell your intimate other about the incompleteness, the lack [you] see in her?" Gencay said that he writes his true feelings in poems, and he shared with her a poem that he had written in an earlier time of their relationship to acknowledge the acute self-division this intellectual incompatibility had created within him: "wanting both to separate/break from her and wanting to stay connected because of his sexual desire for her," as he put it in the poem. Indeed, only the pleasures of sex, their compatibility in this realm, allowed for the continuance of the relationship. He theorized that had they not had sex, he would have been more likely to have ended their relationship. He knew that she was intellectually passive and silent early on, but he discounted the significance of these attributes because of the pleasures and intimacy of their sexual relations.

According to Gencay, his girlfriend's passivity is a function of being intimidated by her former macho boyfriend. Gencay seeks to avoid power imbalances in his relationship with her, because they prevent him from experiencing full pleasure. Explicitly describing this desire, he claimed, "I am seeking an equality of desires so that I won't feel superior. . . . In order to have pleasure, I need to feel that there is a balance."

This link between selfless girls and efforts to reject male dominance in the relationships established by Gencay and others contrasted sharply with the narratives of a small group of men who embodied vulnerable masculinity.

Vulnerable Masculinity

The group on whom this section will focus is made up of young men on the path toward upward mobility who negotiate the tension between, on the one hand, longing to remain organically connected to conservative values and histories that underwrite the patriarchal construction of masculinity as protective and dominant and, on the other hand, the desire to surrender to the seduction of sexual and gender modernity, to renounce the oppressive, protective dimensions of masculinity, and to be recognized as desirable. These men's negotiations of discrepancies between the values and lifestyles of their families of origin and their own upward mobility, with its rich possibilities of new experiences and feelings, bear the marks of vulnerability. I employ the term "vulnerable masculinity" here to refer to a mode of male subjectivity that inhabits an anxious boundary between belonging and unbelonging, displacement and placement, relatedness and autonomy, identification and dis-identification. It is important to underline that this notion of vulnerable masculinity should not be equated with marginalized or subordinated masculinity in Connell's model of hegemonic masculinity, the cultural ideal. I use it descriptively rather than as a static designation in order to explore the interplay of different masculinities in the process of self-making. As Tony Coles (2009) points out, one of the shortcomings of Connell's model of hegemonic masculinity is its failure to account for the way masculinities that are marginalized or subordinate in relation to the cultural ideal can be lived as dominant in particular contexts and might epitomize and be received as dominant masculinity. Particularly, with this expression, I want to capture the dialectics between, on the one hand, dependency on a "valued self" ("charismatic self") rooted in the patriarchal family but received (and felt) as marginal in the new environment and, on the other, a competing effort to define an ideal self. The lack of dependency on a reliable other who recognizes and affirms their upwardly mobile existence and idealized selves as they build adult identities renders heterosexual intimate relationships particularly crucial for this group of men. Accordingly, we must read these projects of newly formed masculine self-makings as equally critical to the efforts among young women to craft themselves and a new femininity.

Bearers of vulnerable masculinity straddle the space between, on the one hand, the overbearing presence of a new world permeated by middle-class values and gender relations and, on the other, attachment to familiar and familial images, values, and symbols that uphold parental conceptions of gender and sexuality. These men come from provincial backgrounds and experience dissonance between a sense of distinction and superiority due to their placement in Boğaziçi and a sense of lack, social inadmissibility, and exclusion. They are socialized for economic mobility, with educational and professional ambitions to pursue higher-status occupations than those of their fathers, but not social and cultural mobility. The pursuit of upward mobility through educational achievement places them within new spheres of sociability, but their expectations and predispositions, constituted largely through their gender and class habitus, sit uneasily with the requirements of creating upwardly mobile selves. Particularly, their personal histories, punctuated by homosocial socialization into masculinity and their sexually conservative upbringing, render them vulnerable in negotiating emotional and sexual intimacy, which I consider a defining component for building a middle-class subjectivity.

I examine the terrain of these anxious boundaries and how they are experienced from the point of view of four young men: Altan, the most conservative man I interviewed, who considers himself *tutucu* (meaning "holder of traditions") in matters of gender relations and sexuality; Barlas (22), who also considers himself *tutucu* but whose loyalty to patriarchal ideals is challenged; Haydar (22), who has rejected values that support patriarchal constructions of manhood; and Oktay, who actively seeks to escape oppressive masculinity in his self-making but finds himself waging a battle with himself. Their stories provide a different perspective on upbringing in conservative families, both underscoring its impact and powerfully foregrounding the conditions under which ambivalences about patriarchal values arise. Specifically, their stories suggest that departure from parental sexual mores owes its existence and direction to a force produced by liberated girls. Oktay's story, in particular, illuminates the complexity of the relationship between the desire for recognition and the desire for male domination.

Inhabiting Vulnerable Masculinity: Altan, Barlas, and Haydar

Altan's romantic longings are organized around his desire to inherit the protective, dominant, masculine self. Although his gender conservatism is exceptional and without nuance, he is not uncritical of why his views on gender hold power over him. He traced his conservatism to his upbringing and described how it has carried over into his young adult life, leaving him rigid in his views and psychologically ill equipped for any kind of transformative work. For him, there are intractable difficulties inherent in changing one's values:

I cannot abandon them. . . . I know I should be more flexible; I studied at a University, at Boğaziçi. In the near future, I want to go abroad. In order to increase my communication with different people, I have to be more social, and flexibility is a must. In my personality and in my psychology, I cannot achieve this. Ultimately, because of my upbringing and because of my culture, there are values I have accepted, and those will never change. They are going to stay with me wherever I go.

He attributed his desire for control and protectiveness to being born male. Being a man in Turkish society assigned him the dominant role and status as head of the family, giving him jurisdiction over his wife and children and, not incidentally, holding him accountable for the safety and financial security of his children. Accepting his own psychological inability to conceptualize alternative gender frames and identities outside of his patriarchal family structure, he envisioned building a family based on male dominance, mirroring the gender dynamics and relations of his family of origin. His children will be under his control, including financially, even in the event that his future wife works and brings home money. "If she contributes financially for expenses related to our children, I'd feel like I was impotent/weak [aciz]." It will also be up to him to decide "where we live, in which city." This decision-making power and authority, he noted, should also cover her associations with other people: "I don't want her to make friends with people I don't like, including her girlfriends." In sum, the woman in his future will be subordinate to his desires and will follow him, while he will act on his own interests and desires without taking hers into account. His patriarchal perspective endorses a commitment to obedience from a subordinated female who will surrender to his will: "I don't want to fall in step with her, instead she should fall in step with me. . . . I am extremely ambitious." Altan drew an analogy between being a movie star and being the head of a household, forcibly pointing to his need to be dominant: "If we think of life as a movie, I am the main star of my movie. I don't want to enter somebody's life as a supporting player."

When I talked with him, Altan was not in a relationship and had only had very limited preludes to romantic relationships with a few girls, the longest of which, he said, lasted three weeks. He developed a distrust of girls during his senior year of high school, when he fell in

love with a girl who did not return his interest. This distrust was ampli-
fied in college when, as he was about to develop a relationship with a
girl (they went out for about three weeks), he made the mistake of failing to pay proper attention to her because he had an important exam
on his mind. When she refused to see him later, he texted her with
"messages filled with *aşk* and love." She replied, however, with, "Don't
pretend as if there was anything special between us. There was not such
a thing. Where are you coming up with this?" Explaining the absence
of romance in his life despite his desire for it, Altan theorized, "Maybe
because I am too ambitious academically, I am unable to fully devote
myself to girls and the area of romance." More specifically, he identified
his tendency to silence women as the "fatal flaw" that made him unap-
pealing to potential romantic partners: "I speak too much; I don't allow
girls to speak up. I know I have to give them an opportunity to speak
up because girls like men who give them the opportunity to speak. But
I couldn't do that."

Altan was interested in a particular girl at Boğaziçi because she invoked his ideal of feminine passivity:

> I liked her character a lot—quiet [*kendi halinde*], innocuous, demure, and
> she had not had a relationship before. This was a wonderful thing for me.
> To be able to maintain a relationship that can progress to marriage with
> a girl who hasn't had a relationship before is paramount for me. The girl
> I marry should not have had a relationship before me. I want to be her
> first man in her life.

Altan largely equates the preservation of virginity with self-mastery of
passion/desire: "If a girl knows how to be patient and has will power and
has never had a sexual relationship before marriage, she will not have
extramarital relations in the future because she possess will power. . . .
In this way virginity is a measure of trust. . . . I believe this." Altan feels
that girls who remain virgins until marriage will also remain honorable
when they are married. The explicit assumption is that once virginity is
lost, its forsaker could manipulate the truth about her sexual past. The
intact hymen, in this sense, becomes the bearer of the truth. When I
asked Altan if he could imagine himself being with a girl who had gone
out with other men in the past but who was still a virgin, he explained,

If there was a respectful relationship within certain boundaries in her past, I could accept that. But, as I said before, if she kissed, slept in the same bed with a man, even without intercourse, I could not accept that. And for this expectation, I think I am also making some sacrifices. I also don't engage in sexual relationships with girls before marriage. I can date and kiss a girl, but I cannot have a sexual relationship with her, because I would regret it afterwards—she would be damaged.

It is important to underline that Altan's sense of masculinity carries the "protective" dimension of patriarchy—he understands it to be his duty to "protect" girls "without will power" from the effects of their own desire.

Because of the nonhegemonic status of his gender ideology (at least among his Boğaziçi peers), Altan frequently, and anxiously, reflected on the sources of his gender and sexual conservatism. He ruminated over the personal and public dimensions of his attitudes toward virginity and premarital sex, attributing them to a personal fixation and, in the same breath, to his family and the larger society in which he lived. He pointed out that his attitudes were "obstacles to happiness during the joyful times of youth" and lamented that Turkish youth "cannot do certain things like the youth in the West." When asked how these obstacles might be overcome, he theorized that this would happen when the ties between generations were ruptured, when the younger generation found what the older generation told them insignificant, although, from his perspective, this generational rupture would be "bad for the country."

Like Altan, Barlas could not imagine easily transcending the values of his parents, although he sees himself as socially versatile. He does not hint at any tensions he feels between himself and those around him who don't share his values. Although he considers himself part of a "minority" of individuals who are uncomfortable with sexuality, he claims he could also form friendships with the sexually permissive "majority." Citing the "incredible love" of his parents and older brother, Barlas has committed to the terms of the conservative sexual mores constructed by his upbringing. He believes that a sexual relationship without a long, intimate connection is unacceptable. He dismisses all types of sexual engagement outside long-term love relationships as deviant. Barlas's uncomfortable stance toward sexuality is strongest in his disgust with hook-up practices, which he considers to be animalistic activities. The hold of parental sexual mores in his narrative is strong, and he has upheld their standards dutifully thus far. However, his first serious relationship upset his inflexible adherence to traditional values. He explained, "I am now understanding that this [his acceptance of conservative sexual mores without exception] might not be right." This impetus to reexamine "his acceptance without any exception" of conservative mores arose from the tension he feels between his (impossible) desire to embody sexually conservative values in his relationship and his girlfriend's sexually permissive values. Losing their status as unquestionable truth, the values of his upbringing can no longer serve as normative guides for his actions.

At the time of his interview, Barlas had been in this relationship for two months. Before this, he had had only two casual, short relationships. Although their relationship is young, it is already tense. Barlas is preoccupied with the deepening romance, because becoming sexual with a girl, for him, is part of a process of deepening intimacy that should culminate in marital sex:

> I see sexuality as the end point of *aşk*, or a huge love. Sexuality should be shared with someone you are closely attached to, to such a point of bonding that you see that person as a spouse . . . sex is the last point of passion. You share everything with that person, and at the end you share that too. If I had experienced sex before I was married, I would marry that person. In my mind, I am already married. What is important is what you think in your head; it means, in any case, I was already contemplating marriage.

Barlas's girlfriend's desire to have a sexual relationship threatens his desire for romance unaccompanied by sex. As he described it, his girlfriend is an emancipated young woman with her own apartment, not subject to any significant parental controls. However, her success in establishing freedom to live her life as a single woman and her openness to pursuing sexual pleasure bother Barlas: "Her friends coming to her place, my being there all the time, her desire to invite me to her place constantly etc., these things for me are wrong. . . . I disapprove." While he wants the public visibility, the public recognition of their romance, "She doesn't want to be in spaces where people socialize, places people go to see and to be seen." He theorized that the reason she loves to stay in and socialize at home is that she loses her self-confidence when she is out. Working to cultivate a shared emotional closeness, Barlas hopes to maintain a romantic focus in his relationship. His passion for romance is not shared by his girlfriend. Barlas described how he tried to elicit a romantic reaction from her:

> I asked her, "what would you do if I cheated on you with another girl?"— the worst thing one can commit in my opinion; she says, "no I wouldn't get angry at all. I would be only sad because if you were cheating it would mean the love between us is over, and there is nothing I can do if love ends." . . . She is very comfortable in this regard—there is nothing like "I would cry so much, I would kill myself," words like that.

Barlas's prioritizing romantic experience and his aversion to becoming sexual with his girlfriend present challenges to the relationship. As he put it, "Because I have some problems with sexuality and she has none, we have problems. She is so open to sex, and I am not. I am putting up some boundaries. Indeed, I am not ready to do certain things, this is creating a problem." He asked his girlfriend several times if this was a problem for her, and she said that it was not important. As Barlas sees it, her acceptance of his sexual boundaries is not a result of her fear of him breaking up with her but of the fact that "she is ashamed of saying so." Barlas's sense of his girlfriend's supposed shame seems to be linked to his inability to view her desire for sex as anything other than a female transgression, his belief that she should have felt embarrassment or even shame for wanting sex.

While Barlas viewed sex and love as inseparable, his experience has caused him to diverge from his upbringing in that he no longer views marriage as the only institution that provides legitimacy for sex. What counted for him was establishing long-term bonds with a strong emotional attachment. According to him, sex should only be experienced with a person to whom you have such an attachment:

> Maybe you will go out with a girl for one or two years and then have sex, even without getting married. That is, you don't need to get married—I mean you don't need to be married to have sex. You will share so much to the point that you feel so close to that person, you share yourself and

your sexuality. I see the other one [sex without a strong bond] as very problematic. That is, I see people who experience sexuality this way as very problematic, troublesome. This is how I see it. Perhaps I am the person with problems.

Barlas frequently employed the terms "disgusting" and "animalistic" in reference to sex without a strong bond, connoting a perceived loss of will power, control, and normalcy in sexual behavior. Further underlining the importance of fusing sex and love, he offered a hypothetical situation to explain how he defines "disgusting things in sex":

> Let's say I meet a girl and she says, "I am not a virgin." I would ask how it happened. If she says, "I went out with a man, for three years, and we did it"—she was with him three years and she is no longer virgin, that is not important for me. Because throughout those three years, she must have experienced many things, loved him deeply, indeed one cannot go out with a person for three years if there is no love. I would see that situation as very plausible; I wouldn't see it as disgusting. However, if she says, "I was a virgin, but at a party I had a one-night stand and lost my virginity," in that situation, I wouldn't marry such a girl. Virginity is not the problem. You need to know her past, her frame of thought. Otherwise virginity is a stupid biological thing. What was being lived, you need to know that. What is important is how virginity loss is experienced.

Altan's and Barlas's upbringings have led them to maintain sexual sobriety until marriage and to act as "holders" of patriarchal gender relations. While Altan recognized that his rigidity and his desire to dominate has failed (and will continue to fail) him in his romantic explorations and is undesirable in the context of his aspirations for upward mobility, he sees no escape from it. Barlas, who claimed a more versatile self, seems to successfully hide certain values when interacting with sexually permissive social groups, though he acknowledged the difficulty of maintaining this flexibility. As he put it, "Not everybody can do this, an exceptional ability." The familial foundation of gendered selfhood and the continued importance of this connection as a basis for future enactments take place in a dialogical setting and with the seductive power of immediate experiences. Their (potential) departure from parental sexual mores is

influenced by young women, like Barlas's girlfriend, who are less bound
by sexual controls. Their narratives signal that the parental norm could
be compromised and that girls play an integral and constitutive role in
making masculinities that protect or reject patriarchal ideals for men.
Thus, femininities and masculinities emerge as relational frames for
selves in these men's narratives.

Haydar's story presents a different, and perhaps more complex, view
of how young men handle the influence of conservative family upbringings. For Haydar, intimate emotional and sexual encounters with
liberated girls helped him reject values that supported his patriarchal
constructions of manhood. Haydar, who represented himself as forward looking and open to learning and experimenting with different
things, claimed that his conservative family values had lost their hold
on him and that he does not feel like a person tied to cultural values.
Raised socially "inadequately" by his parents, Haydar "cultivated and
completed" himself at the university. In his estimation, his experiences
with relationships and sexuality went beyond anything that the men in
his family, including his older brother, had ever experienced. He is not
detached from his family, but, as he described it, his identity-building
explorations are being realized apart from his family. For him, family
had lost its significance as a mean of creating a sense of belonging. He
views himself as irremediably different, "extreme," and considers it impossible to incorporate his radically divergent views into the boundaries
of his family.

When he came to college, he found himself in a world traversed by
intimate encounters with girls, and he met a girl in his first year who
freed him from the trajectory toward a masculinity tied to his own class
and upbringing. Haydar felt it was significant that he had his first sexual experiences, including coitus, with an emancipated girl who came
from a sexually permissive family, with whom he had an intense twenty-
month relationship. Although he had lost a year academically, what he
had gained from this relationship was priceless: "I sexually experienced
everything there is to be experienced with the opposite sex first with her.
I learned about the other sex through her, sexually and body-wise." He
also learned "the female discourse against virginity preservation" and
her approach to men. According to him, she claimed, "I would never
be with a man who seeks virginity in girls." His experience underscores

how male views, particularly those of men who are already inclined toward openness, are constructed by the girls they meet and romance.

Haydar encountered male peers complicit in what he called "macho discourses." Seduced by his own curiosity to explore other girls, he gave in to macho discourses that voiced, "It has been more than a year [that you've been with this girl], when are you going to break up? There are more beautiful girls." This, combined with the conflict he and his girlfriend experienced over their differing class positions (she came from an upper-middle-class background), led Haydar to end their relationship. He later recognized that this pressure was premised on sexism, and regrets his complicity in it. He dismissed macho discourses with ease during his interview. He referenced a low-level dispute arising from one of his male friends' comment that his "old girlfriend is going out with another man" and that a real man wouldn't permit his old girlfriend to be with another man. Haydar noted that "of course he mixed it [his comment] with humor, but it is embedded in his unconscious, the idea of possessive, protective maleness—a type of man who is ready even to deal with the burden of an ex-girlfriend being with another man." When asked how he responded to his friend's remarks, Haydar reported, "I said it is not my business, you are talking about finished business."

Having already gained some practice in balancing sex, love, and academic work, Haydar continued to accumulate sexual and romantic experience. Sexually inexperienced, his current girlfriend was ambivalent about losing her virginity. According to Haydar, they moved slowly toward coitus, delayed by an extended negotiation about sex and love. According to Haydar, she puts up boundaries about how far to go, but he sees progress as her boundaries become less rigid. To wit, he said, "In the past, even the phrase 'making love' was so distant to her. Now she is using it much more comfortably."

The impact of family values on the men I interviewed depended on the quality of prior family relationships. For Haydar, who always felt he was "extreme" in his family and described growing up with the sense that he would never be able to be himself among the people who had raised him, rejection of parental values might not cause too much pain. For others, like Altan and Barlas, continued emotional connection with family as the locus of their valued selves is extremely important, and any perceived deviance could take an emotional toll. This reality can be a major source of tension and conflict for these young men, who are vulnerable to feelings of divided loyalty. Barlas has a strong but already ambivalent relationship with his family. He feels torn between values and beliefs that provide a link to a geographically distant past and a relationship that seems to point toward the future. Altan feels almost ontologically forbidden to change his views. The extent to which Altan's inhabiting of the terms of a distinctly patriarchal masculine frame is vulnerable to the unsubordinated girls he might end up meeting is open to question.

Now, we turn to Oktay, whose story will spell out additional complexities of protecting or rejecting patriarchal constructions of manhood in self-making.

Oktay: Caught between Two Selves

Oktay's story underscored the role women play in coauthoring masculinity. Unlike Altan's almost nonexistent romantic experiences and Barlas's fresh relationship, Oktay's three-year relationship provided a more in-depth examination of the anxious boundaries between protecting and rejecting patriarchal selves.

Oktay declared that "the woman I will marry [will] have a different life than my mother's" to emphasize his desire to self-consciously and actively reject oppressive paternal masculinity. An ambitious, high-achieving 23-year-old, Oktay was raised in a traditional home structured by patriarchal gender and sexual values. According to Oktay, dominating intimate female others is central to his father's identity. Oktay described his mother, a homemaker with limited formal education, as a typical selfless mother who "sacrifices herself for her children and her husband." In our interview, Oktay revealed that he does not feel he really knows his mother, a fact he attributed to her total selflessness: "Because, I think, it is not permitted to know her; she makes herself obliterate, puts her desires in the background, because she is someone who sacrifices herself for her children and her husband." Although Oktay blamed the larger cultural patterns of male domination and the all-consuming role of motherhood for women's selflessness, he had nevertheless lost personal respect for his mother: "After I reached twenty, I lost my respect for my mother. I cannot receive/gain anything from my mother anymore. . . . I still ask my father about his opinions, and he asks me about things." What troubles Oktay more is his mother's docility and willingness to submit to him: "She obeys me, which is something I never wanted to happen." He attributed his mother's obedience to him and deference to his wishes to fear, believing that his mother is afraid of him becoming angry with her. He added, "Maybe she loves me so much . . . maybe she doesn't want me to be unhappy." Embodying perfectly Benjamin's caution against the self-obliteration posed by limitless maternal indulgence, her inability to "set a boundary" accords Oktay traditional male privilege and entitlement. Through her uncritical deference, she pushes "him back into an illusory oneness."

In rejecting his mother's selflessness, Oktay simultaneously rejects the mode of masculinity upheld by his father. His efforts to reflexively constitute an alternative masculinity are thus steeped within a rejection of the mutually reinforcing traditions of selfless femininity and patriarchal masculinity. From his perspective, his father is an authoritarian man who "oppresses women and girls around him; his sisters, his mom, my mother, and my sister." Intimately observing the impact of his father's controlling behavior on female others, especially his sister, affected Oktay deeply and gave shape to his desire "not to become like his father." Oktay became aware of the implication of his father's oppressive masculinity while he was away at college. Oktay's disconcerting awareness that his sister did not love his father provoked a fear that a future daughter might not love him. Imagining himself as not being loved and admired remained his emotional point of reference for his romantic aspirations, development, and identity. While Oktay described himself as someone who, unlike his father, knows how to apologize and question, he does see himself as sharing his father's tendency to become easily irritated and angry. Perhaps because of the difficulty he has imagining himself ridding himself of that tendency, Oktay noted, "Ultimately I might not be able to become that different from my father."

Oktay met his girlfriend, Sezen, during their freshman year at university. According to Oktay, they love each other deeply, and Oktay values her in large part because he can be totally himself around her:

> I can self-disclose and share many things. Anything I can experience and
> feel I can tell her without becoming uncomfortable because I think she

understands me. That is, I can let myself go. When I have a problem and
after I share that with her I am relaxed and comforted, even if I cannot
find a solution to that problem.

They have been together for three years and explore embodied sexuality, but they haven't experienced sexual coitus. A key episode of their
relationship was an eight-month separation, linked, as Oktay puts it, to
his "curtailment of my girlfriend's freedoms." Despite his resistance to
inheriting his father's oppressive masculinity, Oktay consistently sought
dominance in his relationship with Sezen. As dominance is conveyed
and practiced within relationships, it can be contested, accepted, challenged, or assimilated with complete acquiescence or all-around conflict.
Oktay and Sezen's experience was all-around conflict. Because Sezen
refused to be an object of his will, Oktay was forced to silence his desire
for domination in order to preserve his bond of intimacy with her. His
desire for masculine control and protection did not disappear—rather,
it was carefully managed by Oktay, at great cost to his own sense of satisfaction in the relationship. Oktay was frustrated by Sezen's inability to
verbalize the way she felt Oktay challenged her freedoms. Oktay disapproved, for instance, of Sezen visiting male acquaintances and friends
at their houses to play cards or staying out later than she promised. His
desire to restrict Sezen's freedom upset her, but, according Oktay, "She
wasn't telling me because she feared that I'd be angry. And because we
love each other, we avoid fights." Instead, she apologized for her "transgressions" so as not to upset him. In time, however, "She realized that
her freedoms were curtailed and she found herself apologizing to me
too much because of my reactions." According to Oktay, she eventually
couldn't stand to remain quiescent while her freedoms were subjugated,
and she left him.

Despite his professed rejection of the masculine practices of domination, Oktay' s motivation to control Sezen's mobility and relationships
arose out of a discourse of masculine protection. Oktay has cast himself
in the role of "the protector" (the critical but unnamed term in his narrative) who must guard Sezen from potential harm because she is unable to protect herself. In Oktay's view, Sezen's unsuspecting and warm
personality and her inclination to get close with people easily (the exact
qualities that made Oktay fall in love with her) render her vulnerable

and in need of his protection. For instance, he said that he has no objection to Sezen's socializing and staying out late with friends in their own circle: "She can do anything with friends I know." He saw the issue as Sezen' s innocence in dealing with outsiders and her tendency to approach people with open arms without recognizing that men might have ulterior motives. Therefore, Oktay's demand for deference to his desires stemmed from his lack of confidence in Sezen's self-control.

Integrating their daily lives together over time diminished social and psychic distance between them, increasing the emotional and sexual intimacy they share but also, according to Oktay, greatly magnifying their competing desires. Oktay developed an intense preoccupation with Sezen's selfishness, which, over time, fostered feelings of insignificance in him, leading him to seek reassurance from Sezen that he was desired and important. As he put it, "I desire to feel important. I desire to feel she loves me. I desire for her to respect my values. Maybe even, I want her to live by my values." A variety of situations connecting with his desire "to feel important" surfaced in Oktay's narrative, indicating that Sezen's "selfishness" was, in Oktay's estimation, a function of her prioritizing her own desires. To this effect, Oktay referenced an incident involved cooking together:

> Even cooking together can be a problem. For instance, she likes spinach and I don't like it. It was the cause of our big fight. We were cooking together. I love pasta. She was taking care of the spinach dish when I asked her to watch the pasta, but she didn't hear me because she likes spinach. I coded this as evidence that she doesn't value my desires; she values her own desires. And we fight a lot for this.

In this cooking incident, Sezen's desires signified a selfishness that is individualistic and therefore totally at odds with the selfless stance of Turkish mothers.

Oktay's need for Sezen to reassure him that he is desired by her even extended to the academic environment they share—Oktay reports feeling jealous when Sezen pays too much attention in lecture, ignoring him: "We are taking the same classes; she is listening to the lectures, and taking notes. She is disinterested in me during classes." Oktay feels entitled to constant, publicly visible assurances that he is the most important person in Sezen's life and the center of her attention: "For instance, let's say five of us are studying together and trying to understand something at the same moment. If she understands first, I want her to explain it to me first. That is, I want to know that I am the top priority among other people in her life." Importantly, Oktay valued Sezen's attention precisely because she was a modern, nonmaternal, unsubordinated woman. She could provide the recognition he craved—the love, desire, and understanding of a high-achieving, independent woman. Yet paradoxically, these same qualities meant that Sezen prioritized her desires over his, making him feel unimportant, unloved, and unrecognized.

Oktay's eight-month separation from Sezen helped him gain a critical distance on his relationship. It clarified for him how much he loved and valued Sezen and led him to reassess how he should deal with his intense desire to control her. Knowing he would need to change his behavior in order to rekindle and preserve their romance, he committed to quashing these controlling impulses. Now back together with Sezen, however, he sees himself as keeping his desires "captive":

> Our fights in the past emanated from my desires, that is, Sezen's unresponsiveness to my desires and, in turn, my angry response to her unresponsiveness. I don't like fights; they were starting to touch my soul. I was constantly in an agressive mode. But I don't want these fights anymore. For this reason, I am keeping some of my desires captive in the background to avoid problems.

In addition to "keeping his desires captive," Oktay said that in order to avoid too much togetherness and full integration of their lives, he and Sezen were also trying to break some of the relationship rules they had established and practiced in the past, such as texting each other before going to sleep if they were not spending the night together and seeing each other every day, even if just for ten minutes.

While separated from Sezen, Oktay had a brief affair with another young woman described in his narrative as an innocent and sexually inexperienced girl, but he claimed that he avoided sexual intimacy, even though he wanted it, because he did not want to ignite hope, desire, and passion in her, being fully aware that he would never return those feelings. However, Oktay claimed that this brief affair further reminded him of Sezen's value and the exclusiveness of his devotion to her. During the separation, he also imagined the possibility of being happy with a girl whom his mother chose for him: "If I cannot be with Sezen, I can be with a girl whom my mother chooses for me—a girl exactly like her [his mother] because that girl would do everything I desire/realize all my desires." When I asked him if Sezen also engaged in another relationship when they were not together, he said that she hadn't but that he wished that she had: "I would have probably felt intense hate imagining that she held his hands and kissed him. But for the sake of her understanding of my specialness, I would have liked her to have had a relationship with another man."

Backgrounding his desires offered Oktay a solution to sustain his relationship with Sezen without infringing on her freedoms. However, he claimed that he could not help but continue to think about Sezen's selfishness, and this trait haunted him when he envisioned his future with her: "Selfishness is not something I can forgive. In an ideal relationship, in a marital relationship, selfishness would bring harm to the relationship." Tellingly, Oktay's descriptions of his hypothetical future marriage to Sezen intertwine images that both break with and reinforce certain patriarchal gender practices. For example, he envisions "dropping off Sezen at work in the morning and picking her up after work," at once seemingly fulfilling his promise that his wife will have a different life than his mother's (by affirming Sezen's status as a woman who, unlike his mother, would have professional pursuits outside the home) and placing her in circumscribed spaces under his protective, dominating impulse (by suggesting that he would control Sezen's movements by transporting her to and from work). This unbroken association between protection and maleness also emerged in Oktay's discussion of his ideal imaginings of his future family. According to Oktay, he wants to have four children: two boys and two girls, with the first and the last born being boys because "the first boy will protect all the younger siblings; the sisters in the middle will be great friends and I will love the girls to death; and I will spoil the youngest one."

Oktay's narrative about his three-year relationship with Sezen introduced a host of contradictions. He had to work through the emotional, intersubjective, behavioral, and relational implications of attempting to escape oppressive masculinity in his self-making. His sense of self was negotiated in the context of his relationship with Sezen, who, as Oktay sees her, is a "selfish," unsubordinated young woman. The intimate and sexual bond they shared allowed Oktay to try out a different approach to gendered adulthood. During this process of having a relationship filled with the adult emotions of love and jealousy, anger and passion, he grappled with the painful separation he felt between his idealized and actual selves, the chasm between the ideal, nondominating self and his failings and insecurities in creating and managing a nondominating self.

Oktay's relationship with Sezen was permeated with paradoxes that mirrored and reproduced some constitutive elements of oppressive patterns of masculinity. His "curtailment of Sezen's freedoms" to protect her served and reflected practices of male domination that he found deeply troubling. To break with patriarchal conventions and make himself into a nondominating man, he needed Sezen to be a selfish woman with her own independent identity—the opposite of the selfless mother. Yet it was difficult for Oktay to recognize and honor Sezen's autonomy.

Oktay's narrative raises important questions about the nature of young men's attempts to reject paternal masculinities: What will it take to obliterate/disavow this desire for control, so seemingly at odds with the principles that dictate escape from oppressive masculinity? What will happen to Oktay's transgressive, yet imaginable, project of producing a masculine identity different than his father's? How do we understand this disjuncture between wanting egalitarian, "modern" relationships and being unable to let go of the desire to protect and control women?

Oktay comes across as brutish and narcissistic, consumed by his desire to be recognized as singular and special and driven by open displays of superiority—he even expressed a subversive desire for Sezen to be with another man in order for her to better understand his specialness. This narcissistic stance can be understood as a specific expression of the more general phenomenon of the desire for recognition: it is symptomatic of an uncertainty of rank and status and of porous and changing dividing lines between different types of masculinities. The autonomous self, as Benjamin and Joseph argued, is still an essentially connective self who is dependent on the recognizing response of another. Men like Oktay, who are struggling to form upwardly mobile masculinities, are often attracted to others suitable to recognize and affirm their idealized selves.

For these men, who lack familial others with "suitable selves" for conferring recognition, the intimate, gendered other becomes crucial to the development of the self. The significant others in Oktay's life, especially his mother, are experienced as negating sources of recognition for his upwardly mobile identity. Because she herself lacks an authentic, fully articulated and modern self, Oktay's mother cannot provide the recognition and affirmation that he craves. That is, her subservience to patriarchal domination and uneducated status render Oktay's mother without a "suitable" self with which to confer recognition and assertion for the man Oktay wants to become. Although Oktay's father represents a token of male power that counters the powerlessness of his mother, he too lacks a suitable self for conferring recognition on Oktay, precisely because his power and agency derive from his subordination of women. Indeed, just as he rejects his mother's selfless femininity and limitless love, Oktay defines his ideal self, in part, explicitly against his father's oppression; he wants to be a man who is loved and admired by women for his nonoppressive behavior. This dimension of ideal masculinity is one that neither his father nor his mother is equipped to affirm.

Oktay's story challenges assumptions we may make when we constrain our analysis to the gendered dichotomies of yearning for love and sex that prevail in the literature. Longings for love and sex are not independent from but in fact are complicated by other significant longings—like the longing for recognition. This longing for recognition can lead to masculine domination and control when, as Benjamin suggests, young men wish to be recognized as subjects without returning that recognition. Oktay's story not only highlights practices of domination but may also help nuance the dialectics of male ambivalence when girls claim selfishness in relationships and refuse to make "meaningful the feelings, actions, and intentions" (Benjamin 1988, 21) of the masculine self.

By stressing the simultaneity of connection (the pleasures of attunement) and separation (the pleasures of being recognized as a subject by another subject), Benjamin argued that the relational tie to the other was neither a tie of identification nor a tie of subjection. By experiencing intersubjectivity, the place "where two subjects meet," in Benjamin's words, these young men have the power to disrupt the patriarchal script of male domination. In the Turkish case, this "meeting" would suggest a challenge to both selfless maternal femininity and oppressive patriarchal masculinity.

Conclusion

Gender scholars often approach their research in various geographies equipped with various theoretical tools gleaned from Raewyn Connell (1987, 2002), particularly her concepts of hegemonic masculinity and emphasized femininity. Connell's theory provides a critical framework for understanding the relationship between gender and power. But, in one of the most insightful critiques of Connell's theory, Michael Moller (2007) argues that "the conceptual mobility," the widespread utilization of Connell's typologies of hegemonic, complicit, and subordinated, "may also conceal important aspects of the knowledge thus produced; namely the exclusion of those practices, statements and feelings which do not fit this typology of masculine objects" (268). In addition to encouraging a kind of disciplinary tunnel vision that overdetermines and oversimplifies male behavior, in Connell's theory, femininity is always organized as an adaptation to men's power (1987, 188). Connell defines "emphasized femininity" as "compliance with subordination" and argues that it "is oriented to accommodating the interests and desires of men" (1987, 183). Her conceptualization of the relationship between hegemony and femininity remains underdeveloped (in fact, she herself acknowledges this underdevelopment in a footnote), chiefly because femininity is treated as a residual category, conceptually subordinated and conceptualized with no sustained attention to different forms of patriarchy in different cultural settings, especially in societies, like Turkey, where historically patriarchy strongly articulated with state and individual forms of paternalism. As we have seen in this chapter, the paternalistic construction of masculinity, defined by the value of protecting women, presupposes and is contingent upon a construction of masculinity as selflessness. In other words, Connell's hegemonic masculinity in societies where the paternalism and patriarchy is interlinked is also, like femininity, aligned with selflessness. Indeed, as we have seen, the young men described in this chapter not only pursue a desire to escape from male selflessness but also express new feelings of "oppression" engendered by the relationships with "selfless" women.

Instead of a traditional, narrowly defined, protective paternalism embodied by the paternal generation, young men are expressing a desire for masculine self-expansion and enrichment. This new model of masculinity hinges upon rejecting the self-denials of the father, putting into question boundaryless maternal adoration, and in so doing creating layered, protean selves. How this self-construction was articulated, and inhabited, as well as its ramifications, was therefore intimately and organically linked to a new vision of femininity in intimate relationships. This vision of femininity emerges in an interplay of contradictions between the selfless (positive girls) and the selfish (charismatic, independent girls), with their mutual antagonism and respective incompatibilities. In most instances, the selfless/selfish binary plays out as negative and positive polarities, centered most commonly upon the normative coding of subordinated, maternal selflessness against unsubordinated selfishness. But what was repudiated (selflessness) could not be eradicated, because it also constituted a desired source of energy needed to support masculine selving. Instead, the binary was deconstructed to make the polarities fused and less discrete. Male desire for the selfless female still survived, only it did so alongside, or beneath, a more explicit, public desire for "selfish" females. It was this dependency on *both* selfish and selfless female selves that aligned the structures of connective selving with neoliberal selfhood in the support and formulation of a new masculinity. The creation and legitimization of male self-expansion could not be achieved without gendered coauthors, mutual participants in the creation of a new male selfhood. Its realization required recognition, and that recognition could only come from the newly articulated selfish self who gave equal importance to her own desires.

Heterosexual romance and courtship was a significant site for the cultivation of masculinity as well as femininity. The longings for love and sex in these narratives were not independent of but rather were complicated by another significant longing: the desire for recognition, a desire found in the public sphere of romance more than in the intimate private sphere of sex. This longing itself often led to masculine domination and control. Oktay's story encapsulated the complexities of young men's efforts to reject the pattern of protective, dominant masculinity they learn from their fathers, and his story suggests a collective biographical context in which the pleasurable embodiment of masculinity is deeply tied to being recognized as an object of female desire. Speaking to Benjamin's argument about the deep intertwining of love, recognition, and domination in the self-making of young men, his story crystallizes, in dramatic form, the central aspects of masculine domination practices as they are intimately tied to the desire for recognition through intersubjective connection. It also shows how self-construction is an ongoing struggle negotiated in relation to the gendered other: the contradiction Oktay felt between his real and ideal selves could not be resolved independently of his intimate relationships with women. As we saw in the previous chapter, women's own struggles to articulate new feminine selfhood is equally, *mutually,* and inextricably connected to these masculine projects. Indeed, their own struggles for self-creation in relation to a desired other and their efforts to eschew the conventions of selfless femininity highlight the "two-way street" of intersubjective connection.

Vulnerable Masculinity and Self-Transformation: Ali's Story

I focus on Ali, for his narrative most fully articulates a sense of self-invention as a dynamic, transformable, lived experience. At the center of Ali's narrative lies a chronicle of a failed romance and the language of self-transformation. Ali's reflexivity, in the sense of a self-conscious identity project, emerged from the negotiation of discrepancies, distance, and dis-identification he experienced between the values and lifestyles of his family of origin and his own path of upward mobility, rich in new experiences and memories. His narrative bears the marks of a vulnerable masculinity capturing the dialectics between dependency on his "valued self," rooted in family origins and duty, and his competing efforts to define himself amid a new middle-class masculine subjectivity. A marked tension and liminality between identification and dis-identification are expressed within Ali's lexicon of "here" and "there."

An examined reflection of where he came from ("there," in his lexicon) and where he is in the present ("here") provided the framework through which he evaluated and gave meaning to his new cultural milieu, particularly the class and gender patterning of his new environment. Rather than taking his particular narrative as representative in content, I draw on it here to bring into the foreground a complex terrain of intimate transformations predicated upon gender relations and sex. Analyzing Ali's failed romance is particularly important, given its linkage to the creation of a new self, suggesting that the realm of romance is central to the project of self-invention.

Ali moved to Istanbul for his education at Boğaziçi four years before we talked in 2002. He was twenty-four years old at the time of his first interview. The place of his upbringing, especially his school environment (sponsored and financed by a religious group geared toward educating a consciously Muslim generation), did not offer a rich environment or opportunities for intimate gender interaction and sexual expression. At home, the most stereotypical representations of boyhood were glorified, and his socialization into masculinity was shaped by a homosocial environment. By contrast, his arrival at the university introduced Ali to a range of new masculinities. Like others, Ali mobilized the antinomy of constraint and freedom to evaluate his community of origin and his current destination in Istanbul. He viewed the cultural fabric and mentality of his town of origin from the prism of its gender and sexual prohibitions and portrayed it as a "closed milieu" (*kapalı ortam*). In contrast, he associated Istanbul with the cultural realm of freedom and permissiveness, providing ample opportunities for the sexes to mix freely as an established part of urban life, the most salient aspect of an "open milieu" (*açık ortam*), so far off from the place of his upbringing. He fell in love with this open environment and its openness to discursivity around gender and sexual intimacy:

> I loved it when I heard that one of my female friends could talk about her intimate relationship with her boyfriends, everything, with her mom. She gets advice from her mother about these things. And another female friend sent her boyfriend to meet and entertain her brother when he came to town and she couldn't meet him. These are things that surprise me . . . these are the kinds of things that are very outrageous for us, my hometown community [*bizim orası için*].
>
> When I first arrived, for example, to me a boy and a girl living together [without being married] was abnormal. But now I feel it is very normal. . . . In the same vein, having a girlfriend is so natural, so normal, and it is not something viewed negatively.

In his first year in Istanbul, Ali spent his free time off-campus, almost exclusively in a homosocial group composed of his old friends from the religious high school he attended and with new friends from his town of origin. They often hung around social geographies of Istanbul that are considered provincial. He found that he had increasingly less and less in common with his old friends and especially became uncomfortable with strongly religious friends whose understanding of the world was diametrically opposed to his. As he became conscious of the limiting boundaries of the homosocial group and was able to articulate its limitations for his growth, he pulled away from some of his old friends. His detachment from this group marked an important transition for him. I probed the reasons for his detachment:

> They have their own truths, not to mean to say it in a formulaic way, but a given lifestyle that doesn't fit me. It requires restrictions that don't sit well with me. I want to be free with everything. You

are unable to do something because it is sin, I don't know, but even if it is sin I should be able to do it if I wanted. Everything should be originating from me.

His rejection of power, religious or otherwise, located external to the individual, coupled with his emphasis on self-empowerment, or power arising from within, gave shape and direction in the project of self-making. He started exploiting the opportunities the campus provided: he expanded his social and extracurricular activities on campus, signing up for numerous clubs, and started playing tennis to enhance his claims on urban middle-class culture and acquire a cultural shape and identity. He focused on discarding things about his past self that made him uncomfortable in his new surroundings:

I tried to get rid of a lot of things, and that is not a wrong thing to do. You are coming to a new environment, it is so different from what you experience here and there. Rights and wrongs are changing, and there are things that make you uncomfortable. Right now I am doing things that bothered me a short time ago when others did them, and it feels so natural.

When I asked what he wanted to discard about himself the most, he said,

There was a lot of timidness and diffidence, I tried to be enterprising and gained the ability to express my own ideas. When I first came I couldn't talk much in a social group. People who live in Istanbul are so forward [yırtık], they say whatever they want to say. It took me two years to be like this: to be able to state my own ideas, perspectives, and desires and to be where it makes sense to be capable of discussing them.

Ali became unrecognizable to his old friends. They told him that he had become "freaked out" (uçmuşsun), and "disaffiliated" (kopmuşsun). "They started behaving towards me as if I were a stranger." But he found pleasure in being able to still connect with his friends with his newfound middle-class self. His changed appearance also contributed to making him unrecognizable. Needless to say, constituting and representing the self through consumption practices is a major strategy for creating middle-class individuality. But for someone like Ali, who straddles two worlds—one that demands expression of the self, and the other that demands representing not oneself but one's family—the task of changing appearance was not so straightforward. He said he gained taste and self-confidence to dress himself in a manner that allowed him to express his individuality and his personality. He likes to dress conventionally, to fit in but be himself: "I don't subscribe to the idea that I should dress differently so that I can get attention."

A considerable shift in his style was achieved by his changing taste in clothes. He said he introduced color to his wardrobe, which in the past was full of clothing all in shades of green because he liked the color green. He stopped buying things because they were inexpensive, and instead he started opting for quality and discovered the world of outlet malls where one can buy designer clothes inexpensively. His leisure-consumption habits increasingly included going out to outlet malls with his friends and making more careful selection in consultation with others, even returning whatever he ended up disliking. But because his new appearance bore witness to his transformation, marking his differentness from his family and peers back home, when he went back home during holidays and breaks, he only took his old clothes with him and always made sure that he shaved his stylish beard before he arrived. Ali carried his old self in appearance to give the image that he still belonged. In Istanbul his style expressed individuality, his personality and creativity, while in the public space of his town of origin he had to produce a representation not of himself but of his family.

His model of an ideal girlfriend also drastically changed: now he says he never would consider going out with a girl who embodies his past ideal. His past ideal was "a 'dignified' [oturaklı] girl," embodying the type of qualities attached to so-called marriageable girls. "I want the opposite now. A girlfriend with whom I can have fun, go out with, and share sexual intimacy." Throughout his interviews Ali repeatedly promoted an image of himself as a gender-egalitarian man, making comments about wanting to see the liberation of both genders and about the naturalness of premarital sexual pleasure for both women and men. This appeal to gender equality represented a psychic departure and emotional split both from his family of origin and from some of his male friends.

Then Ali fell in love with a girl named Arzu. For about a year, Ali pursued Arzu, but his love was not returned. She gave confusing and conflicted responses: one day she would be warm towards him, and the next day, she would treat him with indifference. One day she would agree to see him, but she wouldn't show up on the promised day, nor would she respond to his phone calls or text messages. In the course of courting her, he bought her flowers, gave her poems he found on the Internet, even got a charcoal portrait of her made. When they bumped into each other on campus, she avoided him. One time, they had planned to spend the next day together after one of her exams, but she never called. Ali, in fact, learned that she left town after her exam. Another time, she invited him to join her and her friends for dinner, but on the evening of the dinner, she claimed to "forget" to phone him to arrange the meeting. After realizing that they had left campus without him, Ali felt very badly about his exclusion but still went ahead and joined them at the restaurant. Every time she rejected him, he was devastated: "I had no such thing as pride left." When she communicated and interacted with him in front of her own friends, "She didn't grant me any importance. On the contrary, she was humiliating me, telling her friends that she didn't like me." But still, in his relentless pursuit, a pursuit that may even be considered as obsessive as stalking, the resourceful Ali continued to plot "accidental" sightings. For example, one time when he learned that she was going to go to a concert, he also went and approached her, inviting her to walk back to their dormitories together. She refused him in front of her friends.

Sick of these types of betrayals, Ali decided to forget Arzu and even made several attempts to see other girls, but couldn't get her out of his mind. He said she was damaging his psychological health and academic work. He was losing control of his life. He was failing his classes, missing exams. He started seeing a psychiatrist who gave him tranquilizers. Recounting bouts of weeping that went on for days, he said he didn't think he could ever get over her. He was obsessed with her. No longer recognizing himself or being recognized by his friends, Ali gave himself pep talks, set objectives—"be more social, don't stay in the dorm, don't take numbing tranquilizers, don't call her again, make contact with other girls." Instead, he found himself "in bed and lying there for days and wishing that [he] just didn't have to think about her."

Ali went home to forget Arzu, to avoid seeing her around. For the first time, he shared the experience of being in love and his pain with his father. In response, his father reaffirmed the patriarchal privileges of masculinity: "There are a lot of girls for you [*Sana kız mı yok?*]." When he cried, his father said that "a manly man would never cry [*erkek adam ağlar mı?*]; is it worth crying for a girl? [*Ne olacak bir kız için ağlanır mı?*]." His father's comments obviously were meant to boost Ali's ego and to downplay the importance of girls to one's self-esteem, but, because this type of ego boosting was informed by sexist attitudes, it didn't comfort Ali anymore. For him, it was a recuperation of a model of masculinity he experienced not only as oppressive but also, more importantly, as no longer appropriate to the needs of his changing self. At home, he also consulted with a female cousin whom he considered experienced in these matters, because she herself had made a love marriage. Her interpretation of Arzu was that "she is playing hard to get." After he came back to Istanbul, he learned that like him, Arzu was going to stay on campus for summer session. He called her and said that he still wanted to be her friend and to have fun with her over the summer. They made a pact to see each other and have fun and then to cut the ties permanently after the session was over.

The limited time frame (during summer school) lessened the tension between them and proved to be a turning point for the relationship. According to Ali, because he said to her "let's be friends," it made her comfortable. They started hanging out together. One night they went out at 12:30 in the morning and stayed together until 5:30 a.m., but most importantly, according to Ali, they started talking about themselves and their families, revealed things about themselves. That night, for Ali, marked the beginning of going out (*çıkmak*). Ali's interpretation of why she finally agreed to go out with him advanced two theories: "I went after her for a long time, and she never went with anybody before, and now she was sure that I loved her deeply, and her circle of friends finally told her positive things about me, encouraging her to go out with me."

They kissed on the second day of going out. He hadn't expected kissing or any sexual intimacy to happen that soon: "I was thinking that perhaps in two months I would be able to hold her hands." He wasn't prepared for the kiss—he was too focused on his goals of developing an emotional relationship first. His expectations for a meaningful relationship did not exclude sex, but the relationship script he imagined had an order of first sharing ideas and emotionality, culminating with sexual intimacy, but according to Ali, she was sexually curious. "There was no idea sharing, emotionality was very little, the thing that made the relationship go forward was only sexuality." By the third day of "going out," there was only sex: "We would go to a place where there is usually no one around. Without even talking we would start kissing. I cried that night and told myself I didn't want this kind of relationship." Later that night he texted her to say, "Let's not see each other for a couple of days" and "from now on there shouldn't be sexuality in this relationship."

They started spending more and more time together. Without the pressure of heavy coursework and exams, they had fun: went to different places, listened to music, and danced, but "sex continued to be the driving force of the relationship, because we were mostly talking about sex and trying different things sexually. You know, like the expression, 'yiyişmek' [eating each other, screwing without coitus]." And he said he felt so bad when one day she declared, "I wonder if I am using you for my sexual needs." For him, the best moment of the relationship occurred when one night they were sitting together talking about love. "I said let's increase emotionality and I leaned on her shoulder. I stayed liked that for a while and then she touched my leg, that was a wonderful night." Before the fall semester started, Ali went to a summer camp and Arzu went home. When they both came back to campus, they continued seeing each other but with less frequency. One day he had a serious problem and wanted to talk with her. He called her, but she never came. Her lack of response when he was most in need of emotional support was the last straw for Ali. It was over.

According to Ali, neither of them was subscribing to a traditional idea of love—one true love that lasts forever and should be cultivated toward marriage. They both wanted to explore their romantic and sexual selves without a sense of permanency. Indeed, one particular episode that underlined, for Ali, her changed attitude toward him ("she changed: she didn't want to be alone with me") related to their very first and only interaction in a domestic space. Ali and Arzu's social and economic configurations afforded no privacy for sexual intimacy: they both were staying in sex-segregated dorm rooms with others. What they were having in the quiet public places at night (like club houses) was "clothed sex," not "naked sex." They hadn't even seen each other naked. They were experimenting with sexual intimacy without privacy. One day, they arranged to stay overnight at a friend's house. They were going to sleep in the same room but in separate beds. She trusted him and said, "You wouldn't do anything I don't want." They had talked about virginity before: "I said 'it is not important for me, but it is important for you, I would respect you. I don't want a relationship that involves penetration. We don't need to exaggerate.' Besides, there was no possibility. We couldn't do it in a public place." But during the night, Ali asked if he could join her, just to snuggle. Snuggling led to more elaborate things, but they didn't go all the way. Arzu later told him that she felt that Ali was like her husband, referencing the image of Ali holding the remote and zapping TV channels. The image of a married couple they projected when they were in a domestic space disturbed her. Six weeks before they broke up, Arzu also told him that that night proved that "his love for her was not pure/innocent as he claimed to be."

Ali enjoyed a strong sense of belonging and attachment to a group of female peers with whom he could share his sexual and romantic initiatives freely. Claiming to have a "phobia of loneliness," he said that he did not like hanging around alone, especially on campus: "There must be someone with me always, preferably girls." Throughout his painful period, Ali advertised his pain and collected understanding and support from his female friends. Those friends evaluated his moves and experiences with Arzu continuously, working out strategies with him. But what he sought to understand the most by talking with close female friends was how Arzu felt about him, how she felt sexually. For example, after the first kiss, he went to two of his close friends "to ask them how they felt with their own first kisses." He asked them "how I should behave when my girlfriend has her period." Puzzled by Arzu's resistance to her breasts being touched, he again talked with his female friends; they said that normally she is supposed to take pleasure in this, "but she was very uncomfortable, she never allowed her breasts to be touched." In consultation with his female friends after the breakup, Ali arrived at the conclusion that because Arzu was sexually naïve, she allowed him to go far sexually; as he put it, "We exaggerated sexually." To dramatize this point, he said, "Let me put it this way, she will not allow her next boyfriend to do things that I have done with her."

Although Ali actively sought out girls as his confidantes, his narrative was also marked significantly by the absence of his male friends. While he monitored the feelings of his female friends and seemed to possess a lack of anxiety over expressing his vulnerabilities in front of his female peers, he concealed his emotions from male friends and hid his sobbing from his roommates. Although Ali's references to how he related to his male friends indicate that he seemingly distanced himself from orthodox norms by rejecting the tropes of hard masculinity such as virility, power, and machismo in gender performance, it is open to speculation how much the interactions with his male friends and the way he narrated himself to them in relation to his romance actually represent attempts to define himself against more stereotypically and overtly sexist masculinities. But what clearly emerges in his account is a conscious strategy of nonengagement: his elusiveness and unwillingness to make his exploration of romance and sex a subject of male talk. Again, we might speculate that disengagement may also represent a strategy to avoid brandings of romantic or sexual incompetence or being marked as a man who is unable to rely on traditional power dynamics or masculine strategies to seduce women. Alternatively, we might consider that through disengagement, he was able to mitigate his rejection by playing down the importance of Arzu as well as his own feelings of disappointment. But it seems to me that through strategies of nonengagement, such as nonchalance, detachment, silence, and façades, Ali was trying to escape competing discourses and the tension between performances of romance and performances of hard masculinity. For the sake of protecting Arzu's reputation, he said he never told his inquiring male friends how far they went sexually. For example, when Ali spent a night with Arzu in a friend's house, his male friends were curious and quizzed him about what went on. But he didn't tell them the truth. Instead, he fabricated that at the beginning of the evening Arzu and he had an argument, so nothing happened sexually. While comments like this are important insofar as they suggest Ali's uneasiness at occupying a hegemonic space, his rationale behind his façade vis-à-vis his male friends relied on the gendered sexual inequality produced and enforced by the invocation of protective masculinity. It is also telling that one of his best friends, to whom he was comfortable admitting his romantic failure, gave him the advice that he should "forget about Boğaziçi girls." The implication of his friend's statement, which didn't sit well with Ali's aspirations of mobility and self-transformation, referred to a core class dynamic: "Boğaziçi girls are out of your league." Even though Arzu also shared the same class identifications and a similar family background with Ali, Ali's friend's comment reflects women's common avoidance of men like Ali as romantic and sexual partners, as they are prefigured and presumed to be inhabiting oppressive masculinity by young women of all backgrounds who also have their own aspirations of gender and sexual as well as class mobility.

Ali represented his romantic failure with Arzu as his worst personal failure: "For the first time in my life, I wanted something so much, but I couldn't achieve it." What was his desire that did not get achieved? The production of what he called emotionality, not sex, was what he wanted. He understood emotionality as an enactment of a connective relationship. Becoming the object of desire was his desire. He wanted to be desired as a caring lover. And only a meaningful relationship based on emotionality, not sex, was capable of transforming him into the object of desire. In the act of being recognized as a lover, he was going to recognize himself as capable of making someone other than himself happy: "I will make you happy, and when you become happy I will be happy," he said to Arzu. In order to be able to embody the new subjectivity he had invented and fantasized for himself, he needed to be desired as a lover. For him to become the object of his newly created desire, he needed Arzu to be into emotionality and love, but, as we have seen, the Arzu that appeared in Ali's narrative was uninterested in love; she was into sex. Perhaps, she was struggling to get rid of the forced sexual modesty of her own upbringing. She was contesting the "traditional" expectation that women want love when men want sex, and maybe it was this social script of gender she actively wanted to rewrite.

In the course of making a place and identity for themselves, young men like Ali use the realm of heterosexual romance as a map on which to orient themselves to navigate gender sociability and negotiate intimacy and sexuality. It is one of the grounds upon which heterosexual middle-classness operates, as a means of measuring one's self, as a way of monitoring one's social place, signaling one's position to others, and marking masculine identities by accumulating such key experiences and memories as being accepted and rejected. But, most importantly, the realm of romance provides the framework within which one develops self-feeling, an internalized sense of knowing one's self. One cannot know the self without also knowing the other, but also without knowing how one is known and felt. Ali depended on love and romance for recognition, but he never understood "what she felt about me."

Neoliberal selfhood is articulated through the development of a stronger awareness of one's self and a rise in one's level of affect control and self-regulation—the calculating, flexible management of sexual desire. Feelings of worthiness or worthlessness, being recognized as desirable and undesirable, lovable and unlovable, are made within the landscape of romance. Part of being a successful middle-class subject is knowing—awareness of one's feelings and emotions, being able to see a reflection of self in formation. While sex is a site of private activity, the symbolic and material practices and routines of courtship contained within the landscape of romance present young men with a wider framework and horizon to interpret and validate the new male identity as they struggle to transcend the boundaries of what they consider traditional masculinity.

The pursuit of upward mobility through educational success placed Ali in a psychic and material world of a metropolitan location that incited him to become the entrepreneur of himself, and he invested this task with tremendous desire. The way he understands self-transformation is inextricably linked to the realization of a project of acquiring literacy and competency of cross-gender sociability and intimacy. He desires to form an individualized, liberated identity to set himself apart from men of his social origins who inhabit culturally dominant models of connective manhood, representations of nonindividuality. Developing such an alternative identity is not just about crossing borders of economics but also centrally involves integrating and practicing what he imagines as the norms of an open and free milieu into his biography in order to live according to the values of gender and sexual modernity while rejecting family frames of reference.

The unfolding intimate transformation of Ali cannot be described as a seamless makeover or easily fitted into a framework of "before" and "after"—of an easy transition to neoliberal subjectivity. As insightful studies (Lucey and Walkerdine 2003) powerfully point out, upward mobility by definition contains inherent tensions and is lived through a constant psychic and material reinvention, and this reinvention becomes a site of contradiction, or what Zygmunt Bauman calls "ambivalence"—defined by Valerie Walkerdine as "a slipping or sliding, an ambiguity between classifications" (Walkerdine 2003, 247) invested with both desire and threat. Mobility represents a trajectory of self-realization imbued with the promise of pleasure but also a threat—the threat of inevitable failure and also the threat of losing all material and emotional connections to one's past, representing a fundamental dis-identification with those who authored him, or, conversely, of not being able to distance oneself enough from that past. The ambivalence that this position forces is, according to Walkerdine, "absolutely central to [the neoliberal subject's] beingness" (244).

Ali applied the dichotomous tropes of "open" and "closed" to "here" and "there," attributes and locations saturated with meanings of gender and sexual enlightenment and permissiveness of sexual communication, on the one hand, and sexual restriction and repression, on the other hand. However, the complexity of the distinctions and choices he made challenges any conveniently simple notion of a unitary attitude toward "here" and "there." Nor can his varied and selective exposure and utilization of "open" and "closed" be conceptualized as assimilation or rejection. Choices structured by these oppositions of "here/open" and "there/closed" compel Ali to become a participant in a process where he comes to see himself as a project of self-realization with a deep self-reflexivity, dissecting and monitoring his every move and emotion with respect to their belongingness to either "here" or "there." Empowered by his elite education in Istanbul, he traverses between competing subjectivities constructed by radically different worlds, experimenting with the flexibility to claim to be part of both worlds. But in the process of making himself an identity and a place, he is also subjected to experiences of exclusion and rejection, since men like Ali are already prefigured as culturally marginal and as representing "backward" masculinity by virtue of their origins and are addressed in ways that involve coming to recognize themselves in descriptions of themselves as culturally marginal subjects or phonies.

Moving between the frameworks of "here" and "there" with competing claims of male subjectivity, Ali understands himself in essentially individual and psychological terms in order to manage the tensions and emotional dissonance he faces. As we have seen in his self-account, he rejected religion as an authority, yet not only did he continue to hang out with his pious friends, but he also prided himself on being able to be in their company with his newly invented differentness and continued to fast during Ramadan. His movement between the frameworks of here and there was expressed in a telling way when he desperately needed help in dealing with the pain of rejection. He utilized the therapeutic and drug culture of "here" by going to a therapist and becoming a member of a self-help group. The help from the therapeutic culture was often accompanied by ego support provided by his nonthreatening female friends, and by his newly gained habit of writing in a journal to work out his emotions and to self-probe feelings of inferiority and superiority. But he also went "there," home to metaphors and structures of emotion that inform ways of being a man that he desires to unsubscribe to in relation to his upwardly mobile self. Yet, paradoxically, this is also a home of filial parental connections and relationships that cultivate and are supportive of recognizing his important and highly valued self attributes. Likewise, we also have seen with the manipulation of his appearance that he is not willing to annul his connected self, his affinal identity: the nexus of social relations that identify and locate him as a member of a collective as "so and so's son"—one of the constraining principles of the social structure of "there" that he desires to reject. It seems to me such negotiations of a fractured desire conducted in a wide context of differences represent a new demand of neoliberal Turkey: a flexible self.

I suggest that entering the realm of romance and embodied sexuality provided Ali with a "generative grammar" (Weitman 1999, 74) through which to search for the boundaries of his flexible self and to negotiate the complex and contradictory space he occupied as an upwardly mobile man. Not easily discredited (discreditable) was his deep attachment to and dependency on the precious self-feeling that he is special and charismatic, a self-perception authored and cultivated by patriarchal socialization. This deep formative effect on him as the recipient of love, importance, and adoration acquired in the course of growing up as a boy in a patriarchal family was also consolidated with his high educational success: his being able to be placed in an elite university, which also marked the distance he achieved from his family roots. Guided by habitus dispositions of specialness and charisma acquired "there," he is now dependent on new others in his new life to continue enjoying this precious sense of his specialness—deserving and commanding the best things in life. But in his quest for discovering women's innermost secret desires, he finds himself excluded, unwanted, and unloved. The people who populate his new life also gave him a taste of a world of new frustrations, humiliations, and torments. In this way, the realm of romance becomes one constitutive resource/grammar by which men like Ali "police" the boundaries of their flexible subjectivities.

Ali declared that his relationship with Arzu produced feelings of self-denigration and of worthlessness and oppression. "That girl oppressed me," was how he put it. However, even these negative feelings have contradictory implications, I should point out, because they are often the same feelings that internally motivate Ali's success in self-invention. He considered being aware of and understandings one's feelings to be a great contribution to the reconfiguration of his new self. In this regard, Ali compared Arzu to his old self in a telling way: "She was me four years ago. . . . I never knew what I felt . . . for instance now, I feel degraded [aşağılanmış], I can tell this to myself and I feel better. That girl absolutely did not know what she felt and was never sure of her emotions." Ultimately, this complex interplay between pain and motivation serves as a reminder that the flexibility of neoliberal masculine subjectivity is primarily built in an uneasy emotional domain.

When I talked with Ali last (a year after our first sets of conversations), he was pursuing new strategies and objectives to disturb the progressive-intimacy script (first romance and deepening emotionality, then sexual intimacy) he once embraced fully to bring happiness and fun to his life. He talked about playing the field—one girl after another—just fooling around to shield himself from pain. But he worried that having sex without feeling any desire or affection and pursuing sexual relations with girls who had no desire for him might also bring him pain and loss. He was indecisive about whether he should choose one of the bedrooms or the living room as his room in an off-campus flat he planned to share with other men. The largeness and airiness of the living room suited him better, but the privacy of a bedroom promised possibilities, in case. Ali's self-reflections and imaginings of what kind of man he will be without the pleasure (or pain) of an ontological security and membership in a rising culture of neoliberalism continue to be steeped in the realm of romance and sex.

3

New Pious Female Selves

The Feminist "Vein" Within and the Troubling Gender Divide

At the main gate of the Boğaziçi campus, where student identification cards are checked, there is an unmarked cabin. To an untrained eye, this cabin appears to be a prefabricated, oversized port-a-john. In this cabin, "the covered girls"[1] who arrive at the campus dressed in various sartorial choices that keep the contours of their bodies hidden and sporting large scarves tightly covering their hair and chest change to a hat or turban that reveals their necks but still tightly covers their hair. After their transformation from "religiously covered" to "secularly covered," they are granted permission to enter the university.

This "dressing cabin" at the entrance of the university marks the boundary between secular/public and religious/private. The presence of this cabin animates a constellation of desires and anxieties that are themselves constitutive of the social psychology of the boundary between private religion and public secularism. While accommodating the conflicts and contradictions of the secular headscarf ban (the legal prohibition against wearing religious headscarves in schools), this cabin signals that religiously headscarved women have come to threaten the stability of rigid Islamic/secular, public/private, and modern/traditional binaries in Turkey's cultural landscape. This cabin happens to be painted in the color of Islam—green. This irony seizes the imagination of both secular and pious students as a fitting symbol of their respective sentiments. It is branded by the secular students as "the reactionary cabin" (*irtica kulübesi*) to mockingly evoke the threat associated with the longing to reverse Turkey's history of secularism. It is also mocked by the women who are obliged to inhabit it in order to appear "secularly Muslim" as the "green tomb" (*yeşil türbe*). The cabin's presence also creates an unlikely analogy among these interlocutors in which pious women transform their public identities á la the comic hero Superman.

Pious young women, who contest the sanctioned boundary between private religion and public secularism, are the subjects of this chapter. Like this cabin's presence and the associated mocking remarks, this new pious female identity is being formed in a complex field of tension with the secular order where exclusionary policies, such as banning the headscarf, dramatically undermine gender equality and any notions of pluralism. These women employ a pious identity as a means to create an Islamic authenticity for themselves that can withstand the challenge of Republican secularism and also uneducated, ignorant (*cahil*) masculine religious interpretations. Their identity is formed to set themselves apart from close female others, such as mothers and sisters, who inhabit two distinct culturally dominant models of womanhood: the "backward" Muslim women who are restricted to private spaces by Islamic religious patriarchy and the acquiescent "secularly Muslim" women. For them, developing such an alternative identity involves importing Islamic norms into their biographies to live according to true Islam but also means rejecting family-sanctioned frames of references and role models. Thus, they try to free themselves from the path of blindly reproducing either secular Muslim or backward Muslim identities in producing new selves.

The rise of new Muslim subjectivities in Turkey is by no means a new topic in studies of the country. Previous studies contribute in important ways to our understanding of new Muslim women's agency in applying Islam to everyday life (Göle 1997b; Saktanber 2002a) and of their contribution to the successes of grass-roots Islamic movements and political parties during the 1990s (Saktanber 2002b; Keskin 2002). Writings on new Islamist women concerning the secular headscarf ban and protests against it (Olson 1985; Ozdalga 1998; Gocek 2000; Arat 2001; Secor 2002; Komsuoglu 2004; Marshall-Aldikacti 2005; Keskin 2002; O'Neil 2008; Saktanber and Corbacioglu 2008) reveal the deep fracture among secular feminists about covered women's participation in the public sphere. New pious women were also studied as subjects of Islamic consumption culture (White 1999; Navaro-Yashin 2002; Kilicbay and Mutlu 2002) and as embodying Islamic modernity (Göle 2000, 2002, 2003) and Islamic individualism through fashion and participation in leisure-consumption culture (Genel and Karaosmanoglu 2006). A substantial proportion of the commentary on new Islamist women in Turkey has been specifically concerned with the gender tension within the Islamist movement (Göle 1996; Ilyasoglu 1998).

In contrast, in this chapter I focus on the less visible signs of this emerging identity. What are the significant biographical resources that help the new pious woman achieve distance from earlier (and other) models of being a woman in Turkish society? What are the tensions she must negotiate in this process? Our understanding of emerging female identities in periods of rapid societal change must include the differentiation that is implied between generations, especially the maternal generation. According to Mannheim, generational location points to "certain definite modes of behavior, feeling and thought" (1972, 291), and individuals who are born in the same historical and social context and exposed to similar societal and personal experiences during the formative years of early adulthood share the same generational location.[2] While Mannheim clearly distinguishes "generation as actuality" from mere "generational location," he demarcates the boundaries of a generation monolithically, without any attention to how gender inflects and frames his understanding of generation. In contrast to shared location as an unconscious, passive, and inactive one, he defines a "generation as actuality," whose members are differentiated by their exposure to and participation in the "social and intellectual symptoms of a process of dynamic destabilization" (303).

The new pious woman both troubles and illustrates this definition of "generation as actuality" in Mannheim's model, because she has developed an original consciousness distinct from the normative cultural heritage represented by earlier generations—that is, her parents' generation—a Muslim subjectivity created by secularism in the historical context of dynamic destabilization during her formative years. These new pious women have become agents of social change by rejecting traditional interpretations of the role of religion in people's lives and of the way it should be practiced and by offering alternative designs for "how we should live our lives" (Saktanber 2002a). They also set themselves apart from many of their contemporaries—the "passive generation," in Turner's terms (2002), who embrace the cultural heritage of older generations and align themselves with the members of this older (secular) generation.

Within a "generation as actuality," Mannheim also recognizes that differing or opposing forms of response to the particular historical situation may emerge. Thus a generation as actuality is likely to be internally stratified by a number of "generation units" (304–12) characterized by divisions and oppositions among contemporaneous individuals. The Turkish case reveals the importance of this internal stratification by gender within the new Muslim generation. This gender fragmentation raises an important question: To what extent does the gender divide jeopardize the new Muslims' potential of becoming "generative of the conditions of thinking and action of subsequent cohorts" (Turner 2002, 19)?

On the basis of an analysis of the thirteen narratives I collected, I aim to demonstrate the closely connected roles of generational location and gender in producing this identity. The generational and gender consciousness among this group of young women derives from a strong critique of their parents' generation's submissiveness to two powerful societal forces: Republican secularism and the male-dominated gender order. This gendered generational consciousness finds its expression in new subjectivities that dictate a lifestyle according to Islam while rejecting Islamic masculine patriarchal constructions of Muslim womanhood. I argue that it is the cosmopolitan pedagogical and cultural environment of Boğaziçi and the wider context of Istanbul that allows these women to actively cultivate, advance, and validate this new Muslim identity in relation to a wider collective of differences. Their rejection of the legacy of their mothers' generation brings them closer to feminism and secular young women while simultaneously accentuating the gender antagonism between themselves and their male Muslim peers. The realms of romance and love, and the narratives and practices articulated in this arena, offer a privileged vantage point from which to view these pious women's configurations of the self, marriage, motherhood, and sexuality. In particular, the narratives articulated at this site express many of the contradictions of identity making as a pious woman, a project of self that deems the enactment of premarital sexual intimacies singularly inappropriate for pious selves.

I begin by contextualizing the role of the secular headscarf ban and the parental generation's response to the secular state. Unpacking this background before turning to the narratives of the pious young women I collected is central to understanding the historical context of the dynamic destabilization that occurred during my respondents' childhood and formative years.

A Short History of the Secular Headscarf Ban and Protests against It

For many, the covered female head as the embodiment of Islamic morality is the primary signifier of female submission and subjugation. More than anything else, the presence (embodied or imagined) of veiled women animates public debate and has triggered legislative reforms in some Western European societies with large Muslim diasporas, such as France, Great Britain, and Belgium.[3] Islamic headcovering has been and remains socially and politically charged terrain in Turkey since the foundation of the Turkish Republic as a secular nation-state in 1923. Most particularly, the new public visibility of the religiously headscarved woman beginning in the mid-1980s has become both a symptom and a symbol of Turkey's destabilized identity as a secular republic. Sharpening the divide between the two opposing camps of secularists and Islamists, the headscarf forms a core imaginary of a resurgent Islam for secular Turks. Especially for the older generation of Turks, it dramatizes the changing trajectory of the country from secularly Muslim, modern, and Western to antisecular and Islamist. For them, the headscarved woman embodies antimodernism and the attempts of a political Islam to overturn Turkey's secular regime.

Precisely what kind of headcovering is considered Islamic or religious depends on how the scarf is tied, what kind of woman wears it, and where it is worn. The mode of tying generically referred to as "Islamic" and subject to the secular ban aims to hide both the hair and the neck and shoulders, adhering to the principle of Muslim religious headcovering. Wearing such a headscarf in public places such as schools, courts, hospitals, and Parliament is prohibited by the Turkish Constitution. By contrast, the method of tying that is referred to as "traditional" (*geleneksel*) or "cultural" (*kültürel*) and is not subject to the secular ban exposes the neck and shoulders and is less disciplined in terms of hiding hair. This type of cultural covering is generally practiced by rural, formally uneducated women; rural migrant women confined to the low-income neighborhoods of cities; and older women. The exact number of women who practice either Islamic or traditional covering or who do not cover at all is hard to determine. In the same vein, there is no reliable historical data tracking women's changing practices in this realm. However, a

2007 country-wide survey indicates that the percentage of women who don the Islamic headscarf increased from 3.5 percent in 2003 to 16.2 percent in 2007. This survey also demonstrates that 52.9 percent of women in Turkey cover their heads in a traditional manner disassociated from religious devotion whereas 30.6 percent of women are not covered at all (see *Milliyet* on December 3, 2007, cited in Saktanber and Corbacioglu 2008, 533–34, footnote). Quantitative data concerning this issue is problematic at best in today's deeply class-stratified Turkey, where young women with rural family origins flaunt chic-style Islamic coverings to distinguish themselves from women who cover culturally and project an image of lower-class traditionalism (Secor 2002). As merely one class-aspiration marker, this gesture has a different significance than the expression of religious devotion. Thus, closely linking particular forms and styles of headcovering to an increasing or decreasing pattern of religious piousness would be misleading.

One can certainly begin a history of the headscarf ban in Turkey with the ironies and contradictions of the present day to point out how earlier historical moments in the secularization process continue to shape gender constructions and Turkish political and religious life. It is ironic that since 2002 Turkey has been governed by a political party, the Justice and Development Party, known as the AKP, with roots in political Islam, and the wives of the president, the prime minister, and members of cabinet are Islamically covered. But the headscarf ban in universities, classrooms, and public offices is enforced. Indeed, after only six years of coming to power with a landslide victory in 2002, the AKP introduced amendments to the Constitution in 2008 to lift the secular headscarf ban in higher education. The amendments passed the Parliament, and the president, who is a founder and former member of the AKP, ratified it. But the main oppositional party went to the Constitutional Court for their annulment. In annulling the amendments to the Constitution, the Court cited these amendments for violating the principal of secularism guaranteed in the Constitution. Today the headscarf ban is still in effect, although on March 22, 2010, the AKP launched its campaign to overhaul the Constitution. The proposed deep constitutional changes target the judiciary and the military institutions, which are widely seen as the pillars of Turkey's secular state and the enforcers of a strong separation between Islam and the state. The AKP claims that by strengthening the power of the executive branch in the Turkish body politic, the proposed changes will further democratize the country and bring its Constitution in line with European norms, thus helping Turkey pursue full European Union membership (see Arsu 2010).

The secular ban on "headscarves" and protests against the ban are inextricably linked to the processes of secularization and the cultivation of private religiosity in Turkey. My brief recounting of this history below provides an important context for the analysis of the women's narratives that follow. The biographies of all these women bear the marks of an era of Islamization and secular challenges to it. Particularly, the educational aspirations and decisions present in their girlhood biographies were shaped in complex ways by the headscarf ban as a site of either conflict or accommodation in family dynamics. The ways in which these women and their families made and altered decisions about education were frequently responses to some dimension of the fractured cultural and political landscape. Furthermore, these women's and their parents' worldviews are embedded in this history. Examining this history brings into sharp relief a range of issues key to comprehending the impact of the headscarf ban on women's identity constructions as pious women as well as the intersecting forces of generational identity and gender.

As I detailed in the introduction of this book, the processes of radical secularization in Turkey laid the foundation for the equation of religious expression (especially the headscarf) with backwardness, ignorance, submission, and traditionality and the equation of uncoveredness with civilization, enlightenment, and openness to modernity. In other words, being covered or uncovered came to define an essential difference between different categories of women: uneducated/lower-class/traditional/religious and educated/middle-class/modern/secular. This is why today university students who combine the Islamic headscarf with education are seen as transgressing a "fixed" cultural and legal boundary. To put it differently, they are representing an inversion of the construction of the religious woman from one who is submissive and ensconced in the private sphere to one who is in the public, educated, and urban. This is the most threatening dimension of the public visibility of the headscarf.

This context of Islamist visibility has endowed the headscarf with the power to signify the battles between Islamists and secularists. The Republican regime viewed the veiling of educated, urban Islamist women as the epitome of "the intolerable practice of veiling" (Komsuoglu 2004, 100) and as a direct threat to their vision of secularism. The Higher Education Council, a new regulating body established after the 1980 military coup to curb politicization of universities, in 1982 banned the wearing of headscarves along with men's beards and mustaches, which were seen as representing ultra-nationalist, Islamist, and leftist identities (Saktanber and Corbacioglu 2008). However, the way in which this ban was imposed and enforced resulted in a great deal of variation, not only in the dichotomies of private and public but also in the meaning of being covered. In 1988, "by interpreting university students' headscarves as modern turbans rather than Islamic attire," the Parliament passed a law allowing for the "covering of head and body on the basis of religious faith." Soon after, in 1989, the Constitutional Court ruled that this law did not apply to the headscarf, because the headscarf was a political symbol—a symbol of the politicization of religion. The controversy that followed came to a head with the dismissal of Merve Kavakci, a covered woman elected as Istanbul deputy by a pro-Islamic party. Kavakci's attempt to take her seat in Parliament while wearing her veil upturned the sanctioned boundary between private religion and public secularism (Göle 2002). The Parliament would not tolerate her expression of religion via her headscarf and prevented her entry.[4]

During the 1990s, a strong Islamist movement among university students marked the political landscape in Turkey. Sit-ins, demonstrations, and hunger strikes placed headscarved women in the glare of the spotlight, and the secular headscarf ban was taken to the European Human Rights Commission by a university student. As the Turkish Constitutional Court did in 2005, the commission upheld the ban as necessary to protect secularism, gender equality, and democracy in Turkey, noting that the impact an individual wearing headscarf could have on those who chose not to wear one had to be taken into consideration.

The secular ban was relaxed during several political junctures, particularly when the pro-Islamic Refah Party (RP)—which, under the leadership of Necmettin Erbakan, espoused the top-down Islamification of society and polity—was in power. This party was closed down by the secularist courts in 1998 but resurfaced several times under new names. As the leading party in the governing coalition, the Islamist RP brought about another military intervention on February 28, 1997. This event, dubbed a soft military coup, aimed to fight threats against political Islam. After this soft coup, the headscarf ban was more rigidly enforced in universities and public institutions in the broader context of fighting against the rise of political Islam.

As discussed earlier, in the introduction, the shift from the politics of Islamism to the politics of post-Islamism has taken place within the context of a vastly liberalized economy and culture and increasing globalization, but also within the European Union accession process over the past decade. European Union accession has demanded a reform process aimed at radical legal changes, including amendments to Turkey's civil and penal code and protection of minority rights, to bring the country in line with European standards. Within this institutional transformative milieu, the headscarf issue has become a debate with global referents. In particular, the politics of European integration have shaped the aims and objectives of those who defended the headscarf: arguments for lifting the ban are now couched in the language of freedom of expression and freedom from restriction on individual liberty, and the state's interference and surveillance of headcovering is linked to human rights abuses. Forming a new discursive space, the Internet has also played an important role in spreading the voices of women who wear Muslim headscarves (Seckinelgin 2006, 761), as well as in the evolving history of discourses against their prohibition, which, during the Islamist mobilization of the 1990s, was associated "with Islamist activism [and] was also marked as the political symbol of the Islamist movement" (Saktanber and Corbacioglu 2008, 525).

The Islamic radicalism in Turkey during the 1990s distinguished itself by the visible presence of covered university students at the forefront and has contributed to the emergence of a new crop of Islamist women activists and intellectuals as well as bolstered Islamic women's participation in pro-Islamic parties, greatly contributing to the successes of the Welfare Party in 1994. Yet this participation did not bring women much empowerment due to the Islamist patriarchal elite who accepted women's political labor without promoting those women to higher organizational positions (Keskin 2002; Saktanber 2002b; Acar 1995; Ilyasoglu 1998). If we look at how feminists in Turkey have approached and addressed the question of headcovering and the participation of covered women in the public sphere, we see a particular tension and a complicated engagement. Those feminists who primarily identify with the Republican ideology (called Kemalist/secularist feminists) assert that the headscarf is the manifestation of an oppressive religion that seeks to disenfranchise women and is therefore the antithesis of secularism. These feminists thoroughly reject the Islamist woman's vision of "an equal but different womanhood," thereby denying covered women agency (Keskin 2002). From this feminist perspective, it is argued that Islamist women face double jeopardy, as they are oppressed by their Islamist brothers and their secular sisters: both attempt to exclude headscarved women from public spaces.

However, the headscarf issue both accentuated the already existing differences among feminists and created new divisions along two sharply defined oppositional principles: one that seeks to reconcile feminism with Islam to promote a civil society and another that seeks to defend secularism against Islamists (Arat 2001). Recently, a co-authored campaign by some feminists and headscarved women strove to enter into more transformative relationships with the diverse identities of women using the slogan "let's make a pact to look out for each other" (*birbirimize sahip çıkalım*). This feminist call invites women to denounce the divisive and sexist definition of each group of women, such as the characterization of covered women as "Islamists dupes" and of uncovered women as "immoral sexual objects." Their demand for a discrimination-free public sphere for every woman, where different identities can intimately intersect, interact, and communicate with each other, signals feminism's engagement with women's religious identities from a more complex standpoint.

The emergence of a rapidly growing Islamic middle class as modern consumers of an Islamic fashion culture and the increasing commodification of the Islamic way of life, as well as the class-based hierarchies among pious women, continue to problematize Islamic self-expression. Access to a public world of communication, media, fashion, and technologies allows the middle-class pious new Islamist woman to "circulate among different publics with ease" (Göle 2003, 822). Furthermore, these covered women's adoption of the symbols of modernity reduces the social distance between them and the secular elites (823). Also, a new Islamic individualism embodied by educated headscarved women in the big cities helps to blur the distinction between religious/traditional and secular/modern by breaking the headscarf's association with ignorance and tradition while signaling its own distance from Islamic fundamentalism and anticonsumerism. Yet the issue of how enacting the identity of a "new Muslim woman" could correspond with the fundamentalist vision of female chastity and public decorum remains a complex question.

Adding to this challenging issue, the trend of diminishing social distance between the headscarved women and secular women is also marked by gender interaction in the public sphere. The sight of headscarved women sharing private affections with men in very public places has become rather common. Amorous displays that go beyond hand holding and hugging in city parks and the leisure-consumption sites of cafes and malls draw the attention of secular Turks who pejoratively regard public displays of affection among Muslims as hypocritical, while for more conservative Muslims, such displays represent the dark side of enlarged freedom and the decline of the segregation of sexes, embodying a breach of the confinement of women and their sexuality to the private sphere. Social imaginaries for the public sphere continue to make shared, collective locales profound sites for the articulation between Islam and secularism, private and public, and modern and traditional in the production of new selves distinct from Western secular or orthodox Islamic identities.

Crafting Pious Selves

Viewed from a chronological perspective, the collective history of "headcovering" among my narrators identifies three educational onsets (middle school, high school, and university) as specific junctures of headcovering, almost neatly dividing these thirteen women into three subgroups. Although seductive with its offering of a neat inventory of headcovering and a medium for classification, a chronological model falsely asserts linearity and continuation where there is none and fails to capture many emotional experiences, negotiations with self and others, and contradictions. Indeed, there are multiple problems with attempting to use a linear chronological model in classifying experiences of covering. First, it falsely unites divergent experiences. Second, it obscures the significance of shifting definitions and policies concerning women's headcovering produced by the state and/or ignores experiences of temporary episodes of uncovering. Third, importantly, although headcovering is a significant manifestation of piousness, it does not necessarily always signal the beginning of piety, nor does the practice of uncovering always mean vacating a pious-identity construction. Such a linear chronological account limits our understanding of the intersection of family, educational aspirations, and state policies in women's lives. In the same vein, classifying parents' attitudes to their daughters' covering as either "encouraging" or "oppositional" would falsely impose a firm separation, when, in fact, both encouraging and oppositional stands are enacted by the very same actors at different times. My descriptions below aim to expose these nonlinear histories and often contradictory and altered stances.

Yasemin (22) began covering during her first year of college, even though she was pious before. Having been covering for four years at the time of the interview, she indicated that she thought her first year of college would be the perfect time to start with a new identity. She feared that had she started the college uncovered, she wouldn't be able to cover during the later years of her university education. Her parents' reaction was distinctly negative and explicitly articulated through a threat to reject Yasemin as their daughter. Ironically, when Yasemin was in middle school and she reached puberty, her father wanted her to cover, but she gently rebelled against him. Yasemin's narrative recounted how her twelve-year-old self pleaded to her father, "None of my friends are covered. If I am covered, I would experience psychological problems. I am going to be extremely discomfited: everyone will laugh at me; all my friends will leave me if I am covered; no one is going to want to be my friend." This appeal to her psychological health, accompanied by her sobbing, worked because Yasemin said her father loved his girl and couldn't stand her crying and being unhappy. He said, "Okay, we will wait until you grow up a bit more." In contrast, Adalet (23) couldn't wait to be twelve and covered. When she was little, she loved to play with her "toy" headscarves—bandanas. When her father took her shopping to pick out her first headscarf, she chose two with the brightest colors. The daughter of a first-generation "consciously Muslim" family, she was sent to religiously inspired, private all-girls schools. Her mother had primary-school education, whereas her father possessed a university education. Adalet was the only woman in the group who was married.

Like Adalet, Alanur (20), who was also raised in a "consciously Muslim" family environment, donned the headscarf when she was twelve. Her covering/uncovering practices at university were the most unusual in the accounts: in classrooms Alanur was uncovered, in open spaces of the campus she put her hat on, and outside the campus she was religiously covered. Born and raised in Istanbul, both of Alanur's parents were professionals with university degrees. Her recently retired mother had a profession in a field in which the secular ban was strictly observed, and thus, despite her desire, in her professional life she was uncovered. Although Alanur's two older sisters covered after high school and her mother never said to her "you are going to be covered" but "only gently inquired if [she would] like a headscarf," Alanur covered at the age of twelve. Alanur wanted to grow up by donning the headscarf: "It was like I would like to wear high heels. I covered myself knowing exactly why." In contrast, for Akalin (23), the memory of her first scarf formed a sad description: "It was such a big scarf and a huge overcoat like a lampshade, and I was so little." Uncovered on campus but covered outside, Akalin grew up in a traditionally religious environment in a modest family. Her father, a high-school dropout, was very authoritarian and only allowed the furthering of her education after mandatory primary school on the condition that she was going to be sent to a religious middle school. Akalin pointed out, "I always struggled against my father's opposition for education." Her struggle as a child was supported by her homemaker mother.

Oya (22) lost her father when she was eight years old. Raised in a very secular family milieu with her mother uncovered, she covered in the second year of her university education, although her interest in pursuing a religious way of life started when she was in middle school. She had a large circle of friends and saw one of her friends performing the ritual prayers of Islam (*namaz kılmak*), and she was very impressed by her friend and asked her certain questions and understood that she herself also had an interest. She became religious but never dared to be covered until she became a university student. She explained her logic this way: "Ultimately I believe this is the right thing . . . if I don't live by what I believe, I will start believing what I live by. Besides, I thought, 'I am not harming anyone, and I have nothing to lose.'" Her decision to don a headscarf created a turbulent period in her family. In objecting to Oya's covering, her mother said, "I raised you to develop yourself and to learn about the world." However, "after realizing that I am still the same only my appearance has changed," her family relented. She thinks that had her father been alive, she wouldn't have even dared to cover in the university because her father was a big champion of Ecevit, the late iconic leader and former prime minister of the major secularist party in Turkey.

Canan's (19) parents showed a similar response to Oya's when Canan covered upon graduating high school. Raised in a working-class family and a traditional but secular family environment (her mother is traditionally covered), Canan lived "alone and free" in Istanbul during her high school years after she won a scholarship to study in a state-run boarding school. Her parents said, "Live by the rules, otherwise the headscarf will close your path to mobility." Although she showed determination against her parents' forceful objections, for her deciding to cover was a very hard decision to make: "I was raised with the idea that 'you are going to get educated and not be oppressed.' In Turkey's conditions, it is not guaranteed that one with a headscarf can get educated, anything can happen and you may not be able to continue . . . there is always this fear: your path is going to be blocked." Because she arrived at the conclusion in her "thought structure" that an obligation to cover was central to her faith, she was able to dismiss her parents' dissent and her own ambivalences.

Born and raised in Istanbul in an upper-middle-class family, Ceda (23) had been covered for eleven years when I met her. Her mother, who in the past had experimented with the headcover for three years between the ages of thirty-one and thirty-four, and her sister are both uncovered, and they are not particularly religious. Her parents do not exhibit any oppositional stand towards Ceda's piousness: "They don't expect me to live like them, because I don't like how they live their lives." Attending the private, religiously inspired girls' schools that the "Islamic bourgeoisie send their kids to" had allowed Ceda to be covered continuously since her middle school years. Even as a little girl, Ceda actively sought schools leaning toward a lax enforcement of the secular ban and urged her parents to transfer her to another religiously inspired school when she disliked what she considered the rigidity and the curtailment of individual freedoms in her middle school, sponsored by the Gülen community. Ceda openly protested the enforcement of the headscarf ban in her high school. Her protest happened on a day when inspectors were anticipated to arrive in order to investigate whether or not the secular ban was being violated by her school at a time when the pro-Islamic party and its leader, representing the political Islam of the 1990s, were on the rise. Her action was equally a protest against her father, who, upon hearing of Ceda's intention to stage a protest, said, "I don't permit you. If you do it, I will never look at your face." In response, Ceda said, "I didn't ask you. You don't have any right to intervene." Ceda's protest made her very popular in school. Another participant, Zehra, also refused to obey the headscarf ban in high school and as a result was expelled. Forced to interrupt her education for two years (she earned her high school diploma through distance learning), Zehra refused to listen to the emotional appeals and threats of her family (her father refused to talk with her for three months), as well as of sympathetic teachers:

> I was firm in my determination. No matter what I wasn't going to be forced uncovered; no one has a right to come to me and say "open your head," and, in the same vein, no one can come to an uncovered girl next to me to say "cover your head," she can even come to school in a bathing suit if she desires to do so, you cannot intervene in that either.

Zehra (22), covered since age twelve, when she started attending a religious middle-school (İmam Hatip *okulu*), was born and spent her early girlhood in a village. Her "traditionally" religious family is working-class.

The youngest of five children, Mahrem (23), like Zehra, was born in a small village to scantily educated parents. Because he regretted his own lack of education, her father's biggest aim became "to see his kids educated." Indeed, in raising educated daughters, he transgressed the gender conventions of his own side of the extended family. Mahrem's mother, a pious woman since her girlhood, had three years of schooling. Mahrem described her father's and mother's divergent expectations of their children: "My father wants us to earn good livings, my mother wants us to be good mortals [in relation to God]." After graduating from the İmam

Hatip school, Mahrem donned the headscarf. Mahrem's older sister is uncovered, but her younger sister is covered.

Ayşe covered three years ago, during her freshman year of university. She described her father as "conservative but not oppressive by any means because he is university educated." Surrounded by neighborhood friends who went to "normal schools," Ayşe didn't want to be sent to a religious middle school, because she desired to be like her friends. Because her neighborhood friends made fun of her, she experienced what she called a "psychology of inferiority." At her mother's insistence, and in order to increase her chances of receiving a high score on the university entrance examination, she was sent to a normal high school. Ayşe's mother, who dropped out of high school to marry, was covered. Her younger sister was also covered when she was twelve, whereas her older sister was never covered.

Aknur (23) grew up in an unusual family arrangement by Turkish standards due to her parents' separation, a separation caused by her mother's inability and unwillingness to live as a conscious Muslim despite her husband's pious wishes. Aknur "grew up with her father's Islamic values" but was raised in her mother's household. She, along with her female cousin, donned a headscarf when she was twelve years old because she and her cousin very much admired and were influenced by a female teacher at a Koran course and because as little girls they wanted God to love them. A university graduate, Aknur's mother is one of two mothers in this group with a professional career. The uncovered mother and her covered daughter are met by puzzled looks in public: "My mother find herself in an inferior place, like as if I am a 'high/sublime' saint and on the other hand my mother is this woman who couldn't transcend certain things and who could not become covered. And of course, sometimes the reverse is true."

Derya (22) grew up in a midsize, conservative Anatolian town, as the only girl in a mainly modest middle-class family. Her parents' marriage forged together two individuals with different backgrounds. Her father, who had a middle-school education, was raised in a secular family, whereas her mother received a religious upbringing. With the influence of her mother, Derya's father became religious over time. Swayed by the strong influence of her primary school teacher, Derya never wanted to go to İmam Hatip. But her father was vehement about sending her to a

İmam Hatip middle school: "My father himself cannot read the Koran but feels it is important. He thought that I would get such an education at İmam Hatip. He didn't want to raise us the way he was raised." Derya's mother was not eager to send her to İmam Hatip and was unhappy to see Derya engaging in something she did not desire. Nevertheless, she worked hard toward "warming" Derya up to İmam Hatip by pointing out nice scarves and promoting İmam Hatip, telling her "how İmam Hatip school is a charismatic one: you will learn English in prep school and you will see how religious studies are combined with lots of science classes."

Despite her initial strong opposition, Derya ended up loving her school. And ironically, when the time arrived to decide which high school to attend, Derya desired to stay at İmam Hatip while her parents wanted to send her either to a very prestigious high school specializing in sciences (Fen Lisesi), for which she scored high on the entrance examination, or another prestigious high school. Her parents "won again." Donning a headscarf at the age of twelve "did not carry any meaning" for Derya. She wore it "because [she] had to. It was an accessory without any special meaning." Headscarves were not required in İmam Hatip, but she still wore one because she saw it as "an extension of the school uniform." "Most of time when I was out playing, like biking, I did not wear it. It gained meaning later." In her high school, she was uncovered.

Most of these daughters were raised in traditional "secular Muslim" families in which religion was practiced privately and women were either not covered or covered traditionally. Only two young women, Adalet and Alanur, came from families who consistently supported a religious upbringing and who seemed to be one of the first cohorts of families that chose to live Islam as "conscious Muslims." According to the discourses of their daughters, these parents felt the tensions of Turkish modernity and secularism deeply, especially with respect to bringing up their children with Islamic norms and knowledge, because they had experienced the conflict between a secular school culture and a religious family background. Besides this seemingly clear-cut division between those who grew up in "consciously Muslim" families and those who were raised in "secular Muslim" families, there are those whose family backgrounds present more complexity with regard to intimate religious environments. A chief example is Aknur, who was raised by a secular mother but with her father's religious norms. Similar but less pronounced is Mahrem's family background, which displays a divided orientation between her mother and father. On the other hand, Ceda's family history reflects a trajectory of change from subscribing to religious devotion to abandoning it, a trajectory clearly reflected in her mother's experimentation with covering for three years and in the initial patterning of Ceda's education in private religious schools. At the time of her interview, Ceda was the only one in her family who was pious. This overall diversity is a microcosmic representation of the social geography of Islamization in Turkey, bearing the marks of ambivalent transformations.

Sociologist Nilüfer Göle, who conceptualizes the headscarf as the most visible and provocative stigma of a Goffmanian framework, points out the irony that Islamist women have become assertive by adopting a symbol of gender subservience and stigmatization (Göle 2003, 817). The educated woman can claim the headscarf as a new prestige symbol that signifies her morality and provides a means of distinction and dignity. The head-covered woman communicates that she is more pious than secular Muslims who relegate their religiosity to the private sphere. She broadcasts that she will no longer be restricted to a traditional role and private spaces but will participate in public urban life. In Göle's formulation, the head-covered woman reinterprets the stigma that brands her as inferior. The young, covered Islamic woman's status gives her a "subaltern advantage" (Göle 2003), a position from which she can voice dissent against the secularist definition of modernity and education: one must abandon "Muslim habitus" to achieve both.

The covering experiences of the women described in this chapter centrally highlight the salience of the connections between a visual Islamic feminine display and an internal self, an issue to which Göle's brilliant formulation of stigma is indifferent. Commentaries on the genesis and meaning of veiling for women, as well as on whether it is a religious requirement, have repeatedly pointed out that the Koran does not contain any specific prescriptions for veiling, although the dominant interpretation of two particular verses informs the Koranic position on this question and provides guidance to religious adherents. One of these two verses (Surah al-Nur, verses 30–31) urges women to cover their bosoms and jewelry. Another verse (Surah al-Ahzab, verse 59) recommends that the wives of the Prophet wrap their cloaks tightly around their bodies, so as to be known and not molested in public (Hoodfar 1997, 251). Some scholars see veiling as a technique of self-realization (Mahmood 2005), while others see a trajectory within Muslim communities that gives less and less significance to the connection between veiling and Muslim womanhood, claiming that Islamic piety does not hinge on the veil (Bartkowski and Ghazal Read 2003).[5]

For my narrators, Muslim headcovering is rooted in the concept of *hidayete ermek*. The *Oxford Turkish-English Dictionary* translates "*hidayet*" as "the right way to Islam; searching for the right way," and "*hidayete ermek*" as "become a Muslim." In the continuous process of coming closer to God, the religious commitment of many Muslim women manifests in daily prayer and the study of the Koran and the practice of headcovering—a means to developing a more modest self. As one wrestles with an inner struggle to get closer to God, she becomes a participant in a process of deeply embedding religion in her daily life. Head and body covering serves as an important marker of this process of finding the correct ways to conduct oneself. Some among my narrators advocated the interpretation that daily prayers (*Namaz kılmak*) were more "decisive" vis-à-vis headcovering in the pursuit of religiosity.

It is also important to note that in this visual economy, an Islam-prescribed feminine appearance extends beyond merely donning a headscarf. It centrally includes women cultivating their bodies with modesty, disciplining their gestures and their demeanor—what Marcel Mauss, in his discussion of "national habitus," calls shared "techniques of the body." This appearance is accrued through education and emulation and is displayed through physical gesture and movement, denoting a common belonging to a "Muslim habitus." This belonging represents a rising demand for self-regulation: the woman must lower her eyes in front of men, move in a subdued manner, never laugh too loudly or be boisterous in public.

Thus, becoming "covered" (*tesettüre girmek*) is an important part of constructing a Muslim identity and communicating that identity to others. Donning a headscarf both distinguishes women and locates them in the Muslim habitus. The headscarf shapes their interactive space and determines forms of social interaction in this order. For example, it protects women from the unwanted intrusions of modern manners and customs—such as men and women kissing each other on the cheek when they are introduced for the first time. It also shields them from one of the common idioms of youth: openness to cross-gender touching as a means of expressing modernity. On the other hand, it denies them entry into certain interactive spaces or forms of interaction, for instance, going to a social gathering where alcohol is served. Locating oneself visually in the Muslim habitus also means becoming a subject of discriminatory practices. For example, Yasemin was completely convinced that even though she was overqualified academically to get into a graduate program (she passed the written exam with flying colors), she was rejected after her interview. And as Oya narrated, her professor did not invite her along with her classmates to apply to a coveted internship in an ad agency because she was covered, and the professor thought that the ad agency wouldn't be interested in hiring a covered woman. These women also feel the impact of being covered in that others identify them by referencing their Muslimness rather than identifying them as individuals. Ceda narrated her classmates' inability to imagine her beyond her religious identity: "When you are covered, people attribute a certain kind of worth to you, as if whatever you say has a distinctiveness in their mind. This is an uncomfortable situation. . . . My classmates focus on Muslimness—they always desire to understand you in that box. I am also myself—they don't see that unfortunately."

As I explained earlier, the increasing proliferation and diffusion of Islamic fashion in the last decade has contributed to the fracturing of the pious women by class, and embodied consumption particularly has become a main strategy for creating class and status distinctions. There are now many versions of being a covered Muslim woman. This diversity is apparent in my study group. As university students, they aim to show their unique personal expression in the way they dress and cover their heads. For them, the way they dress is a significant site of class disidentification, an attempt to escape and defy easily recognizable class-based looks. In creating a stylish, authentic look, they generally avoid two class-based dominant appearances. They dismiss a contrived, overly styled look often associated with wealthy, bourgeois Muslim women who are outfitted with brand-name clothing, high heels, and expensive silk scarves. It is also the kind of appearance that many of them cannot afford financially to emulate. They equally avoid what some consider the look of *overlukçu* girls (referencing those young women who work as operatives of overlock sewing machines). Dominated by a combination of light pinks and blues, this *overlukçu* appearance for them signals an uneducated status and thus something that should be avoided. In stark opposition to these two styles, they dress with a sense of irony and seek out unusual accents, particularly with regard to their "secularly Muslim" headgears. Several of them had hats specifically designed and made for them, thus making these hats their signature. A minority of these women clearly articulated a tension between Islam and fashion and chose sartorial modesty by dressing plainly (*sade*)—long, loose overcoats accompanied by large scarves—arguing that consumption undermined their claims to Islamic piety and modesty. The appearance of this minority in my study group announces the practice of renunciation of Islamic consumption, while signaling ambiguity on the part of these women with regard to their educational status.

As we have seen above from their profiles, structured by the moving boundaries of private and public and shifting definitions by the state of what constitutes headcovering, what some experienced was a sequence in which they initially covered when they were twelve, then uncovered for three years during high school, then re-covered for a one-year period in the first year of university when the ban was temporarily lifted. Also, during their covered periods, there were many instances when they were compelled to be uncovered, for example, when they participated in internship programs, were employed in public offices, took university entrance examinations, or went to job interviews.

How do these sartorial transformations affect/configure identity construction? Being in a state of complete nakedness is the dominant imagery evoked in these young women's descriptions of how they felt when uncovered. Phrases such as "being as a different person," "an artificial person who is not herself," "a hyper (*sanal*) person who is not me," "deceptive and untrue representation of myself," and "self-deceiving but also deceiving others" dominated their narratives of coming out of the "dressing cabin." Also, because the styles of headcovering define what female beauty is and how they project "techniques of the body" through demeanor, wearing a headscarf is associated with beauty, while the hat is considered "funny" and unflattering.[6]

Wearing the hat/turban or being completely uncovered is unsettling because it creates a breach between these women's interior and exterior selves. Because the hat is not a true representation of their authentic selves, it embodies betrayal of their interior selves. According to these women, then, being uncovered or donning a hat engenders an experience of stigmatization and disempowerment, because these sartorial shifts and the ambiguity of a hat represent a vacillating/unformed/ambivalent self to others, despite the fact that they stand apart from other women and their hats make them unmistakable as pious women. In fact, some of the women expressed that they would have preferred to be completely uncovered, because they disliked the liminal look that a hat projects, yet they felt pressured by their peers not to be uncovered. Akalin, who chose to put on a hat because her friends do, explained that she would have preferred discarding her scarf completely because "that image [the image with a hat on] is such an in-between, undefined image: it is not clear what it represents to people." Especially those like Derya, Ayşe, and Adalet, who came to the campus in their first year with headscarves when the ban was not enforced, found it very hard to enter the university uncovered in their second year. Their narratives underlined a profound sense of displacement, describing how they couldn't feel a sense of belonging, how they felt inhibited in displaying academic performance, and how, as a result, their grades suffered. Drawing a contrast between her high school self, who was an assertive and active participant in class when she was uncovered, Ayşe claimed, "Now I am someone who sits in the back of classroom, never speaks, always wishing no one will ask me a question. I am trying to learn like this." Their experiences suggest that the stigma for these women is grounded in the ways they are forced to respond to the secular ban and the way it impacts their ability to maintain and project authentic selves, rather than the stigmatizing meanings inscribed in the headscarf by secular forces.

The Parental Home

To sketch a generational profile of my participants' parents, I pieced together various pieces of information the women shared with me about the lives of their parents. Their parents were all born roughly between 1950 and 1960, had lived their formative years (youths) during the mid-1960s and mid-1970s, married in the mid- and late 1970s, and started having children in the late 1970s and early 1980s.

These parents were born and raised either in villages or in small towns, but they all experienced geographical mobility in early adulthood by moving to larger urban areas. The absence of high educational attainment (such as high school or university education) among many of the fathers is one of the most salient aspects of this cohort, and it must have contributed a great deal to their status as members of the economically and socially subordinated classes in Turkish society. These fathers had secure employment in state-run factories or government offices in working-class jobs with the provision of lifelong employment, reflecting the important role of state-run enterprises in the economy and employment structures prior to the open-market economy of the 1980s onward. However, these jobs were low-paid, and although some of these men owned small businesses or shops in Anatolian towns, these small businesses did not seem to facilitate a transition to a higher class status. Yet for a small group of fathers, geographical mobility when they were young brought with it upward economic and social mobility through educational attainment, and they became part of the group of well-to-do professional families.

The women's mothers were not highly educated and had little employment experience, with the exception of two mothers who had professional jobs, one of whom had a university education and the other a high school education. The other mothers, who deeply regretted their own lack of education, made huge emotional and practical investments in their daughters' education. It seems the most important gender conflicts in the marriages of these women revolved around their daughters' education. After these daughters had completed the mandatory primary school education, the decision concerning their further education was not only about how far they should go in their schooling but also about where they should be schooled: in "normal" middle/high schools or İmam Hatip schools, where the curriculum combines courses in religious topics with regular academic subjects. For most fathers (religiously conservative or not), the İmam Hatip system offered a good educational opportunity for their daughters. However, because the İmam Hatip schools did not give students the right to enter the university system on an equal footing with the graduates of the normal high schools, the mothers fought hard not to send their daughters to İmam Hatips. It is important to point out that these mothers tried to convince fathers of this choice not on the basis of religious belief but on the basis of the limitations that an İmam Hatip education would put on their daughters.

It is very clear from the daughters' narratives that their mothers continued to be active advocates for their education and often worked hard to elicit consent from their fathers to expand the educational opportunities for them. For instance, attending private prep schools in preparation for the centralized university examination greatly enhances one's chances of obtaining a high score on this exam. If fathers were reluctant to send their daughters to prep schools for financial or other reasons, it was the mothers who convinced them otherwise. Or when it came to the choice of a regional university (in the home town or close to home) or a university in Istanbul, the mothers fought on the side of the daughters to support their decision to attend a university in Istanbul. If their daughters wanted to live on campus or in shared accommodation with their friends in order to avoid long commutes or to free themselves from parental supervision, it was again the mothers who persuaded the objecting and resisting fathers.

These high aspirations for the education of their daughters also meant a shift in the role these mothers played in the gender socialization of the daughters: they tended to relieve their daughters of the domestic tasks of cleaning, food preparation, etc., while they were growing up. Indeed, many of these young women claimed that when they came to the university, they didn't even know how to boil pasta or crack an egg.

Renouncing Parental Acquiescence

The daughters conceptualized their parents' religious experience as "empty," recurrent social practices or rituals structured by tradition in the absence of publicly taught and expressed religion, which had been eradicated by the secularization process in Turkey.[7] My narrators recall men going to mosques only on religious holidays, parents teaching their children about prayers but failing to teach them the meaning behind them, and women veiling themselves but ignoring other religious requirements. They see these empty practices as part of an unquestioning acceptance of religion, something that they contrast with their own experience of faith. According to them, this empty Islam is an inevitable consequence of Turkish modernization and secularization.

Emphasizing the habitual and automatic aspects of tradition, the young women suggest that habits and customs do not require conscious thought and therefore facilitate a relatively effortless reproduction and maintenance of a religious identity and faith. Oya's comment on religiosity in her family reflects this point well: "There is not an absence of religion in their lives [referring to her family members]—that is, they believe in the existence of God. They have this knowledge and faith, but they don't think about religion: how should we live our lives or what should our lives contain for this religion? They do not ask these questions." The women also became harsh critics of their own secular education and its noted absence of any teachings of religious knowledge. As Derya put it, "We don't know [the prophet Muhammed's] life, and we don't know him as much as we know Tolstoy or Aristotle. It is better to belong to Tolstoy's or Aristotle's religions. If you don't know your prophet, then there is a problem between what you believe and what you practice."

This cultivation of private religiosity promoted the spread of an uneducated Islam, what Ernest Gellner (1989) and Serif Mardin (2006) call "folk" or "low" Islam. On the basis of these women's understandings and experiences, it is tempting to advance a more gender-based analogy and argue that the process of relegating Islam to the private sphere has resulted in the "feminization of Islam"—its banishment to exclusively private spheres where it is ritualized as an unquestioned tradition and stripped of its charisma, dynamism, and power. However, the cultivation of a private religiosity by the secular Republic has its obedient subjects. In the daughters' narratives, the mothers and fathers come across as weak and subordinate: obedient to the secular establishment and its ideas. These women characterized their parents' generation as conformist and silent, passively integrating into a secular society and unquestioningly adopting secularism.

It seems that the daughters' characterization of their parents as obedient paralleled an oppositional stance with respect to the secular headscarf ban. As we have seen, a number of the young women I interviewed chose to don the headscarf (even though they were pious but unscarved before) in their senior year of high school or when they became university students. They explained that because they were entering a completely different social universe, they wanted to participate and forge connections from the start as pious women, instead of suddenly donning a scarf in the middle of their undergraduate years. Becoming "covered" is an important part of constructing a Muslim identity and communicating that identity to others. Fearing that their daughters would lose the hard-won opportunity to attend the most prestigious universities in Turkey, parents (both fathers and mothers) often begged their daughters not to wear the headscarves. Yasemin recounts an experience with her mother:

> When I first put a headscarf on, all hell broke loose at home. [My mother] got very angry with me. We almost reached a point where she was going to reject me as a daughter. Because according to my mother, donning a headscarf equals regressing to second-class citizenship in society . . . she said, "they will belittle you, even if you are well educated you will not be noticed, you will remain invisible."

Here, Yasemin's mother was referring to the way a headscarf is taken by many secular Turks to be a sign of backwardness and submissiveness. Similarly, after her decision to cover, Zehra's father did not talk to her for three months, lamenting, "How could you do this [referring to her insisting on going to school in a headscarf]? You have the capacity to become a doctor."

The young women heard family members say, "Don't fight with the state" (*devletle kavga etme*), "do whatever the state says," "pass as uncovered until you achieve your educational goals," and "your professors will discriminate against you, if you are covered." These clear messages and warnings from their parents represented to the women a call for obedience to secular rules, a call for the generational continuity of a culture of acquiescence. However, it would be quite superficial to understand this intergenerational drama merely in terms of conventional generational differences or the ordinary conflicts of growing up; the daughters' stance is something different from normal processes of rejecting paternal power.

My interpretation is that the daughters' narratives suggest that the parental call for obedience to the secular state has a deeper salience and emotional content for these young women, one that is not primarily about generational differentiation. Yasemin's recollection of her mother and Zehra's of her father both illustrate that the parental discourse always draws its logic and language from the dominant secular mental map, which equates covered heads with covered minds, submissiveness, tradition, and backwardness and the uncovered head with enlightment and modernity. For the daughters, then, these parental discourses express a strong form of obedience to secular ideology, one that lies deep in the structure of thought through which their parents define them.

I think that on top of these young women's recognition of how deeply parental obedience is internalized and how much their parents subscribe to the secular definition of covered girls, there is another, class-related factor that contributes to parents seeming weak and subservient in their daughters' narratives. In a sharp counterpoint to middle-class parents who are overly involved in their children's educational lives, the uneducated parents of these women lack skills and competencies in the realms of education and career, and these daughters are not able to fashion their success after their parents. As we have seen earlier, these parents have often made enormous financial sacrifices and efforts to send their daughters to the university, including, in some cases, moving the whole family to Istanbul. A deep appreciation of the sacrifice their parents made (sacrifices that ultimately widen the psychic and intellectual gulf between parent and child) and of the emotional support and encouragement they received from their parents permeated these young women's narratives. However, at the same time, their parents' low levels of education meant that they could not be a source of authority, and these women's need for parental experience and guidance, especially when making important educational decisions, was left unmet. Instead, what they constantly heard from their parents was, "You know better than us." Therefore, they often found themselves in situations in which the parents willingly submitted to their daughters' opinions and decisions. Parents' weakness in these regards made the daughters feel insecure and created a sense of having to "make it alone"—that is, the sense that they had to overcome unusual obstacles to get where they were and that they had to do it without the aid of a network of people who understood them. It seems that their feelings of aloneness in negotiating the complex and contradictory space that they occupy as upwardly mobile women reinforced these narratives of parental weakness.

A Site for New Identities: Boğaziçi and Istanbul

The vibrant cultural and intellectual student life at Boğaziçi University reflects and actively articulates the culture of urbanism and modernity that, with its ethnic and class-based diversities and sophistication, characterizes Istanbul, a metropolis of fifteen million residents. This culture offers a strong contrast to the local, insular, or provincial specificity of the origins of the majority of the narrators in this chapter. Martin Stokes observes that "Istanbul continues to emblemize modern Turkey more than anywhere or anything else. . . . It has lost none of its contradictory force as an image of the East in the West, and the West in the East" (Stokes 1994, 21). Zehra recounted how she and her father were in total awe of the Boğaziçi campus when they arrived five years earlier. She remembered her father saying, "This place is like Texas," expressing the vast contrast between Boğaziçi and any other place he knew. In order to describe her own reaction, Zehra used a different interpretive lens, one that her five years of educational and cultural experience equipped her with: "I thought, 'Wow, it is such a postmodern space,'" an expression that marked the growing distance between the way father and daughter see the world.

Boğaziçi provides a new home in which to nurture a new identity, creating the possibility of encounters between students from different places and political and moral persuasions who in other circumstances would never have met. This allows the young Muslim women I interviewed to forge social connections based on a recognition of separateness, while also searching for selective forms of sociability, intimacy, and safe encounters with their secular Muslim counterparts. Only in a setting like Boğaziçi can these women occupy the kind of physical and discursive spaces that they need in order to build (and communicate to others) an identity that is centered on values of openness, liberalism, and a tolerant acceptance of diversity and heterogeneity. Mahrem explains, in response to me asking if she ever considered dropping out when the university enforced the headscarf ban,

> I wanted to be here because I wish to do things to beautify this world, not just because for the sake of getting educated. . . . I want to be here with my thoughts, even without my headscarf. . . . In order for people to see

whether I am prejudiced or not, I needed to be here. If I am a person who prays five times a day, I can be friends with those who do not. We can share the same social milieu and be friends within a framework of love and respect. I wanted to show people this possibility.

Similarly, Adalet, who employed the analogy of there being many colors and shades of color and who defines herself as one of the colors, said, "If we don't want sameness, we need these differences." She illustrated Mahrem's point above more concretely when she talked about how her *iftar* dinner (the fast-breaking dinner in Ramadan) included secular friends:

If you accept someone with her/his identity and she/he accepts you, then whatever commonality that brings you together creates a unity. . . . When you start knowing that person, you start understanding, and you understand there is nothing to be afraid of, and a while later when you start realizing that there are things you can learn from this person, there can be a mutual interaction.

When I asked Zerrin (21) whether religiously devoted people and secularists would be able to live together, she introduced the concept of ghettoization into the conversation:

I am totally against the ghettoization of Muslims. What does ghetto mean? Ontologically, it means because you feel insecure, you would like to be with those who are like you, with those who would not question you, and not challenge you. For this reason you would like to be always surrounded by people like that. You close and isolate yourself. However, I don't think there is any reason why Muslims should lack confidence or feel insecure.

As these quotations demonstrate, these women pursue their religious identities in relation to and as part of a wider value for a collective of differences. Thus, the differences embodied in this university setting present these women with a wider framework and horizon in which to interpret and validate the new pious identity as they transcend different group boundaries and experience inclusion or/and exclusion. For these young women, attending Boğaziçi University, and living in the larger context of Istanbul, was vital to the formation of their new selves.

The "Feminist Vein" Within

The young women I interviewed did not engage with any organized feminist groups, except for having a few secular feminist friends. However, most identified what they called a "feminist vein" (*damar*) in themselves, and it is through this vocabulary of feminism that they perceive and understand their gender consciousness. More importantly, it is also through this vein that they reject the selflessness of their mothers' generation and develop a critique of the masculine understanding and interpretation of gender relations in Islam.

It appears, then, that these young women, like their counterparts in many other national contexts, embrace feminist ideas and possess gender consciousness but refuse to take on the label of "feminist." Some feminist scholars describe this contradiction as the central "paradox" of contemporary feminism (Misciagno 1997). However, if we consider the definition(s) of feminism in the local and historical contexts of countries such as Turkey, where feminist movements have to struggle to carve out an independent political space vis-à-vis other political movements as well as against (or with) state feminism (Sirman 1989), then what feminism represents, who represents it, and how it is represented become significant questions, rendering it difficult to explain these women's relationship with feminism merely as a contradiction or a paradox.[8]

These young women's responses to feminism are structured by their perception of feminism in Turkey and occur against the backdrop of issues of compatibility with Islam. Their understanding of feminism in Turkey is quite plural, but not in the sense of identifying different political orientations within feminism. Rather, they put feminism and feminists on a continuum. As Oya puts it, "Feminism . . . [is] a huge spread like a fan" (*geniş yelpaze*), ranging from feminism that protects women's rights to feminism that is "against men." Those who disapproved of feminism (despite their feminist vein) did so sharply on the basis of a definition of feminism that, to them, meant "the annihilation of the male race" (Adalet) or "women's egoism" (Alanur), which they considered to represent the extreme end of this feminist "fan."

In fact, any feminist stream or discourse that implies a call for female dominance over men and/or rejects the family as the foundational unit of social order can never be part of these women's feminist vocabulary. They have no use for such an interpretation of feminism, as it is neither relevant to nor compatible with the Islamic social order, which is founded on complementary gender roles and the family—the only institution within which women's sexuality can rightly be expressed and their sanctified role, motherhood, realized. The idea that women and men are created to complement each other is sacred in the Durkheimian sense of the term. It is inviolate—cannot be modified or revised in the light of any new reading or new interpretation of Islam.

The following fragments from Aknur and Adalet illustrate why feminism is merely a vein in these women's thinking and why a complete embrace of feminism is not possible for them:

> If I am going to defend women's rights, I should do it from within my Islamic identity. I don't want to take feminism and subsume it under Islam. I know from an outsider's perspective when I defend women's rights I am called feminist. . . . If women are oppressed and they are oppressed, their rights too should be defended. (Aknur)

> I completely agree with feminists for their advocacy of women's rights and on many other important issues they tackle. . . . As I mentioned before, in fact, a good Muslim woman would not need to have a separate banner of feminism; had we lived in a good Islamic society we wouldn't need feminism. Islam gave Muslim women certain rights, if we live it the right way. (Adalet)

The excessive and repeated reference to "women's rights" in their discourses is not accidental: men are not given any rights by God to determine, dispose of, or withhold rights from women—it is God, not men, who determines a woman's rights and duties. An educated reading of Islam, they argue, reveals radically the depth and breadth of women's rights contained within it. They refer, for example, to a woman's right not to breast-feed; not to do housework; to have the power to dispose of her property; to be able to trade and not have to give a share to her husband; and not to allow her husband to use her money if she doesn't want him to. Therefore, according to them, Islam already contains gender equity.[9] In their discourse, they also imply that defending rights is already consistent with elements of their Islamic identity.

How, then, do we understand these young women's claim to a feminist vein within themselves? The vein as a symbol of the nature of their feminist sensibilities seems especially fitting when we consider that these young women first and foremost define themselves as Muslim and have adopted an externalization of that religious identity with the headscarf. Veins, on the other hand, lie below the surface—yet are not entirely invisible either. The feminist vein evident in the testimonies of these women surfaces and asserts itself in their subtle opposition to their own mothers' acquiescence to patriarchal marriages, but also to the hegemonic Muslim male identity they see represented by their male peers. These feminist impulses, imagined as veins flowing from within, are claimed by the women not only to label and reject their disadvantages and vulnerabilities in the face of male privilege but also to articulate alternative identities as pious women.

Mothers without Selves

It is through their personal experiences of the gender dynamics in their families that these women developed a critique of male exploitation of Islamic principles. This connection is especially clearly expressed in Adalet's narrative about her father, a close model of the authoritarian Muslim man:

> For years, my father committed this mistake: he made every decision, every move on the basis of religious values. For instance, it sounds extraordinary to everyone when I say this: my mother had been at home for twenty years, she never went outside. It was forbidden to her—my father didn't want her to and he justified this as forbidden [haram]. [He said,] "Strange men shouldn't see you," but it was completely an individual desire on his part.

Adalet's father is an exceptional case. More importantly, not only are fathers identified as a problem, but mothers are also criticized for their conservative gender ideology. Canan offers an illustration of her mother's perspective: "For example, she thinks that in mixed-gender company, women should not talk too much, and a woman should not play soccer, girls shouldn't play soccer or ride a bicycle. She thinks that it is not a normal thing for a woman to ride a bicycle. She gives tremendous importance to what other people would think." My analysis of the daughters' narratives about their parents and their marriages suggests that the daughters are more interested in questioning and critiquing their mothers' subjectivities (as we will see shortly, due to the pivotal role of motherhood) than in merely criticizing an abstract, all-encompassing Islamic patriarchy.

These women all see their mothers in the same way: as the selfless female devoid of the subjective experience of an independent self separate from her status as mother and wife:

> My mother doesn't have a life of her own, a life in which she can be herself [her own person] . . . everything she experiences contains children. . . . If I married and had children, I would like to keep a small life within it that just belongs to me. (Akalin)

> When I look at [my mother], she doesn't have a life of her own. She becomes happy when she does something for our home or for us children, not for herself. It is the same thing for her. (Alanur)

However, it is not only this quality of selflessness that defines their mothers and renders them undesirable models of womanhood. It is also the way this form of womanhood subjectively experiences the wifehood—as compliance and submission to the husband's power and authority—that makes it subject to criticism. The following quotations from Yasemin and Ceda elucidate this point well:

> In my family, whatever my father's wishes are, they happen. My mother submits to my father's wishes. . . . Everything is done with my father's permission. When he does not permit, it doesn't happen. (Yasemin)

> [My mother] gives great importance to whatever my father says—that is, by definition a woman should always be on the side of her husband, support him and his decisions regardless of the content of his decision. . . .

My mother is always like this: if my father makes a point he must have a good reasoning. She always showed us things like this. (Ceda)

This twin rejection of the selflessness of the mothers' generation and the mothers' acquiescence to the power of their husbands is pivotal in fashioning the religious and gender identity of these young women. Without ambivalence, these women rejected the model of the "selfless feminine" represented by their mothers as a model for their own self-making, not only because it represents the restriction of women to the roles of wife, mother, and homemaker and thus the subordination of one's needs to the needs of others but also because it represents the way women live by others' (fathers and husbands) choices and are left with no selfish selves with which to desire or create. This understanding of selflessness perhaps explains the resentment of the mother model.

However, these women also approach this model with a mixture of gratitude and awe. On the one hand, their mothers' collusion in their own subordination emotionally disappoints these women, even though they know the impossibility of their mothers escaping from their conditions of existence. On the other hand, the mothers' strength and resilience in raising educated children, like them, under intolerable gender and class conditions with material deprivations in what these women consider troubled marriages inspire awe in them. Paradoxically, then, the mother model also reveals itself as profoundly seductive, a force capable of creating anxieties in the process of dis-identification. As a model embodied and enacted by their mothers, it is at once a source of profound gratitude and a high standard deserving of emulation. Indeed, many of them expressed the fear that they might not be strong like their mothers. They know that they have to draw or have already drawn upon the resources of this female tradition of endurance. Even though it did not surface clearly in their narratives, they must also recognize that raising educated daughters and preparing them for very different lives of their own might have given their mothers a feeling of power and a sense of agency and of personal efficacy that they don't get anywhere else. Also, while they don't see themselves identifying with the silent mother (*suskun anne*), they see their mothers as the ones who understand their selves the most. The most telling detail in this regard came in addressing my question, "If your mother chooses someone for you, would that per-

NEW PIOUS FEMALE SELVES | 201

son also be the person you chose for yourself?" With a few exceptions, all the participants gave affirmative responses, stating that their mothers knew them best.

This gendered generational ambivalence is very much shared by these women's secular sisters. But unlike their secular sisters, who, as we saw in the previous chapters, claim sexual freedom and develop an antipathy toward marriage and maternity, these women's quest cannot be one for an individualized sense of self and sexual self-determination and autonomy. Before exploring this issue in detail, we first need to see how these women employ the vocabulary of their feminist vein in rejecting the hegemonic Muslim male identity.

Rejecting the Hegemonic Muslim Male Identity

More than a decade ago, scholars such as Göle (1996, 2000) and Ilyasoglu (1998) argued that a comprehensive understanding of Islamist politics and religion during the Islamic mobilization of the 1990s not only enabled Islamist women to question their prescribed roles as mother and wife but also allowed some of these women to reject the "moralizing definition of woman in Islam" and the "pseudo protection of women" as constructs that reassure men and confine women to the private sphere (Göle 2000, 100–101). Göle claims that these Islamist women's identification of Muslim men as part of the problem and their consequent demand for independence creates a truly radical cleavage between women who unquestioningly acquiesce and those who fashion new, unique self-definitions not recognized by holistic Islam (101). My narrators not only expand the parameters of marking out the problem with the hegemonic Muslim male identity but also, as we will see in the next section, imagine, construct, and elaborate on an ideal Muslim man.

Since women construct their selves under the pressures of a secular society and since their life strategies, unlike those of their male peers, are subject to interventions by secular outsiders, they, not Muslim men, bear the burden of representing Islamic identity. The active appropriation and presentation of religiosity in the public sphere is achieved through them. They point out that it is their headscarf that transmits the religiosity and social difference, while discrediting and excluding them from many educational and professional opportunities. Muslim men, however, don't have to clearly assert their religious difference in the public sphere. The young women I interviewed found this unfair. For example, Alanur explained, "I am really angry in this regard because a man, a religious man, also has a lot of restrictions on him—should have restrictions, yet, in terms of his appearance there is nothing to make him different. Therefore, I think, they have it easy." Moreover, the women insist that Muslim men take advantage of their vulnerable position and use secular restrictions as an opportunity to confine women to the domestic sphere and exploit their labor. The following testimony from Canan strongly voices this concern:

> [Muslim men] use [secular restrictions on Muslim women] as an advantage for themselves. For instance, because she does not wish to be uncovered, she is not going to be able to work outside; she will be used to labor for men at home. Muslim men are appropriating the absence of many employment opportunities for Muslim women as an advantage for themselves, but it shouldn't be this way. Men don't have any right to use this.

These women identify the lack of male self-reflection on their identities and roles as Muslim men as the biggest problem. They insist that men should conform to the same religious obligations as women and that Islam should be defined equally through the prism of male Muslim identity as it is through the prism of female Muslim identity:

> Men, Muslim men, are overly defining women; they are constructing their religiosity over their wives, daughters, sisters, and other Muslim women. . . . However, how a husband should behave towards his wife, or what a man really does for the purpose of getting closer to God, and how far he works on himself are also very important things. These matters should be foregrounded to define himself rather than how much power he establishes over his wife. (Aknur)

I suggest that this intense interest in rethinking the Muslim male identity is intimately related to one of these women's central life strategies: desiring to become "mothers with selves" in their future marriages. For them, the shift from a female Muslim identity domestically enclosed to an identity bound up in the public sphere demands a life partner who is equally committed to creating a Muslim male identity that is compatible with aspects of secular modernity and plurality of identities. The following quotation from Yasemin exemplifies this shared concern:

> Muslim men want to marry high school graduates, not too-knowledgeable ones, so that they can oppress them. They still see women as second-class citizens. For instance, the first thing they would inquire [about a woman] is, "is she a good cook?"—it is not what we are going to share: for instance, do we read the same books? It is not that.

Their unique position allows them to renounce the patriarchy embedded in uneducated Islam, but it also creates an important gender cleavage between them and many of their Muslim male peers, their potential marriage partners. In other words, from the perspective of upwardly mobile Muslim women, Muslim men and women have different answers to the pivotal question of how one should live in keeping with an Islamic way of life in a secular society.

Dangers of Aşk (Passionate Love)

Islam prohibits the exercise of certain activities, one of which is mixing of the sexes—stranger sociability with men. Thus, the practice of actively disengaging with stranger men in gesture, demeanor, and bodily conduct is thought essential to a fully pious female existence. In this regard, marriage assumes crucial importance as the only (religiously) legitimate locus within which intimacy with men can be realized and women's sexuality expressed. Also, it is especially in the arena of socializing with stranger men that pious selves mark their distance from secularly Muslim counterparts who, as we saw in chapter 2, express desire for embodied sexuality and strive to carve out a new female identity in Turkish society as nonvirgin unmarried women between girlhood and womanhood. The university years for both groups of women (pious and secular) reflect the liminality of their independence, constituting a time during which they realize their intellectual odysseys. As a marker of significant difference in orientation, the domain of romance, love, and sex gives different shapes and directions to pious and secular women's liminality. Because of pious women's ontological commitment to marriage, emotional and affective processes of mate selection and marriage form a core terrain of identity making—from their perspective, a terrain in need of transformation. In other words, they, more than any other group of young Turkish women, have high stakes in redesigning the meaning of marriage and the relationships within it. The narratives of *aşk*, love, and the ideal mate that I explore in this section crystallize the dilemmas they deal with, in particular the threat posed by falling in love. The definition of the ideal pious man also comes forward with more clarity in these narratives.

As we saw in earlier chapters, young Turks' discursive and experiential repertoires in the realm of romance and sex make a distinction between *sevgi* (love) and *aşk* (passionate love), each fulfilling different needs as well as having a varied relationship to sexual desire. My narrators in this chapter also agreed on the division between *aşk* and *sevgi*, but their narratives contained greater elaboration and clarity about separating *sevgi* from *aşk* and the relationship between the two. Formulations of *aşk* and *sevgi* common to all separated the two on the dimension of attainability and unattainability. *Aşk* is a fantasy, imaginary, and antisocial whereas *sevgi* is real and social. Canan, who doesn't believe in the realization of *aşk*, defined *aşk* as a feeling "engendered by the impossibility of attainment." Referring to her own *aşk* experience in high school, she suggested that "had I attained that person—thought that he was mine, it was going to end. There was going to be nothing remaining." But to her, *sevgi* for family and friends has an enduring quality: "With your love for them, you attain your family and friends, but still the feelings you have for them are unending." Claiming that her definition of *aşk* echoed Lacan's notion of fantasy, Aknur drew the contrast in this way:

> Love is two people being in mutual sync [bond] with each other in order to support each other—the name of this is love. . . . But for me *aşk* is about attachment to a fantastic object: it can be a platonic ideal, and you can be in *aşk* without really knowing that person. *Aşk* is realized through attributing exalted qualities to a person or an object.

Aknur believes that in our inner worlds, we have a quest for perfection and we desire to find this perfection in somebody else or in an object. Searching to fulfill the desire for perfection residing inside of us makes *aşk* an obsession (*tutku*) for "a fetishized object." Although Aknur has enjoyed "loading people and objects with meanings" since she was a little girl and "relish[es] to live life with romanticizing it, living it like a movie," she thinks that one cannot escape from obsession "as long as that object of desire remains undestroyed—until you start realizing that he lacks perfection." Oya experienced *aşk* with one of her teachers but "lived it inside of" her, as she lives other powerful things inside of her. She described it as feeling as though she "cannot live without this person":

> In this life what we desire most is tranquillity. Even when you feel un-happy and uneasy when you are with that person but still want to be with that person, then I think you are in love. Also, admiring that person's qualities, not being able to see his bad qualities even after a certain period of time, I think it is *aşk*.

Yasemin, who also lived all of her *aşks* inside of her, defined *aşk* as follows: "You see from other people and start thinking that this is a need, there must be this need for me too. By thinking that I must be also in love, you attribute *aşk* to someone who fits your criteria." This disasso-ciation of *aşk* from an embodied person is echoed in Ceda's definition. After being rejected by a man she was in love with for three years, Ceda discovered that "depending on the person you fall in love with, the qual-ity and meaning of *aşk* also changes." She offered the comparison: "In my first *aşk*, I felt disconnected/ruptured from life. . . . I felt locked, ob-sessed, as if I was glued to something that I could not move away from. Now I feel inside of me butterflies and birds flying, I am feeling very positive but I am not defining this as *aşk* yet." She elaborated further and quoted lyrics from a poem by Özer Bal:

> The source of the intensity of emotions I experienced was not about him but was rooted in/emerged from the nature of *aşk*. Of course there is some connection, there is something in him that awakens things in you. But on the other hand, the capacity to live/experience that *aşk* belongs to me:
>
> > The meanings I give to you
> > Don't think they are you

> You will be deceived
> You with those meanings
> Only exist in me
> If I am in love
> You are only an excuse [pretext].[10]

Despite its disappointments, *aşk* both breaks one's relationship with reality and activates pleasurable emotions that are unnoticed and unused in daily life, and thus these women admitted that falling in love played a critical role in enriching selfhood.

In Aknur's and others' formulations, love is a derivative of *aşk* because after the person is attained, "*aşk* is transformed into a strong love and that is much healthier." According to Aknur, love is healthy because it is something that "sustains and makes practical life easier." Adalet, who obtained her object of desire, was the only one who disagreed about the transient essence of *aşk*: "*Aşk*, as long as you don't put any inhibitions on its expressions, *aşk* inside of you does not die. Indeed, provided that spark is inside of you, that excitement is not constrained/oppressed, it continues to continuously glow." And in her concrete illustration, she clearly tied an enduring *aşk* to the enactment of sexual desire. Speaking of her relationship with her husband, she said, "Even if we are outside, if I desire to embrace and kiss him, I do it. I don't like to restrain things that arise from within me, I want to act like what is coming from inside; he is also like me." It is important to note that for this group of women, *sevgi* is also a powerful force emanating from within but with an altruistic purpose: to create good in the lives of others. In this regard, the enduring quality attached to love is related to an ethics of care. While *aşk* is antisocial, love, in contrast, is social—it is the glue that binds individuals together and makes life easier through meeting collective obligations of care.

Because as a fantasy *aşk* resides in the realm of the most inner self, encouraged by freedom of imagination where, it is presumed, moral predicates cannot be applied, it blinds us. *Aşk* is dangerous: one can easily fall prey to a temptation to compliance. As Canan puts it, "It is such a different feeling, you don't think anything else; everything, all your principles could be destroyed, the values you believe in up to that point can get contradicted with each other." What makes *aşk* dangerous is its destructive capacity in disempowering reason, leading one to go to undesired places and relationships. *Aşk* should be disciplined. Bringing in religion as her main narrative resource, Sultan emphasized that

> in religion, there is the idea of disciplining of the cravings of the flesh [*nefis terbiyesi*]. The cravings of the flesh should be restrained; you have to strengthen your will [*irade*] not to obey/give in to everything your flesh [self, essence] wants: self can interpret everything as cravings. Using your reason—studying and interrogating—allows you to question your desires.

Concretely, for these women, the danger of *aşk* lies in its power to derail their educational plans and professional aspirations, inviting a dangerous anticipation of the broken promise of education. The dangers of *aşk* assumed more poignancy for them, because when it happens, when it is enacted, it needs to be carried to marriage. Acting on the feelings of *aşk* competes with their real object of desire: education.

How did these women discipline *aşk* or, alternatively, fail to do so? At an early age, Aknur was determined to shield herself against *aşk* long enough to ensure the attainment of educational sucess and to avoid it resulting in an early marriage, resolving in her mind,

> I shouldn't fall in love and have a relationship with a man until I reach a certain age. [Because] when it happens, the ideal situation is to transform [carry] that love/relationship to a marriage. If something like this had happened in high school years, I couldn't take it to marriage, and therefore, falling in love was not a desirable thing.

But at eighteen, despite this firm resolve, Aknur fell in love. She explained, "I tried to develop a cold behavior towards the person I fell in love with, I tried to avoid communication and attachment." However, against the force of considerable determination to keep her *aşk* residing in her imagination, she became consumed with love for this man. I asked her if he knew her feelings. She said, "Yes, because I couldn't carry it inside of me," attributing her weakness to her eighteen-year-old self. Importantly, Aknur acknowledged that her avoidance of a connection with this man was also about preserving her fantasy of him: "Because the more I knew him better, the more the persona I constructed in my mind would be destroyed/spoiled. In order not to disturb that persona, I did not approach him too much." At the same time, she imagined that "he would understand my *aşk* for him without me approaching him." "But," she admitted, "I learned that men are not like that."

Sultan's (21) analysis of her experiences with a man she saw for two months (whom she called her boyfriend in her narrative) powerfully captures the way the desires of different forces—family, education, and religion—are at play in these women's lives. As Sultan described it, she experienced neither *aşk* nor *sevgi*; what she felt toward this man was *hoşlanma* (liking), the mildest emotion in the pecking order of *aşk*, *sevgi*, and *hoşlanma*: "When I first felt an awakening [*kıpırdanma*] of love I gravitated towards him. It would have never happened, had I said no outright, but I never said I love you, etc., either; there was always a boundary between us, but we desired each other." She broke up with this man after reading two verses of the Koran at a time when she was uneasily pondering whether or not to continue the relationship. She explained her dilemma: "There [was] no real attachment, only liking. On the other hand, I wanted to continue because I desired the experience of a high-quality *aşk* and *sevgi* so to speak." Her pondering became intense when her boyfriend openly declared his love and said he wanted a response from her. Interestingly enough, the first note of discord also emerged at this time: "Our first quarrel was about my going home during weekends. He said, 'you never allocate any time for me.' I was like, what he is talking about? We just started seeing each other. He was already being resentful/touchy [*alıngan*]. I had to make a decision."

The decision Sultan refers to was not just about whether or not to break up with this particular man, but about whether to stay in that space of exploring her feelings and desires. She said she asked herself, "What [is] going to be my criterion in making this decision?" She talked with her younger brother, with whom she was very close intellectually and emotionally (a contrast to her older brothers, who exerted authority over her, even placing a curfew on her when she went to her home town, in spite of her objections that she was twenty-one years old and lived in Istanbul). She and her younger brother "both agreed that [they found] it unacceptable when girls had relationships, but on the basis of what? On the basis of custom and tradition, not on the basis of a principled criterion." They went back to verses of the Koran. "The verse we consulted did not state that this is certainly something you should not do, but it said it should not be conducted clandestinely [*gizli kapaklı*]. It said don't do it clandestinely." Adopting this criterion, she ended the relationship, knowing that if she revealed her relationship to her family, they would insist on her taking it to marriage. To her, the dilemma she faced was between a romance inevitably resulting in a path to marriage and the continuation of her education:

> Had I continued, my family [her father, mother, and two older brothers] was not going to know, I couldn't tell them. It was going to be clandestine. I was losing in that regard. Had I disclosed to my family, "I have a boyfriend," they were going to say, "*let sözleyelim*" [enact an oral agreement between the two families constituting a binding promise to wed].

Sözlemek makes a relationship public, unclandestine. However, this was not an option for Sultan, since it meant a commitment to marriage: "I am only in my first year of college, I have dreams of postgraduate education, and he would prevent me from continuing because he wanted to get us married immediately." However, she did not reveal her reasoning to her boyfriend:

> Had we married, he wouldn't have permitted me to continue my education. Had I given him this reason, he couldn't possibly understand, and he would have tried to find alternatives. No, he would have definitely prevented me continuining my education. In order to be able to study [in a university] I went through too many hurdles. I couldn't allow him.

Despite this expression of her strong determination to choose education over romance, Sultan invoked and pondered the crucial question of the power of *aşk*: "Perhaps I could have found a solution, had I really loved him."

The story of Adalet's marriage is what others in this chapter desired not to happen, but with a happy ending. Married at the age of eighteen, Adalet, married for three years at the time of my interview, met her husband through e-mail in their last semester of high school. What seemed to be a school-related e-mail correspondence about an extracurricular cultural event turned more personal. When they met face to face for the very first time, he proposed marriage. Adalet quoted her husband: "As far as I can tell from your appearance and what I know about you, I cannot invite you to flirt with me or suggest that we should go out, but I want to see you and I don't wish to lose you, therefore, I propose to marry you."

Adalet's desciption of how she fell in love with her husband invoked the Islamic framework of inadmissibility of stranger sociability and how her feelings for him allowed her to trangress it:

> With Islamic sensitiveness, when you talk with a man face to face you inevitably feel an uncomfortabless inside of you. . . . But when I first saw him I did not feel any fear. On the contrary, I felt such a different sense of warmness and trust towards him, as if I have known him for years. I didn't find him unfamilir [*yabancı*]; I didn't regard him as a strange man. It is a peculiar thing, but for me in the first instance he was such a man [familiar-seeming man]. After that nothing had any significance.

Adalet offered the following description of *aşk*: "You don't feel the need to inquire what it is behind this, you only love, you only want to be with this person all the time and to marry him and to spend a life together." Her father approached her relationship warmly and said he would give her hand if she wanted to marry. In contrast, Adalet's mother worked very hard to prevent her daughter's marriage:

> Because I was so young, she feared that I wasn't capable of making the right decision. My mother realized that I fell in love with him, but also she knew my dreams—my university education, my desire for postgraduate education. She was afraid that I was going to give up on all my dreams, if I got married. I wouldn't be able to realize all these; she thought that a lot of aspirations would remain unrealized. Also, she worried that I might have chosen the wrong person, because she herself suffered so much in her own marriage. But I always told her, "I am not going to make a marriage of logic" [referencing her mother's "logical marriage" to escape from her own family of origin]. I prefer a love marriage, because when you are in love, it is easier to accept certain things.

As Adalet recounted, her husband's father also raised objections to the prospect of his son's early marriage, but her husband convinced his father, arguing that in recent years he had developed tendencies toward living a consciously Muslim life, and that because Adalet was a covered girl she would help him to realize his religious aspirations. After their engagement, they planned to wait for four years to complete their respective educations before getting married. But because of some problems in his family, he had to drop out of school, and they ended up getting married.

Scenes from Adalet's happy marriage included her biking on weekend mornings while her husband ran by her side, intensely sharing ideas instead of watching TV at night, cuddling up with their books and reciting poems to each other, him helping her with her papers by translating English words and typing up her papers on the computer, and sharing the burdens and pleasures of cooking. But the most important component of this happy marriage for her was how her husband enabled her educational success: "I wouldn't be able to continue my education without him." Happiness also materialized in their major decisions, how they decided to give priority to Adalet's education and postpone having children until they both finished college. Her husband seemed to personify the archetype of the Muslim man narrated in the next section: "He reads more than me"; "He is open to change: he stopped giving hugs and kisses to his old female friends"; "If we happen to attend to each of our own preoccupations after we come home, we terribly feel the lack of our interaction."

Hermeneutic Curiosity: Defining the Ideal Muslim Man

These women's definitions of the ideal man differ in some respects and in emphasis, but their accounts converge in many important ways. By definition, the ideal man with whom they would like to build a life is one who is committed to living by Islamic norms:

> For me [his commitment to Islamic norms] is an essential criterion both in terms of his life ideals and his ideals in relation to our creator. That is, someone who will want to walk on the same road, and we will support each other on this life road and in realizing our religious ideals. (Aknur)

I am basing my life on Islamic norms. According to those norms I am either limiting my behaviors or transgressing certain things. I want him to also take Islam as a core and revolve himself around that center. I would expect him and his actions equally to follow the way I live and the restrictions I observe. (Canan)

First, he should live his life by Islamic norms. This doesn't mean that he has to fast outside the Ramadan, go to mosque every day, never miss *namaz* or memorize the Koran. He has to have the fear of God, he should possess consciousness of God—there is God and he created me and I am afraid of God. He has to have this consciousness. (Sultan)

As hinted at by the quotation above from Sultan, the parameters of the profile of a religious man who lives by Islamic norms are not drawn only by religious devotion. A gift for imagining and reasoning is a central dimension of the ideal man for this group of women. Described in strikingly similar words by the women, this ideal man sees things from other points of view, enters imaginatively into what he first takes to be undesirable, adopts a caring and respectful attitude toward others who represent difference from him, shows genuine interest in the reality of others, and possesses both desire and motivation to recognize others.

Aknur's detailed description below encapsulates richly a permutation of these desired characteristics and how and why they should be combined:

I want someone who is really good in human relationships, possessed of a high emotional IQ, and with a powerful capacity for empathy. This is very important to me: understanding other people and giving them value and respect. . . . Not the type of person who has the stance that "I solved life and there is nothing new I need to learn." He should be someone always open to learning new things and to accepting the fact that there are always going to be things that he doesn't know, he can't comprehend or understand. That is, when he hears or encounters difference or a different thing, he should be able to say, "Yes, this could be also possible." He should keep this possibility in a corner of his head. That is, instead of believing that he solved the meaning of life and the right road

people should walk on, he should consider the possibility that there can
be different alternatives and these alternatives can offer truths better fitting one's circumstances. He should be someone open to different truths.

Curiosity about difference defined the essence of the ideal man for
Canan as well. Canan's image of this ideal has its roots in her own curiosity about different people and lives:

> I don't have any curiosity or love toward people that live like other people.
> But I am curious about people with longings to be different, about those
> who want to have a different lifestyle. For instance, in my culture of up-
> bringing, a man who grows long hair is viewed as very abnormal and
> unacceptable, but I had longing for these things, or I was curious about
> this type of person the most. I wanted to communicate and relate to this
> type of person. The person I fall in love with should be like that. . . . In my
> high school years, I imagined him long-haired and sporting an earring,
> etc., but [on campus] there are too many non-normals.

In her further elaboration of the man she desired to fall in love with, a
replica of herself, a self marked by the experience of change, emerged:
"He should be someone who has experienced great changes in his life
and transformations in his thought structure—change from one thought
structure to another one. I would be curious about such a man—what
changed him?" Alanur's definition of her ideal man is also a man of
curiosity: "Someone who is curious about learning new things . . . neither combative/embittered [hırçın] nor dull/inanimate [sönük]." Oya
also wants a man who is "versatile [çok yönlü], like [her], someone who
would like to discover new things, and vibrant," suggesting that it is
important to ask, "How would one marry someone and live with that
person for forty–fifty years?"

The man Sultan wants to build a life with would also possess a character endowed with curiosity. Like the others', her description emphasized that the core virtues associated with this type of man can only
be found in an educational equivalent who has an interesting mind, is
endowed with a cosmopolitan education, values the aesthetic dimension
of life, and speaks English:

If he doesn't speak English, then I am not going to express myself comfortably. . . . I don't like this kind of limitation. . . . He should be someone with high ethics and morality, or strives to construct and live an ethical life. Not to say that he should be perfect; nobody is perfect. His possession of knowledge—I don't mean only religious knowledge—is also essential. He has to be curious about different things, such as philosophy and history. . . . I will be a college graduate; he could be someone engaged in a trade, that is not the problem, but he must be someone who would read and be cultured. Imagine this profile: he is wealthly because of what he does or is an inheritor of money but uneducated—a high school graduate. What I am going to talk about with such a spouse? "Oh, honey," etc. [cicim] at the beginning is nice, but it has its limits. We should be able to engage in intense debates. Like, in solving a mathematical problem he should be able to challenge me: "That is not the correct way to solve this problem." And he should show genuine interest in my areas of interests.

It is not surprising, of course, that love also comes into play with respect to the image of the desirable man. Oya's statement, "I want him to love me to death and I should love him equally," sums up the way they all stressed the importance of mutual love. Love is the essential key to a man understanding the value of a woman, that "a woman has desires and needs of her own" (Yasemin). Because only a man who loves her would be able to recognize this value of a woman, the emotional contribution of a man to a woman's growth is realized through the medium of love. His love spoils her, bolsters her confidence, incites her growth, and supports her in pursuing desires and needs of her own.

I also asked these women to describe the qualities embodied in what they considered an undesirable man. When discussing the qualities associated with an undesired profile, as opposed to the ideal man, they drew upon more real-life examples of peers, brothers, and other male relatives or men they see around themselves. These descriptions also exposed how the ideal man is articulated against men who enact and display lower-class, nonurban, sexist masculine gestures. Citing the model of a man who dominates a conversation, who after exiting the mosque after a Friday prayer gazes at women in the street, who constantly plays with and displays his prayer beads (tesbih sallamak), and who dons nothing but pants made of fabric (*kumaş pantolon*, as opposed to jeans or khakis, signaling stagnation, traditionalism, and a rural background), they profiled unwanted dimensions of masculinity. Different emphases depended, in part, on whether they reflected on class dimensions, but overall the gendered and sexual inequality produced and enforced by traditional masculinity defined the contours of the undesired male profile for these women.

Ceda was very vocal in expressing her class-based preferences, referring to class habitus: "The extreme peasant look/appearance repulses me. He could be a nice person but he could not be the person I carry with me and call my boyfriend. I am also, of course, including conversation style, etc. As a woman I can intervene with his appearance. But his interactive style is very important." She elaborated on what she meant by interactive style, an inherited lower-class disposition: "The type of man who is troubled if a woman knows more than him . . . you knowing a bit more than him would irritate him, that kind of man—he tries to answer you and if he can't, he would try another thing. . . . I never like this type of man." Similarly, a "self-centered man in every aspect" defined the profile of an undesirable man for Yasemin. She said, "I look at the sentences he composes. The one who starts his every sentence with 'I,' I consider such a man repulsive [*itici*] and egoist." Derya deployed an interesting analogy when describing the characteristics of a man that she finds very unattractive: "A man who uses his wife like a purse to be opened when he needs to use it, and if he doesn't need it, he keeps it closed by his side." Ayşe defined such a person as "a man without will power: who looks at every woman and goes after every woman . . . a man with a lot of dialogue with girls."

The description of the ideal man intersects contradictorily in several important ways with the way these women see that God created men. Men are created by God, so to speak, more crudely, lacking in finesse and compassion. Therefore, the materialization of this ideal manhood is clearly contingent on men working on themselves. In other words, these women place the labor of (re)making masculinity on men: they need to produce themselves as tolerant, open to change, gentlemanly (*kibar*), and refined. They should be willing to vacate the position of male privilege, displayed in terms of unearned authority and inflexibility to the formation of new values.

I suggest that the visionary impulse that animates these women's definitions of the ideal man bespeaks the ideal man at once concretely (for themselves) and abstractly (for the formation of new values for pious living in a society characterized by plurality). The quality that was most seriously desired and that formed this archetype of the ideal man was the ability to align his own personal identity with his claims to be a Muslim man. The overarching principle, perhaps we can call it a foundational value, is the embrace of hermeneutic curiosity, the possession of a motivating desire to search for different truths.

Corporeal Compatibility

In these descriptions of the ideal man, the significance or insignificance of sexual compatibility in marriage, for the most part, was not addressed head-on, except by Derya and Yasemin. I addressed and explored this question with all of the women through a Turkish idiom of "corporeal compatibility" (*tensel uyum*), a notion pertaining to whether two individuals are capable of connecting with one another sexually. In addition to examining whether this corporeal compatibility indeed forms a significant dimension of marriage for the young women, another related and crucial question for me was their experiences in this realm—whether or not they explore this dimension of compatibility and how. So I also used our conversation on this topic to explore the ideals and practices regarding what might be described as "courtship," the overture to marriage, a transitional period during which partners are expected to explore their compatibility. How do they define and draw the boundaries of opportunities for and limitations on courting possibilities, such as those for being alone together and for physical intimacy, like holding and touching? Is corporeal intimacy excluded or included in courtship? Are physical intimacies explored and experimented with?

Derya referred to the incredible thrill and excitement she felt in the presence of the young man she was in love with in high school. His mere presence produced in her a vibrating tremor throughout her body: "My hands and legs were shaking." She described it as a state of being that she had never experienced before. For such a thrill to be felt by her sensually, she said, "He didn't need to touch me. We didn't need to touch each other." For Derya, the production of this same feeling became essential for her mate selection: "If I don't feel a similar thrill with the man I am about to marry, I won't marry. I will wait for the one who affects me with the same excitement and thrill."

Yasemin described the significance of corporeal compatibility by recounting a recent conversation she had had with a close friend who disclosed to Yasemin that she had fallen in love with a man and that they were very much in sync. Yasemin quizzed her friend: "But I asked her: 'can you see this man as your spouse [eş]? By spouse I meant *tensel uyum*, 'corporeal compatibility' [fleshly, sensually]." She told her friend, "Okay, you can be compatible in every respect, but if you cannot see that person as spouse—for example, when he is lying down by you in bed when he touches you and you feel revulsion [*iğrenme*]—then there can be nothing like marriage, this is not marriage." In elaborating her point of view, Yasemin stressed that "marriage is not just about intellectual compatibility, and shared tastes in things . . . if there is no fleshly compatibility, marriage cannot be realized." She made a clear and crucial distinction between feeling and needing to enact corporeal compatibility:

> I don't touch, because according to Islamic rules a man and a woman can not realize such a touch. I wouldn't even shake hands [with the man she will marry]. But this corporeal compatibility, you feel it in your heart toward that person, only after you get married you experience such a need [corporeal touching]. You don't need to rehearse this.

Others also joined Yasemin and Derya in subscribing to this theory of not needing rehearsal. Oya's explanation further illustrates this theory. Claiming that she is not a sensually developed person, Oya said she generally doesn't like giving people hugs and kisses. The absence of such physical engagements ("I haven't embraced them and I don't know the taste of their kiss") is not a loss for her. Indeed, she describes that she has people in her life "whom [she loves] dearly despite the fact that [she doesn't] like to touch, embrace and kiss":

> I didn't discover that I love these people because I first smelled and kissed them. On the contrary, because I love them, I like to smell their smell. I think it is going to be the same way with the man I marry. If he is going to

be the man I love, that thing we call corporeal compatibility will happen. Because of love, that need arises and is felt inside people.

Contrary to this firm theory that excludes the process of trial and error, so to speak, by distinguishing feeling corporeal compatibility in the heart and needing it in the flesh, Akalin's narrative revealed ambivalences. On the one hand, she advanced that corporeal compatibility is something that cannot be understood without trying: "There must be a way of knowing it." She gave the example of the multitude of women being in marriages without this dimension of compatibility. Referring to some women she knows who don't have *tensel uyum*, she explained, "I am surrounded by women [like this]: she reaches the age of fifty and still cannot find that in her husband, but there is nothing to do. She cannot even slightly consider divorce." But then, she drew a disassociation: "If you love that person perhaps you don't care about that aspect." It is possible to attribute Akalin's ambivalences to her *aşk* position: she is the sole member in this group who claimed she doesn't know *aşk* experientially. But the distinction between knowing and needing is also complicated by Ceda, who was madly in love for three years and who was developing strong feelings for a man when I interviewed her. A particular constellation of expectations defined Ceda's notion of corporal compatibility: "You can understand compatibility, if there is electricity, from a gaze, how he is holding a glass, how his contact/touch is with other things." But she also added that she would try to determine if there was compatibility by using her imagination: "In my imagination pictures emerge, I scan the moments of togetherness." Yet, the imagination has its own limitations. Ceda expected that at least some intimacies, such as *kol kola yürümek* (walking arm in arm), should occur during a period of getting to know someone and that if it went further than that, she said, "there is an easy solution: *İmam nikahı* (religious wedding), getting married with God's permission" as a way of religiously receiving license to become intimately physical. I inquired as to what happens if a suitor pushes the boundaries of the desired intimacy:

> I have this world in my imagination as to my expectations. If he is someone who pushes/pressures me, then it means that he doesn't have the same sensitivity like me. Then my trust would be shaken. . . . I would lose

my respect for that person. And I would put it on the table, and I would ask him, "how would you legitimize it?"

Ceda's description of withstanding and responding to the violation of intimacy boundaries in the context of a courting relationship was echoed, almost in identical language, across the board.

These narratives on and around corporeal compatibility acknowledge the sensual love and carnal desires of women as well as express strong aspirations for sexual congruence as a core component of the ideal marriage. Trusting in love's power to orient their desires and the power of marriage to create the need for enacting those desires, these women strive to make their romantic and sexual selves congruent with Islamic principles. Their narratives also suggest that they orient themselves to similar codes of self-regulation, in which bodily and erotic impulses and emotions are banned from courting interaction. However, the way they draw boundaries in this realm ranged from not even shaking hands (Yasemin) to wanting to display bodily touch in public (Ceda). It seems that there is a subtle process of negotiation for expanding the spectrum of accepted boundaries of intimacy toward dismantling the neat division between feeling corporeal compatibility in the heart and needing it in the flesh. However, as expressed by Ceda's point of view, the making of a new Muslim courtship regime primarily relies on a reinvention of legitimacy granted by a religious marriage, which can be utilized as a façade of respectability. This sort of religious marriage, involving a public declaration of intention in front of two witnesses, is not legally binding and is not recognized by the Turkish civil code, and none of these women are willing to engage in a marriage devoid of such legal protection. Indeed, the appeal to religious marriage should be understood as a strategy of pursuing and exploring feelings and desires in a publicly and religiously recognized domain that carries the promise of respectability.

Mothers with Selves: From Marriage of Logic to Marriage of Compatibility

These women articulate and defend a paradigm shift in marriage from marriage of logic to marriage of compatibility.[11] What my narrators called the "marriage of logic" refers to the marriage of "classical patriarchy," in which women, in order to be virtuous, must be legally, economically, and morally dependent on men. Deniz Kandiyoti (1988) describes women's relation to this system of male domination as "bargaining with patriarchy." Women who enter this form of marriage as dispossessed individuals receive "protection and security in exchange for submissiveness and propriety" (280). Logic in the "marriage of logic" thus refers to this unequal exchange. Their interpretation of women's rights in Islam, coupled with their strong critique of both the male-dominated marriages of their parents and the hegemonic Muslim male identity, lies at the heart of these women's conceptions of a desirable marriage of compatibility. For them, a radical reframing of marriage very much depends on women and men entering it on equal terms, without imbalances in age, resources, and taste. It is a marriage that brings together intellectual equivalents who share ideals of religious devotion and corporeal compatibility.

A reflection on the circumstances of their parents' marriages of logic animates the project of transforming marriage for these women. From their vantage points, their mothers and fathers were disturbingly out of sync with each other in age, interest, education, and religious devotion, which imposed a stifling life and limited choices on their mothers. Their claim, as I understand it, is that the organization of family by a marriage of logic with strict gender-role division cannot fulfill a desire for a richer and more complex terrain of human relationships and intrasubjective experiences or a desire for religious realization.

Their application of a new framework to marriage, a central institution for them, clearly foregrounds the intersection and interconnection between home and participation in the extra-domestic sphere. As we have seen, these women do not find the home an adequate site for the cultivation of rich female subjectivities. Explicitly identifying the public sphere as one essential place for women to express and extend the God-given quality of female tenderness and to apply their epistemic authority to the formal domains, they argue that the public sphere should occupy a central place in women's lives, because pursuing education and a career allows for developing potentialities within themselves that would otherwise remain dormant. In other words, they see the risk that women who don't participate in the world outside the home will uncritically accept the world according to others (husbands). This high commitment to the cultivation of a public self is also clearly exemplified in the women's response to my inquiry about whether or not they would be willing to shed their headscarves if the professional jobs they attained required them to do so. With the exception Aknur, they all said yes, as long as those jobs/positions were ones they truly desired.

I identified in these women's narrative three crucial components that were both common to all the women and illustrated in a concrete and unambiguous way. First, all of these women wanted a marriage in which the wife was allowed to experience individual growth so that she could enjoy an identity apart from that of being a mother and wife. As Canan encapsulates this sentiment, "Even if you get married, you should make your own decisions to continue your own life—a common life, but there should be a personal life along with it."

Secondly, they did not want their husbands to exercise arbitrary authority or force them to do things against their free will, including requiring them to always stay home to raise their children. Third, they wanted a marriage in which the wife had an extra-domestic life and made her own decisions about that life (such as decisions to work or not, or to cover or not). Zehra explained, "I will be dead if I must stay home. . . . All of my accumulated knowledge would dissappear as I plunged into housework. I need to work, to be outside of home, in the public and to show myself off to shine."

They used the Turkish word "*ikna*," which means "persuasion" and "eliciting consent through rational discussion," as the thread that connects each of these requirements and the foundation upon which democracy at home can be built. Their usage of the term "*ikna*" is important here, because they transport it from one of the foundational principles of Islam. Islam does not allow the forceful imposition of religious beliefs and tenets on others. Thus, these young women believe that their Islamic faith helps lay the path for the democratization of the private sphere. But also, they trust the power of persuasion and epistemic authority they have gained through their elite education.

What is the role and place of motherhood in this project of making marriage a nonrestrictive institution? Women's identities as mothers are pivotal in the conceptualization of gender in Islam. "Motherly mercy and affection" defines the core of women's God-given natures (Saktanber 2002a, 41). Saktanber explains the phenomenon of mothering in Islam in relation to men:

> In so far as women were thought of as having been created with the innate qualities of motherly mercy and affection, they were also expected to give rest and comfort to men, who in return were expected to take care of women. More important among the benefits that men gain through the medium of the merciful nature of women, men can learn how to love, that is, they can be helped to appreciate divine cause and grace, and thereby be helped to approach God. (2002a, 41)

It is this expanded and spiritually charged role attributed to a woman's mothering that justifies and legitimizes the traditional division of labor, which dictates that women's place is in the home, but without equating confinement with subordination.

The women in this chapter reaffirmed the natural differences between men and women and this God-given quality of female mercifulness. However, they also recognized that this quality of mercifulness is subject to manipulation and exploitation, especially in a marriage of logic. Furthermore, in keeping with their critique of the model of motherhood represented by their own mothers, they no longer see womanhood and motherhood as synonymous identities and categories of experience. Neither do they see mothering, as the nurturing and caring task, as necessarily the exclusive domain of women, especially in cases where women have employment outside of the home. After Ayşe stated that she definitely wanted to share domestic responsibilities with her future husband, I pressed her to find out if she also desired the same kind of sharing with respect to child care: "Of course, I want to. When the baby cries every night, I am not going to be the one who gets up every night. The father should also get up. Yes. Okay [tamam] [one might say,] 'but you are the one who gave birth,' but he is the one who caused it too."

At first glance this alternative, new way of being a mother, which combines a professional interest and identity with a public presence that does not result in a subjectivity of selflessness, might seem contradictory to the way Islam defines the role of the mother and might even sound like a project of individualization. However, if we recall these women's overall vision of a pluralistic society and the place of pious Muslim identity within it, we can see this form of motherhood as an adjustment that can support their Islamic faith. Within the context of a modern society that emphasizes differences, it is, indeed, a positive adaptation that will allow them to raise a new generation of truly "conscious" Muslims. These women's children, raised by mothers who will teach them how to deal with difference without feeling insecure about their own identity, will carry their Muslim selves with confidence and assert their Muslim identity without any inferiority complex. In the context of Turkey's radical secularism, which made even walking next to a covered woman shameful for earlier generations of secular Turks, this project of disassociating the Muslim identity from inferiority and insecurity underlines the interconnectedness of gender and generational consciousness.

Conclusion

The new devout Muslim woman in Turkey has been inaugurated as an icon of Islamic modernity in recent scholarly accounts (Göle 2000, 2002, 2003; Genel and Karaosmanoglu 2006). She is celebrated for her power to erase important individual and collective identity-defining demarcations: the traditional Muslim and the secular modernist. She distances herself from the older-generation Muslim women's reputation for subservience by voicing dissent against Islamic patriarchy, while her adoption of symbols of modernity through consumption and especially her education delete the social distance between her and secular women. In this chapter, I have attempted to situate sociologically and explore the less visible aspects of this new female identity in Turkey by focusing on the confluence of gender and generational experiences and by examining the narratives articulated at the site of romance, love, desire, and marriage.

This new pious female identity is being formed in a cultural and political landscape fractured since the mid-1980s. My analysis illuminates the paradoxical significance of the secular headscarf ban: it has produced a heightened criticism of gender inequality in masculine interpretations of Islam and of Muslim male identity alongside a critique of secularism. It has also accentuated a process in which daughters renounce their parents' obedience to the secular order. This twin criticism, engendered by the secular headscarf ban, is central to the gendered generational consciousness. Another important aspect of this paradox is these young women's empowerment in gaining authority in religious knowledge through their secular education. Not only have they, like secular women, gained access to the public arena largely as a result of secularist reforms but also their secular education has enabled them to become educated and to probe sources of Islamic knowledge and practice. More importantly, their education in a secular milieu has provided them with the intellectual, emotional, and practical resources necessary to imagine and affirm a new Muslim female identity that is not relegated to the private sphere.

Yet, by limiting their participation in the public sphere, the secular ban restricts the range of professional roles they can play. In practice, this often results in channeling these young women into "Islamic workplaces and offices" where they can pursue work lives with their heads covered, while devout Muslim men have already become dominant political and economic actors in Turkish society. This not only implies narrowed choices and opportunities for these women but also means that they are experiencing this new pious female identity within a context of segregation, contrary to their pluralistic worldview and their desire to coexist with other identities.

I will address this question of integration and segregation in more depth in the conclusion in relation to the production of other identities and Turkey's global neoliberalism, but now I would like to point out that this question has great significance, not only politically but theoretically as well. These young women's Boğaziçi experiences revealed accommodations in the language of affirmation by their peers, unlike their experience with elderly secularists who show intolerance to their presence in public. It seems to me that when an interpenetration happens, as it has in this university setting, the subjects, Islamic and secular, can no longer perceive one another in terms of rigidly defined anonymous social categories that carry information about the other's moral status and views. In fact, this interpenetration in daily life helps to break down the preestablished consensus about the meaning of these categories. The Turkish case clearly urges us in our theorizing and research to concentrate on coexistence and interpenetration. Educated young Muslim women are strategically positioned to breach the irreducible divide that lies at the heart of the historical conflict between Islam and secularism in Turkey in that they are instrumental in helping both to transform.

As always, it is difficult to address the relationship between consciousness and action. The degree to which these women's new subjectivities challenge and change Muslim gender relations and refigure the "Muslim habitus" in Turkey is an open question, and given these women's firm demand for women's active and sustained participation in public spheres, it is inextricably linked to the processes of altering the meaning of secularism in Turkey as well as the meaning of piety.

Under what societal and personal conditions do the new subjectivities that these young women create become malleable and open to change? Mannheim privileged the formative years in the development of a person's identity, because he believed that individuals carry their identity with them as they grow older. Conway suggests that even in the face of modifications, "the original generation-specific self remains the self with which all later selves must be negotiated" (Conway 1997, 2145).

A more immediate and relevant question in the light of my research is to what extent these women will be able to enact and embody the new subjectivities they have invented for themselves. My analysis of their narratives suggests an obvious response: theirs is a subjectivity that is still without subjects. Women cannot become full subjects without male spouses within religious Muslim life; full subjecthood can only be materialized through marriage and motherhood. For them to become subjects of their newly created subjectivities, a new type of Muslim man must emerge, in addition to a host of other conditions necessary for the ideological maintenance of this subjectivity. As we have seen, the Muslim men that appeared in these women's narratives do not approach the ideal men they imagine building their lives with. To my knowledge, there is no empirical, in-depth study of pious, educated men in Turkey, and as I explained at the beginning of this book, despite my consistent and determined efforts to interview educated Muslim men in order to give voice to their perspectives and experiences, I was turned down. They are only known from their appearance in fiction and autobiographies. It is ironic that while covered women have been the subject of intense commentary, their male peers have mainly been the subjects of fiction. Sociologists who analyze the fictionalized accounts of new

Muslim men point out the transformative power of love, which can alter Muslim male identity from militant to moderate (Göle 2000; Saktanber 2006).

It is safe to assume that the question of love will figure significantly in the crystallization of subjectivity, despite Ayşe's rejection of the transformative power of love: "A woman should not be a man's slave even if she dies from loving him. A woman should not give up her own truths; she should be strong and powerful." Since these young women are on the threshold of a new stage of life—the transition to wifehood and motherhood—matters of love will play an important role in their trajectories. Marriage is not an individual affair in Turkey; it brings together two sets of extended families. Even those who experience a sense of growing distance and feelings of alienation from the world of their provincial family background and family circles will have to bring their families back into their lives. Their differing trajectories in this regard will add to the already existing diversity among rising Islamic middle classes.

Theoretically speaking, the Turkish case brings into sharp focus the issue of gender polarization within a generation unit, members of which, in Mannheim's model, are by definition united because they share a common consciousness across all kinds of divisions and differences. In line with Mannheim's argument, a common worldview (contesting earlier generations' understanding of the role religion plays in society) unites young Muslim women and men and differentiates them from other generation units in Turkey. But Mannheim's "fundamental integrative attitudes and formative principles" about the identity of Muslim women and about gender relations in Islam divide them. Mannheim emphasizes fundamental integrative attitudes, because, as he writes, "they alone are 'the primary socializing principle' really capable of becoming the basis of continuing practice" (Mannheim 1972, 305). Indeed, this gender divide should be considered highly significant in the formative principles of a desired new social and moral order in which the conceptions of gender and sexuality are pivotal to its establishment. A systematic exploration of whether Mannheim's conceptualization of "generation unit" can accommodate a gender breach also requires in-depth studies of young Muslim men. The post-9/11 period has created an intense concern and interest in young Muslim men and in the differences that separate them from earlier generations of men, especially in Western Europe. I think that the notion of generation we inherited from Mannheim is still relevant, but as the Turkish case demonstrates, it needs to be elaborated through the critical prism of gender.

The Turkish case also points to the necessary task of developing a sociology of gender through the critical prism of generation. A cultural setting such as Turkey, where strong relationships between mothers and daughters exist throughout different stages of women's lives, poses important questions about young women's roles in transforming patriarchy as well as about intergenerational continuity and change in women's identities. As we have seen, the young women in this chapter renounce their mothers' model of identity, not to spite their mothers but because their mothers primed them to do so. These young women often referred to a feminist vein in themselves. It would be correct to assume that these daughters have inherited this feminist vein from their "selfless" mothers, who deeply resented their lack of secular education and who socialized their daughters (emotionally and practically) to envision a female subjectivity not tied to domesticity. In this way, the mothers are the first authors of these women's subjectivities.

Becoming a *Sade* Pious Woman in a Secular Society: Aknur's Story

Aknur identifies herself foremost as "her father's daughter." Fully embracing at an early age the religious path her father charted for her formed the most significant force (influence) in her self-making: "I was determined that I was going to raise myself as a girl and a woman the way Islam desires." At twenty-three, Aknur personifies a *sade* (pure, simple, and frugal) identity in her totality. Her *sade* appearance is an assertive counterstatement against the grain of mainstream middle-class Islamic chic; her ideals and aspirations are completely connected to altruism and other-directedness; and her day-to-day conduct is antimaterialistic. Hers is a self-making that not only responds to Islam's call but also articulates anticapitalism and a complicated understanding of feminism.

Aknur grew up in an unusual family environment by Turkish standards due to her parents' separation, a separation caused by her mother's inability and unwillingness to live as a conscious Muslim. As Aknur described it, she was raised in her mother's household, but "grew up with her father's religious values." At a very early age Aknur, a precocious only child, felt a "competition" between her parents over her. But eventually, the father took the dominant role in her upbringing: "My mother did not intervene much because my father was better educated and better read and had a strongly developed life philosophy. My mother is also a university-educated professional, but she is more inner-looking and less self-assured. She also knew my fondness for my father."

For her father, Aknur's education and "what kind of individual she [would] become" were paramount, and he was preoccupied with every detail of her upbringing and education. Officially divorced years later, her parents separated when she was twelve. During her girlhood, Aknur acutely felt the tensions in her parents' marriage, particularly the differences between her mother and father and their drastically divergent views about how to live their lives, the underlying cause of their divorce. As Aknur explained, "My father is a more pious person and he emphasized my education and upbringing according to Islamic norms, whereas my mother was more relaxed because she comes from a modernized and westernized family background." Desiring to inhabit highly contrasted spaces and lifestyles from one another, her mother wanted to be a modern, secularly Muslim woman and enacted the practices of what constituted modern and secular femininity, such as putting on a bathing suit to swim, using make-up, and getting her hair permed, while Aknur's father wanted his wife to be plain and modest. These and similar contradictory desires created problems in their marriage, producing for Aknur a home world of open or muted conflicts. Because during her girlhood years divorce was very rare among her friends' families, she hid her parents' divorce from them: "Instead I would show them that everything was normal because perceiving myself so different was intolerable, as if I was from outer space [uzaylı]." During the separation, Aknur's father moved to another part of the country while Aknur stayed with her mother and paternal grandmother in Istanbul, only seeing her father during summer vacations. In Aknur's experience, her mother was less vocal in defending her life choices, while her father sharply indicated how a pious woman should properly behave. He introduced Aknur to the desirable models of piety in women in his own circles, in addition to the direct religious teaching Aknur received from her father and other family members on the paternal side.

Aknur used the word "ambivalent" to describe her mother's religiosity and classified her as part of the cohort of women in Turkish society who personally experienced the contradictions of Turkish modernization. Aknur's mother was rooted within a large, heterogeneous family network, including those leading active religious and secular lives. Her grandfather was theologically oriented, debating fine points about the Koran and Islam at home, but Aknur's mother's education and the circles she inhabited were steeped in "enlightenment and modernism." In order to be accepted by that modernist milieu, she "couldn't apply her father's norms in her practical life" in her early adulthood. Now, according to Aknur, her mother feels pious but claims "she cannot align her life practices to what her tongue [dili] utters." In other words, she feels religious but is unable to live her life as a "conscious" Muslim. Significantly, Aknur's birth was a turning point for her mother with respect to how she was going to live her religiosity, and she recalled to Aknur a strong feeling of unwillingness to enact her husband's ideals of piety after becoming a mother.

Aknur was very forthcoming in describing the contradictions she felt as she traversed the world of secularly structured school culture, where the exclusion of religious education was willed and concerted in multiple

ways by the Turkish state, and the world of her father's religiously inspired worldview and anti-Western attitudes. Dubbed by Aknur as both
nationalistic and religiously conservative, her extended family, particularly the paternal side, embraced Ottoman heritage. The Ottoman sultans, from their perspective, were "very valuable, and reverend figures"
while, in contrast, in school, Atatürk's abolition of the Sultanate system
was applauded. Aknur was confused by this contradictory conceptual
environment: "Of course I wanted to give more importance to what was
taught in school; the teacher had power because of her institutional authority, so whatever she said was true." She also felt the contradictions
of these separate cultures, a secular school culture and a religious home
culture, more personally because of her parents' opposing views. For instance, Aknur cited the example of New Year's celebrations: her teacher
taught that the new year is celebrated in Turkey not because it is Jesus
Christ's birthday but because it marks the welcoming of a new year: "I
remember vividly coming home one day and telling my parents the real
truth behind the New Year's celebrations and declaring to them that 'I
will celebrate the new year and I don't believe you.'" There were no New
Year's or birthday celebrations in her home, because, as Aknur put it, "My
father was against it; quote-unquote because these traditions were coming from the West." But her mother wanted to celebrate: "There were lots
of fights about my birthday celebrations when I was little." As an inquisi-
tive child, whenever she felt a contradiction between home and school
cultures or if something remained unresolved in her mind, she always felt
free to go to her father and question his authority: "My teachers tell me
this and that; why are you teaching me the wrong things?"

Aknur's reconstruction of her girlhood was replete with references
emphasizing how "childhood religiosity is really different and wonderful." When she was growing up, her father would take her on many out-
ings exposing her to his pious circles. "I developed admiration for plainly
dressed and covered women, and my father supported this model of
womanhood." This fresh contact with new Muslim women, who were
becoming assertively visible in the public sphere of early 1990s Turkey,
provided her with "personally acquired" memories in the cultivation of
her identity. As Mannheim (1972) theorized, acquired memories and
knowledge are much more powerful, because they are created directly
in real situations and, therefore, they "stick" and have binding power,

compared to appropriated memories "taken over from someone else" (296). A Koran teacher formed another early and significant fresh contact for Aknur. She was sent to a Koran course taught by "a very modest and sweet" female teacher. She and her cousin very much admired and were influenced by this teacher, and because as little girls they wanted God to love them, at age twelve she, along with her female cousin, made a pact that they would both cover on "such and such day." And since that day she has never uncovered. The uncovered mother and covered daughter are now met by puzzled looks in public life. She describes the sentiment: "My mother finds herself in an inferior place, like as if I am a 'high/sublime saint' and on the other hand my mother is this woman who couldn't transcend certain things and so could not become covered. And of course, sometimes the reverse is true."

It is an intriguing question why Aknur favored, valorized, and took as her role models the pious women her father praised, not her modernist mother, through her growing-up years. How does this idiosyncratic self-making call into question connective selving or put it in a new frame? It is also striking that Aknur's narrative about her effective acceptance of the pious women in her father's circles was marked by the absence of any expression of feelings of being torn between competing modes of femininity, her mother's and the pious women's. On this question, Aknur alluded only briefly to the idea that who we become is shaped by the people we admire, as with her admiration for her father. Perhaps what rendered her mother's identity nonemulative is simply that it was a problematic female identity that produced conflict, fractured her family, and eventually led to a divorce. But more importantly, even though her mother could not herself enact such an identity and did not even attempt to "intervene" in the way her husband raised Aknur, there were many instances in Aknur's narrative that emphasized that her pious self-making was fully "approved" by her mother. For instance, Aknur's mother told her, "Years ago I knew you would be covered. In fact, when you were small, I met a covered university student and told her that 'if my daughter covers like you, I will buy her many colored headscarves.'" What comes across here is her mother's pleasurable connection with Aknur's religious identity, despite her ambivalent stance toward her own. Aknur's mother also assigns perfection to her daughter, a high form of maternal affirmation: "My mother thinks that I am a perfect individual, and she is sure that because I am such a perfect person, I am bound to make a good marriage and definitely expects me to marry a good man." Even more intriguing was Aknur's claim that even though in practical terms her mother and she are different, they think alike, and because there is a good, constant mother-daughter dialogue, her mother perfectly understands her: "I don't see myself as different from my mother because my mother is not covered or does not pray. Because I know the structure of our minds overlap, I don't see myself as different than my mother." When I probed further about what made her different from her mother "in practical terms," apart from being covered, Aknur assessed the situation in relation to men: "In terms of our different sensibilities regarding physically segregating/putting physical distance from men [erkeklerden kaçınma], I am more sensitive," an acknowledgment of differentiation based on one of the most important Islamic principles.

The expression "thinking alike," which Aknur used, is crucial, for it located sameness, not seeing herself as different from her mother, in the mind. This category of identification and connectivity emerged even more powerfully when I asked her whether, if her mother and father chose a suitor for her, this person would be the same person she chose for herself. Without any reservations, Aknur's response was, "It would completely overlap with my mother because she knows me perfectly well." However, her father's choice would differ from hers in an important respect, as her father would choose a suitor whose structure of mind was identical to his own. According to Aknur, her father is "a type of man—even though he objects to this characterization—who feels whatever he thinks true is true," the exact opposite of Aknur's ideal suitor, a man who is "open to different truths."

The word "sade" dominated Aknur's narrative. "Sade" in English means "plain, simple, frugal, and pure." All her desires and aspirations in her self-making are intimately tied to being sade in appearance and action or conduct. Sade appeared in Aknur's narrative in multiple ways: she has respect for women who dress sade, she was attracted to sade religious women when she was a little girl, she desires to pursue a sade lifestyle, she feels herself only when she dresses sade, she wants to have a sade work life without titles and office signs, and she respects and interacts with those who are sade with no materialistic ambitions.

Indeed, *sade* in her lexicon clarifies and makes concrete the organizing principle of her religious self and what she strives for in this life: "I don't want to lead a materially rich life; materiality, living in a self-contained and selfish way, is something I try to escape. My endeavor is to strive to make myself not to embrace this [materialism]. Let me say this is as an ideal, but I don't know how I am going to live." Aknur practices what she preaches. Until very recently, it was her mother who cut her hair: "I see going to a hair dresser or a beauty salon as a luxury. Every time I go to a hair salon, a voice inside of me says, 'Are you going to spend this much money on a haircut while people cannot even afford a loaf of bread?'" Similarly, she likes to dress plainly:

> I dislike wearing colorful clothes, attention-grabbing ones. Even if I cannot accomplish it myself, I feel respect towards those women who dress plainly. For me wearing a *pardesü* [long overcoat, the most commonly worn outdoor attire] is not an unquestionable requirement for a woman to be religiously covered, but I feel tremendous respect for a person wearing an inexpensive *pardesü* in a non-attention-grabbing color, and a pair of sporty shoes, combined with a nonexpensive headscarf.

Aknur defines herself in opposition to the figure of the bourgeois Islamic woman, the newer members of the Islamic middle class in Turkey who are offered as a model to the rest of the religious women in mainstream culture. She dresses inconspicuously so as to totally express her *sade* religious identity, separating her from the image of these bourgeois Islamic women, an image blending fashion with Islamic identity, whose enactment requires considerable material resources ("a headscarf costing as much as a wedding gown"). Aknur also dislikes "the look of a business woman." Referencing her mother's desire to dress her up, Aknur told of the time her mother bought her a colorful skirt and headscarf to go with her solid jacket for her graduation, complete with matching shoes and purse. She said to her mother, "I don't feel like myself in those clothes because they don't express me. And I don't want to own many outfits." But her mother insisted that it was for a special occasion and that she would wear "these things only every forty years."

Because "the occasion required" it, Aknur put on the outfit her mother assembled for her, even though she felt uncomfortable. Indeed, Aknur said, "I feel I can follow some dominant norms" without compromising too much. This is consistent with the way she constructs herself as a *sade* person. According to her, because too much resistance equally makes one stick out and attract attention, it is undesirable for her to be too rebellious.

When she first came to Boğaziçi, Aknur sensed an air of privilege: "This is a school for people from wealthy backgrounds, a school for upper-class people." She was covered and did not see a single covered woman around and felt very lonely. Her feeling of alienation had not diminished over time. Speaking of other covered women, she told me,

> We were always made to feel that we are an unwanted minority. It was like this: a security guard following you to point out how under your hat your headscarf was still visible. Professors always distancing themselves from me: I was always made to feel I was different in front of the professors. When you are faced with ill treatment, inevitably you attribute it to your headscarf: "am I subjected to this bad behavior because of my headscarf?"

More significant was the form of social distance produced through the conscious efforts of secular students and faculty: "[They fit] you in the stereotype of the identity of a covered girl in their head. They only define you through that, and thus they don't need to know you." Despite all these experiences that she considered alienating, she did not feel like "a fish out of water" because she "[came] from a heterogenous extended family background" and "grew up in Istanbul." Pursuing her religious identity in relation to and as part of a wider collective of differences in cosmopolitan Boğaziçi allowed Aknur to know lots of different people: "people who come from Anatolia, those who come from margins of Istanbul, and those who come from segments of the Islamic bourgeoisie." Encountering people who, like her, are dealing with differences but also people who think like her in the university setting presented her with a wider horizon within which to interpret and validate her Islamic identity as she experienced inclusion or/and exclusion. As a result, Aknur explained, "If I am going to accomplish something with my Islamic thought in the name of religion, I think my education and training, and my past experiences here, will feed me richly."

In recounting her experiences and perspectives, Aknur chose narrative resources that reflected her intellectual power, gained by her secular education at Boğaziçi. For example, in response to my question about whether and how she makes a distinction between passion and love, she framed her response with the notion of fantasy and referred to Lacan. While talking about her relationship with her mother, she referred to a point Virginia Woolf made on mother-daughter relationships. "God is dead," a quotation from Nietzsche, came up in connection with her perspective on the schizophrenic educational environment in relation to secularism. I do not simply interpret Aknur's references to Lacan, Woolf, and Nietzsche as evidence of her desire to mark herself as intellectual. These are the cognitive, and sometimes emotional, resources through which (or against which) she frames her experiences and beliefs. As such, I consider them important influences, figuring significantly in the construction of her subjectivity.

Aknur's close friendships are built around exchanging ideas and interrogating "the macro structures of capitalism" with people who attempt to organize their lives on the basis of such macro critiques. Aknur has also formed friendships with those who "come from the Islamic bourgeoisie, those who went to private Islamic or secular schools and never experienced any financial hardship, and therefore had not developed sensibility towards others," because of the common thread of closeness: religious identity. However, she is more interested in interacting with individuals who see the world differently from most people. She feels close to individuals who are sensitive to and more aware of global and local sufferings, injustices, and class-based inequalities, people who assign a major role to altruism—the kinds of people who, like her, ask and reflect on questions to gauge their deeds, such as,

> What do you eat and wear, simple or flaunting? Who else is able to eat what you eat? Can poor people eat the same things or is it a luxury? Do I really need to buy that ice cream with the exotic taste? Yes, it is made and sold in that pastry shop, but where does the sugar in that ice cream come from? Who labored to produce it?

According to Aknur, liberalism and capitalism contradict Islam's essence, and she views the AKP's pursuit of a neoliberal capitalist agenda as a dangerous current compromising Islamic sensibilities. For her, under neoliberal capitalism, the pious people in Turkish society are sacrificing their religious ideals and going further away from Islam, and this is a signal of their willingness to reconcile with other sectors of the population. She finds it problematic that "on the one hand, religious conservatism is going parallel with capitalism and the right politically and, on the other hand, the left is separated from Islam" and "there is no tradition of Muslims criticizing capitalism." While Aknur never explicitly identified herself in this way, her voice is situated within an emerging movement of "anticapitalist Muslims" in Turkey. Aknur is hopeful because she observes that the exalted linear narrative of successful self-making—running like a horse after a predetermined educational path, going through the extreme stresses of competitive entrance examinations for coveted private high schools and universities, quickly reaching top positions, making astronomical salaries, owning luxury cars and homes—is now being challenged by her cohort: "We will be coming out of materialism, because we are the first cohort that is experiencing that materialism does not bring happiness and there is no end to career ambition, while there are other important things in life." In her view, there is an emerging new approach to self-making steeped in searching for more spirituality, more understanding, and openness to new things. And her cohort is "ready to get out of the box."

In the realm of love and intimacy with men, Aknur's mother had always been very comfortable with the idea of her forming romantic relationships and in fact always desired Aknur to have a boyfriend. Not surprisingly, her father had contrary views:

My father raised me strict in this realm or, more correctly, he did not do anything to be strict with me—he never intervened in any nonromantic relationships I had with men. But my father's life philosophy affected me most, that is, "the person who holds your hand first should be the person you will be marrying." Because in Islam it is a sin to be in a sexual relationship before marriage and because I was a religious child, my father did not tell me anything explicitly. Therefore, there was no reason for my father to put forth and exercise any prohibitions.

Aknur lived out the Islamic rules of sexual purity before marriage without subverting them. Aknur expressed that she had never felt pressure to have a boyfriend, because, as I recounted in the preceding chapter, she always carried the objects of her desire inside of her as "platonic ideals." Between father and daughter, the emotional and experiential dimensions of Aknur's romantic and sexual subjectivity never became a topic of conversation and always remained a "taboo" subject. Citing her father's extreme discomfort in this regard, Aknur said, "Even today, if there is a talk like about my future marriage in the family, my father becomes red in the face. He is never comfortable." Equally, Aknur was always terrified by the idea of her father hearing about the men she liked. She drew a contrast with her cousin to illustrate this point: "My cousin's father is not like him—my cousin can openly say, 'I like this man.' If I liked someone and happened to tell my cousin, it would terrify me that this knowledge would go to my father's ears." Men she liked had to remain hidden because "according to my father, one should have priorities. For example, girls who have boyfriends cannot succeed in school, advance educationally. They just leave school and get married, something that ordinary people do, what is important is education and doing science." This paternal view is reflected in how Aknur avoided falling in love and developing any attachment with the men she liked. As I referenced in the preceding chapter, to protect herself against falling in love until she attained educational sucess, Aknur resolved when she was younger,

> I shouldn't fall in love and have a relationship with a man until I reach a certain age. [Because] when it happens, the ideal situation is to transform [carry] that love/relationship to a marriage. If something like this had happened in high school years, I couldn't take it to marriage, and therefore, falling in love was not a desirable thing.

Yet she deviated from the firm resolve she made with herself (and her father) by falling deeply in love when she was eighteen. Aknur would like to articulate love with religious spirituality: love is the concretization of one's desire for God through (over) another (embodied) person.

Aknur "dislikes" the concept of gender equality insofar as it represents to her an erasure of what she sees as fundamental and innate differences between the sexes: "I subscribe to the concept of complementarity of the sexes, as the *fitrat* defines it," the *fitrat* being a core tenet of Islam that attributes distinct and divinely ordained natures to men and women. Invoking frequently cited examples of an "apple and pear" (one is not superior to the other but they are different) and a "pair of shoes" (a single shoe is useless without its matching pair), she put a premium on difference—how the sexes are created differently—and the importance of their complementarity. According to Aknur, God creates in females a heightened capacity for mercifulness and empathy. Consistent with this religious gender conception, for Aknur, to be a woman means to possess mercifulness and affection and to look at the world from a different perspective. This feminine perspective looks at life through a more somber, melancholic lens to see some details that men cannot see.

Interestingly, Aknur attributes this melancholic identification at least in part to women's socially constructed roles and identities. As she explained it, "Women gain wounds and unfinished grieving from life and, therefore, tend to reflect and interrrogate intensely what they go through." Thus, Aknur understands this feminine outlook not simply as a natural disposition but as a social construction, a projection of women's societal condition. By suggesting a conception of gender as socially and contextually constructed and different from the religious essentialist notion, Aknur posed an interesting contradiction and pointed out that "this competition of conceptual frameworks, what should be deconstructed as constructed and not constructed, the nature and nurture debate, is a question that I can't clarify in my mind yet." In a similar vein, she described men's God-given nature in explicitly essentialist and binary terms: in contrast to women, men are created raw; thus they are insensitive, carefree (*vurdum duymaz*), thick-skinned, and lacking in affection and mercifulness. But by insisting on the importance of men building empathy to develop openness to differences, she also challenged and inverted the terms of this essential differentness and complementarity. As discussed in the previous chapter, it is imperative that the man Aknur will build a life with be committed to live life by Islamic norms to realize religious ideals. Yet equally important for her is a man with the capacity for empathy, "a high emotional IQ," and a willingness to work on himself to achieve that capacity.

It is a must for Aknur that her future husband be involved at home, sociable, and other directed. Interestingly, she identified her father as the source of her egalitarian ideals about the gender division of labor:

> I am a daughter of an egalitarian father. My father could tell me bring me a glass of water but I also equally can ask him to bring me a glass of water. My father never ordered me around in a servile way. If my future husband comes from an environment where women are oppressed and he tries to oppress me, I think I can reject that.

But more importantly, her feminist vein takes on a meaning of refusing to conform or tolerate it if her future husband claims and exercises a right to intervene in her life, tampering with her path toward the realization of her ideals: "If I organize my life according to Islamic norms, he has no right to intervene in the realization of my ideals." Because she is not in favor of a situation where married people lead different lives, the question of whether she can meet a "suitable mate" for herself is a significant source of anxiety. This includes class anxieties. Because she desires to pursue a "simple life," I inquired what would happen if she met a man with a wealthy family background, and she responded, "If I meet someone whose family is well off, that would make me think: Do they give importance to the status that money brings? Would he and his family intervene in how I dress and what kind of life I want to lead? Would they want me to buy a jacuzzi?" Aknur's feminist vein also surfaced when she shared her views on virginity. She articulated her analysis of virginity norms in religious terms: "Only after a legitimate contract of conjugal union can a woman give her virginity." However, she is very critical of the way in which the virginity loss is lived out: "If virginity loss is a problem, this is not only a women's problem, it is also a men's problem; if she loses her virginity she is made to lose it. From my perspective, it is a crime committed by both sides. Yet the woman pays a price and this price can even extend to her murder."

For her, postgraduate life is like "a black hole." Because she cannot imagine her future, she often attributes her lack of imagination to an admittedly silly thought: "Maybe I will die after graduation." Two major sources, personal and societal, make her future undefined: her headscarf and her lack of a marriage prospect. She would like to pursue postgraduate education, but it is not clear whether she would be accepted, and more importantly for her, she "cannot become an academician with [her] headscarf." Her determination not to uncover under any circumstances is consistent with her desire not to be complicit with any system or person in her life that counters her ideal of embracing a *sade* religious identity and pursuing a *sade* life. In this regard, it is instructive to recount our conversation about her cousin's trajectory. When I inquired about what happened to that cousin, whether she remained covered or not, Aknur explained,

> She remained covered until a month ago—throughout her higher education, she was uncovered in the university, but covered outside. Recently she found a job at an educational setting and if she takes that job, she is required to be uncovered. Besides, regardless of this particular job prospect, her degree is in one of the STEM fields, and therefore she is going to experience the same demand in other job offers. There is no workplace where she can practice her profession covered. And at the same time she got married and said, "I don't want to feel this tension anymore" and became uncovered.

The cousin came to Aknur to elicit her opinion: "Would it be too bad if I uncovered?" Aknur said, "I will not intervene. I will not say anything. I don't know." I also inquired about her cousin's mother's reaction:

> She felt sad. However, because she gives enormous value to her daughter, whatever the daughter's decision is, it is acceptable. In her eyes, her daughter is the one who can pursue things she herself couldn't, and because she always felt the lack of education in her life, she lives vicariously through her daughter, filling her own gap with her daughter. For this reason, she is putting her daugh-

ter in a supreme place/position—whatever the daughter says is acceptable.

Aknur wants to find a place for herself in a nonprofit, nongovernmental organization. Because her goal in life is not to make herself comfortable but to be useful to other people, work in a nonprofit organization offers her a vital medium through which acts of altruism, caring, and compassion can be enacted. Her less ideal fall-back plan is to do freelance editing or writing out of her home. Building a career in a traditional sense and being a class climber has no appeal to her: "Having a job title, occupational prestige, business cards, a big office, a job considered to be prestigious, and nice business outfits . . . none of these things are important to me." What is essential for her finding satisfaction and being able to "continuously develop" herself is altruism: "I want to do things useful for other people and contribute to the eradication of inequalities and injustices. I don't desire to be someone who only works towards her own comfort and well-being."

Being on a path of becoming a conscious Muslim commands a whole way of life, including a strong family orientation and motherhood. Aknur views becoming a mother as a central component of her life ideal and aspirations, as she is motivated by a desire to raise pious children against materialism and individualism. Her offspring will learn how to deal with difference without feeling insecure about their own identities and will carry and assert their Muslim selves with confidence and without any inferiority complex. In this regard, mothering provides a crucial template of moral choices and religious education. Shaped by her own positive experiences of childhood religiosity, Aknur strongly believes that religious knowledge should be inculcated when children are small, including instruction in Arabic. However, she holds a deep and realistic fear that "not having someone" in her life currently to build a lifelong conjugal bond with will place her ideal of becoming a young mother out of reach. It is important to underline that although the ultimate priority for Aknur is becoming a mother and building a family, she doesn't see her self-making as being limited by motherhood: "Not to work, just to be a homemaker and caregiver is not what I want. I don't want all my educational capital to go to waste."

Aknur's account, along with the other stories in chapter 4, marks the significance of marriage and motherhood as the critical and inseparable ingredients in becoming "a woman the way Islam desires." The acutely felt tensions Aknur is experiencing epitomize a gender dynamic whereby a firmly carved path toward self-making as a devout woman rests a great deal on the success of finding a partner who is committed to a shared religious trajectory and a particular brand of feminism. The tension between agency and not being able to be a subject of that agency powerfully underscores this gender dynamic.

4

Desire between "Doing" and "Being"

İbne *(Faggot) and* Gey *(Gay)*

This chapter takes up a deceptively familiar observation—the emergence of "*gey*" as a category of identification by men who practice same-sex sex—in order to consider how this borrowed "global" category is given substance and localized in Turkey. Most scholarly accounts of *gey* identity construction in Turkey operate within the key paradigm of the history of homosexuality in the West, focusing on the processes precipitating the development of gay subcultures and identity there: the transition to modernity, individualism, relocation to urban areas, reorganization of family structures, and a deemphasis on kin relations (Weeks 1985). This broader history also focuses on the immense transformative power of global capitalism—the global circulation of commodities, cultural products, and connections—as it refashions non-Western same-sex sex practices from "doing" (behavior) into "being" (identity).

Building on Suad Joseph's notion of "connectivity," I problematize this sequential narrative and argue that understanding gay subjectivity in Turkey requires a fuller picture of the way familial ties and kinship shape individuals' self-identities, senses of status and class, and feelings of honor and shame. The accounts of *gey* identity construction in Turkey that dominate the literature on the subject tend to uncritically view the emergence of a global gay identity through models of selfhood based on individual autonomy. By contrast, Joseph's model of connectivity allows us to see how *gey* subjectivities in Turkey are given particular meaning through the way individuals "invite, require, and initiate involvement with others" in shaping their own identities (Joseph 1993, 468).

In this chapter, I explore how men practicing same-sex sex in Turkey manage love, desire, and the closet (or "coming out") in order to explicate what a global gay identity entails for the men who adopt it.

In doing so, I pay close attention to how these processes are shaped by individuals' embeddedness in larger social collectives. My intention here is to explicate how connectivity shapes the meaning and implications of a *gey* identity in Turkey, giving local inflection to this imported global category.

In doing so, I place this explication in the broader context and content of the identity formation of upwardly mobile, educationally advantaged young men in Istanbul who embody the contradictions and quandaries that Eve Sedgwick (1990) in *Epistemology of the Closet* theorizes as the simultaneous existence of two irreconcilable accounts of homosexuality: the minority and the universal. In the first—the "minority" account— homosexuals are understood as having essential differences that distinguish them from their heterosexual counterparts, and homosexuality is thus defined as a discrete and definitely identifiable category of minority. In the second—the "universalizing" account—homosexuality is understood as a universal potential for everyone, and same-sex desire is not seen as an essential part of one's identity. As I will demonstrate, this conundrum assumes a special potency in Turkey, where notions of self inscribed by connectivity (as opposed to ideals of autonomy or independence) work against both "minority" accounts of homosexuality and living as openly gay.

Investigating silences that are not permitted to be spoken or analyzed presents a difficult task for empirical investigation.[1] This chapter draws upon interview data from seven educationally advantaged, upwardly mobile gay men, between nineteen and twenty-seven years of age, born amid the social and economic transformations of the 1980s in Turkey, as well as two focus-group interviews.[2] All of the interviews and the focus groups were conducted between 2002 and 2004. The narrators in this chapter were undergraduate and graduate students who identified themselves as secular Turks raised in secularly Muslim families. The contradiction between Islamic morality and homosexuality was not mobilized in their narratives as a source of important conflict or disjuncture for articulating their sexual identities.

My interviews were designed to collect narratives about the participants' sexual histories and conceptions of gender and sexual identities across generations as well as their views on and participation in gay communities and gay activism. Specifically, I constructed my interviews to answer the following broad questions: How do these men negotiate competing global and local cultural constructions of their roles and identities? And how and in what manner do they perceive, evaluate, and import various models of gay identity and sexual relations into their biographies? Although I used a uniform interview protocol, my interview design allowed me to probe more deeply into questions that encouraged respondents to reflect on conflicts and contradictions, such as how they position themselves within particular discourses (coexisting and contradictory) related to the closet/coming out and how they balance their own individuality against the interests of their family and social class.

Sociologically speaking, because my sample is small, my argument is suggestive rather than conclusive. Rather than draw definitive conclusions, my aim here is to explore and outline the main parameters of the complex and paradoxical processes of an unfolding identity construction.

Troubling the Global Adoption of a Western Gay Identity

As many scholars who study sexuality and globalization have noted, non-Western individuals engaged in same-sex sexual practices are increasingly adopting the linguistic, lifestyle, and political markers of a Western gay identity[3] (Adam, Duyvendak, and Krouwel 1999; Altman 1996, 1997; Bereket and Adam 2006, 2008; Jackson 1997; McLelland 2000; N. Miller 1992; Whitaker 2006). This trend has led a number of critics to challenge the dominant Eurocentric paradigm of gay identity and history on several fronts. Focusing on the efforts of the Gay International and other global gay movements in non-Western national contexts, critics such as Joseph Massad (2002) have troubled the role these movements have played in reshaping the sexual and political climates of many non-Western cultures previously characterized by their diversity of sexual practices, including unmarked, often nonstigmatized, homoeroticisms. As Massad notes, in an effort to liberate individuals from constraints and repression, these movements have deployed gay rights discourses that compress culturally permitted sexual indeterminacy and culturally and historically unique same-sex practices into a fixed, "open" gay identity. In doing so, Massad argues, these discourses often replace culturally accepted models of sexual fluidity with rigid homo-hetero binaries and problematically conflate "doing" (participating in same-sex sex) with "being" (having a gay identity).

In confronting Eurocentrism, other scholars have sought to demonstrate the ways in which homosexuality operated as a visible identity category in premodern Muslim societies. In a volume exploring the different facets of homosexuality in Muslim contexts, Stephen O. Murray and Will Roscoe (1997) question the assumption that "'identity' and 'subculture' are uniquely modern and western inventions" (5). Through historical, anthropological, and literary studies, the volume's contributors attempt to document how practitioners of premodern homosexuality were able to articulate identities based on their practices and how they created networks among themselves by achieving sufficient density and localization to be noticed in various Islamic societies. In a recent article, Serkan Delice (2010) gives us an insightful analysis cast in terms of interrogating the limits of a linear historicism that neatly divides the past and the present and premodern and modern at the service of constructing "a hetero-normalized past" to "naturalize a hetero-normative present" (104). Specifically, he argues that narratives produced by historians about the ways in which the Ottoman Empire shaped the categories of gender and sexual identifications and the same-sex intimacies between men, as well as the ways those relations were perceived and lived out by people from different backgrounds, should be understood as "ideological and political deployments of history." In other words, the stakes in question are contemporary ones.

The contradictory presentations of the Ottoman sexual order are illustrated by Delice's juxtaposition of the historical narratives inspired by the Kemalist nationalist ideology[4] and Islamist conservative scholarship's rejection of such narratives. According to Delice, by reappropriating Orientalist constructions of the Ottoman sexual order, the Kemalist nationalists depict the world of the Ottoman elites as "governed by pleasure and perversity, a world that recognized no moral boundaries," and "the imperial harem as a space of boundless lust and rampant sexuality, a perverse space where the voracious and debauched sultans committed all kinds of abominable acts, including homosexuality" (105). In stark contrast to this depiction of a world of decadence, the Ottomans in the discourse of Islamic conservatives were sexually decent and the Ottoman Empire was marked by "a golden age of purity unblemished by so-called degenerate elements, such as homosexuality" (106). Notably, Delice also argues that the modern Turkish LGBT movement also turns a historical gaze toward the Ottomans in order to provide a set of references to resignify "Ottoman culture and society as a more sexually permissive era, an era that supposedly came to an end in the nineteenth century, when the already institutionalized homophobic culture of the West infiltrated Ottoman-Turkish society as a consequence of Westernization and the construction of the nation-state" (106). Vis-à-vis this point, Evren Savci (2011) makes the argument that the modernization and Westernization projects of the Republic had heteronormalizing and heterosexualizing effects. She cites, for example, how the banishment of polygamous marriages and households during the modern, secular, and Western nation-building process removed "multiple adult bodies from the domestic sphere, . . . only leaving the heterosexual parental couple" (70). Similarly, she argues, when the early Republican leaders outlawed *tekke* (which served as a home for a religious leader and his male followers), this secularizing measure also meant erasure of "a same-sex place that has been reported as a key male homoerotic space during the Ottoman era" (70). In the same vein, replacement of the *hamams* (public same-sex baths) with the modern bathrooms in family homes produced "the slow erasure of a historical location for same-sex sexuality" (71). While it is beyond the limits of this chapter to review this pivotal debate in depth, the question of whether under globalization gay identity achieves sameness in different national and cultural contexts is an intriguing one (is, for example, the Turkish notion of *gey* the same as the Thai adoption of "gay"?), and it invites us to elaborate a new perspective on the relationship between globalization and the adoption of a seemingly homogenized gay identity.

The most recent literature on globalization, particularly that on the vexing issue of how the global and the local interact, has acknowledged and used rich empirical research to evidence how globalization is actively constructed rather than passively received in many different cultural contexts, an insight that suggests that despite globalization, self-production continues to be inscribed by cultural particularity. As Carla Freeman (2010) has suggested, because "globalization itself is imbricated within cultural forms and meanings," we should examine how the global operates "in and through the stickiness and particularities of culture" rather than view globalization as a singular and homogenizing force that "operates outside the fabric of culture" (578). Similarly, in an effort analogous to my own, Lisa Rofel (2007) disrupts the global/local, sameness/difference binaries underlying the model of a singular global gay identity to present a dynamic vision of the transcultural production of gay identities in modern China.[5] Reading gay identity in China as a category closely articulated with a desire for cultural belonging, she suggests that gay men there invoke the ideal of a global gay identity not to become passive bearers of that identity, but to place themselves and their sexual identities "within Chinese culture in temporal, spatial, linguistic, and substantive terms" (96–97).

Conceptualizations such as Freeman's and Rofel's that accord a prominent role to the specificities of the local in informing and forging new concepts of the self also reject a stale and undifferentiated notion of culture or "the local." Instead, they invite us to historicize our studies of the local while paying attention to both the continuities of cultural ideas and the ruptures caused by globalization, urging us to see the deep structures of culture as internally pluralistic, capable of containing and exhibiting contradictions. Bringing this cultural and historical specificity into better focus, as Sanjay Srivastava (2007) suggests, "may invite unique readings" (26) of what seem to be common practices or homogenized identities.

My intention in this chapter, then, is to foreground the more opaque (and deeply internalized) instances of cultural particularity in Turkey via Joseph's concept of connectivity. While recognizing the evidence of individualizing forces and the erosion caused by major transformations in Turkish society of certain practices that used to cultivate connectivity, I suggest that connectivity plays a meaningful role in regulating the closet and that the concept of disembedded or autonomous selves in the construction of an open gay identity is problematic.

The following pages begin with a description of the social and cultural context of emerging gay identities and gay culture in Istanbul. From there, I move on to discuss the popular understanding of homosexuality in Turkey in order to highlight the charged role this understanding plays in redefining homosexuality and in the adoption of *gey* identification. I then focus on two vital aspects of *gey* identification—desire management and love, and social class—to show how these domains give substance to a *gey* subjectivity that is at once fashioned on ideals of globalism and inflected by cultural particularities. I explore the implications of the culturally specific dynamics of connectivity for the closet or coming out. I conclude that connectivity, closely articulated with class reproduction, informs, fashions, and regulates selves in ways that might not sit well with the global demands of an open gay identity.

Emergence of Gay Visibility and Politics

Whether or not we refer to the existence or formation (*oluşum*) of a *gey* community, there is clearly an increasingly visible *gey* subculture and a growing general discourse around non-normative sexual identities in contemporary Turkey. Mainstream newspapers routinely feature articles on gay issues as well as interviews with gay activists and writers. Adored by mainstream audiences, gay singers and entertainers are a ubiquitous presence on television programs. Gay/lesbian/trangender organizations in Turkey are developing ideological perspectives and bringing individuals together through Internet networking and organizing events and discussions. These groups publish journals; organize activities, protests, and marches; engage with other political movements in Turkey; and organize international and national academic and nonacademic conferences. In June 2013, the Lesbian and Gay Pride march in Istanbul, which had previously only attracted a few hundred people, became an immense parade and protest of thousands of people with a large participation of straight allies.[6] And gay men and women in Turkey have increasingly become the subjects of scholarly work.[7]

For Turkish LBGTQ individuals, Istanbul (which, with its fourteen million inhabitants, is a truly cosmopolitan city) offers the kind of urban existence that allows for the growth of a gay subculture. The Taksim district of Istanbul has become the heart of gay subculture, offering locations and opportunities for leisure-consumption practices ranging from elegant clubs, high-end restaurants, theaters, and bars to shabby eateries, *hamams* (bath houses), movie theaters, and street prostitution.[8] Gay men are visible and make intensive use of the streets of Taksim, frequenting spaces defined as gay as well as mingling openly with the city's more mainstream crowd. Different groups, divided by class and regional origin, mark and identify certain clubs and cafes as their own.

Poor but handsome young men from the margins of the city, squatter settlement districts of Istanbul, also populate Taksim's bars and clubs to make their livings as "rent boys"[9] for wealthier upper-class gay and straight clients.

However, the increased visibility of gay men and the relative openness of gay life in Turkey's metropolitan cities has not necessarily translated into a growing acceptance of homosexuality. Although homosexuality is not criminalized in Turkey (there is no law that bans homosexuality), military service, which is mandatory for all Turkish males, is strictly prohibited for anyone who claims and provides medical/psychological evidence of homosexual orientation. In a measure initiated by Turkey's efforts at accession to the European Union (EU), the legislative framework of the Turkish Republic was radically changed in the early 2000s: in 2001 the Turkish Civil Code was renewed, and in 2004 the Penal Code was revised. A new article criminalizing discrimination based on sexual orientation was drafted, but during deliberations, the ruling party, AKP, removed this article, and a new article on obscenity (acts against public morality) was passed. This article built antihomosexual bias into the Turkish criminal code and can be interpreted in such a way as to limit individuals' freedom of expression and legitimize discrimination based on sexual orientation (WWHR 2005).

Moreover, the intensified visibility of gay culture and the growth of a self-assertive gay consciousness have, rather than diminished homophobia in Turkey, in many cases actually produced new societal anxieties and violence against gay, lesbian, and transgender people. According to data collected by the 2007 Pew Global Attitudes Project, in 2002, 22 percent of Turks reported believing that homosexuality was a way of life that should be accepted by society, compared to just 14 percent in 2007 (both of these figures are drastically lower than the acceptance rate among Americans, which was 49 percent in 2007) (35–36). A recent study (Gerhards 2010) investigating the value orientations of the citizens among EU member states and Turkey (a candidate country) asked participants "whether homosexuality can always be justified, never be justified or something in between" (9). With a mean value of 1.6 on the ten-point scale, Turks endorsed virtually no support for the justification of homosexuality (10). Surveys among Turkish university students also report negative attitudes toward homosexuality, especially toward male homosexuality (Gelban and Duyan 2006), although reports suggest that female students are more likely to have more positive attitudes towards homosexuality. My own representative survey among Boğaziçi students replicated the gender polarization found in such surveys: roughly 40 percent of my male respondents endorsed defining homosexuality as an illness and agreed with the statement that "homosexuality shouldn't be tolerated," compared to roughly 20 percent of my female respondents. However, reflecting the strong culture of familialism and connectivity in Turkey, a high percentage of both my male and female respondents said they would not cut off their relationships with their sibling if he or she came out as gay to them.

According to most observers and my respondents, differences in gender and religious beliefs influence value orientations toward homosexuality, with men and religiously devoted individuals showing stronger negative attitudes toward homosexuality and women and less religious people (as well as those with more liberal attitudes toward sexuality in general) holding less negative views. Indeed, the overwhelmingly negative attitude toward homosexuals in Muslim-majority countries seems to have a strong connection with orthodox Islamic religious beliefs. Like Christianity, orthodox Islam views homosexual acts as conflicting with reproduction and the complementarity of the sexes, an idea often tied back to a line in the Koran: "How can you lust for males, of all creatures in the world, and leave those whom God has created for you as your mates. You are really going beyond all limits" (qtd. in Duran 1993, 182). Negative attitudes, prejudice, and hatred toward homosexuals also manifest in acts of physical violence and police harassment against gay men and women in Turkey (Yüzgün 1993). The recent tragic murder by his father of 26-year-old gay man Ahmet Yıldız in Istanbul is considered the first gay honor killing in Turkey.[10] Turkey's LGBT movement is hoping that the trial of Ahmet's father will bring attention to the country's attitude toward homosexuality and help highlight the lack of state protection for lesbian, gay, and transgender individuals in Turkey. Similarly, a recent string of murders of transgender women has rallied national and international organizations to call on the Turkish government to enact antidiscrimination protections, institute programs to combat hatred, and repeal laws that permit the police to harass gay, lesbian, and transgender people.

İbne (Faggot); Gey (Gay)

In their attempts to redefine homosexuality and change the public understanding of their identities, gay men in Turkey draw upon and import global definitions of homosexuality and localize them by giving substance to the term "*gey*." First introduced to the Turkish lexicon in the late 1990s, this term has allowed men to articulate their same-sex desires and practices in terms of a more global, flexible gay identity and, as such, has become an important category for organizing selfhood and politics of resistance in Turkey. One important context for understanding the incorporation of this global gay identity into Turkish culture is formed by the rigid active/passive, feminine/masculine binaries that have historically structured understandings of homosexual identities in Turkey. These binaries, which, among other effects, have supported the stereotype of the *ibne*[11]—or faggot—exercise a special potency in the public understanding of homosexuality in Turkey, and adopting a *gey* identity has become one key way in which Turkish men practicing same-sex sex distance themselves from and challenge this public construction of homosexuality.

As in many other societies, in Turkey, homosexual encounters take place among heterosexually, in addition to homosexually, identified men. Rather than being predicated on the anatomical sex of one's partner, sexuality in these contexts is organized by active/passive sex-role binaries (denoted, respectively, by being the penetrating or penetrated partner). These roles, in turn, are associated with particular gendered connotations and stigmas. The partner who adopts the active role of the *aktif* (or "inserter") does not have his manhood/masculinity compromised and is not considered homosexual, while the partner who adopts the passive role of the *pasif* (or "receiver") is effeminized and marked as homosexual. Because one of the ways homosexuality is constructed as deviant is through the feminization of the figure of the male homosexual by reference to his passive/penetrated role, this binary operates to define homosexual/heterosexual identity and allocate stigma accordingly.

In Turkey, "*ibne*" has historically referred to the penetrated/*pasif* partner and is used to connote passivity, unmanliness, femininity, dishonor, and shame. Employed to talk about both identity and conduct, "*ibne*" can be attached to even the most exalted figures of masculinity.

For example, a successful soccer player who happens to miss a good opportunity to score a goal is readily subjected to insulting shouts of "*ibne*" by his fans in the stadium. More than a homophobic colloquialism or a referent for a fixed identity, "*ibne*" operates as a regulative discourse, simultaneously defining, circumscribing, and patrolling forms of behavior deemed inappropriate or outside the boundaries of proper masculinity.[12] In this sense, "*ibne*" embodies what Judith Butler theorizes as the constitutive outside—the "threatening specter" (Butler 1999, 3) that the dominant cultural grid renders and recognizes only as a failed, unacceptable gender that must be continually iterated and repudiated.

Through interviews with twenty Turkish men who have sex with men (MSM)[13] from a range of socioeconomic backgrounds, educational levels, ages, and sex-role preferences, researchers Bereket and Adam (2006) have demonstrated that an increasing number of Turkish men practicing same-sex sex are moving away from identifying themselves as either *aktif* or *pasif* in favor of a more flexible *gey* identity. By appealing to this *gey* identity, these men are constructing their homosexual subjectivities as distinct from the *ibne* and asserting ideals of more fluid (and, as I will demonstrate, often more egalitarian) roles for themselves and their partners. As Bereket and Adams argue, beyond the simple adoption of a term, the acceptance of a more global, flexible gay identity significantly shapes identities, group life, and gay activism in Turkey. Also, *gey*-identified men tend to hold liberal views concerning religiosity, while "the men who identify themselves as being exclusively *aktif* or *pasif*, and, thus, adhere more closely to the traditional constitution of same-sex bonding, tend as well to be influenced by Islamic teachings and are more troubled by their 'inability' to resist the homoerotic, anticipating punishment after death" (Bereket and Adam 2008, 218).

The appeal to a *gey* subjectivity, as opposed to a homosexual subjectivity based on active/passive sex roles and stereotypes of the *ibne*, is significantly reorganizing the strict gendered binaries structuring the relationships between homosexual men in Turkey, transforming the mentalities and self-fashioning of men practicing same-sex sex. One of the most profound changes this shift has brought is the fact that one's sexual preference is no longer just a habit or practice, but a way of living and thinking that is incorporated into one's personality and identity (Bereket and Adam 2006). Piecing together a coherent picture of the meanings attached to *gey* identification is not an easy task. However, in this section I will approach and begin to unpack the multivalent meanings this label acquires in Turkey through two pervasive and overlapping concerns: (1) desire management and love and (2) class formation. In doing so, I will show how this transformation from "doing" *aktif/pasif* into "being" *gey* entails particular ideals of love, equality, and middle-classness that mark *gey* as a privileged category, permitting, as one of my respondents suggests, every *gey* man to be homosexual, but not every homosexual to be *gey*.

"Every Gay Is Homosexual, but Not Every Homosexual Is Gay": Ideals of Love and Middle-Classness in *Gey* Self-Making

In the context of globalization, homosexual men in Turkey who are urban, young, educated, English-speaking, and middle-class are being confronted with the active/passive question more frequently, intensely, and personally than ever before. As they increasingly direct themselves to globalized norms of desire management, these men are using ideals of versatility, equality, and intimacy to forge new models of homosexual relationships and transgress the rigid boundaries between *aktif* and *pasif* homosexual identities.[14] For these men, forging relationships defined by versatile sex roles, equality between partners, and ideals of love and intimacy has become an important element in constituting a new *gey* identity.

For one of the young men I interviewed, Celal (23), negotiating the active/passive binary requires sensitivity to and a willingness to accommodate his partner's desires. Although in the past Celal has shared active and passive sexual roles evenly with his partners, he explains that in his current relationship he most often assumes the passive role because his partner prefers to be active:

> Before meeting my current boyfriend, my preference in bed was what is called versatile style, both active and passive, but [my current boyfriend] is more selective in this regard and would like to be active. I don't like to push anyone into doing something they don't want to. . . . I never forced my boyfriend either. Nevertheless, you have your own desires. He acted with consideration: he said he wanted to [take the passive role] with me,

despite having no experience with being passive. But I don't want [to switch roles] because I know he doesn't enjoy it, so I am not demanding. I am more passive and he is active so we are drawing boundaries like that, even though I would have preferred the other kind [versatility] . . . we switch roles sometimes. He understands that I would like to take other roles, but it still creates problems, since I don't want him to put up with it because he loves me. He insists that he is taking pleasure, but I am not relieved [*içime sinmiyor*] because I know for sure he is doing it because he loves me.

Here, Celal clearly articulates the way versatility has become a strategy for negotiating desire in homosexual relationships, as well as the way partners negotiate the passive-active balance to meet the particular needs of a given relationship. As this account suggests, this twin process of pacification and activation between partners involves mutually expected self-restraint.

The discursive and practical presence of this binary, however, is not limited to negotiations in personal, intimate relationships. The issue of "who is active, and who is passive" in a relationship also dominates conversations among gay friends. More importantly, the coming-out narratives I collected suggest that this binary is accorded special importance when one discloses his sexual orientation to heterosexual others for the first time. Indeed, my respondents reported that the first question they encounter when they disclose their homosexuality to friends and acquaintances is often whether they are active or passive. Overall, these men report that the heterosexual individuals to whom they come out read performing the active role as a marker of masculinity, and they suggest that coming out as an active gay man affords one a greater degree of acceptability in peer groups. One member of the focus group articulated the sentiments of his heterosexual peers:

I know from my [heterosexual] friends, for instance, in a conversation if I emphasize I am active or my being active is alluded to, they listen to me with more sympathy. They take me more seriously [*kaile alınmak*], they even love me. [It goes like this]: "you are homosexual but at least [*bari*] don't be passive, at minimum be a man."

As this account suggests, negotiating active and passive roles also has important implications for the way one negotiates and distributes certain gender roles and ideals within one's relationships, as well as the way one communicates those roles to the outside world.

Overall, this shift toward decreasing (displays of) passive/active inequality seems to be the central constitutive element of *gey* subjectivity, and *gey* identification can be understood, in part, as a search for versatility. Without extensive data, it is impossible to ascertain the exact extent to which this binary is actually transgressed and versatility desired and achieved in intimate relationships and the extent to which it remains an unpracticed theory. Nevertheless, expectations to live up to this ideal of versatility appear to be giving substance, at least discursively, to the culturally and linguistically empty identity category of *gey*.

Importantly, this appeal to a more even distribution of domination and submission within relationships should be understood as operating through and alongside another ideal of *gey* subjectivity: the egalitarian partnership. Without exception, my respondents stressed the importance of equality within intimate partnerships both in terms of age and in terms of social class. Efe, who is twenty-two years old, stressed that he would not date anyone over twenty-five, explaining that "anyone who is above thirty, I consider old . . . we live in a fast changing world, even a five-year age difference amounts to a generational difference." Efe also gave a lucid account of the importance of finding a partner from a similar class background to his own, stating that he "would never go out with someone above or below [his] class—this is the rule." He explained, "Your life perspectives are different. I don't want to have any relationship with those mannerless, vulgar wealthy men, except for sex. There wouldn't be any shared topic we can talk about." Referencing such an encounter, he recalled, "He [the wealthy man] kept talking; I said, 'let's go fuck' because he was talking about radically different things . . . when you come from the same class you have the same aspirations, same desires, and same point of view." "But," Efe added, "I also equally discriminate against those who are below my class." Efe is here expressing a very common pattern in the organization of *gey* identity that is fundamentally linked to class distinctions. Class-related cultural attitudes and interests place a psychic distance between men of different classes, powerfully communicating the significance of class in the production of *gey* identity. Upwardly mobile middle-class men like Efe rely on class norms, behaviors, and dispositions in the process of distinguishing themselves from other men who engage in same-sex sex but are located further down in the class hierarchy, lacking in middle-class material resources and cultural values.

Another of my respondents, Akın (20), similarly described believing that mutually satisfying, egalitarian relationships were impossible between individuals with significant differences in age and life experience. As he explains of his own ideal partner,

> It is a must that he is a university student, and I am twenty and he must be in the 19–21 age group. I don't even talk to people outside these parameters, because I don't think we can get along. This is what I don't want to see happen: that person [an older partner] anticipating my mistakes and behavioral paths because he already traversed this road—who clearly would see what you would do and exactly where and how you would screw up. Hypothetically speaking, you can be with a 27-year-old, but that relationship would strictly be based on sex. I don't want that kind of relationship.

For Akın, like Efe, ideals of egalitarianism significantly influence what he looks for in a partner as well as how he distinguishes his same-sex desire from homosexual relationships based purely on sex.

As Akın's repudiation of a relationship based strictly on sex suggests, in addition to versatility and equality, ideals of love and intimacy centrally underlie the construction of *gey* subjectivity in Turkey. Indeed, for the young men I interviewed, what it means to be *gey*, as opposed to *ibne*, is inextricably tied to the ability/capacity to be in love with another man, and the privileging of love and intimacy over sex significantly contributes to their formation of a positive, affirmative self-identity that is distinctly *gey*. As Celal stated when I asked him what it means to be gay,

> "Gay" means to be able to fall in love with someone of your own sex. Because in sexual terms in Turkey, a man can use another man sexually, but that doesn't mean he is gay. To be gay is to be able to really love a man; to fall in love with him; to be able to think about him all the time, well, you know, when I close my eyes or when I am alone if [my current

boyfriend] is on my mind and I am making plans in relation to him; and if I am happy about being with a man, especially if I could pronounce his sex to others with complete quietude of heart [*gönül rahatlığıyla*], that is what it means to be gay. It is not what a lot of people perceive as to be effeminate, or sex-focused.

Here, appealing to the ideal of love allows Celal to distance his own identity as a gay man from stereotypes of homosexuals as deviating from the norms of gender and sexual desire. In affirming his *gey* identity and repudiating stereotypes of the sex-focused *ibne*, Celal also draws a distinction between having sex for emotional reasons and having sex purely for bodily satisfaction. To this end, Celal attributes the strength and longevity of his relationship with his current partner to the fact that they waited for two to three weeks before they had sex, a decision he suggests allowed them to form a deeper emotional attachment and make sex more meaningful:

> [My boyfriend and I] shared meals, went to movies. . . . While spending time with him, I realized that I liked him. He also felt the same way about me. . . . The first time we coupled [*birlikte olduk*], what I felt was so incredibly intense. I imagine that had we had sex on that first night, I wouldn't have been able to experience those moments of intensity. To me it is more beautiful to have sex with someone when there is an emotional connection between you than having sex with someone you only desire sexually. . . . Gays meet with each other for the purpose of sex, "oh this guy is beautiful, I should sleep with him." That is the purpose of meeting, it is never a consideration of "let me go out with him and establish a shared life with that person." When you have sex immediately, that possibility is even stolen away. The sex you have with someone you don't know doesn't carry any emotionality; it is only for bodily satisfaction.

Another of my respondents, Ahmet (24), similarly emphasized the importance of love and intimacy in distinguishing gay from homosexual identities, but his account also underscores the ways in which the recognition of same-sex love becomes a domain of struggle for gay men:

Homosexual is different from gay. Every gay is homosexual but not every homosexual is gay. Being gay is an identity. I accept it as an identity, that I am not only a man who loves men [but] it is also a struggle—it is a struggle for liberation. At this point to be gay as a homosexual man, it is a political stance towards life. This is a revolt, in fact; it is a quest of justice. This is gayness to me.

Ahmet's account clearly illustrates the way becoming gay is a process of identification as opposed to a pattern of behaviors. It is not just the act of same-sex sex that makes one gay as opposed to simply homosexual but also the capacity to share love with another man and the centrality of that capacity to the way one thinks about and structures other aspects of his identity.

Given the role love plays in the formation of gay identity, it is particularly important to note that love is a complicated realm that brings with it all kinds of tensions and negotiations over a host of concerns, particularly in relation to the confinement of sexual desire/activity to monogamous relationships. As more and more men adopt a global gay identity, love and sex are increasingly imagined in terms of committed and long-term relationships, and impersonal, transient encounters between men are being subordinated to ideals of gay couplehood and domesticity. In this regard, comments like Akın's below were echoed by others:

It seems what we have is an endless consumption of bodies without the possibility for gay kinship or commitment. [Kinship and commitment] are important: we can't reject them because heterosexual relationships are based on them. [Sexual] morality is not well defined. I don't know, but it seems to me that it remains unnamed and very fluid. You can see the person who was with you yesterday with somebody else the next day, or all the possible permutations are being tried. This does not sound good to me.

As this account suggests, negotiating the place of heterosexual ideals of love and commitment in homosexual relationships remains a central concern of those men fashioning their new gay identities.

Overall, for the young men I interviewed, cultivating a *gey* subjectivity through ideals of versatility, equality, and love has helped expand a group feeling and identification around homosexual practices. However, the growth of a collective *gey* identity has, for the most part, failed to cross class boundaries or weaken urban/rural distinctions in Turkey. Indeed, class and urban/rural distinctions structure and mediate another, more visibly pronounced meaning the identity label "*gey*" assumes in contemporary Turkey: in middle-class homosexual vernacular, if you are middle class, you are *gey*; if you are not, you are *ibne*. As this discrepancy suggests, membership in the *ibne* or the *gey* category is not predicated simply on the transgression or maintenance of the active/passive binary. On the contrary, it is mapped on complex and rigid class and urban/rural–origin distinctions, whereby "*gey*" comes to mean "middle-class."

As I discussed before, class identity—"a sense of one's place(s) in a cultural economy of meaning" (Bettie 2003, 43)—has multiple registers in Turkey and is expressed through a combination of an individual's level and type of schooling, English-speaking ability, work identity, income, and leisure-consumption practices. In Turkey, as in many other national contexts, leisure-consumption practices in particular become a significant domain in which gayness gains public visibility and different bodies are alternately included and excluded from a collective *gey* identity. Indeed, the expression of *gey* selfhood through one's use of and relationship to commodities and leisure activities is a central practice in contemporary Turkey, and *gey* subjectivity has increasingly become rooted in a middle-class lifestyle in which individuals are expected to embody their class privilege through certain physical ideals—being young, beautiful, athletically built—as well as through their ability to purchase and wear the most fashionable clothing and to frequent sites of leisure such as gay clubs and bars. In other words, class acts as a powerful way of making *gey* identity. Thus, in addition to the ideals of versatility, equality, and love that structure individuals' desire, *gey* identity is also substantiated and articulated in Turkey through expressive cultural styles that assert one's inclusion in an urban middle class and distance from a stigmatized *ibne* identity.

In contemporary Turkey, young homosexual men are increasingly appealing to the borrowed category "*gey*" to distance themselves from certain undesirable homosexual identities and assert particular ways of being gay rather than simply participating in stigmatized sex practices. In doing so, they substantiate and give meaning to an otherwise empty term by aligning it with ideals of global identification, versatility, masculinity, cosmopolitanism, flexibility, and middle-class belonging—a process that, in turn, marks local identification, rigid active/passive roles, femininity, rural origins, stasis, and lower-classness as undesirable traits belonging to a stigmatized *ibne* identity.

But are these disclosed or closeted *gey* identities? And what is the relevance or irrelevance of the closet/coming out to giving substance to *gey* identification? In the following section I will consider the process of coming out in Turkey as it relates to a *gey* subjectivity shaped by the particularities of connected/relational selfhood. Reading the closet through Suad Joseph's model of connectivity, I will suggest that the strong emphasis put on kinship networks and the role familial relationships play in shaping individuals' senses of self in contemporary Turkey is an important (and often overlooked) factor influencing the way *gey* men there understand and publicly represent their sexual identities.

Coming Out through Connectivity

Conceptualizing the notion of *gey* identification within the perspective of family associations is imperative in cultural contexts such as Turkey, where collective and relational selves are more salient than the autonomous self. The linear story of gay identification under globalization, with its emphasis on the diminishing importance of traditional frames of reference for identity development, misses this strong presence of connectedness in contexts like Turkey. I make this point not to suggest that we ignore evidence of individualizing forces or ideologies of the autonomous self emerging in Turkey. Rather, I make this point as a way to refocus our attention on those aspects of cultural life and those identities that are excluded from this "before-and-after" model of modernity, a category that includes those gay men in Turkey who are negotiating the tension between the desire for relatedness and the desire for untied autonomy.

Because connectivity as a cultural form is diffuse and fluid, I did not actively seek out stories that represented the absence or presence of connectivity in the lives of my respondents. Only detailed and close readings between the lines of their narratives provided windows into the complicated workings of connectivity in their lives. Celal, for instance, tapped into connectivity when narrating the differences between himself and his father:

> I don't believe in family values too much—well, you know, the belief that kinship should bond us together. . . . My father is strongly connected to his family—his brothers, his dad, and his children. I love my aunt very much, not because she is my aunt, but because we can talk and share things together. This is why I love her deeply . . . but my dad doesn't have this kind of relationship with his aunt. He loves his aunt and respects her because she is his aunt.

My respondents also indirectly alluded to their continued dependence on their mothers. For example, when I asked him about the last gift he had received from his boyfriend, I inadvertently learned that Celal's mother buys his underwear: he reported that it was a pair of shorts because the boyfriend didn't like the boxers, "suitable for a fifty-year-old man," that his mother kept buying him. My respondents' desires for continued parental attachment also emerged through the way considerations for their parents factored into large life decisions. Despite the fact that his professional future realistically might lead to life and work abroad, one of my respondents, Efe, indicated that because he was the only child in his family, "it would be very hard to separate from [his] family." As he explained, "It is okay to have my own home here, but that kind of distance would be very hard."

Regardless of the specific examples cited or referred to, the narratives I collected overwhelmingly indicated that mothers are routinely involved in their sons' social and extracurricular lives and are primary sources of emotional caring and practical tending for their sons. Living in the parental home and being embedded in the routines of daily living there play an important part in this involvement. These young men's acceptance, rejection, or negotiation of their mothers' high level of involvement in their lives underline a dialectical tension between autonomy and connection, openness and closedness. Their accounts also sharply revealed how this level of engagement creates the need for deep lies. As Efe, who is in the closet to his mother, noted, "My life revolves around lies. My mother asks: 'Where did you go?' 'I went to such and such bar.' 'Which bar is that?' 'That bar'—I am lying about the bar.

'Whom were you with?' 'I was with my friends,' 'Which friends?' 'This friend, that friend.' More lies, or I was 'with my girlfriend.' Lie."

Ergen's (21) story dramatizes even more vividly the challenges involved in managing the closet when one lives in the parental home and the upper-middle-class parents' involvement in one's educational and social lives is quite intense. Ergen remarked that the day before I interviewed him, his father, while using Ergen's computer, found his c.v., which he had prepared for a class assignment. In his c.v. he listed his membership in a gay-lesbian civic organization, and under extracurricular activities mentioned that he "organizes queer parties." Confronting him directly, Ergen's father said, "I couldn't understand the meaning of this [referring to the c.v.]. If you are hiding your inclinations from us, if there is such a thing this is a very serious matter. It should be talked about." Ergen told him a white lie: "This c.v. is fictional because the professor is gay. I wanted to get a good grade." In addition to this event, his mother found a book, *Homosexual Dialectic*, in his room. She immediately asked, "What is this?" Ergen said it was a book for a paper for a psychology class. Before this episode, in fact, Ergen's mother had also found a flyer on violence against gays in his backpack and had asked him where he had gotten it. He told her, "It was given to me on the street and I was going to throw it away but I forgot." Ergen also recounted two other events in which he was very close to being caught. After his first sexual relationship with a 27-year-old man whom he met through an Internet site, he got panicky despite the fact that he didn't have anal sex. He took an HIV test and all the other tests for sexually transmitted diseases. He went to a private hospital without thinking that the bill would go to his father. After a huge bill arrived, his father called the hospital to inquire about it, but they did not reveal the nature of the tests because of doctor-patient confidentiality. Ergen's father then confronted him by asking, "Is there something serious with you because this is a huge bill; I want to know." In another incident, when his parents were out, he brought home a gay friend to have sex. His parents arrived home early, just two minutes after his friend left. Because he knows he is being closely watched by his parents, Ergen tidied up his "closet" to the point that he even got rid of the list of books he had checked out from the school library and erased from his computer his typed-up thoughts on gay/lesbian-themed movies he had watched.

Besides the lies they tell about their daily routines and associations, what pains these individuals is their self-imposed inability to confide in their mothers about what they experience and feel in their own intimate relationships. Ahmet's mother knows he is gay but refuses to acknowledge this fact. As he told me, "From time to time she alludes. There is this discourse: I know, but you don't tell me . . . I don't want to hear." He lamented the fact that while in the past he used to elicit and enjoy the pleasures of his mother's company, now whenever he and his mother have conversations about relationships, love, and sexual intimacy, he finds himself veering off into generalizations or shifting the conversation to other topics. This issue is particularly complicated for Ahmet because he defines coming out as something sacred: the best form of gay activism. Because of his staunch stance on this issue, he is quite vocal about it in the gay community. He also practices what he preaches: for example, he detailed how he came out to a large class during a class discussion. However, the discrepancy between actively advocating rejection of the closet and his inability to come out to his mother pains him tremendously. In this regard, he referenced an argument with one of his gay friends. Ahmet was arguing for the significance of coming out for gay visibility, and the friend he was arguing with confronted him with the fact that he himself was still in the closet in relation to his family. The friend said, "You cannot tell to the one who gave birth to you, how dare you talk about activism around coming out?" Ahmet noted, "[What he said] hurt me so much and still it hurts. It is always about this oppression of love: your love for the people you love overpowers any gay politics." For him, only connecting love for the mother with another type of love makes the coming out meaningful: "I want to directly come out to my mother when [it will come to a time when] I introduce someone to my mother and say, 'look mom this is the man I love.'" The pain caused by this growing distance surfaced in the words of many of the men I spoke with and serves as a significant emblem of the tensions and ambivalences of remaining in the closet.

Open Secret/Secret Subject

The connected mode of being and belonging adds further significance to the closet/coming out in Turkey, particularly when we define the closet as a metaphor for social interaction that organizes and manages knowledge around homosexuality, rather than as a metaphor to register a single state of being out. Aptly identified and conceptualized in literature[15] as the dialectics of the "open secret," the metaphor of the closet in Turkey is also governed by the familiar dynamic of knowing the secret subject but refusing to acknowledge it (Miller 1988). That is, the closet yields its repressive authority by making the secret subject's presence absent. In this sense, the closet decisively structures gay life/identity, not because it hides it, but because it serves as a means of controlling its presence.

Although experiences of being "in" or "out" of the closet incorporate diverse practices, both contextual and contingent, one consistency I found across my interviews was that my respondents' decisions to conceal or disclose their gay identity involved a deep consideration of the threat this exposure posed not only to themselves but also to their significant others. The cultural and familial expectation of connective selving—"thinking about yourself in relation to others," "seeing yourself as an extension of intimate others," and "the subordination of individual interests to the interests of a larger familial collective"—means considering the radical effects one's actions have on others and understanding that the respectability, honor, and shame of one's significant others are inextricably linked to oneself. Cem (27), who is out to his parents, referenced one particular instance when his father arranged a highly sought-after appointment for his serious medical condition with a specialist through his CEO. Cem said he refused to see this doctor because "there was this danger that this doctor, who is a close friend of my dad's CEO, could have outed me to my father's boss. I couldn't risk it."

With paradoxical effects, coming out to one's family is regarded as "the epitome of coming out" by my informants, embodying, for them, the true essence of what it means to be out. Not surprisingly, family relationships have a profound effect on how open these young men are able to be with others. Indeed, remaining closeted to family members inhibits individuals in coming out to others, for fear that doing so would inadvertently result in their parents learning their secret. Thus, disclosure to one's family significantly regulates the ways in which social interaction and relationships are managed. Akın elaborates on this issue in relation to the way his coming-out process would have been slower had he stayed in Ankara, where his extended family lives:

We don't have any relatives in Istanbul, and the number of people we socialize with as family friends is very limited. Our social circle was in Ankara. . . . You know Ankara, there is only Kızılay [center city] where everyone can see you, you are too visible, you are under a spotlight. Istanbul is better, and I am lucky because I only have my parents here. To give you an example, one of my gay friends says, "on one side of Istanbul I have my mother's relatives, and on the other side I have my dad's relatives, what can I do? Where can I go?"

Yet, paradoxically, when one comes out to his parents, this process neither marks complete outness nor promises a life beyond the closet. On the contrary, disclosing one's homosexuality to one's parents can actually support the closet, implicating parents as coparticipants in protecting this secret knowledge. Moreover, knowing parents often closely scrutinize their sons' daily routines and relationships in an attempt to ensure that they manage their closet "properly," suggesting that connectivity plays an important role in ensuring that the open secret remains secret.

What we observe here is, perhaps, the disempowering effects of connectivity at multiple levels. A society that forms and organizes selves instrumentally and emotionally by connectivity makes those who vacate the closet/leave home seem as though they have lost their foundational grounding, especially when there are no alternative sources of embedding and belonging. Living out completely, being enclosed in a gay world of cafes and bars, does not offer individuals a secure base from which to move forward and form other professional and personal relationships. Even a gay couplehood existence, relatively insulated from what is considered the jealousy-filled gay world, has limited appeal if one partner is completely out, because this openness inhibits one's integration into the larger society. Akin highlights this desire to be integrated into larger social networks:

I am not going to be with only one person because I am in a relationship. Spring doesn't arrive with the blooming of a single flower. He shouldn't be someone who plucks me from my social life. We should be both able to remain integrated. The guy I went out with for a while—two months— was completely out in his own circles and was very comfortable [*rahat*] because he has no family in Istanbul. His being that out made the relationship difficult for me because I couldn't go to places with him or introduce him as a regular friend to other friends or to my parents.

A quick exposition of Cem's discursive context and the content of his sexual identity development fleshes out the closet/connectivity suggestion I have discussed so far and helps us interpret one of the salient dimensions of the coming-out narratives I explored: the tension created when coming out to one's friends and family means having one's selfhood inscribed by an essentialist gay identity.[16] Cem, who came out to himself, his parents, and some of his friends (but not to extended relatives) at the age of seventeen, now, at the age of twenty-seven, explains his dis-identification with a gay identity:

> In recent years, I have come to the conclusion that I don't want to define myself as "gay," "homosexual," "*ibne*," or with any other adjective. That's partly because of my personal history, but also because I believe that human behavior is much more complicated than these definitions . . . and I think I don't find myself in one of these definitions.

Tracing Cem's movement to what we might consider a queer identity predicated, in part, on the rejection of identity labels is, of course, complicated. But at the core of Cem's narrative is a foundational theme shared by the others I interviewed: the problems and frustrations of coming out to others who are accepting and loving yet seem only to accept an essentialist gay identity in which gay is always, everywhere relevant and omnipotent and being gay is framed as an intrinsic constant and the sum total of one's parts. In this regard, Ahmet's narrative echoes Cem's:

> I don't like my homosexuality taking the center stage. Because to the person you came out to you are homosexual and you always remain as a homosexual. After you come out you cannot control this. The person [you came out to] loves you, but, for instance, let's say he introduces you to someone. I bet afterwards he tells that person that I am homosexual—not necessarily in a homophobic sense, but you cannot break away from the homosexual label in those moments.

For Cem, being categorized under and controlled by the label of homosexuality reduces his personhood/selfhood to a single criterion, an authentic homosexual core regarded as constituting his defining essence and character, and erases all other aspects of his identity. What Cem is rejecting, in other words, is subjection to a minoritizing understanding of homosexuality. As described in the introduction to this chapter, Eve Sedgwick (1990) powerfully theorized the simultaneous existence of two fundamentally oppositional, irreconcilable understandings of homosexuality, what she distinguished as "minoritizing" and "universalizing" accounts: on the one hand, an understanding of homosexuality as a distinct, definitely identifiable, largely stable minority, and, on the other hand, an understanding of homosexual desire as a universal potential of everyone, a universally available possibility. Holding these accounts together with their mutual antagonism and respective incompatibilities, she argued, "has been the single most powerful feature of the important twentieth-century understandings of sexuality[,] . . . has been deeply constitutive of our very resources for asking questions about sexuality," and has been "an issue of continuing, determinative importance in the lives of people across the spectrum of sexualities" (1990, 1). Cem's refusal to be trapped in a (globalized) minoritizing understanding of homosexuality describes the personal contradictions of this "incoherent dispensation."

I suggest we delicately reserve judgment on the implications of Cem's practice of queer theory and not foreclose or generalize his embracement of a "universalizing" discourse. Nevertheless, we do need to articulate the implications of category abandonment, particularly with regard to how it could contribute both to further typification (passing) and invisibility and to the expansion of the closet. Cem's latest policy of "neither telling nor hiding" his love and desire for men does not necessarily secure a life beyond the closet, but actually puts him in danger of becoming invisible.

There is another significant question here: How should we understand the class-based identity implicit in Cem's rejection of categories? It is not a stretch to conclude that a class-based, elite, professional integration into the social order, like Cem's integration, serves as an important bulwark against processes that encourage living "out" a minoritizing understanding of homosexual identity and gay activism, which jeopardizes one's social and economic upward mobility. Cem's self-reflexive, examined, and lived understanding of what it means to be gay and his consequent refusal of identification has profound consequences for gay politics and activism. In particular, it acts against those types of politics that advocate a version of identity politics with a core assumption based on a minoritizing, separatist account of gay identification that denies embeddeness/connectivity.

Conclusion

In its short history, gay visibility and culture in Turkey has produced what might be described as its most authentic globalized gay subject, branded as "*kaşar*." Paradoxically, "*kaşar*" embodies the most stigmatized gay subjectivity, inviting aversion and distancing for *geys*. "*Kaşar*" literally refers to a type of hard, aged cheese, but its adjective form gives clues to its constitutive elements and the cultural meanings it conveys. In everyday Turkish vernacular, the widely used adjective "*kaşarlanmış*" attaches a negative attribute to individuals who are considered hardened and therefore insensitive and even proud of their callousness and brazenness. In the gay world, the figure of *kaşar* is marked by a reputation of being too out and having excessive sexual experience. A *kaşar* has a permanent presence in segregated and segregating virtual and real gay spaces and is always dressed up, is ready to party and cruise, and is totally globalized with his wireless connection. As Cenk Özbay notes in his study of rent boys in Istanbul (2006), "A *Kaşar* gay gives the impression that he is as comfortable in a queer space as if he is in his own home. He never seems shy, bored, or isolated" (34). I suggest that the figure of the *kaşar* is a powerful, controlling cautionary tale, because he is a reminder in the flesh that becoming *kaşar* can be unavoidable for anyone who vacates the closet and leaves the family associations that embed him relationally, making the gay world his only home and space of sociability and connectedness. The *kaşar* violates the norm of connective selving, defies and refuses to participate in the tenuous achievement of managing desire between doing and being. He is stigmatized because he lacks the shame of being orphaned by vacating the closet, not because he is too out, but because he is comfortable being out.

The Classless Penis

Preamble

"The Classless Penis" is an exploration of gay identities and lives with three interlocutors: Cem, Can, and Devrim, who have been close friends ever since they were teenagers. In their early thirties, these self-identified gay men self-conceal or -disclose their identities to varying degrees to different publics, such as extended family and the professional world. They confront and engage with the conundrum of "secret subject, open secret" in myriad ways. In order to carry on a dialogue about salient facets of their lives in the intersecting realms of family, work, love, and sex, we recently conversed over Skype for close to five hours.

The specific questions I pursued with them are motivated by my desire to understand their experiences and perspectives as they are poised at a moment in their life course when an undisclosed gay identity collides with the societal/professional and familial expectation of heterosexual marriage and family building. To this end, some of the questions I considered were as follows: How do they perceive and act on others' expectations? What are the particular dilemmas facing them in their personal and professional lives at this juncture, and how do they respond to them? How does their status as upwardly mobile men inflect their gay identities, and how might these class advantages position them to live out their sexualities more easily? Are they able to integrate their gay identities into their familial relationships, or are their lives as gay men totally ruptured from their families of origin? Have they experienced the loss (or gained the support) of family ties—with parents, siblings, extended family? How do they experience the opposition between the desire to express themselves and the obligation to be silent in the workplace? How do they experience romance, love, and sex?

The men in this group share a high level of professional success, the prime measure of their high educational achievement and class status. Upwardly mobile, they are all already in managerial positions in their chosen careers. Fluent in several languages and connected globally through their work, they are visible global actors. Their chosen careers, however, are in strikingly different fields. Cem works in banking and finance, a highly conservative sector, while Can is in the fashion industry (business side), which has the reputation of being a gay-friendly workplace. Devrim's work is at a big transnational foundation geared toward developing policies and solutions to global societal problems.

Posessing ambitious dispositions and oriented toward professional success, they all experienced educational advantages afforded by their parents' class privileges, such as private tutors to prepare for school entrance examinations; instruction in foreign languages such as English, French, and German; and internships or similar educational experiences in foreign countries in their teens. Both Devrim and Cem spent a considerable amount of time in Europe in their mid- to late twenties for undergraduate and postgraduate education. As children, all of these men inhabited upper-middle-class milieux, characterized, for example, by vacations in family summer homes, travels abroad, and the presence of family maids or house cleaners in their homes.

However, their coming-out/closet stories are not identical to each other's. Cem came out to his immediate family when he was seventeen. Devrim, who came out to his older sister at age twenty-three, is still in the closet to his father (his mother passed away when he was twelve). Can claims that he never came out in a classical sense. His parents and extended family do not know that he is gay, though he believes his mother is beginning to suspect. Their love lives are also marked by dissimilar trajectories: while Cem coupled twelve years ago and created a home with his partner, Devrim and Can are still in search of "the one," a class equivalent, to forge a lifelong partnership with. These significant commonalities and differences in the men's biographies provide a lens through which to view their journeys in self-making as gay men.

GUL: Let's start with mapping out how each of you are open or closeted vis-à-vis immediate and extended family. Who knows you are gay? Who doesn't? Who suspects but does not talk about it? Who was the first person you came out to? Who helped you in this process of coming out? Were there moments you regret that you came out? Are there any people or situations that you would like come out to but you cannot?

CAN: I think I'm going to pass this question. I have never come out to anyone. So, I have never had a negative reaction. People figured it out.

CEM: I first opened up to my best female friend in high school, the day my brother accidentally found it out. I was in a big panic, and

I needed to talk to someone. She was very supportive. A couple of days later, I came out to my aunt.

DEVRIM: My first important coming out was to my sister. After living in Paris for three years, I moved back to Istanbul when I was twenty-three; then, I opened up to my sister. It went pretty smooth. I had sent her an e-mail. She called me the next day and told me that she loved me a lot. I guess I have been very lucky in all my coming-out stories. I never lost anyone. Instead, I became much closer with them. I have a situation about this though, if you want me to explain further.

GUL: Please do.

DEVRIM: I occasionally rent one of the rooms in my house on airbnb.com. There is this guy who is interested in renting it for six months. Should I tell him that I am gay? In principle, there is no need, as straight people do not specify that they are straight out of the blue.

CAN: I agree.

DEVRIM: But if I do not tell him, he may turn out to be a homophobic or conservative person who would not be very comfortable with the idea of me having sex with a guy in the next room.

CAN: If he turns out to be homophobic, that's his problem. In the worst case scenario, he would leave and lose his money.

DEVRIM: This year I rented a room. A mother and her son from Brazil. When they came to check the room I told them that I am gay, they said that it's not an issue for them, and they rented the room. However, my ex-boyfriend did the same thing with a Spanish guy, and he literally changed his mind.

CEM: I think it's not something that you need to tell people who will rent a room in your flat.

DEVRIM: I think it's not . . . but in practice . . . I do not want someone homophobic under my roof either.

CEM: Well, as a better scenario, you can help a homophobic person overcome his fears and turn him into a gay-friendly one.

CAN: In my family, no one knows that I am gay except my cousin—my paternal uncle's daughter. My sister is suspicious, actually, I think she knows, but we have never talked about it. I think all my friends know too. The number of those who do not know is less than the ones who know, anyway. In my former job, everyone knew. In my current one, no one knows yet.

DEVRIM: I am open to almost all my friends, including close colleagues and even the director of my department. My sister and her husband know that I am gay. Those who are not aware are only my dad and my stepmom.

GUL: Can, why don't you see the need to open up to your sister?

CAN: No one comes out of the closet because he/she is straight. I do not see why I should. If someone asks me, I say yes. But I have always found it somewhat ridiculous to make someone sit in front of you to make a declaration. I never did that. Instead, I confirmed it when those with suspicions asked me.

CEM: I am out to my nuclear family—my mother, my father, and my older brother. My father has not talked about it for years, though.

GUL: Devrim, would you like to open up to your dad and stepmom?

DEVRIM: I wish my dad and his wife knew. The reason why I do not come out to them is that I cannot assume the burden, even if it would be for a short period. My father has always been very open-minded regarding male-female relationships. My sister has introduced him to her boyfriends since high school. But when it comes to being "gay," things change. I'm sure he would be very upset, and he is seventy-two now.

GUL: Cem, what about your extended family? Your cousins, aunts, uncles, etc.?

CEM: One of my aunts knows. Actually, she is one of the first people I came out to. And she has been very supportive throughout the years. As for my other aunts and cousins, I think they suspect it, but they don't want to accept it. Instead, they prefer to consider me as a very gentle, polite person. The fact that I lived abroad for a long time also helped them in this regard. I do not fit in the stereotype of the classical Turkish man. I actually think about coming out to my cousin, who moved to Istanbul a couple of years ago, occasionally. He is close to my age and we grew up together. But if I become out to a family member, I fear that this would be spread to other family members almost automatically. I cannot trust him really, as I think he would tell his mother. And his mother would tell everyone else. On the other hand, I am not really sure about how my cousin would react either. And, ultimately, I think that my mother and my father might be disturbed by the situation.

GUL: Can, I wonder why they do not ask?

CAN: I do not know. . . . Maybe I seem inscrutable to them. In general they steer clear of me; they avoid asking me questions, maybe on this issue too. I have been living in a different city for eight years; maybe they don't find the right moment when I visit them every two months. I do not think that my dad suspects it, my mom and sister do.

GUL: Devrim, what kind of problems do you confront with your father in terms of keeping your identity secret?

DEVRIM: I think I am quite lucky, as my father has never pressured me for marriage. The thing is, I just got so used to being "open" in Istanbul that it saddens me not to be able to share everything with my dad and to mention important aspects of my life when I visit him. I want to add something about this: there is something that I have been observing in many families, especially in my home town, İzmir. Even though they are very open-minded regarding male-female relationships (premarital sex, etc.), being gay is considered as a "failure."

CEM: Yes, I agree with this.

CAN: Yes, I witnessed many conversations supporting this in my family. I have a specific personal experience with this. Let me briefly explain. I think I was in college. Murathan Mungan [a renowned Turkish writer who is openly gay] was on TV. Both my mom and my sister are Mungan fans, but this was the first time they saw him talking on TV with his effeminate style. They were quite shocked, and my sister said something like "this is the worst thing that can happen to a man." Somehow I cannot forget this family scene.

DEVRIM: I have similar memories too. It is very similar actually. My sister and I have many gay friends that my father and stepmom know as well. They seem like not judging and actually appreciating them. But at the same time they have this "God, this should not happen to anyone" approach.

CAN: I agree with Devrim. At the same time, I am pretty sure that people's approaches change once they know that I am gay. People are always scared of the unknown. They get used to it and even embrace the idea.

DEVRIM: Yeah, right.

CEM: I think they do not completely embrace the idea. They always have that feeling "this can happen to someone else's child, but not to mine"—the "failure" theory that Devrim mentioned earlier.

CAN: That's true.

CEM: Furthermore, in Turkey, especially in our families, parents invest enormously in their children. Most of them started their lives with nothing and managed their way up the ladder. They are first-generation upper-middle-class, and they want their children to climb even more. A gay child spoils all these plans. I observe that, among my gay friends, those who are from low-income or more pious families go through more comfortable coming-out processes. This is a general observation, of course.

DEVRIM: This is also due to the fact that the general social approval is very important in Turkey. What would the others say, etc. Everyone's son got married, and we are always single. This is somewhat weird for people.

CAN: Yes, I think the "weirdest" period of our lives is commencing on us due to our ages.

GUL: And of course, your "singleness" is startling and gives you away.

DEVRIM: To me, the "giving away" scenario is not bad at all. Because behind it there is the idea of "no one should know that he is gay." I think my father does not even suspect it. I wish he did.

CEM: People used to ask me a lot of questions about me being single—at work, in my extended family. I have recently noticed that they no longer do. I don't know if this is a good or a bad thing.

CAN: Yes, no one asks questions anymore.

GUL: Can you tell me more about these façades/fronts that are created to overcome these weird situations? In the family context in particular.

CEM: As I am open to the family, I think we create these façades in cooperation with my mom. Such as "Cem has a French girlfriend." She even had a name, I cannot recall now, I hope no one asks about her! Also, my mother often helps me out by, for example, changing the subject when the conversation goes to dangerous territories. Or she says things like "do not meddle in young people's lives," etc. The other day, I was on the phone with my father, and they had friends visiting them. He persistently asked me about this photograph I had on Facebook: Who was the girl in the photograph? Was she French? He sounded like he wanted to show his friends that I was fooling around with girls.

DEVRIM: In general, I try to avoid the conversation in order to not be obliged to lie. I have this "lying by omission" practice. Apparently, my father asks my sister if I have a girlfriend from time to time. She helps me out by replying like, "he lives his own life, he is not obliged to get married," etc.

CAN: I have never created and talked about a fake girlfriend. But I do not necessarily deny it when people make jokes about me and girls either.

GUL: Devrim, if your father somehow learned, would he remain silent or would he ask you questions?

DEVRIM: Gul, believe me, it is a big question mark for me. I can't tell. Actually, maybe I do not know my father that well. If my mother was alive (I lost her when I was twelve), I think I would have been definitely open to her. We were very close. But not with my father.

CAN: Mine would come see me with a shotgun, in my opinion. Another thing is, I am often held back by the eventual traumatic situation that the person would go through if I disclosed my identity. My mother is sixty, why would I inflict something like this on her?

GUL: Can, why do you think your father's reaction would be different (and violent) compared to Cem's father's reaction? What makes your dad and Cem's father different? Had your father lived in Istanbul too, if your lives intersected more, would it have been more difficult then?

CAN: Yes. But my parents are divorced. If I have five units of time with mom, I have only one with my father. So, I guess it would have been more or less the same even if he lived in Istanbul. My father is more rigid compared to Cem's. He used to say things like, "I will cut your ear off if you have an earring one day," the same thing about tattoos. I did all, by the way. As he got older, he became milder actually. But still, I think he still thinks I am going to get married. My mom on the other hand helped me out the other day when there were too many marriage questions in the air. I think she really understands that I am gay. My aunt's husband was joking during dinner, saying things like "when are we going to get this one married?" etc. My mom said, "I won't give him to anyone, he will stay mine." Later in the evening, when the same topic came up, she said, "Well, he is not obliged to get married, I already have one grand-child"—my sister has a son— "that's fair enough." She said things like this for the first time.

DEVRIM: By the way, speaking of façades, I invited two of my ex-boyfriends to my father's house in İzmir, as regular friends of course.

CEM: I swear I did not take anyone to my parents' house!

GUL: Cem, of course, it makes sense because as you are open to your family, you have a kind of special restriction in that regard.

CEM: Right, when they learned, for the first couple of months, they suspected any straight, gay friends of mine of being my boyfriend. That reminds me of an episode: years ago, my father had picked me up from a place in the center city in Izmir. I was waiting for him with Can, who he had never seen before. He continued looking at him even after he began to drive away, he was literally driving with his head turned backwards!

CAN: Somehow knowing/half-knowing/suspecting, they manage to explain it away. Ignorance is bliss.

CEM: I think there is a kind of common trauma-prevention mechanism/agreement in my family as well. In fact, everyone tacitly adopts it. Sometimes things can be very obvious but too far out of sight at the same time. It is a sort of a public façade. Another example is my flat in Istanbul, where I have been living with my boyfriend, pretending that he is my flatmate. I never invite family members to my place, which is very unusual in Turkish family culture, and yet they wouldn't say anything about it. We have a big bedroom with a king bed, and a tiny second bedroom with a small bed, actually that's all there is in this room. I had invited my cousin and his wife once. When she saw the flat, she made jokes like, "you must be really hating your flatmate, you put him in a tiny room." It's so obvious that the room is not occupied, but everybody plays the game.

GUL: I want to ask you how it feels not being able to share your private life with your family members: your joys, disappointments, and boyfriends?

CAN: Gul, you understand this lack when you write about it or think about it. You do not realize it as something that you have never done, that you have never experienced. Now that you have asked, I realize that this is a big lack, of course. It is a huge lack, because there are specific situations, moments, and events in my imagination in which I put a man I love and my family in the same frame. But that frame cannot be realized in real life. Coming out means risk. If they accept you, it doesn't mean they accept your lover. Let's say even if they did, living those ideal moments in my head would not be that easy. That's why I choose not to tell them. I do not want to go through a traumatic experience both for me and for them. Furthermore, if I tell them that I'm gay, they will think of many other things as well—I won't have a child, I will grow old alone, and the risk of AIDS, etc., etc. They will constantly ask themselves what I'm doing with whom. Yet, I feel like it would be much easier if I found the one to share my life with, and took him to my parents to say, "I am gay, and this is my lover, and we are very happy like this." Maybe I will gain strength from the existence of a second person. I always felt like this. Maybe this would legitimize me being gay.

DEVRIM: Gul, I think this is very saddening in general. Why would gays be not able to present their partners to their families? But when I think of my family, I already do not share many details about my life with my father. So it is not a big issue if I do not tell him about some other things.

CEM: I do share some details with my mother and to a certain extent with my brother.

DEVRIM: But there is one thing that upsets me about this. I'm experiencing this with my sister and her husband as well. My relationships are never considered to have the same status as straight relationships somehow.

CEM: Yes, this is absolutely true.

DEVRIM: For example, when my sister and her husband invite me somewhere, if I reply, "I have plans with my partner," they say, "Devrim ditched us." If it were a girlfriend, they would have replied, "Of course, she is also invited." I mean, your gay relationship is always considered as a mischief; it is never legitimate enough. Some straight couples who live together without getting married experience the same thing I think.

CEM: Yes, I experience the same thing with my friends when I tell them about my problems in my relationship. They act like mine are not real problems. Even my brother and his wife behave the same. I am not sure if this is the case because they are afraid to ask me, or if I'm too secretive or just if they do not take it seriously. Some of my straight friends have this "you are gay, one partner goes, the next one comes, it is not an issue in your circles" approach.

CAN: I think they just do not consider this as a legitimate issue. We have this image of constantly-having-fun guys with three-days-long love stories.

DEVRIM: You know, if I told people that I am going on vacation with my girlfriend, they would say, "of course, great." The answer for the boyfriend version would be, "Oooh, I am sure you will have fun you naughty guys."

CEM: Yes, they do not ask many questions and they do not give the same reactions they would have to a straight friend after a breakup, for example.

DEVRIM: Yes, I talked about this with my sister. She is much more careful now.

GUL: Do you think gay coupling brings a sense of security to families who know?

CEM: Yes, the fact that I have been in a relationship for a long time helped my family cope, I think.

DEVRIM: I had introduced my ex-partner to my sister and her husband. My brother-in-law liked him so much that he hired him. And then we broke up. But my ex had started to work with my brother-in-law and he continued. My brother-in-law was not very delicate during this period. He behaved in a way that he would not have if I had a girlfriend.

GUL: Devrim, what happened? I hope he did not fire him?

DEVRIM: No, of course not. I mean, for example, if I were in his shoes, I would have thought twice before inviting both of us to the same place, considering that we had a bad breakup. He was invited to my sister's summer house; I couldn't go there for three months! I would have consulted me beforehand. My brother-in-law was like, "they are gay anyways, they had their fun, and now it's over." He would have behaved differently if it was a girl.

GUL: I would like to stay a bit longer on this important issue you all are raising: the idea that gay relationships are perceived as more fluid, less intimate, emotional, and therefore scarring. Why is this the case? How should this perception to be countered? What do you personally do to erase that perception?

DEVRIM: I don't do anything special to change this "perception." As with regards to the reasons, there are many things that come to my mind. I'm just thinking out loud. Social circles in which gay people can meet are limited compared to straight people. That's why we have some specific platforms such as gay clubs, websites, social media apps, etc. And thanks to these, it's in fact much easier to meet someone compared to straight people. Most of my straight friends have months of interval between two relationships, whereas we get to meet someone much faster. I have many straight friends who tell me that we are so lucky! But the other side of the coin is that many people in the gay community have this feeling of "I can meet someone much better and easily!"

CAN: I wish I had a dating life like straight people.

CEM: Yes, meeting someone is easy but relationships tend to end easier too, unfortunately.

DEVRIM: Yes, indeed, Can. If things were slower, if, for example, we go out and have dinner the first evening, then two to three days later see a movie. . . . Slowly increasing the adrenaline and the thrill. . . . We spend that adrenaline the first night in general. I am somewhat confused about the "post-date" period. Everything is going so fast that I sometimes do not understand if I'm into him, if he's into me, etc.

CAN: Totally. Having sex puts out the fire. And as you didn't share something else, you do not necessarily want to see each other again. Whereas if things were slower, a smile, a nice conversation, it may help things go further. Well, this is not always the case either. Sometimes you can tell if it will work out after the first kiss.

CEM: Yes, but coming back to your question regarding the perception, I think it's not just about short-term encounters. The fact that straights tend to abstain from asking questions about gay relationships [and] that gay relationships are not in the open as straight ones are [are] also some factors that feed this perception. For example, if your boyfriend leaves you, you do not have the luxury to cry at the office. You cover your wounds by yourself. We are used to that. And this may reinforce the idea that you do not live "profound" relationships.

CAN: I agree.

GUL: So there is this strong desire for love and monogamy?

DEVRIM: I guess yes, there is. Actually, there is also the fact that the more experience you have, the more difficult it gets to start a relationship, and it's the same for gays and straights. Someone who hasn't been in a relationship for years may sometimes jump on the first spark of passion he/she encounters, this may be misleading sometimes. It gets more difficult with experience anyhow as you do not want to create a world that you know will not last. And you get picky.

CAN: Couldn't agree more.

GUL: So, when coupled, if one of the partners is open and the other is not, do you experience any problems?

DEVRIM: If he is very closeted, that can be a problem. "Let's not go there," "if someone sees us, let's invent this story"—"a friend of mine is coming over, you are my tennis partner, ok?"—this kind of stuff. I cannot act anymore!

CAN: I could talk about this for hours.

GUL: Share some examples.

CAN: The last guy I was seeing was twenty-one years old and no one knew he was gay and he had no gay friends. He kind of felt obliged to keep me separated from his straight universe. In this case, many problems arise, of course, when your lives cannot overlap. You cannot go everywhere, you cannot see each other when you want to. After a certain age and life experience, one cannot accept this kind of situation.

GUL: How long did the relationship last?

CAN: Five months. There was nothing I could do; he was a nice guy but this type of relationship is not possible even if you are in love. He couldn't fulfill my expectations of a relationship.

GUL: Do you know people who are completely in the closet like this person?

CAN: Not really in my immediate circle, but I get to meet many in different social situations. There are even married guys. In the gym, for example.

CEM: I guess I do not.

DEVRIM: Most of my close gay friends are out as well.

GUL: Can, what do you expect the most from a relationship?

CAN: I expect what straight people expect from a relationship as well. Not just a "bed friendship." Sharing things, living a common life. And that is not possible with everyone.

DEVRIM: Me too, I would have expected the same thing if I were straight. Actually, I like being alone. If I am going to be in a relationship, it must be worth it. I should really want it. It is unfortunately quite difficult to meet this kind of person.

CAN: Yes, I agree.

GUL: Façades (lying by omission, passing as straight—voluntarily or involuntarily) can be both a form of deception, a form of protection, a liberating means by which to claim a new/different self/identity, and also a barrier precluding the sharing of deeper/inner/truer selves. What parts of yourselves remain hidden (not shared) from your family members or loved ones in general? What parts of yourselves do you wish you could share with members of your family or loved ones in general?

DEVRIM: It's more like a barrier to me.

CAN: I guess the thing I would like most would be taking my partner with me to my family home, so that he could sit by my side at family dinners. Sometimes I get angry at straight people. They are not aware of the luxury they have.

CEM: Exactly my feeling. I would like to take my partner to my parents' house as well.

DEVRIM: Me too.

CAN: Yeah, for example, I would love to hear my dad tell my boyfriend about my childhood. Oh, we will begin to cry if we go on [with] this topic.

CEM: Or just a lunch with a friend or a business dinner. I used to check the invitee list before going to a, say, birthday party with my boyfriend. Now I do not care. But on some occasions I am still obliged to invent several lies.

GUL: I would like to ask you about specific events in which you might wish to include your partner (current or potential) that you currently feel you cannot: birthday party/dinner for a close family member (mother, father, sister, brother, etc.); a young nephew or niece's birthday celebration or school graduation; new year celebrations or Bayram family gatherings; vacationing at family summer house or someplace with family; and company/workplace-related events (dinners and receptions).

CEM: All of them. But because it is currently the appropriate season, I would love to go to our family summer house together in İzmir now.

CAN: My little nephew's birthday party. But I would say all of them actually. A family dinner, a birthday gathering. Just to see my partner chatting and laughing with my family. It sounds like a Ferzan Özpetek [a Turkish film director and screenwriter who is openly gay] movie, but yes, I would really love that. I imagine my partner playing with my nephew, my father giving my partner a tap on the shoulder.

DEVRIM: I would like them all as well. Because my sister and her husband know, I have been to a school ceremony for my nephew with my boyfriend.

GUL: What does it mean to be gay? I know this is an unfair question because we never ask straights the same question, but I have to ask given the fact that we live in heteronormative and homophobic societies.

CEM: A difficult question.

DEVRIM: Being sexually attracted to the same sex?

CAN: I think it can be explained as Devrim did.

CEM: Are you asking what it means to be "gay," the word in English, or what it means to be "eşcinsel" [same sex], the word in Turkish? I think these two do not cover the exact same meaning.

DEVRIM: Is it different? I really do not know.

CAN: I don't know either.

GUL: Cem, I ask both indeed. How do you make the distinction?

CEM: For me, the word "eşcinsel" is more like a definition, a man attracted to a man and having sex with a man. Being "gay" on the other hand is more about an identity. And I think that's why we use the word "gay" too, even though we have a word for this in Turkish.

CAN: I think they are the same.

DEVRIM: I think being gay is "being sexually attracted to the same sex." You might have heard some people say things like, "in fact, everyone's potentially gay, we are all bisexuals in nature etc." There may be some exceptions, but at the end of the day, being gay is being attracted to the same sex, just as being straight is being attracted to the opposite sex.

GUL: How does being "gay" as an identity differ from being "eşcinsel"?

DEVRIM: Cem, do you mean that these two mean the same thing but we use them differently in daily language? Like, "this is so gay!" and not "this is so eşcinsel!"

CEM: Let me put it this way. A man who does not admit that he is attracted to men may have some "eşcinsel" encounters from time to time. But he wouldn't see himself as "gay." Saying that you are gay depicts a kind of belonging to a community.

DEVRIM: But that man would not say "I'm eşcinsel" either.

CEM: Yes, but he would never ever say, "I'm gay."

GUL: Cem, does being "gay" require being out then?

CEM: Yes, I think to a certain extent, but not necessarily. What is important is how you define yourself. I don't know how to explain it, but I think being gay is a kind of political stand and has repercussions on many choices in your life. Even your attire. This is again a generalization, but I really think that these two words do not depict the same thing.

CAN: I have to disagree. At the end of the day, we are men who like men. That's it.

DEVRIM: Cem, I think what you are saying is that "gay" is an expression of a particular social identity whereas "eşcinsel" is a "dry" definition.

CEM: Yes, Devrim. "Eşcinsel" for me is a more clinical term.

DEVRIM: I get it.... But I see both as the same. Although I use "gay" much more often in daily life.

GUL: Which one do you use most often, or does that change according to the audience?

CAN: I guess I never use "eşcinsel."

DEVRIM: Almost never.

CEM: I use "gay" as well.

GUL: In the globalization literature about queer/gay/MSM [men having sex with men] life there are big distinctions drawn between men who have sex with men and men who identify as gay, queer, etc. These are different cultures and reflect different sexual practices with different sexual identities—what do you make of those distinctions—are you bothered by men who have sex with men but don't/won't identify as "gay"?

CAN: I think they are all gay, they just do not admit it.

CEM: Well, being with a man who does not identify himself as gay bothers me. But the distinction between short-term encounters versus long-term relationships we talked about earlier applies here as well. If it's just a one-night stand, it's not that important. You do not speak about these issues with the guy anyway.

DEVRIM: "Men having sex with men, don't/won't identify as 'gay'?" . . . I think these men, as Can puts it, cannot admit that they are gay. I guess this kind of man exists relatively more in conservative countries. I also agree with Cem.

CAN: Yes, indeed it would be absurd to think of a relationship with a guy like this.

DEVRIM: I guess we do not come upon this kind of guy often enough to be "bothered."

CAN: Well, actually we do. The fact is these men are not only those who consider themselves "only tops," you also have "bottoms" like this, though relatively less.

DEVRIM: I think I have never encountered someone who practices gay sex and who says, "I am not gay." That may be because I haven't got close enough to talk about this with everyone I met, as Cem mentioned. By the way, we are not talking about those who admit it but will stay in the closet, right?

GUL: Yes, for example, married men with children.

DEVRIM: My ex had three children, divorced. . . . But he always identified himself as gay, he only kept it secret.

GUL: Is he out now?

DEVRIM: Yes, but it's a complicated story. His ex-wife and he had their three children after his coming out to his wife.

CAN: I know this guy from the gym. We have had sex every two to three months for four or five years. I recently learned that he is actually married, and furthermore his wife comes to the same gym too.

CEM: I think there are two types. The first one is those who have sex with men but do really think that they are not gay, these in general consider themselves "tops." The second type is those who do not embrace "the gay identity." They have a different understanding of being gay, are in general older, and have a kind of nostalgia for Ottoman-style men-to-men relationships.

GUL: What do you mean by Ottoman style?

CEM: Well, there are people who think that it was once considered normal to have sex with a man, especially before marriage, to be physically intimate or to walk hand-in-hand in the street. And that all this changed when we acquired the Puritan values of the West and "invented" the gay identity. In fact, these people are usually not out and I think they reduce being gay to a bed activity.

DEVRIM: Maybe this was happening behind closed doors and they didn't name it. But there are also those who are nostalgic of this "charm," such as some orientalist Europeans who adore the gay life in Morocco, Algeria, and even Turkey.

CEM: Exactly. It's nearly an auto-orientalist approach.

GUL: By the way, do you identify yourselves with a religious identity—as Muslims? If not, does it have anything to do with being gay?

DEVRIM: No, I don't identify myself as Muslim. It would be the same if I were straight.

CAN: No.

CEM: No. I think I resolved this issue in my head during high school years. I think it has nothing to do with being gay. I do not judge people for who they are, but I cannot see how one can be a pious Muslim and gay at the same time either. Or gay and fascist at the same time.

DEVRIM: Well, I know some gays who stop having sex when they hear the call for prayer.

CAN: Or those who perform Islamic ablution ritual just after sex. I want to tell them that it wouldn't go away even if they washed themselves for ten hours, but I cannot.

CEM: Or those who do not have sex at all during Ramadan.

GUL: Is there such a pious Muslim gay population?

CAN: Not really in our circles, but in our beds from time to time.

GUL: Let me pose a new question. In what public/private spheres of life can you be completely comfortable with your gay identity? What are the advantages and disadvantages of being gay in Istanbul?

CEM: I think I am completely comfortable only when I am with my friends. In general, I never feel completely comfortable in what we may call public spheres. I cannot see any advantages of being gay in Istanbul. Maybe the possibility to meet like-minded people, straight or gay, might be an advantage.

DEVRIM: Well, as I said, I'm very comfortable at work. Sometimes I even forget that I have a secret. I limit myself only when I am with my dad. When it comes to Istanbul, we live probably in the best city in Turkey. It's of course not like Paris or Berlin. But it's not very different from Athens either. Of course, everyone's situation living in Istanbul is unique. As I live alone here, I feel quite free. There is no "neighborhood pressure" either.

CAN: I think the hardest period for me was my military service. In Istanbul, 90 percent of my friends are gay-friendly, so I am very comfortable. I think, gradually, I chose to be in comfortable circles. Over time, all the uncomfortable circles disappeared from my life.

GUL: Can, tell us more about your military service. Which circumstances stressed you the most?

CAN: The military is a completely straight-dominated place. Well, the real world is so as well, but at least we are not surrounded by barbed wire. All the jokes in the military are based on homosexuality. Any sign of weakness is perceived as gay. If you fail during exercises, rifle shots, etc., you are considered a fag. "Look at the fag, he couldn't even hit the ball."

DEVRIM: Superb observation, Can. In Turkey, we have this "male youth morality" [delikanlı ahlakı]. The worst thing that can happen to a man . . . you know what it is . . .

CAN: In order to not be exposed to all this, I worked out really hard before my military service. At the end, I had become the one who won many competitions.

DEVRIM: When I did my service, I was older than most of the other guys. So they had a kind of respect for me, their older brother. I did not have any bullying linked to being gay. The only problem I had was getting bored, like anyone else.

GUL: Can, did you try getting exempted by going through the infamous procedure?[17]

CAN: No, I did not, Gul. I have a different stand regarding this issue if you want to hear it.

GUL: Yes, I would love to hear.

CAN: I do not think that one should be exempted from military service because he is gay. Yes, military service is bullshit, but being gay is not an obstacle to do it. We are not physically or mentally inferior to straight men. Exempting gays is humiliating.

CEM: I agree. We are not "rotten."[18]

CAN: So, I never thought of applying for exemption. I just tried to minimize any trouble that I could have had.

DEVRIM: Yes, that's so true. I think the military service should not be mandatory for anyone. If all men are obliged to, gays shouldn't be considered "rotten."

CEM: I did not do my military service because of some medical issues. So, when people ask, I say that I am exempted. There is always a short silence after this. When I add that it's because of my medical problems, everybody seems relaxed. It's as if there was already enough evidence for them to suspect that I am gay, and this would be the last straw to break the camel's back.

GUL: What are the risks of being open or semi-open in business life?

CAN: In Turkey, only a small number of sectors [are] comfortable to be out in. I think I am very lucky in this regard. In my previous job, everyone from the boss to the tea server knew, and I never had a problem. I guess this is an advantage of working in the fashion sector.

DEVRIM: My director knows, she accidentally learned actually. But the general manager does not, and I wouldn't want him to know. You never know. They may see it as a bad thing for the company's image and could take a stand against me.

GUL: How did your director accidentally learn?

DEVRIM: We were abroad for a conference. The wifi password was written somewhere on the wall. I did not have the time to write it down so I took a picture with my cell phone instead. When my director wanted to connect her iPad, she asked me if she could look at the picture I had taken. I gave her my phone and while she was looking at the picture a push text message came from my boyfriend which was instantly on the screen. So she saw the message and his name right away. It was something like "My loveeeee, how is the conference going?" She looked at me, and I replied, "yes, it is exactly what you imagine." Then, we had a coffee and talked about it.

CEM: The sector I work for, the banking sector, is quite traditional and managed in line with old-style hierarchical patterns. For example, it is forbidden to wear something other than a dark suit. Being open for me is unthinkable. But I think many colleagues suspect. I only shared it with a close colleague. She resigned a couple of months later as she didn't like the culture of the company.

GUL: How did these suspicions manifest themselves? Can you give some examples?

CEM: Well, they were not very clear, but as I said earlier, many people stopped asking me questions one day. In group conversations, when everyone shared a story of male-female relationships, I was skipped automatically. Also, the colleague I told you about was kind of spying for me. People were apparently asking her if I was gay. Or they often consulted me on issues that they thought a gay guy would know better.

CAN: I want to add something on this issue. I think homophobia decreases as we go up the ladder in the company. When you are senior, people are either afraid or they just ignore the fact out of respect.

GUL: You mean that higher positions shield your gay status, right? Devrim, Cem, do you agree with this?

CEM: Yes, for sure. I even believe that gays—consciously or unconsciously—work harder to have this shield.

CAN: I agree, Gul, yes. Maybe that's why many gays are overachievers at work. Because we are unconsciously aware that the more power you have, the more accepted you are.

DEVRIM: I think being gay in this society is considered actually as a sort of "disability." The new definition of disability is not linked to the person's medical condition but to the degree of social integration. In this sense, gays are also disabled. As you put it, as you gain power, this disability decreases.

GUL: Why is the world of fashion more gay-friendly, Can?

CAN: Because it is dominated by gays. Creative directors, designers.... There are many gay people in the sector and they are the best. If you look at the international fashion industry, except Chanel maybe, most of big fashion companies are developed by gay people. Fashion does not have the luxury to exclude gay people. Maybe that's why.

CEM: I think it may even be an advantage to be gay in the fashion sector. Do you agree, Can?

CAN: Yes, I think we can say that it's an advantage.

GUL: What does it mean to be open in the fashion world? What is normalized, in other words?

CAN: I can't really explain. . . . But, for example, in our office, there isn't any extraordinary situation either. Gay people do not kiss their boyfriend in the office and they don't wear skirts, for example. It is more accurate to say that people understanding that you're gay is not problem.

GUL: For example: there is going to be a nonbusiness get-together with your colleagues or a colleague invites the others to dinner. Can you take your boyfriend with you? Or is he invited?

CAN: In my previous job, I could have taken my boyfriend, I guess. I do not know for my current job. I guess I could. The real issue is finding the man, if you find the right man, every obstacle can be overcome.

GUL: Which other similar sectors exist in Turkey?

CEM: In general, I would say fashion, communication, and advertising.

DEVRIM: I work in the so-called third sector—civil society. The issue of LGBT rights is on our agenda nearly every day. So, this sector is relatively more open as well.

GUL: How does this "openness" manifest itself?

DEVRIM: For example, we are collaborating with NGOs working in the field of women's rights, gender equality, and other issues. Everyone in our department has a master's or doctoral degree on these issues, and being gay is a nonissue for them now. I went to this year's LGBT march with a colleague of mine. But, at the same time, this is our "department." This does not apply to the general work place.

GUL: While looking for a job or changing jobs, how important is it to find a gay-friendly workplace?

CAN: It's not one of my priorities, but a big plus.

DEVRIM: It hasn't been a criterion for me so far. A gay-friendly working environment is a luxury. I have happened to work in gay-friendly workplaces by chance.

CEM: Currently, I'm looking for a job, and while talking with my partner today, I realized that it's quite important for me actually. Not finding a gay-friendly place, but avoiding gay-unfriendly places, perhaps.

DEVRIM: This is very true: I cannot work in a place that I will have to stand homophobic discourses.

GUL: Speaking of the LGBT marches, I also had questions about gay rights activism. Are you actively involved in a gay organization/club/movement?

DEVRIM: Unfortunately I'm not. Shame on me. I want to, but . . .

CAN: I'm not involved either.

CEM: I'm not actively involved, unfortunately, but I would like to take a more active role in the future. The problem here again is being open or not. Thanks to the Gezi movement,[19] many people who feared being there in previous years, joined the march this year. Me too actually.

DEVRIM: I'm one of them. I attended this year for the first time.

CAN: I started attending four years ago.

GUL: So, the "straight alliance" is important then. When many straight people attend the march, it gets easier for gays to attend. What do you think?

CEM: Yes, absolutely.

DEVRIM: Right.

GUL: Cem, can you explain what you said about the relation between gay rights activism and being open?

CEM: As I am not completely out at work or in my extended family, I think I cannot be actively involved. Many photographs from the LGBT march were printed in newspapers in the past years, for example. Or TV channels show many people's faces. Or if you want to work for an LGBT-related NGO, there is always a risk of exposure. Maybe one can work for an NGO without being out, but I find it somehow ridiculous to be a gay rights activist and say, "I am sorry, I cannot do that as I am not out."

GUL: Have you ever thought of living abroad? What holds you back? I know you all had opportunities.

CAN: I would love to, Gul. I even want to leave and never come back. I would prefer a country where gay marriage is legal, if possible. I want to have a wedding!

DEVRIM: Sometimes I would like to. Especially in these days, given that our names are probably in a file [fişlenmek, to be the subject of a police file].

CEM: I lived abroad for a while. Then I moved back to Istanbul because I found it more attractive to live here. I do not regret my decision. Being out or not is not the central criterion when we make our choices because we live in a bubble in Istanbul, in fact. We do not have serious difficulties in the world we have created for ourselves.

DEVRIM: Due to the bubble Cem is referencing, my life here is not really different from in Paris.

CAN: I think we are living very comfortably in Istanbul, but I am pessimistic about the future. As Devrim said, I think we have been "filed."

GUL: I did not understand this "filing" issue. Does the AKP government have such a system?

CAN: Well, they record everything about everyone. I am pretty sure we are stamped homosexual somewhere.

DEVRIM: If I wanted to have a career in politics, and if I had a serious opponent from the AKP, I am sure that they would use my homosexuality against me. And they wouldn't have much difficulty to find proof.

GUL: You bring up an important issue. In a similar vein, one can hit the "gay ceiling" in careers as well, when you try to become an executive, for example, except some sectors such as fashion.

DEVRIM: Of course. Especially in politics. We can even be a victim of a hate crime. If we are too visible, demonstrating a bad example.

CAN: I agree.

CEM: After you reach a certain level in your career, you begin to have some social obligations associated with your position. You need to go to a work-related dinner with your wife, for example. Then again, as we discussed before, if you are powerful enough, everyone obeys the rule of silence.

GUL: So, to what extent is the bubble you talk about linked to one's class location?

DEVRIM: There are both cultural and economic aspects to class. You need to have a comfortable income so that you can live alone and not with your family. Or you do not have this luxury, but you have a very open-minded family. The latter is nonexistent.

CEM: Well, the relationship between this bubble and class is relevant and not relevant at the same time. We live in certain neighborhoods, and inhabit certain places; we establish friendships in certain circles.

These usually belong to a specific class. However, due to the nature of gay relationships, we are in touch with many people outside our class as well. Class, age, social status are more permeable issues for us compared to straights.

DEVRIM: I want to add something to what Cem has just said. Thanks to my homosexuality, I think I may have met more people from different classes compared to my straight friends. Straights only date in their own environments. We are using many social platforms and can meet anyone.

GUL: Does this permeability between classes cover permanent or temporary relationships?

DEVRIM: A very good question.

CAN: I think it includes temporary relationships only, even just sex.

CEM: Usually temporary relationships.

DEVRIM: Can is right. Exceptions can happen though.

CAN: Zeki Müren[20] had a saying—I apologize for my language Gul, "*sikin mertebesi olmaz.*"

GUL: How should we translate the saying of Zeki Muren into English? Shall we all give it a try?

CEM: "The penis does not have a social class"? As Marx said!

DEVRIM: "Dick does not have the social status."

CAN: I think we did it, Gul.

GUL: Yes, that's great!

CEM: I think it might even be the title of this conversation.

CAN: My *pasha*,[21] sleep in peace.

DEVRIM: Actually, I am going through a similar issue. I started dating this 24-year-old guy recently. His family is very conservative. His mother and sisters are religiously covered. But he is agnostic and a *Sex and the City* fan. He talks to me about movies like *The Hours* or *Angels in America*. There are examples like this guy, who somehow rescue themselves despite the conservatism of their families.

GUL: Did your lover go to college? How did he save himself?

DEVRIM: Not my lover—we just started dating actually. Yes, he is a mechanical engineer. But not from a reputable university, and he doesn't want to work in that field. There is a social-class difference between him and his family in terms of economic and cultural aspects.

GUL: The family does not know he is gay?

DEVRIM: No, and he certainly cannot come out. For example, he can never sleep at my place, he always goes back home even if it's very late.

GUL: Do you see a future in this relationship?

DEVRIM: That's what I'm thinking about precisely these days. I am cautious. I don't want to build up a world together before being sure that it will work and see it break down after a few months. So for the moment, "we enjoy each other." The fact that he is not out at all and that he lives with his family can create problems in the long term.

GUL: Cem, Can, do you have any class-permeability experiences apart from sexual encounters?

CAN: I had some experience, Gul. I had a similar situation with this 21-year-old guy I mentioned before. My experience tells me that this kind of relationship does not work. I mean, the prospect of beginning a common life is very small with all these differences. Sorry, Devrim. So I can be interested in this kind of situation just for sex. If this is called prejudice, so be it.

DEVRIM: No problem, Can, I agree.

CEM: I have had some experience as well. But no long-term relationship.

DEVRIM: There are always some exceptions, of course. In France, or more generally in Europe, it's possible. A Virgin employee or a cashier can turn out to be quite an interesting person. Here, those examples are very limited.

CAN: I totally agree. I gave up because I am sick of trying and trying and failing each time. One shouldn't say amen to an impossible prayer [olmaz duaya amin dememek lazım].

GUL: Why is this more likely in France? Isn't the French middle class a bit snobbish?

DEVRIM: It's linked to the education system and the country's economic health. I met a boy who, for example, was a cashier at FNAC store in Paris. He was extremely intelligent and a real intellectual. And he financially did quite well for himself. Here, we have very few examples like this. We have sharper occupation categories, with each having different and unequal cultural resources and opportunities at its disposal.

CEM: I guess, in France, the material and social divisions do not match [overlap] with each other like here. People in different economic classes or with high or low job positions can be similar in relation to cultural attitudes, intellectuality, and cultural sophistication in France.

DEVRIM: Exactly. I also met an editor, he was like a philosopher, and he never went to college. There is more advanced vocational training in Europe. College is not the only choice; you can choose not to go to college.

GUL: It seems you are talking about things you inherit from the family culture, i.e., the process of socialization, right? Such as how to behave at table, and appreciating a painting, etc.

CEM: Yes, I think these gains are distributed more widely among classes in France. Here, we have sharp lines. At the same time, the relationship you build as a foreigner abroad is different as well. They relate to you in a different way. We may not have been developing these opinions if we were French.

GUL: Speaking of class and appearance, do you think that there is a middle-class gay appearance? Is there such a thing?

CEM: I recently went to Mykonos and I can certainly say that such a thing exists.

CAN: There are some brands that have become like a secret gay signature—for example, aussieBum. If you see someone with aussieBum underwear at the gym, you are 99.99 percent sure that he is gay.

DEVRIM: Wait, I will take notes!

CEM: I think this is not really linked to class. It's about being gay and gay stereotypes.

GUL: These are expensive brands though, right?

CAN: Not too expensive. It's not like Armani. We can call this affordable luxury.

CEM: They can be a bit pricey, but one can save money to purchase them. Apart from brands, I observe a uniformalization of styles— particular types of beard and hair styles, etc.

CAN: Well, everyone is not wearing the same thing, by the way. There are class differences among gays too. You have different types of dress codes for bears, twinks, gym fanatics, etc. They mark themselves with their unique styles.

GUL: Do you have anything to say about lesbians and lesbian relationships?

CAN: Gul, I cannot understand lesbians, how could one live without a man?

CEM: We talk about this sometimes among ourselves. Indeed, we do not have any lesbian friends. Lesbians here live in a closed community I think.

CAN: I have never had one. Though it would be nice.

DEVRIM: I did have a friend. I'm not sure, but I think that their relationships last longer than ours in general. There are fewer lesbian-specific places as well, but this is the same everywhere.

GUL: I wonder why gay and lesbian communities do not intertwine?

CEM: As far as I know, there is a lesbian club in Istanbul and men are not allowed. Well, I think both communities have similar problems. But I think they don't have the same "visibility" problems. And I think there is a problem between these communities over "masculinity" issues, the two communities despising each other.

CAN: I think in general people are more prone to being able to accept the lesbian community.

CEM: Gays usually find lesbians "scary."

GUL: Why?

CAN: Some lesbians are so masculine that you fear them. The way they look at you, the way they behave.

CEM: I know it's a prejudice, but in my personal history, the lesbians that I met when I moved to Istanbul were in general butch types, and I witnessed a few fights between them with a lot of chairs in the air. They were kind of hyper-masculine. And they really despised gays.

DEVRIM: Unfortunately, discrimination is everywhere, even within disadvantaged groups.

CEM: Exactly.

GUL: Which identities/groups are exposed to discrimination the most in the gay community?

CEM: Those who are more feminine, I think. Trans individuals are on the front line of being subjected to discrimination, of course. On gay dating sites, you see a lot of "looking for" columns with messages

such as "I want a masculine, manly man, not a bearded woman," and
so on.

DEVRIM: Yeah, the other day I saw someone who wrote something as a
reply. "You will never look straight with a dick in your mouth."

GUL: Effeminate gays are obligatorily out of the closet, of course.

CEM: Exactly, some also write, "I respect effeminate gays, but I do not
like them." They feel the need to mention that they respect them.

CAN: It may be unrelated, but I read today that we have our very first
gay candidate for municipal elections in Giresun. Although I was
very happy to read that, when I saw his photo and the press release, I
thought that the gay image in people's head is already very effeminate such as Cemil Ipekçi [a very famous Turkish fashion designer],
and this guy is not very different. I was very proud, but at the same
time, I thought it would have been better if he had a more ordinary
look. Then, I was ashamed of myself. He did something that none of
us can, and we are still talking about the gay image.

CEM: I thought the same thing. Then I did not know what to think.

DEVRIM: Right, but in fact we cannot ask someone to act differently
just to fix our image. Well, even the word "fix" is not an appropriate
one.

CAN: Yes, you're right. If we have the courage to do so, we should "fix"
this image ourselves.

DEVRIM: We have the potential, my friends, maybe one day.

CEM: I have a similar dilemma regarding the gay pride march. Maybe
not in Turkey, but in many European countries, one can witness
many "hard-core" scenes, in particular from the BDSM community
[Bondage, Discipline, Sadism, Masochism]. I don't know if this helps
us. But, on the one hand, it's a carnival and a celebration of diversity.
So, I do not know what to think.

DEVRIM: Yes, actually, it's good to show the most radical as well. "I am
very different from you, but I exist as well." But yeah. This can make
some coming-out processes difficult. "My son will be like them."

CEM: I think so too, Devrim. But a couple of years ago, my parents were
on vacation in Rome. Mom called me. They were having coffee with
their friends when they realized that it was Gay Pride Day in Rome
and the march was just in front of them. At the beginning, my mom

thought this would be a good opportunity to speak to her friends about LGBT rights, etc. Then came those scenes I told you about. She was very disturbed. I did not know how to answer her.

GUL: Last question, are there things you want to discuss? Or American readers to know?

DEVRIM: Not just homophobia, but equally every kind of discrimination is unacceptable. And unless it attacks your identity, you cannot judge people because of their identity.

CEM: Actually, I think it's important for the USA readers to know that there is a relatively organized gay community in Turkey. And that one cannot use the same schemes to understand different gay identities and communities in different countries. What is true for USA, the West, or the East is not always valid in Turkey. Many tourists I meet here are too orientalist or some others think that everything should be the same as in their countries. There is no understanding in between.

Epilogue

This rich and stimulating conversation illuminates an increasingly visible new identity in Turkish society. I discuss here my reflections under the headings of constitutive ambiguities and ambivalences; the power of (mis)recognition; the family home and desire for convergences; and class—its privileges and trangressions. In the process, I draw both theoretical and practical conclusions and pose some questions for future research.

CONSTITUTIVE AMBIGUITIES AND AMBIVALENCES

One of the most important realities that this group conversation has revealed is that ambiguity and ambivalence about hiding/disclosing is at the heart of self-fashioning or identity management. The assumption that recognizing and living one's own sexuality is a universal, delineated event or even a process that can be labeled as "coming out" is being questioned by these men's own experiences and the experiences of other men—heterosexually or gay-identified men who engage in same-sex relationships, whose stories also appeared in the group interview. Rather, their experiences demonstrate a back and forth in degrees of openness and a dynamic play of complicated interactions among a variety of personal, professional, social, and familial factors. Even the assumed genericism of the coming-out experience (individuals need to define or label their sexual identities) is dislodged. These men put forward new ways of understanding their gay subjectivity and its public/private face as a contingent process that is always in a state of flux and change, undertaken on many levels, in different practices and sites of experience. Their handling of the demands of a stigmatized sexual identity is marked by what I would like to call a constitutive or generative ambiguity. It is constitutive because ambiguity and ambivalence are serving to generate new practices, understandings, and transformations: new ways of relating to others and new frames for positioning oneself in the world and for inhabiting particular spaces. Their experiences point to a notion of a public persona that is held together by a dialectical tension between alienation and identification, concealment and revelation, the free and the constrained. As they move between these two poles, I sensed both ambiguities and ambivalence. In negotiating their identities in their public and private lives, they are at pains to hide and yet feel compelled to expose (exemplified in the case of Devrim by the question, "Does disclosing your identity to a renter make you subject to violence/insult or help create gay-friendly people?"). They refute public suspicions about their sexual orientation by engaging in practices designed to prove to the world that they are not gay but also by using subtle and silent strategies that allow intimates and strangers to see behind the public façade, as if to remind the audience that the façade is just that—a role, a performance maintained with discipline. This transformative rewriting of themselves, in both empowering and disempowering ways, in relation to shifting interpersonal and professional contexts is also being undertaken by collaborating significant others, both by those who know and those who pretend not to know. For instance, an obligatory or a voluntary act by a mother to provide "assistance" to a gay son faced with others' persistent questions about still being single at the age of thirty can serve to generate a new maternal perspective/positionality, putting into question the significance of the normative imperative in Turkish culture that a mother has to have grandchildren from her son. This is a small step toward subverting the hegemony of heteronormativity. Subtle stories like these signify the unfolding transformations of those who take part in the task of protecting the "secret subject." Considered this way, the scenarios of "coming out" or self-fashioning articulated by these men resonate with the ideas of contemporary queer theorists who suggest that coming out is not a prescribed or singular process but a lifelong negotiation that is more contextual and contingent than is suggested by the linear models. We know little about the feelings of family members in Turkey— how recognition of a non-normative sexual orientation sets in motion a complex process of coming to terms with a stigmatized identity—except for a generic understanding of their responses, ranging from providing support to antagonism and withdrawal. The above conversation is filled with mediated voices raised among family members and significant others in these men's lives.

THE POWER OF (MIS)RECOGNITION

A special vantage point offered by the experience of these men's relationships with significant straight others conveys important insights about the relationship between recognition and "the lives beyond closet" (Seidman et al. 1999). They tell us that significant others (family members and friends) in their lives, who are themselves the products of hegemonic sexual distinctions, and thus by definition lack imaginative identification as subjects of a heteronormative culture, project stereotypes onto their same-sex relationships. The stories they articulated particularly underscore an imagined radical difference between heterosexual and same-sex relationships on the basis of a neat opposition between the categories of permanence and impermanence in relation to the end goal of an intimate relationship. The world over, gay relationships are painted with the stigma of impermanence, reduced to sex and having fun, and thus intense affective bonds between men are deemphasized. These men in the conversation claim that heterosexual culture assumes that gay love affairs do not embody many of the same ideals as those of heterosexual couples. In moving away from this negative opposition between heterosexual and same-sex love relationships, they claim that love relationships are universal in form and meaning, regardless of the sex of one's object of desire. Thus intimate gay relations and their potentialities are signficanly conditioned by this misrecognition and the struggle to negotiate and transcend the perma-

nence/impermanence distinction that casts a shadow over the relations
with straight significant others, who seem to be maintaining a complex
balance of association and distance. It is important to remember that
these negotiations are taking place in a context where these men are
also grappling with the contradictions between their ideals for building
a lasting relationship with a life partner and the limited choices they
face for coupling, often conditioned by imbalances in class and levels of openness. This nonacknowledgment and refusal of gay intimacy
and love exert their power in social interactions as they become deeply
intertwined with attitudes towards gay men, often producing feelings
of exclusion. More importantly, I would argue that at least one of the
serious harms that a failure of recognition perpetuates has to do with
the production of differentness through notions of essential, irreducible
differences, as well as reification of a particular unidimensional image of
homosexual identity.

Because these men give voice to the tension between familial identity
(as sons and siblings, cousins, nephews) and familial misrecognition (the
lack of acknowledgment of love/intimacy in the homosexual couple),
interrogating the uneasy relationship between these familial factors, the
question of how much one needs and is vulnerable to the recognition
given or withheld by significant others emerges as an important issue.
Moreover, the demand for recognition should be viewed as a way of re-
vising the inherited meaning of their identities. It is perfectly clear that
the nuanced complexities of gay self-making is in dialogue with familial
relationships and that the recognition of same-sex love by significant
others is absolutely essential for building lives beyond the closet. Indeed,
the men in this conversation suggest that no genuine life beyond the
closet is possible when their relationships are seen as different. Neither
can it occur when gay men's love for each other is not recognized and
affirmed and is not considered vital for the definition of who they are.
For them, the real family acceptance, true "normalization" or "routiniza-
tion" of these men's gayness, ultimately resides in families' ability to bring
gay men's intimate relations into the life of the family home. As we have
seen, nothing makes this more explicit than the tendency for gay men
to judge the effectiveness of a disclosure, or the worth of coming out to
family members, not in terms of whether they will be accepted as gay
but in terms of whether their relationships are accepted—whether they

are able to bring a same-sex lover to the family home to publicly declare, "This is the man I love."

THE FAMILY HOME AND DESIRE FOR CONVERGENCES

Indeed, as we have seen, the large question that is at the center of these men's aspirations and struggles is precisely the promise of a merger: how to assimilate and converge gay intimacies and affective ties with the "family home" understood as a source of connection with family and kin and past and future, a significant site of belonging. It seems to me there is no desire to ignore family and kinship ties altogether and build social and affective ties completely out of other sets of relationships, such as those based on common, shared sexuality. On this point it helps to recall how these men remain unconnected with lesbians as well as LGBTQ activist circles that might be producing perspectives on "gay kinship" ideologies (Weston 1995) and practicing new, non-family-based, meaningful, and supportive relations with others. These men's desires to privilege connectedness, as opposed to displacement and self-displacement, from the family home, invite us to rethink the value of home, which has been explored as a locus of displacement and/ or self-displacement for gays and lesbians and therefore seen as an important source of gay subordination (Calhoun 2000). Organized through procreative heterosexuality and a domain of kinship, the family home carries profound paradoxical meanings: it can be a site of homophobia and violence (the image of Can's father carries a real or imagined threat of violence) where homosexuality is denied and suppressed, but it also is a site invested with positive meanings because loving, caring, and giving relationships are contextualized within it. Their investment into the intersubjectively shared experiences and lives articulated in the family home in which they have been socialized and have formed their class habitus has great significance. In other words, family home and loving and conflictual relations within it form the background against which their desires and aspirations make sense. Some of the things they value most (ranging from a mother's cooking of a favorite childhood dish to close relationships with younger generations in families) are accessible to them only in relation to participation in family events and rituals. For these men, thus, the family home constitutes a source of limitation and insult but is a valuable part of who they centrally are. The making and sustaining of their identities are always in a continuing dialogue with, sometimes in struggle against, the family home.

Integration into the routines and rituals of the family home with a same-sex partner provides an important environment for cultivating lives beyond the closet. Central to the idea of family integration is participation in a conversational community—intimate access to rituals of remembrance and connectivity in which one hears the stories of one's history reiterated, thereby constructing and retaining affectional ties to the persons, belongings, activities, and life-cycle events that sustain belonging and offer the pleasure of identification.

In order to explicate some of these important issues regarding family home and intergenerational relations that surfaced in the conversation, it is instructive to focus on the idea of home. In another context, Iris Marion Young (1997) argued that while the ideal of home has been historically an important source of women's subordination and oppression and thus the feminist critiques of home are important, there are aspects of the ideal of home that carry critical normative values (she names them as safety, individuation, privacy, and preservation) that support personal and collective identity. For Young, "the proper response is not to reject home, but to extend its positive values to everyone" (159). For our discussion here, Young's two critical values—preservation and safety—are pertinent. For Young, home is ideally a site of preservation of individual and collective history and meaning. Young stresses that preservation can be conservative, but it can also be reinterpretive: "The narratives of the history of what brought us here are not fixed, and part of the creative and moral task of preservation is to reconstruct the connection of the past to the present in light of new events, relationships, and political understandings" (154). As I understand it, the men in the conversation identify with this understanding of reinterpretive preservation of histories, through their telling and retelling, to themselves and to others, in ways that transform them and transform the future. "A father telling the story of one's childhood to a same-sex lover" (as Can encapsulated and others agreed), they have claimed, is more compelling than any other scenario because these retellings affirm both resistance (to heteronormative order) and belonging (fitting in and being seen to fit into a collective body). The importance attached to affirmation of a same-sex relationship's belongingness to a family biography is a significant reminder that transformation of the future remains attached to family homes. Theoretically speaking, these men's perspectives urge us to investigate the permeability of domains of gay relations and family home and their mutual (re)structuring. The actual nature of transformations wrought by such convergences must be examined to deepen our understanding of the kinds of family environments that nurture or constrain the development of these convergences. A productive question is to ask how family homes are transformed in relation to convergences and trace their effects on individuals. We need to examine how the patriarchal family structure in Turkey embeds these new relationships—the extent to which it permits new family relations to emerge simultaneously as radically new and innovative and assimilationist. In sum, we need to examine queering of the Turkish family home.

"Home means a safe place" (Young 1997, 161) is another critical value Young identifies about the ideal of home. Young's advocacy of reclaiming critical values about the ideal home has many inspirations, but she particularly references bell hooks, who gives a positive and political meaning to the idea of home in relation to the critical value of safety. Invoking hooks's concept of "homeplace" as the crucial site of resistance to dominating and exploiting social structures in reference to the historic experience of African American women, Young reiterates hooks's argument that "[t]he ability to resist dominant social structures requires a space beyond the full reach of those structures, where different, more humane, social relations can be lived and imagined" (159). Can the safety of Turkish homes be a site of protection from and resistance to homophobia, when Turkish homes themselves are significant sites of homophobia, insult, and violence? I think these men's varied and contradictory experiences with the family home and their desire for connectedness demonstrate that holding onto the ideal of safety—affirming the value of safety and of home as a safe place—is a crucial personal and political pursuit. Indeed, very recently, Turkey's LGBTQ movement has started to highlight the importance of the parental/family home in safeguarding the safety and identities of LGBTQ youth. With the slogan "Don't touch my child" (Çocuğuma dokunma), the movement articulates a strong protective parental voice against the state and individual forms of violence directed at lesbian, gay, and transgender individuals.

CLASS: ITS PRIVILEGES AND TRANSGRESSIONS

The themes of class identity and cross-class relations running through the conversation warns us against discounting the multifaceted impact of class in gay self-making. These men's accounts of class clarify and make concrete some subtle and some obvious meanings class privilege may have in the lives of gay men. There are three dimensions to explore here.

First, it is significant that they grew up in families in which the project of upward mobility for offspring was at the center of parenting and family life. Brilliance, cultivated taste, good use of elite educational advantages, commanding occupational positions, marriage and procreation—these are the dimensions of a form of upper-class masculinity to which, it was expected, these sons would conform. And in many senses they did: they embraced and collaborated with their parents' life plans for them, with the exception of their sexual subjectivities and proclivities. The conversation stresses that from the standpoint of upper-middle-class parents, a gay child who otherwise is celebrated for his high educational and professional achievements represents "failure," a non-normative sexual orientation compromising all other achievements and thus becoming representative of an unrealizeable potential threatening to interrupt a family's class trajectory. These men also shared an assessment that upper-middle-class parents' difficulty in accepting their children's sexual orientation is bolstered by this perception of "failure." By contrast, they invoked the observation that their lower-class counterparts have an easier time coming out to parents, equating lower-classness with easier parental acceptance. Also, crucially linked to the class location is the parental concern and anxiety about the sons' becoming marked by being too out and visible, potentially leading to experiences of social ostracism and professional ruin. Thus, it seems that one concomitant of this parental anxiety among upper-middle-class parents is a greater emphasis on an enforced double life.

Second, the men in the conversation also point out another dimension of class privilege, making an explicit connection between being in positions of authority at work and protection of the façade, revealing a more complicated picture of gays in professional life, particularly calling into question the (parental) certainty that professional ruin will always be associated with being openly gay. In this conversational exchange, these men show us that the relationship between a professional identity and being open or closeted is more complex, more dynamic, and more fluid than a more simple connection assumes. As their account makes clear, there is a continuum of gay friendliness in workplace culture. While in some workplaces (such as fashion and advertising), gay identity can be visible and nameable, in others (such as banking and finance), disclosure can be damaging. In their view, a major factor protecting them from involuntary outing is, in fact, their superior positions; thus class/ status privilege provides a shield of protection to militate against homophobia and insult. Once again, what we are seeing is the collaboration of others—this time in institutional contexts—in protecting the façade. Overall, these men's differentiated experiences at work provide important clues to the importance of attending to different professional environments and workplaces in future research.

Third, these men's reflections on questions of class identity are also closely linked to transient figures in their lives. The upper-middle-class gay culture is situated in a much larger context involving large numbers of people from quite diverse social backgrounds, a context in which lower-class men, married and/or heterosexually identified men, and pious Muslim men are in contact with each other. This imbrication of gay men from the privileged classess with others enables transgressions of class boundaries in a society in which they are so rigidly respected and preserved by their heterosexual counterparts, who always couple within their own circles. So even on the most superficial level, we can observe intriguing forms of self-consciously adopted romantic cross-class relations that make certain forms of behavior, otherwise prohibited, permissible to gay men of the privileged classes. Although they claim the significance of these class-boundary infractions, it is not clear how the infractions, which are invariably limited to sexual encounters ("the penis does not recognize class boundaries") or short-lived romances, transform them or the others they encounter, other than letting us know that there is always an uneasy affinity with lower-class counterparts who differ profoundly in upbringing and social and economic class. And their own trials testify that class-imbalanced relationships are bound to fail in meeting the requirements of long-term relationships of intimacy and affection; the core conundrum of their lives is intimately tied to the recognition and inscription of their gay identities within the affective family home to create a sense of legitimacy and belonging. Their desire to give same-sex love access to the family home once more articulates the power of connective selving in the construction of new selves in Turkish society.

Conclusion

I was raised by staunchly secular parents. My parents belonged to the first generation of sons and daughters of the new Republic who undertook the project of creating a secular, Western-looking, and industrialized nation. They were great admirers of Atatürk, the founder of the Turkish Republic in 1923 and the main architect of state feminism in Turkey (defined by the inclusion of women in political citizenship for the improvement of the legal, social, and economic status of women through top-down reforms initiated by the state, without notable participation from women). Perhaps more than my mother, my otherwise authoritarian and patriarchal father embraced and experimented with Atatürk's ideals and aspirations for Turkish women during my and my sisters' formative years in the sixties and seventies. Foremost, this meant for him a high regard for girls' education and advocacy for women's full participation in public and professional life, even in the most male-dominated fields. However, his vision for women's emancipation from home-bound lives was full of contradictions, for his investment in certain aspects of the patriarchal tradition of raising daughters was equally as strong as his brand of state feminism.

As a true man of enlightenment, my father also embraced a strong hostility toward religion, and religious upbringing. My father never set foot in a mosque, and I never saw him praying or fasting during Ramadan. I don't think the family owned a Koran. I remember seeing one for the first time in my grandmother's home and wanting to play with it (she took it away from me, saying it was not a toy to play with). When I was growing up, my mother (and my older sisters, and occasionally I) fasted and participated in some ritualistic aspects of Islam when a child was born, when a boy got circumcised, or when someone close died. Only on those occasions when prayers were called for would my mother put on a scarf loosely. We were secular Muslims. Thus, as the narrators of the chapter 3 argued, my parents did not ask deep questions about the meaning of religion in their lives, delegating it to an unimportant place in their life projects.

I benefited from my father's all-encompassing antireligion stance, in which he associated religion with ignorance, dogma, and darkness. As a daughter of a "modern family," I enjoyed the pride and superiority of being nonreligiously raised vis-à-vis my traditionally raised peers, who in our urban middle-class circles were the wives and daughters of the rural-to-urban migrants who supported our middle-class lifestyles with their work and labor as doorkeepers, domestic workers, and small shopkeepers. However, complicated feelings of shame and stigmatization were not absent from my girlhood. Not only would my father refuse to fast during Ramadan, but he would send me and my sisters to the neighborhood grocery store to buy his alcohol (*rakı*, the national drink). The shopkeeper was a typical rural-to-urban migrant. Often hanging around him in the store were men of his profile, and they would look at us with an evaluative gaze and great pity, clearly seeing us as "poor little girls subjected to child abuse by their father." In those moments, I disliked my father's flaunting of nonreligiosity the most. My early internalization of the association between headscarves and traditionalism, ignorance, and backwardness also made me not want to be outdoors with my paternal grandmother, who wore a headscarf in a traditional way. An undefined sense of shame would overcome me when she held my hand in the street. I also remember being confused when this association between the headscarf and tradition was contradicted: one day I saw the teacher of a religious course in my middle school (because the religious course was elective in those days, I wasn't taking it) walking in the street with a woman whom I presumed to be his wife. Not only was her head naked, but she was a bottle-blond in chic modern attire.

My father died young, at the age of fifty-seven, in 1977, without witnessing the growing Islamization of Turkey that has occurred since the early 1990s. However, my mother, who passed away in 2006, lived long enough to personally witness the heightened visibility of headscarved women in her midst and the rise of a more pluralistic Turkish society. She exhibited an elevated sense of her national identity as a secular Turk. For instance, I saw her pinning an Atatürk rosette/pin on her lapel to show her continued affiliation with his ideals.[1] In the last years of her life, shame affiliated with the religious headscarf also (re)entered my mother's consciousness. My mother's caregiver was a live-in, middle-aged woman who dressed conservatively and wore a headscarf when she was outside. My mother was a very social person who always enjoyed the outdoors and found pleasure in striking up conversations with strangers from all walks of life in parks and other public spaces. But on a summer day she declared to us that she had stopped her routine of frequenting the park every afternoon. Alarmed by her cocooning at home, my sisters and I inquired about the reason. Flatly, she said that because of her caregiver's headscarf and the reflection it produced about her, she desired not be seen in public with her.

The last *iftar* dinner (the meal that breaks the Ramadan fast) I participated in was about ten years ago at my male cousin's home in Istanbul, which happened to bring three generations together. My mother and my aunt were not fasting on account of health reasons, but my cousin, a colonel in the army at that time, was. We started eating at the exact moment the *iftar* prayer was called for, but at dinner, beer and wine were served and my cousin sang on his guitar one of my favorites from our youth: the Beatles' *Let It Be*. This dinner was another reminder of the peculiarity of Turkish secularism and the ways in which religious rituals are practiced and "secularly Muslim" identities experienced.

I recently remembered this family episode in relation to the *iftar* dinners organized by a group called "the anticapitalist Muslims" during the Gezi protests. Out in the most crowded streets of Istanbul, they set up potluck-style dinners, called "*dünya sofrası*" (world's tables), participated in by hundreds of antigovernment protesters. The pictures circulated on social media sites showed religiously covered and modestly dressed women side by side with young women in tank tops and shorts. A striking scene showed a huge LGBTQ rainbow flag doubling as a tablecloth, confirming the participation of gays and lesbians. The pious young women of this book always referenced Muslims and seculars coming together over *iftar* dinners as potent symbols of intimate interaction and coexistence. Is it possible for people to form close connections across secular and religious lines and to be comfortable with their own identities in these spaces? Is it possible for secular women to participate in *iftar* dinners in shorts and pious women to frequent a gathering, like a party, where alcohol is served? Or must they reformulate themselves (in appearance, personal decorum, and emotion management) so that they are more palatable to their respective habituses? How can close connections between secular and nonsecular young Turks be sustained amid these contradictions? If we follow Durkheim, we have to say that the integration of social groups requires both the production and maintenance of common goals, gods, and rituals. In other words, rituals and symbols, like *iftar* dinners, do not simply reflect integration or social cohesion but construct them. An examination of the way people engaged in coexistence work in these intersecting environments should be on our research agendas. By bringing these relations/interactions into focus, we might learn that through crisscrossing religion and secularism, people are dulling radical ideologies, both secular and religious.

The young Turks in this study live in a historical moment in which a deeply entrenched secular and Muslim polarization within the context of growing Islamization troubles the transition to a more democratic, liberal, and pluralistic Turkey. Since the beginning of the establishment of modern Turkey on the ruins of a multiethnic Ottoman Empire, it has become a truism in the vocabulary and imagination of outsiders that Turkey is defined by the in-betweenness of the polar opposites of religious and secular, West and East, and modern and traditional. Now insiders themselves are truly finding and recognizing themselves as one or the other identity category, either secular or Muslim, as the historical construction of secular Muslim identity my parents' generation helped to build is being contested by the AKP government and as Islamic identities have become more publicly visible and assertive.

The AKP came to power in 2002 cloaked in emancipatory ideas and with a discourse of protecting human rights and equality before the law. The premise had great appeal among liberals and even among some feminists who wanted to see freedom for religious expression and a diminished role attached to the military. Opening the way for voices outside the center that have been disempowered by exclusion from democratic processes and by social and cultural discrimination (among them the Kurdish ethnic minority, the religious minorities like Alevis, and religiously covered women) was considered truly transformative. The AKP hardly lived up to expectations, treating its electoral success as a mandate for majority rule and a call for an illiberal democracy articulating economic neoliberalism with an increasingly authoritarian state. As happens with many authoritarian leaders, the political orientation of the AKP's leader, Prime Minister Tayyip Erdoğan, and the aggressive drive for economic neoliberalism, have trumped democratic concerns.

As David Harvey notes, the core "substantive achievement of neo-liberalization has been to redistribute, rather than to generate, wealth and income" (Harvey 2005, 17). The central force here is "accumulation by dispossession," and the main dynamics of this dispossession are the corporatization, commodification, and privatization of hitherto public assets and the opening up of "new fields for capital accumulation in domains hitherto regarded off-limits to the calculus of profitability" (160). Within the context of integrating the Turkish economy into the neoliberal global order, the AKP has followed this formula exactly, at great human and ecological cost. These costs now significantly animate antigovernment protests also led by those new middle classes created by the openness to global neoliberal economic and cultural currents. Even if there was much in the earlier Republican rule designed to foster a monolithic Turkish populace (organized by patriarchy and patrilineality, Turkishness, radical secularism, and heteronormativity) that ought to have been abolished, the AKP has promoted religious piousness and criminalized dissent in the process.

The long-awaited so-called democratic package was unveiled by the prime minister on October 13, 2013. It lifts the ban on headscarves in public offices, except for judges, prosecutors, police officers, and members of the army, and punishes persons who discriminate against those donning headscarves for religious purposes. The package also includes partial relaxations on the Kurdish language instruction. The student oath, which starts with the words, "I am Turkish, righteous, and hard working," will also no longer be read in schools in recognition of the existence of non-Turkish ethnic groups. However, as noted by many,[2] not only is the package half-full (it is completely silent on protection from discrimination for LGBTQ individuals or recognition of the cultural expression of non-Sunni religious groups, for example), but it was also designed without any input from civil society or parliamentary participation. No doubt lifting the secular ban on headscarves is a positive step for many women who choose to lead an Islamic way of life. The immediate question is this: Will the young, educated pious women in this book help protect the rights of secular women to express themselves in the ways they desire without being subjected to discrimination and exclusion? Will they let their "feminist vein" surface in order to ensure the vitality and durability of different selves for heterosexual women, gays, and lesbians and the establishment of a true liberal democracy in Turkey? Will these different identities safeguard each other from the forces of homophobia, sexism, and intolerance for religious identities?

Judging alone from the budgets allocated to different ministries, the AKP has been steadily devoting increasing resources to its Islamization project. For example, the budget of the Religious Affairs Directorate has increased steadily since 2002 and doubled in a single year in 2007, greatly enhancing the capacity of this state institution.[3] More importantly, in 2007 its budget was equivalent to the combined budgets of the eight ministries and the twenty-two state-funded universities. There were 67,000 schools and 85,000 mosques in Turkey in the same year, and there was one hospital for every 60,000 people while there was one mosque for every 350 people. There were 77,000 doctors, 90,000 religious personnel, and a reported deficiency of 250,000 teachers in schools. These numbers convey how thoroughly Turkish society has been refashioned by the AKP's twelve-year rule. The state's top-down measures promoting Islamization are also backed by religious civil-society organizations. There were 35,000 mosque-building associations (*cami yaptırma derneği*) in 2007. When compared to other civic associations devoted to establishing venues for art and performative expressions (for instance, one association for opera, eleven for ballet, ten for sculpture, eighteen for painting, eighteen for cinema, and thirty-eight for theater), the figure of 35,000 is truly glaring. Indeed, a religious nongovernmental organization (Tüm Din-Der) recently invited and attracted eight thousand 6–12-year-old girls and boys for a public prayer at Fatih mosque in Istanbul.[4] When I read the posters for this event, I particularly thought of Aknur, who greatly emphasized the importance of childhood religiosity, and I imagined how she must be pleased to see thousands of children flocking to this event. But there was a capitalistic twist to the program: the attending children were given various material gifts (prayer beads and rugs, and headscarves), and the first arrivals were even promised gold coins. I wondered if antimaterialist Aknur would approve of this method of promoting childhood religiosity.

The most important government-initiated Islamization project relates to the educational system—vital to the design of a hoped-for pious generation or, in the words of the Prime Minister Tayyip Erdoğan, to "raising a religious youth." The course on religion that I escaped from in middle school is now mandatory for all middle-school children (only Christian and Jewish students are exempted) in addition to several elective courses that my narrators in chapter 3 wished to have available when they were growing up, such as courses on the life of Prophet Muhammed and on Arabic language instruction. However, secular parents have started registering the complaint that their children are forced to take more than the single required religion course because the other elective courses are never available, allegedly because of a lack of instructors or demand, even in school districts populated by secular middle-class families. These parents also note the infusion of Islamic perspectives into math and science courses. It is not far-fetched, then, to imagine that the undergirding of the project of "raising a religious youth" will be fractured on the basis of a socioeconomic-class-based polarization, the public/private school split.

At a dramatic level, the AKP's desires and actions for fostering piety based on Sunni Islam are animated by the top-down imposition of Islamic morality, legislating virtue intimately associated with gender, sexuality, and women's bodies. Attending to the cultivation of piety by focusing on gender relations and sexuality, the new state policies are designed to facilitate a pro-nationalist agenda of sexual reproduction, promotion of (heterosexual) marriage, gender segregation in the public sphere, and the control and regulation of public life—particularly the elimination of sexually animated environments.

The ruling party's own definition of permissible gender and sexual mores is presented and gradually enforced as society's Puritan norms and values. It disregards the values, desires, and objections of those who do not wish to embrace an Islamic way of life for themselves and their children. It makes no allowances for alternative lifestyles and actually attempts to suppress them, encroaching on civil rights and liberties. In recent years, the country has encountered the regulation and legislation of virtue in various schemes; some have been merely proposed as a set of instructions by public discourses while others are already codified and implemented through legal means. To give just two recent examples of a host of informal practices enforcing piety: very recently (October 24, 2013) Victoria's Secret lowered its shutter during the opening ceremony of a mega mall in Ankara attended by Prime Minister Erdoğan, and a female TV host was fired after the AKP spokesman criticized her for wearing an outfit that was too revealing (coincidentally, on the day after the headscarf ban was lifted). There are many examples of the prime minister criticizing individuals sharing physical affection and intimacies, such as holding hands and kissing in public spaces, for acting against public morality and decency. A lawyer and an Islamic thinker on the state-owned TV station declared that it was immoral, disgraceful, and aesthetically displeasing for pregnant women with huge bellies to reveal themselves in public.[5] He suggested that after seven or eight months of pregnancy, expectant mothers should go out with their husbands by car to get some fresh air. This comment prompted the Religious Affairs Directorate to issue a statement saying that Islam requires no isolation of pregnant women and that being a mother was a gift. Even so, the directorate's statement still reminded pregnant women that they should be more careful with their dresses, not wearing clothes showing their bellies or backs.

When we think of the comments of this lawyer, which immediately prompted huge protests led by feminists, in combination with the prime minister's desire for Turkish women to have more than three children and his recommendation that new mothers breast-feed for at least eighteen months, it is not too much to imagine that the religiously inspired conservative design for women is for them to stay in their homes to have and raise children. In the educational realm, there is the example of a school principal revealing his plans to create separate stairways for boys and girls in his school. There are also government-initiated proposals to convert all the state-controlled dormitories for university students into single-sex units. According to Reuters, the prime minister said that "the government had already shut down mixed accommodation in 75 percent of state-run student dormitories and would continue to do so."[6] On November 2, 2013, while commenting on the inadequate number of dormitories for university students, the prime minister remarked, "Female and male students are living in the same house. This is against our tradition/structure, which is conservative-democratic." He added that his government should "one way or another inspect and supervise" the situation.[7] The government recently revised the building code to ban the construction of studio apartments in order to discourage the "bachelor lifestyle." Indeed, government policies to actively encourage marriage have multiplied. A new piece of legislation will exempt married students from dormitory fees and provide student loans (with no obligation to pay back) to those who are married. Student loans of already-married students will be forgiven by being converted into scholarship.[8] Another legislative proposal that will be brought to the Parliament would incentivize marriage by offering financial aid for marriage in the form of a lump-sum loan. The proposal further stipulates that the marriage loan for those couples who have children within the first two years of marriage will be forgiven.

A state polity led by the desire to create a new pious generation (possessed by powerful self-restraint to create and enact selves that are virtuous, sober, and sexually restrained until marriage) is very much tied to the question of political legitimacy and controlling the reins of power. Whether the AKP is willing and able to use the full weight of its electoral power (around 50 percent) to bring more change toward Islamization is a question with no easy answers. However, it seems that the more radical action the AKP takes and the more it uses the rhetoric of "pious-moral/impious-immoral" to polarize society, the more it delegitimizes its claims of bringing democracy to Turkey and of respecting different lifestyles, as well as its repudiation of the past as undemocratic. The more it radically awakens civil society, inspiring dissent among more groups (including some devout classes), the more its interventions may become self-defeating.

It is safe to say that in its project for cultivating and raising a pious generation, the AKP has gained access to the formal institutions of power during its twelve-year rule, but it has by no means gained total cultural hegemony and consent. Yet, as the Gezi protests powerfully demonstrated, dissent is being criminalized in an effort to nullify resistance. A report by Amnesty International on the Turkish government's response to the Gezi protests points out the Turkish government's large-scale human rights violations: "the wholesale denial of the right to peaceful assembly and violations of the rights to life, liberty and the freedom from torture and and ill-treatment."[9] As some scholars have started pointing out, the new Turkey is becoming a police state and the Violence Law is being used to "oversee the entire population: wholesale detentions and *ex post facto* indictments have emerged as the preferred method of intimidating, marginalising and criminalising dissenting groups *en masse*."[10] Despite this bleak picture, the voices of the young Turks in this book tell us that we should not ignore the promising contingency of the future.

Studying recent Turkish transformations from the perspective of upwardly mobile young Turks underscores some deep desires and anxieties about changing Turkish patriarchy, which has historically intertwined with state paternalism and has been directly and powerfully constitutive of gender identities and sexual selves. The transformation of this complex and connective system in which normative femininity is intimately linked with the maternal role of selflessness and masculinity with protection and providerhood cannot be viewed as a total shift. It presents both challenges and opportunities to those young Turks, who actively negotiate its transformation in their self-making. The narratives I have recounted in this book have explored in some detail the forms and content of that negotiation process.

Like the many mothers who appeared in the narratives of their daughters and sons in this book, my mother also confirmed conventional gender expectations and roles: she was a stay-at-home mother and utterly dependent on her husband for her economic survival. For her, the self and the family were coterminous—although her marriage involved, if only partially, breaching the boundaries between gender roles, compelling her to refer to herself as being "both the woman and the man of the house." These breaches came about because my father was away from home for long stretches of time due to his job, causing my mother to complement, and more often replace, my father's socially assigned gender role. I think that because my father's absence from home necessarily made her independent and autonomous, my mother never came across to me as a selfless mother or a female model of deference and acquiescence, and thus my family situation nuanced the normative system with the deviance of my lived experiences. Perhaps this impression was also related to the fact that I was keenly aware of the importance my mother's domestic talents (especially cooking) played in her self-realization and how these talents gave her high status in the female hierarchy. She experienced utter financial dependency, but through the home she created and the five children she raised on her own, she expressed her individuality, her taste, and her quality. Like many of the mothers of the daughters I studied, she heavily invested in my and my sisters' education, and she encouraged us to increase our value and financial independence through education.

My mother's dependency and the subsuming of her identity under my father's was supported by the state's protective paternalism (as I explained in the introduction, now dismantled by the privatization of healthcare and pension systems under new neoliberal policies), and because my mother never worked outside the home, this dependency was always present in her life. My mother, who battled and survived cancer twice and was afflicted with Alzheimer's in the last years of her life, benefited from a public healthcare and pension system through her social identity as a wife. I witnessed a crystallizing moment of her identification with patrilineality when, in her old age, she became suspicious about a possible Kurdish ethnic background in the family. She lived in an era in which the ethnic differences were suppressed and normalized to the point of invisibility in Turkey. One summer when I was home, she practically whispered in my ear, the ear of a sociologist, the question of whether there was any possibility of us being Kurdish, since my father was born in a town currently inhabited by Kurds. "Us" here is significant, signifying my mother's identification with my father's suspected non-Turkish ethnic identity, despite the fact that her family had had roots in Istanbul for multiple generations. Indeed, the Turkish state merges women's identities with the identities of their husbands—when a girl marries, her records are transferred and merged to the husband's records. The struggle for my generation of feminist women was to denaturalize these mergers in women's lives and to reject marriage and the sanctified role attached to motherhood.

In this book, we have seen the existence of open or clandestine practices of cohabitation among young Turks that were hardly permissible during my early adulthood. I was the first one in my family who attempted to reject marriage as a bourgeois institution (a particular blend of Marxism and feminism defined my early adult worldview) to try to cohabitate with my partner. However, we were compelled to marry by our respective families (a huge financial incentive being attached to marriage by my partner's family). Nevertheless, we refused a traditional wedding. Rejecting the white gown, I went to my marriage ceremony in jeans. Two of our friends were our witnesses. The marriage officiant had a standard preamble to recite; he trained his gaze on the groom and started saying, "He is the head of the household . . ." I couldn't help myself and started laughing uncontrollably, which made him stop the ceremony to say, "Look, young lady, there are three important moments in one's life: birth, death, and the between— marriage—and only at the moment of marriage is one conscious of what is happening." Although, thanks to feminists, the new civil code of 2001 abolished the concept of man as the head of the family and equalized the status of husband and wife in the conjugal union, marriage continues to be an important institution for transitioning to adulthood and for enacting certain gender identities and roles in Turkey, especially the roles of motherhood and fatherhood.[11]

As we have seen, the young women (both religious and secular) view their parents' marriages, which they associate with male power and female selflessness and strict gender-role divisions that impose stifling and limited choices on women, in strongly negative terms. For them, the home is not an adequate site for the cultivation of richer female selves. Patriarchal marriage represents not only the subordination of one's needs to the needs of others but also the obliteration of women's selves through acquiescence to the choices of others (fathers and husbands). Wifehood is experienced as compliance and submission to the husband's power and authority, leaving women with no selves with which to desire or create. These young women's application of a new framework to marriage clearly foregrounds a high commitment to the cultivation of public selves. Both secular and devout young women articulate and defend a paradigm shift in marriage—in the pious women's vocabularies, a "marriage of compatibility" over a "marriage of logic"—although this ideal is elaborated much more in the pious women's narratives because of the ontological importance marriage has for their identity as Muslim women, while many secular women expressed desire for independent, single lives. Women cannot become full subjects without male spouses within religious Muslim life; full subjecthood can only be materialized through marriage and motherhood.

The narratives of the gay men in this book underscored a similar ontological imperative: the embodiment and enactment of a gay identity as a full subjecthood, as opposed to the identity of *ibne*, which reduces gay men entirely to sexual beings, can only be realized in the context of a gay couplehood in which attachment is forged through same-sex love. Such a union is the only route to being out and being recognized and integrated into the familial sphere and larger society. I have suggested that the dominant connective culture remains the reference point in their self-making as gay men. In other words, just as the pious women's marriages to desired hermeneutic Muslim men are critical to the realization of their identities as Muslim women not confined to the home, so is couplehood—forging a lifelong relationship—critical among upwardly mobile gay men to authenticating their same-sex desires and establishing the legitimacy of their identities as gay men.

One of the most important shared desires among the young Turks I studied, sometimes underlined and explicitly articulated and at other times emerging in the recounting of relationship dynamics, is pleasure found in equality of desires. Feelings of shared experiences and Bourdieu's "structured and structuring dispositions" with intimate others from the same class, ethnic, and religious background significantly determine whom these young men and women love and desire and the intimacies they create. This was true for the secular heterosexual men and women, the gay men, and the pious women. Their most intimate connections are profoundly shaped by existing societal distinctions. The moorings of gender and class, urban/rural, religious/secular are not being cast aside in the new premarital sexual culture, because these intersections in contemporary Turkey have not lost their ability to define a social and political hierarchy, thus motivating their reproduction in intimate relationships.

What do young Turks' experiences suggest about contemporary self-making? First, and perhaps most importantly, they show us that the selfless feminine and the protective masculine are repudiated. One of the most striking features of the gender transformation across all classes is the merging of young men's and women's desires for expanded selfhoods beyond the selflessness implied in both the protective masculine and the maternal feminine models. Hegemonic masculinity in Turkey is historically identified with the values of protection and providerhood. Men are deemed appropriately masculine when they are protective and carry the power to define the boundaries of action and conduct of the girls and women under their protection. The renunciation of this model by the young men in this book is propelled by Turkey's neoliberal turn within the context of globalization and the changing structures of career trajectories as massive privatization orients these men toward aspirations for creating layered, protean selves defined by risk taking in careers, ambition outside the professional realm, male passion and expressiveness, and creative interests geared toward self-actualization. The majority of young men link their self-making to their claims to be free from protective paternalism—independent from the dependency of others and the selfless/altruistic effects of protecting others and providing for them. However, the building of male self-expansion is organically linked to and dependent on a vision of the feminine other who provokes and nurtures these male desires for layered selves. The male narratives described a vision of desired femininity that was marked by opposing dualities of, on the one hand, ambitious, charismatic, sexually desiring, and self-possessed women and, on the other hand, positive, altruistic, energy-giving "girls." I have argued that both independent and selfless female selves support new masculine selving and have suggested that this male dependency on both old and new femininity should be read theoretically as an instance of the articulation of neoliberal selfhood with connective selving.

The emergence of the new definition of masculinity is simultaneous with the appearance of a new construction of femininity among young women. The young women rejected femininity intimately linked with the maternal role of selflessness. This new femininity constitutes its identity not through maternal roles but through a shared desire for individualized selves defined against other-directedness, self-sacrifice, and female subservience to the desires of others. The desire for self-governance and the rejection of male intrusions on female sovereignty in the name of protection mark the most important constitutive dimensions of the new femininity. Like its male counterpart, this new femininity also has its co-creators. The desired man in the female narratives is constructed dualistically as someone who seeks power and creativity for self-expansion and has strong ambitions to become a dominant actor in society, while simultaneously escaping from gender-based traditional privileges to control and dominate women.

I have argued that these nonpatriarchal identity projects should not be read necessarily as a promise of democratic gender relations. The very notions of desirable femininity, the dialectic between charismatic and energy-giving girls in male narratives that would help make expanded male selves possible, might ultimately undermine young women's claims to a new femininity untied to maternal selflessness and female altruism. In the same fashion, the female constructions of ideal masculinity, the dialectic between power in the public sphere and gender transgression in intimate relations and the private sphere, might actually serve to undermine female desire for noncontrolling men.

Gender ideals are socially and sexually constructed and defined in relation to each other as nonoppositional in the sense that both the young men and the young women embraced the same process of individuation that propels and sustains young Turks' renunciation of hegemonic constructions of gender in Turkey. Behind this development is a new sexual culture powered by the sexualization of love and intimacy freed from marriage. But, in their pathways to claim and enact sexual selves, these young Turks encounter an unbending prohibitive order. I do not wish to assign a transhistorical essence to patriarchy. However, it was striking to observe the resilient presence of a contradictory patriarchal desire in young women's lives that my own generation of girls and young women had also experienced: daughters are to be educated to obtain greater freedom and power in the public sphere but to be sexually chaste and confine sexual expression within the realm of marriage.

My father's Atatürk-inspired feminism was also permeated with this patriarchal paradox: his daughters were to become possessors of high-powered careers in the public sphere but be sexually innocent (no boyfriends were allowed) and be androgynously modest in appearance (no miniskirts, and makeup was forbidden, except a faintly applied, light-colored lipstick).[12] The new emancipated Republican woman should be both modern and chaste, publicly visible yet sexually virtuous, an asexual, nationalistic mother. It is this fundamental contradiction in terms that feminists of my generation in Turkey had to grapple with. Indeed, the modern feminist movement in Turkey has been challenging these patriarchal constructions and has had many legislative victories in constructing women as sovereign individuals and citizens, as I outlined in the introduction of this book.

The posing of feminist demands for women's sexual entitlement and autonomy provides the rhetorical and moral force and the inspiration for the young Turks I studied, even though they do not categorically identify themselves as feminists. As Feray in chapter 1 powerfully articulated, when these young women were growing up, girls were not given a language in which to talk about sexual desire; they were only allowed to dream and talk about marriage while protecting their virginities. Even in my female-dominated family (four girls and one boy—the youngest) led by my permissive mother, who was always helpful with her daughters' façades in relation to boyfriends and miniskirts (it was the early 1970s, and miniskirts were in high fashion), I don't remember ever talking about my adolescent sexual desires, attached or unattached, with my friends or sisters. On the basis of the experiences of those who traversed the most distance in overcoming the silencing of their desires, I have underlined the utter significance of the close encounters girls and young women have with alternative discourses, like feminism, that question, counteract, and delegitimize the silencing and regulation of women's sexual desires and expressions. Equally important, I have emphasized, is the role close embodied role models of the liberated woman play in young women's lives. I arrived at the conclusion that in a patriarchal society like Turkey, where mother-daughter relationality plays a significant role in self-making, only other women permit one another to be sexual without guilt and shame. In turn, the young women who voice, without shame, "I never would be with a man who seeks virginity" become important agents of change for their male peers.

In this book, I have directed attention to those upwardly mobile young Turks with provincial and sexually prohibitive family origins who attempt to create new kinds of identities and relationships very different from those of their parents. They are the Turks embedded in the dynamic interconnection between identification and distantiation with their parental culture/homes and their middle-class destinations—in Ali's narrative, "here" and "there." Vulnerable to either orientation, they experience emotional attachment to those identities experienced as "charismatic" or "respectable" in their familial circles and communities of origin but "marginal" in their new surroundings. I suggested that they are the ones who give the gender and sexual transformations in Turkey their central dynamic. What their stories underscore is an inversion of both a theoretical construct and an everyday understanding of the existence of a hard gender divide between romantic and erotic. I have argued that for the group of young heterosexual men in this book, transgressing socialization in homosocial and sexually conservative environments in the service of a desire for new masculine selves means a greater focus on their romantic ambitions, not sex, being publicly recognized as desired by the gendered other. In contrast, for the young women in this group, these transformations translated into a focus on erotic ambitions, being recognized as liberated and embodying their sexual desires. In other words, for this group of men, new selves are built in the realm of romance, and for women, in the realm of sex. However, vulnerable masculinities and femininities face a unique set of challenges. Female enactments that cross the boundaries of sexual permissibility often result in young women experiencing negative, shameful feelings about themselves and, in turn, make these women vulnerable to male domination and render difficult the repudiation of self-sacrificing maternal femininity in their self-making. For the young men, the desire to be recognized as desirable and important in intimate relationship with young women who have their own desires for recognition can lead to domination, jeopardizing these men's projects of creating nonpatriarchal male identities.

This book has conceptualized intimate romantic and sexual relationships as sites both for the reproduction of patriarchy and for challenges to it. I have viewed romance and sex as an intersubjective terrain from which young people look at themselves, at gendered others, and at society. This terrain shapes their perceptions of who they are and generates experiences that reinforce or contradict the enactments of patriarchal gender identities and sexual selves. Theoretically, I have emphasized the importance of pursuing intersubjectivity, not only because it is a key reflexive relation as an individual comes to feel that "'I am the doer who does, I am the author of my acts,' by being with another person who recognizes her acts, her feelings, her intentions, her existence, her independence" (Benjamin 1988, 21) but also because it epitomizes a reflexive relation insofar as it includes not only the other's "confirming response" but also the way one finds himself/herself in that response, enhancing his/her sense of effective agency. In the context of connective selving, as long as the significant others' (mothers', etc.) desires and expectations enter into that confirming response, even in the most intimate moments of the dyadic relationship, the sense of effective agency is diminished, not enhanced. This is a small reminder from a complicated society in transformation that our prevailing theories of global neoliberal subject-hood centered on self-invention and autonomy should not rely on a truncated and generic understanding of the production of selves.

Table 1.1 Opinions on virginity across sex

		Agree	Disagree	No Opinion	Total
I want to marry a virgin.	Female	14.9	75.9	9.2	100.0 (174)
	Male	51.0	37.7	11.3	100.0 (151)
I am virgin.	Female	64.1	35.3	0.6	100.0 (170)
	Male	49.0	49.7	1.3	100.0 (147)
Premarital sexuality is not acceptable because it is against our traditions.	Female	18.4	74.1	7.5	100.0 (174)
	Male	26.7	62.7	10.6	100.0 (150)

Table 1.2. Opinions on sexuality in general across sex

		Agree	Disagree	No Opinion	Total
It is important to establish emotional intimacy before engaging in sex.	Female	87.6	6.8	5.6	100.0 (177)
	Male	62.0	30.0	8.0	100.0 (150)
I do not experience my sexuality at all.	Female	41.6	43.8	14.6	100.0 (178)
	Male	44.3	38	17.7	100.0 (158)
Young Turkish men are sexually hungry.	Female	79.3	9.2	11.5	100.0 (174)
	Male	87.4	6.6	6.0	100.0 (151)
Masturbation is normal.	Female	74.0	6.4	19.7	100.0 (173)
	Male	82.8	7.3	9.9	100.0 (151)
The one I will marry should have some sexual experience except intercourse.	Female	55.6	19.3	25.1	100.0 (171)
	Male	34.5	42.1	23.4	100.0 (145)
It is not acceptable for me to perform/receive oral sex.	Female	11.2	55.0	33.8	100.0 (169)
	Male	18.1	59.7	22.1	100.0 (149)
If someone is sexually attractive I may have sex without seeking emotionality.	Female	18.4	71.8	9.8	100.0 (174)
	Male	57.6	31.1	11.3	100.0 (151)
For me it is important whether the person I will marry is a virgin or not.	Female	74.9	20.6	4.6	100.0 (174)
	Male	42.3	51.0	6.7	100.0 (149)

Table 1.3. Opinions on sexual experiences across sex

		Yes	No	Total
Have you ever had a girl/boyfriend?	Female	86.4	13.6	100.0 (176)
	Male	76.5	23.5	100.0 (153)
Have you ever had a hook-up experience?	Female	25.9	74.1	100.0 (174)
	Male	31.6	68.4	100.0 (155)
Are you currently in a relationship?	Female	52.8	47.2	100.0 (176)
	Male	39.7	60.3	100.0 (156)
Are you and your partner having sexual intercourse?	Female	47.3	52.7	100.0 (91)
	Male	52.5	47.5	100.0 (61)

Table 1.4. Hook-up experiences

		Yes	No	Total		
Ever had a hook-up experience?	Female	25.9	74.1	100.0 (174)		
	Male	31.6	68.4	100.0 (155)		

		Mean		Total		
Mean of hook-ups in last year	Female	2.12		43		
	Male	2.50		49		

		In a party	In a bar	Already a friend	Through internet	Other	Total
I met her/him	Female	18.6	23.3	39.5	0.0	18.7	100.0
	Male	8.5	17.0	36.2	4.3	34.1	100.0

		Sex above waist	Sex below waist	Oral sex	Sexual inter-course	Other	Total
Content of the experience	Female	43.9	17.1	4.9	29.3	4.9	100.0
	Male	14.6	22.9	4.2	58.3	0.0	100.0

		Completely sober	Slightly drunk	Drunk	Don't remember	Used other sub-stances	Total
Level of sobriety	Female	30.2	39.5	25.6	2.3	2.3	100.0
	Male	34.7	42.9	16.3	0.0	6.1	100.0

		Condom	Birth control	With-drawal	Nothing	Total	
Which method used?	Female	27.3	3.0	15.2	54.5	100.0	
	Male	40.4	6.4	14.9	38.3	100.0	

		Myself	My partner	Just occurred	Don't remember	Total	
Who initiated the last hook-up?	Female	7.0	39.5	48.8	4.7	100.0	
	Male	24.5	22.4	53.1	0.0	100.0	

		SS*	ES	BSSES	SU	EU	BSUEU	Total
General satisfaction about hook-ups	Female	21.9	2.4	4.8	0.0	26.2	45.2	100.0
	Male	56.3	0.0	10.4	0.0	12.5	20.8	100.0

*SS: Sexually satisfying   SU: Sexually unsatisfying
ES: Emotionally satisfying   EU: Emotionally unsatisfying
BSSES: Both sexually & emotionally satisfying   BSUEU: Both sexually & emotionally unsatisfying

330 | APPENDIX I: TABLES

Table 1.5. Opinions on gender roles across sex

		Agree	Disagree	No Opinion	Total
Men are not inclined to do homework.	Female	23.7	74.0	2.3	100.0 (177)
	Male	32.0	64.1	3.9	100.0 (153)
What women really want is a home and children.	Female	7.3	83.1	9.6	100.0 (177)
	Male	14.5	61.8	23.3	100.0 (152)
Fathers can raise children like mothers.	Female	90.2	6.9	2.9	100.0 (174)
	Male	75.0	21.7	3.3	100.0 (152)
Both husband and wife should contribute to the family income.	Female	96.6	1.1	2.3	100.0 (174)
	Male	84.8	10.6	4.6	100.0 (151)
A working woman can care her children properly too.	Female	85.1	9.7	5.1	100.0 (175)
	Male	58.9	27.8	13.2	100.0 (151)
Being a housewife is as satisfactory as working outside of home.	Female	8.0	85.7	6.3	100.0 (175)
	Male	16..0	62.0	22.0	100.0 (150)
Preschool children can be negatively affected from a working mother.	Female	41.9	45.9	12.2	100.0 (172)
	Male	54.1	31.1	14.9	100.0 (148)

Table 1.6. Opinions on virginity in relation to mother's education

		Agree	Disagree	No Opinion	Total
I want to marry a virgin.	Elementary	61.3	29.3	6.4	100.0 (75)
	High	27.6	63.4	7.0	100.0 (123)
	University	18.6	69.8	11.6	100.0 (129)
I am virgin.	Elementary	72.2	27.8	0.0	100.0 (26)
	High	54.9	43.4	1.6	100.0 (122)
	University	50.8	48.4	0.8	100.0 (124)
Premarital sexuality is not acceptable because it is against our traditions.	Elementary	48.0	40.0	12.0	100.0 (75)
	High	14.8	74.6	10.6	100.0 (122)
	University	14.8	79.7	10.7	100.0 (128)

APPENDIX II: SAMPLING PROCEDURE

Table 2.1. Sampling Procedure

Boğaziçi University undergraduate programs. Total number of students in 2001: 7632

Groups

Group 1 - Mathematics - Chemistry - Physics - M. Biology $\Sigma=120$	**Group 2** - History - Philosophy - Psychology - Sociology $\Sigma=120$	**Group 3** - Foreign Language Education - Translation - Western Languages - Turkish Language $\Sigma=120$	**Group 4** - Economics $\Sigma=100$
Group 5 - Management $\Sigma=100$	**Group 6** - Political Science $\Sigma=100$	**Group 7** - Educational Sci. - Computer Education - Primary School Edu. - Science Education $\Sigma=100$	**Group 8** - Chemical Engineering - Civil Engineering $\Sigma=100$
Group 9 - Computer Engineering - Electirics & Electronics Eng. $\Sigma=100$	**Group 10** - Mechanical Eng. - Industry Eng. $\Sigma=100$	**Group 11** - International Trade - Management Information Systems - Tourism Administration $\Sigma=100$	

Random selection of one real, two substitute courses among the all courses—of 30 to 50 students—opened by the department in a group.

For Example:

Group 2 - History - Philosophy - Psychology - Sociology $\Sigma=120$	**Courses** - HIST (XYZ) - PHIL (XYZ) - PSY (XYZ) - SOC (XYZ) Three courses randomly selected from the group.	**Selected Courses** - HIST (YXZ) (Real) - PHIL (ZXY) (S1) - SOC (XYZ) (S2) In the selected course the questionnaire is distributed.

NOTES

INTRODUCTION

1 Over three hundred active and retired military officers were imprisoned for allegedly plotting a coup in 2003 to remove Prime Minister Erdoğan's party from power. In 2012, the court sentenced 324 defendants to up to twenty years in prison, including former air force and navy commanders. The coup plot (called "Ergenekon davası," the "Sledgehammer Case" in English) is considered a driving force in reducing the power of the military. The case initially had broad support from both liberals seeking to curb the military's role in civilian life and pious conservatives. But in recent years, liberals have withdrawn their support amid a growing perception that the government is using the judicial system in a witch hunt to destroy opposition to its rule. The trial played a significant role in deepening the divide between secularists and pious sectors of the population. To read more about the history of this case, see the *Wall Street Journal* online, "Convictions Mostly Upheld in Turkish 'Sledgehammer' Coup-Plot Trial," by Emre Peker, October 9, 2013, available at http://online.wsj.com/news/articles/SB10001424052702304520704579125071654564740 (accessed on October 23, 2013).

2 Several factors have contributed to this reducing desire: accession requirements, the never-ending negotiations, the European public's resistance to Turkey's accession, the diminishing possibility of becoming a full member, and, especially, the nationalist segment's perception that the legal reforms and increasing human and minority rights for Kurds pose a threat to Turkey's national sovereignty.

3 For recent discussions of Prime Minister Tayyip Erdoğan in the news, see Ayla Albayrak in the *Wall Street Journal*, June 17, 2013; Andrew Finkel in the *New York Times*, October 4, 2013; the *Financial Times*, August 6, 2013; and *Hürriyet*, April 9, 2013.

4 *Detraditionalization: Critical Reflections on Authority and Identity* (1996), an edited volume by Paul Heelas, Scott Lash, and Paul Morris, brings to the conversation important propagandists of the detraditionalization thesis and its critiques.

5 Throughout this book I add Turkish words and expressions when no adequate referent for particularly untranslatable expressions and idioms can be found in English.

6 See Julie McLeod (2002) and Lynn Jamieson (1999). Jamieson provides the most substantive feminist critique. She reviewed recent empirical research on intimate relationships in order to examine the extent to which they were similar to or divergent from pure relationships. She argues that many of the relationships are structured by gender inequalities, although "the gap between cultural ideals and structural

inequalities results in a range of creative identity and relationship-saving strategies" (477). A more recent empirical test of Giddens's theory (Gross and Simmons 2002) reports the existence of successful pure relationships. Many of Giddens's critiques accuse him of uncritically embracing psycho-therapeutic literature and self-help manuals at the expense of downgrading sociological explanations and feminist perspectives (see Howard L. Kaye 1994).

7 Öncü (2002) offers a brilliant analysis of the representation of Maganda, an adult male figure with rural origins, in highly popular satirical comic publications. He is depicted as uncivilized sexually (always in a state of sexual arousal and hypermasculinity), in appearance (ugly and ungroomed with excessive body hair), and in conduct (rude and violent toward women), thus consituting a threat to the civilized, urban others.

8 Lisa Adkins and Beverley Skeggs (2004), in the introduction to *Feminism after Bourdieu*, make a powerful argument for Bourdieu's social theory providing a productive ground and a rich resource for contemporary feminist analyses.

CHAPTER 1. VIRGINAL FAÇADES

1 All respondents in this book are referred to by pseudonyms. To further protect the identities of my respondents, I don't identify them with their majors or with physical characteristics.

2 Ironically, the short questionnaire I asked my participants to fill out after each individual interview had a box to be marked either "*kadın*" (women) or "*erkek*" (men). I noticed that a few of my participants crossed out the word "*kadın*" and replaced it with either "*kız*" or "*bayan.*"

3 The focus of this chapter is those young women in my study who self-identified as heterosexual.

4 See Altinay 2000; Seral 2000; and Parla 2001 for various dimensions of virginity testing.

5 Similarly, Goksel (2006) notes that men "associated modernity and Westernization with the ability to approve of, or at least tolerate, women who engaged in premarital sex" (58).

6 James Farrer (2002) discusses remarkably similar attitudes among Shanghai youth.

7 In her comparative study of Dutch and American teenage girls' experiences with sex, "Sexual Subjectivity Revisited," Amy Schalet suggests that there are important cultural differences in the ways teenage girls negotiate their heterosexuality cross-nationally, even among advanced industrial nations. Schalet analyzes differences in the relational contexts in which American and Dutch girls develop their sexual subjectivity, focusing particularly on how parents and peer groups respond to a girl's decision to become sexually active. While American girls often feel the need to keep their sexual selves separate from their role as daughters, Schalet notes that the majority of Dutch girls were able to integrate their sexual identities into their family lives. According to Schalet, not only do Dutch girls "expect to receive parental recognition of their sexuality," but they actually negotiate the proper parameters of that sexuality by

discussing with their parents contraception as well as potential "sleepovers" (317). In contrast, American girls, even when they receive tacit approval for their sexual activities from their parents, generally report keeping their sexual lives private from their parents for fear that they will damage their image as "good daughters." Schalet suggests that Dutch girls have more sexual agency than their American counterparts, a difference reflected, according to Schalet, in the lower rates of STDs and unplanned pregnancies among Dutch teenage girls as well as higher levels of self-reported sexual satisfaction.

8 I put "lesbian" in quotation marks here because every time she referenced her, Alev underscored that her lover was heterosexual.

CHAPTER 2. MAKING A NEW MAN

1 In the dominant male vernacular, young women are referred to as girls. Throughout this chapter, I retain the language of my subjects.

2 For an insightful discussion on categorizing and classfying men and masculinities, see O'Donnell and Sharpe (2000).

3 For the political economy of neoliberal globalization in Turkey, see Balkan and Savran (2002); for cultural aspects of the emerging new middle classes under globalization, see Öncü (1997, 1999); for development of a new relationship between contemporary Turkish citizens and the state as a result of the neoliberal economic policies, see Özyürek (2006), and for the politics of neoliberal globalization and citizenship, see Keyman and Içduygu (2003) and Keyman and Öniş (2007).

4 Men and masculinities scholar Michael Messner (2011) in his recent memoir brilliantly reflects on the complexities and contradictions of father-son relationships among young men of his generation.

5 This is also a line of lyrics from a popular song by a feminist rocker in Turkey.

CHAPTER 3. NEW PIOUS FEMALE SELVES

1 Throughout this chapter, I refer to different forms of Islamic head coverings and/ or body coverings and women who wear them with different words. I use "veil" or "veiled woman" when I refer to a particular body of literature that uses the word "veil" to refer to what the head covering signifies symbolically, such as lack of women's emancipation, not necessarily to the actual forms of head covering. I use "headscarf"/"headscarved" and/or, alternatively, "covered" to refer to the young pious women I studied

2 I follow Mannheim and the sociological convention in my usage of "generation." As noted by Pilcher, "generation meaning cohort remains in wide currency within social sciences" (1994, 483).

3 For some recent contributions to the debate in Europe, see Afsanesh Najmabadi (2006); Judith Ezekiel (2006); Bronwyn Winter (2006); Frank Peter (2006); and Jeanette S. Jouili and Schirin Amir-Moazami (2006).

4 In her insightful analysis of this case, Göle argues that Kavakci was later rejected as the ultimate Other, an unrecognizable, intrusive foreigner (she had a double

citizenship with the United States). Her technical competence, ability to speak English, divorce, composure, and time spent abroad distinguished her as a modern woman, reducing the social distance between her and more secular women. According to Göle, Kavakci's proximity made her all the more threatening because she refused to fully assimilate to Western liberalism. Through the veil, she embodied her religious difference, but in a two-piece suit and rimless glasses, she demonstrated modernity. The ambiguity of her identity, body, behavior, and place make her impossible to categorize as simply Muslim or modern.

5 For some excellent examinations of veiling in different geographies see El Guindi 1999; Gökarıksel and Secor 2010; Hoodfar 1997; Secor 2002; Shively 2002; and Mahmood 2005.

6 See also O'Neil (2008) for the narratives of another group of pious women who chose to go to university completely uncovered.

7 Jouili and Amir-Moazami (2006, 626), in their comparative study of Muslim women in western Europe, also observe that younger women with high Islamic knowledge described their parents as uneducated Muslims who never studied the Islamic texts.

8 Gurin (1985, 1987) distinguished among four components of gender consciousness: identification (recognizing women's shared interests), discontent (recognizing women's lack of power), assessment of legitimacy (seeing gender disparities as illegitimate), and collective orientation (believing in collective action).

9 There is a sizable literature that examines the compatibility of Islam with feminism. See Valentine M. Moghadam (2002) and Anouar Majid (2002) for good coverage of these debates. While Mogdhadam does not see much utility in Islamic feminists' attempt to reinterpret the Koran and Islamic texts in order to rescue Islam from its patriarchal interpretations, Majid endorses the renewed interpretations of Islamic texts by Muslim women to redefine Islam on the basis of more egalitarian interpretations of the Islamic tradition and practices.

10 Sana yüklediğim anlamları / Senmişsin gibi düşünme / Aldanırsın. / Sen o anlamlarla / Sadece bende varsın / Ben seviyorsam / Sen bahanesin.

11 In some other cultural contexts, this type of modern marriage is defined as "partnership/entrepreneurial marriage" (in Barbados) (Freeman 2007b) or "companionate marriage" (in Mexico) (Hirsch 2007).

CHAPTER 4. DESIRE BETWEEN "DOING" AND "BEING"

1 Indeed, only one individual identified his sexual orientation as gay in the representative survey I conducted with 325 students at Boğaziçi University in 2002.

2 The first focus group interview was conducted with four participants. The second focus group had nine participants, including three lesbians, and was designed to generate discussions and interpretations on how heterosexuals view homosexuality and homosexuals that had emerged in the analysis of the representative survey I have referred to in the previous endnote.

3 I should note that my description of the problem here is also couched in terms of an unproblematized, unified Western gay identity, inevitably and regrettably contributing to the reification of this category of identity we find in the literature. For an excellent in-depth analysis of a Western case—the Norwegian construction of gay identity vis-à-vis negotiation of four discourses of gay identification—see Hegna (2007).

4 This political ideology is named after the founding father and the first president of modern Turkey, Mustafa Kemal Atatürk.

5 Specifically, Rofel (2007) suggests that the global/local binary fails to capture the complexity of transcultural productions in four main ways: first, it radically and artificially severs the East from the West; second, it presents culture as "timeless, bounded, homogenous, and unchanging"; third, it assumes that gay identity has a stable meaning; and fourth, it does not adequately grapple with the very meaning and limitations of "globalism" (91).

6 The Gezi Park antigovernment protests played a substantial role in expanding the support of various segments of the Turkish society for the march.

7 The number of nonfictional accounts is quite small, and there are only two research-based studies: Bereket and Adam (2006, 2008) and Özbay (2006) (a master's thesis in sociology). See Armbrecht (2001), a semifictionalized personal essay that focuses on homosexuality and class in Turkey; Hocaoğlu (2002), a collection of interviews with gay men; Özbay and Soydan (2003), a collection of interviews with lesbians; Çekirge (1991); Yüzgün (1986), a psychological study; and Tapınç (1992).

8 For an ethnographically rich description of these social geographies, see Özbay (2006).

9 Cenk Özbay (2010) in his article "Nocturnal Queers: Rent Boys' Masculinity in İstanbul," conceptualizes "rent boys" as heterosexually identified men with low class locations who engage in sex with other men for money. According to Özbay, they enact "exaggerated masculinity in order to negotiate the tensions between their local socially excluded environments and a burgeoining Western-style gay culture while they conduct their 'risky' sexual interaction with other men" (645–46).

10 For details of Ahmet's murder in English, see Bilefsky's November 25, 2009, *New York Times* article "Soul-Searching in Turkey after a Gay Man Is Killed."

11 The word "*ibne*" originates from the Arabic word "*ubnah*." Ze'evi (2006), in his study of medical and sexual discourses in the Ottoman Middle East (1500–1900), discerns two approaches to *ubnah*. Al-Razi in the Abbasid period described *ubnah* (passive male "homosexuality") not as a deviance or a sin but as a genetic defect— attributing passive homosexuality to someone who is not a "perfect" male because "his penis and testicles tend to be smaller and closer to the groin" (38) and who prefers to be penetrated because his erogenous zones are much closer to the anus. Al-Razi's conceptualization was countered by other authors, such as Ibn Sina, who argued that *ubnah* is "a cultural disease, or one spurred by the imagination," arguing that the male passive homosexual should be punished (38). As Ze'evi points out, both approaches focused on the "passive" males, not on active males and homosexuality in general.

12 Pascoe (2005), who also conceptualizes "fag" as a discourse rather than an identity, demonstrates that the fag insult in the North American context is not only gendered and sexualized but also racialized.

13 I retain the authors' description.

14 Men who are described as active because they are the insertive partners can be passive, and men who are receptive can be quite active. Although I concur with those who argue that the more precise lexicon is to refer to insertive and receptive sex, I preserve the language of my subjects.

15 The original formulation of "Secret Subjects, Open Secrets" was conceptualized by D. A. Miller (1988) and later elaborated by Sedgwick (1990).

16 Hegna (2007) uses the coming-out story of nineteen-year-old Michael in Norway to explore the process through which Michael constructs himself and is constructed as a gay subject. Her presentation of how Michael, as a subject of discourse, incorporates heteronormative, essentialist, cultural, and queer (de)constructions in concert with his life experiences is inconclusive. But she suggests that the unavailability of specifically gay sexual scripts and the consequent reliance on the dominant discourse on homosexuality is disempowering and engenders risky behavior (unsafe sex and drug use).

17 It has been the policy of the Turkish military to subject candidates for military service who are seeking exemption on the basis of being gay to physical as well as psychological examination to establish their sexual orientation and practice.

18 "Rotten," "*çürük*" in Turkish, is the official word used for those who are exempted for medical reasons or for being homosexual.

19 The antigovernment protest movement.

20 Zeki Müren was a famous and highly respected Turkish singer and performer known for his effeminate and flamboyant style. His immense popularity and unique style helped increase public acceptance of homosexuality in Turkey and helped open Turkish popular culture to gay and transgender artists.

21 Zeki Müren was affectionately called "*pasha*."

CONCLUSION

1 Esra Özyürek (2006) brilliantly argues that the consumption of Atatürk-laden symbolic artifacts is an important dimension of Turkish citizens' new relationship to the state and expresses emotional and nostalgic attachments to the official ideology of modern and secular national identity.

2 For a good summary in English of various reactions to the reform package, see Yavuz Baydar's "Erdoğan's Democracy Package Gets Cool Reception," *Al-Monitor*, September 30, 2013, available at http://www.al-monitor.com/pulse/originals/2013/09/erdogan-democracy-package-reception-cool.htm (accessed on November 7, 2013).

3 Here my source for these figures is Can Dündar's very influential "Sayıyla Kendine Gelmek" (To Be Awakened by Numbers) column. Since its first appearance on June 21, 2007, this newspaper article continues to be widely disseminated via repostings on social media. Available at http://www.candundar.com.tr/_v3/index.php#!%23Did=5081 (accessed on November 7, 2013).

4 The event was called "I am 7 years old and starting *Namaz*" ("7 Yaşındayım, Namaza başlıyorum"). For a short video of the event, see http://video.cnnturk. com/2013/haber/10/7/cocuklara-namaz-etkinligi (accessed November 7, 2013).

5 For a good summary of this episode in English, see Semih Idiz's "Erdoğan's Crisis with Pregnant Women," *Al-Monitor*, August 2, 2013, available at http://www.al-monitor. com/pulse/originals/2013/08/erdogan-crisis-pregnant-women-abortion.html# (accessed on November 7, 2013).

6 "Mixed-Sex Student Housing Becomes Turkish PM's Latest Bugbear," *Reuters*, November 5, 2013, available at http://www.reuters.com/article/2013/11/05/us-turkey-erdogan-students-idUSBRE9A410N20131105 (accessed on November 13, 2013).

7 *Radikal*, April 4, 2013, available at http://www.radikal.com.tr/politika/kiz_ve_ erkek_ogrenci_ayni_evde_olmaz-1158890 (accessed on November 4, 2013).

8 See article in *HaberTurk*, http://www.haberturk.com/gundem/haber/890249-ogrencinin-ogrenim-kredisi-borcu-silinecek (accessed on November 7, 2013).

9 "Turkey: Gezi Park Protests; Brutal Denial of the Right to Peaceful Assembly in Turkey," *Amnesty International*, October 2, 2013, available at http://www.amnesty.org/ en/library/info/EUR44/022/2013/en (accessed on November 7, 2013).

10 Yağmur Nuhrat and Karabekir Akkoyunlu, "Turkey at a Suffocating Intersection," *Open Democracy*, October 16, 2013, available at http://www.opendemocracy.net/ ya%C4%9Fmur-nuhrat-karabekir-akkoyunlu/turkey-at-suffocating-intersection (accessed on November 7, 2013).

11 According to a recent poll conducted by Ersin Kalaycıoğlu of Sabancı University and Ali Çarkoğlu of Koç University, 72 percent of those surveyed (n=1555) in fifty-nine cities are against unmarried couples living together, and 87 percent shared the opinion that it is unacceptable for couples who wish to have children to cohabitate without marriage. Of those surveyed, 43.2 percent also defended the position that women's employment outside the home damages the family. See *Radikal*, June 11, 2013, available at http://www.radikal.com.tr/turkiye/toplumun_yuzde_72si_evlilik_disi_beraberlige_ karsi-1159335 (accessed on November 7, 2013).

12 I have explored this issue in more depth elsewhere (Ozyegin 2011).

REFERENCES

Aarseth, Helene. 2007. "Between Labour and Love: The Re-erotization of Home-making in Egalitarian Couples within a Nordic Context." *NORA-Nordic Journal of Women's Studies* 15.2–3: 133–43.

Acar, Feride. 1995. "Women and Islam in Turkey," in Women in Modern Turkish Society, ed. Sirin Tekeli (London: Zed), 46–64.

Acar, Feride, and Ayşe Ayata. 2002. "Discipline, Success, and Stability: The Reproduction of Gender and Class in Turkish Secondary Education," in *Fragments of Culture: The Everyday of Modern Turkey*, eds. Deniz Kandiyoti and Ayse Saktanber (London: Tauris), 90–115

Adam, Barbara. 1996. "Detraditionalization and the Certainty of Uncertain Futures," in *Detraditionalization: Critical Reflections on Authority and Identity*, eds. Paul Heelas, Scott Lash, and Paul Morris (Malden, MA: Blackwell), 134–48.

Adam, Barrry, Jan Willem Duyvendak, and André Krouwel, eds. 1999. *The Global Emergence of Gay and Lesbian Politics* (Philadelphia: Temple University Press).

Adkins, Lisa. 2000. "Objects of Innovation: Post-Occupational Reflexivity and Re-Traditionalisation of Gender," in *Transformations: Thinking through Feminism*, eds. Sarah Ahmed et al. (London: Routledge), 259–73.

Adkins, Lisa, and Beverley Skeggs. 2004. Introduction to *Feminism after Bourdieu*, eds. Lisa Adkins and Beverley Skegg (Oxford: Blackwell), 3–19.

Adrian, Melanie. 2006. "Laicite Unveiled: A Case Study in Human Rights, Religion, and Culture in France." *Human Rights Review* 8.1: 102–14.

Alemdaroglu, Ayca. 2007. "Formations of Femininity at the Intersection of Class, Gender, and Age: Young Women in Turkey." Unpublished paper, presented at the 2007 American Sociological Association Meetings in New York, NY.

Allen, Louisa. 2003. "Girls Want Sex, Boys Want Love: Resisting Dominant Discourses of (Hetero)Sexuality." *Sexualities* 6.2: 215–36.

Allison, A. 2000. *Permitted and Prohibited Desires: Mothers, Comics, and Censorship in Japan* (Berkeley: University of California Press).

Altinay, Gul Ayse. 2000. "Talking and Writing Our Sexuality: Feminist Activism on Virginity and Virginity Tests in Turkey," in *Women and Sexuality in Muslim Societies*, ed. Pinar Ilkkaracan (Istanbul: Women for Women's Human Rights), 403–12.

Altman, Dennis. 1996. "Rupture or Continuity? The Internalization of Gay Identities." *Social Text* 14.3: 77–94.

———. 1997. "Response to Donald Morton." *Critical InQueeries* 1.3: 31–33.

Appadurai, Arjun. 1996. *Modernity at Large: Cultural Dimensions of Globalization* (Minneapolis: University of Minnesota Press).

Arat, Yesim. 1994. "Women's Movement of the 1980s in Turkey: Radical Outcome of a Liberal Kemalism?" in *Reconstructing Gender in the Middle East*, eds. Fatma Muge Gocek and Shiva Balaghi (New York: Columbia University Press), 100–112.

———. 1997. "The Project of Modernity and Women in Turkey," in *Rethinking Modernity and National Identity in Turkey*, eds. Sibel Bozdogan and Resat Kasaba (Seattle: University of Washington Press), 95–112.

———. 1998. "Feminists, Islamists, and Political Change in Turkey." *Political Psychology* 19.1: 117–31.

———. 2001. "One Ban and Many Headscarves: Islamist Women and Democracy in Turkey." *International Social Science Review* 2.1: 47–60.

———. 2004. "Rethinking the Political: A Feminist Journal in Turkey, *Pazartesi*." *Women's Studies International Forum* 27.3: 281–92.

Armbrecht, Thomas J. D. 2001. "The Cucumber Seller: Homosexuality and Class in Turkey." *Gay Men's Fiction Quarterly* 3.4: 51–61.

Aronson, Pamela. 2003. "Feminists or 'Post-Feminists'? Young Women's Attitudes toward Feminism and Gender Relations." *Gender & Society* 17.6: 903–22.

Arsu, Sebnem. 2010. "Turkey's Governing Party Proposes Changes in the Constitution." *New York Times* (Europe), March 23, available at http://www.nytimes.com/2010/03/23/world/europe/23turkey.html?_r=0.

Asad, Talal. 2003. *Formations of the Secular: Christianity, Islam, Modernity* (Stanford, CA: Stanford University Press).

Atasoy, Yildiz. 1997. "Islamic Revivalism and the Nation-State Project: Competing Claims for Modernity." *Social Compass* 44.1: 83–99.

———. 2005. *Turkey, Islamists, and Democracy: Transition and Globalization in a Muslim State* (London: Tauris).

Ayata, Sencer. 2002. "The New Middle Class and Joys of Suburbia," in *Fragments of Culture: The Everyday of Modern Turkey*, eds. Deniz Kandiyoti and Ayse Saktanber (London: Tauris), 25–42.

———. 2008. "Migrants and Changing Urban Periphery: Social Relations, Cultural Diversity, and the Public Space in Istanbul's New Neighbourhoods." *International Migration* 46.3: 27–62.

Balkan, Nesecan, and Sungur Savran. 2002. *The Ravages of Neo-Liberalism: Economy, Society, and Gender in Turkey* (New York: Nova Science).

Bartkowski, John, and Jen'nan Ghazal Read. 2003. "Veiled Submission: Gender, Power, and Identity among Evangelical and Muslim Women in the United States." *Qualitative Sociology* 26.1: 71–92.

Baslanti, Ugur, and D. Betsy McCoach. 2006. "Factors Related to the Underachievement of University Students." *Roeper Review* 28.4: 210–15.

Bauman, Zygmunt. 1990. "Modernity and Ambivalence," in *Global Culture: Nationalism, Globalization, and Modernity*, ed. Mike Featherstone (London: Sage), 143.

———. 1991. *Modernity and Ambivalence* (London: Sage).

———. 2003. *Liquid Love: On the Frailty of Human Bonds* (Cambridge, England: Polity).

Beauvoir, Simone de. 1972. *The Second Sex* (Harmondsworth, England: Penquin).

Beck, Ulrich. 1992. *Risk Society: Towards a New Modernity*, trans. Mark Ritter (London: Sage).

Beck, Ulrich, and Elisabeth Beck-Gernsheim. 1995. *The Normal Chaos of Love*, trans. Mark Ritter (Cambridge: Polity).

Benjamin, Jessica. 1988. *The Bonds of Love: Psychoanalysis, Feminism, and the Problem of Domination* (New York: Pantheon).

Bereket, Tarik, and Barry Adam. 2006. "The Emergence of Gay Identities in Contemporary Turkey." *Sexualities* 9.2: 131–51.

———. 2008. "Navigating Islam and Same-Sex Liaisons among Men in Turkey." *Journal of Homosexuality* 55.2: 204–22.

Bettie, Julie. 2003. *Women without Class: Girls, Race, and Identity* (Berkeley: University of California Press).

Bilici, Mucahit. 2006. "The Fethullah Gulen Movement and Its Politics of Representation in Turkey." *Muslim World* 96.1: 1–20.

Bourdieu, Pierre. 1977. *Outline of a Theory of Practice* (Cambridge: Cambridge University Press).

———. 1984. *Distinction: A Social Critique of the Judgement of Taste* (Cambridge, MA: Harvard University Press).

———. 1998. "The Essence of Neoliberalism," trans. Jeremy J. Shapiro. *Le Monde Diplomatique.*

Bourdieu, Pierre, and Loïc J. D. Wacquant. 1992. *An Invitation to Reflexive Sociology* (Chicago: University of Chicago Press).

Buğra, Ayşe. 2012. "The Changing Welfare Regime of Turkey: Neoliberalism, Cultural Conservatism, and Social Solidarity Redefined," in *Gender and Society in Turkey*, eds. Saniye Dedeoglu and Adem Elveren (London: Tauris).

Buitelaar, M. W. 2002. "Negotiating the Rules of Chaste Behaviour: Re-Interpretations of the Symbolic Complex of Virginity by Young Women of Moroccan Descent in the Netherlands." *Ethnic and Racial Studies* 25.3: 462–89.

Butler, Judith. 1999. *Gender Trouble: Feminism and the Subversion of Identity* (New York: Routledge).

Calasanti, Toni, and Kathleen Slevin. 2001. *Gender, Social Inequality, and Aging* (Walnut Creek, CA: Altamira).

Calhoun, Cheshire. 2000. *Feminism, the Family, and the Politics of the Closet: Lesbian and Gay Displacement* (New York: Oxford University Press).

Cancian, Francis. 1990. *Love in America* (Cambridge: Cambridge University Press).

Carpenter, Laura. 2002. "Gender and the Meaning and Experience of Virginity Loss in the Contemporary United States." *Gender and Society* 16.3: 345–65.

Çekirge, Pinar. 1991. *Yalnızlık adası'nın erkekleri: Psiko-Sosyal açıdan eşcinseller* [Men of Lonely Island: Homosexuals from a Psycho-Social Perspective] (Istanbul: Altın).

Cinar, Alev. 2005. *Modernity, Islam, and Secularism in Turkey: Bodies, Places, and Time* (Minneapolis: University of Minnesota Press).

———. 2008. "Subversion and Subjugating in the Public Sphere: Secularism and the Islamic Headscarf." *Signs* 33.4: 891–913.

Cinar, Menderes. 2006. "Turkey's Transformation under the AKP Rule." *Muslim World* 96.3: 469–86.

Cindoglu, Dilek. 1997. "Virginity Tests and Artificial Virginity in Modern Turkish Medicine," *Women's Studies International Forum* 20.2: 253–61.

Coles, Tony. 2009. "Negotiating the Field of Masculinity." *Men and Masculinities* 12.1: 30–44.

Collier, Jane F. 1997. *From Duty to Desire: Remaking Families in a Spanish Village* (Princeton, NJ: Princeton University Press).

Collins, Patricia Hill. 1991. *Black Feminist Thought: Knowledge, Consciousness, and the Politics of Empowerment* (New York: Routledge).

———. 1993. "The Meaning of Motherhood in Black Culture and Black Mother-Daughter Relationships," in *Double Stitch: Black Women Write about Mothers and Daughters*, eds. Patricia Bell-Scott et al. (New York: Harper Perennial), 42–60.

Connell, Raewyn. 1987. Gender and Power (Stanford, CA: Stanford University Press).

———. 2002. Gender (Cambridge: Polity).

Conway, Martin A. 1997. "The Inventory of Experience: Memory and Identity," in *Collective Memory of Political Events: Social Psychological Prespectives,* eds. J. W. Pennebaker et al. (Mahwah, NJ: Lawrence Erlbaum).

Dagi, D. Ihsan. 2004. "Rethinking Human Rights, Democracy, and the West: Post-Islamist Intellectuals in Turkey." *Critique: Critical Middle Eastern Studies* 13.2: 135–51.

Dayıoğlu, Meltem, and Cem Başlevent. 2012. "Gender Aspects of Income Distribution and Poverty in Turkey," in *Gender and Society in Turkey: The Impact of Neoliberal Policies, Political Islam, and EU Accession*, eds. Saniye Dedeoğlu and Adem Elveren (London: Tauris), 65–86.

Dedeoglu, Saniye, and Adem Elveren, eds. 2012. *Gender and Society in Turkey* (London: Tauris).

Delice, Serkan. 2010. "Friendship, Sociability, and Masculinity in the Ottoman Empire: An Essay Confronting the Ghosts of Historicism." *New Perspectives on Turkey* 42: 103–25.

Demetriou, Demetrakis Z. 2001. "Connell's Concept of Hegemonic Masculinity: A Critique." *Theory and Society* 30.3: 337–61.

Douglas, Mary. 1989. *Purity and Danger: An Analysis of the Concepts of Pollution and Taboo* (London: Ark Paperbacks).

Duran, Khalid. 1993. "Homosexuality and Islam," in *Homosexuality and World Religions*, ed. Arlene Swidler (Valley Forge: Trinity Press International), 181–98.

Edmunds, June. 2002. "Generations, Women, and National Consciousness," in *Generational Consciousness, Narrative, and Politics*, eds. June Edmunds and Bryan Turner (New York: Rowman and Littlefield), 31–51.

Edmunds, June, and Bryan S. Turner. 2002. "Introduction," in *Generational Conscious-ness, Narrative, and Politics*, eds. June Edmunds and Bryan Turner (New York: Rowman and Littlefield), 1–13.

El Guindi, Fadwa. 1999. *Veil Modesty, Privacy, and Resistance* (Oxford: Berg).

Erdur, Defne. 2002. "Seeking the Truth of Sex: Narratives of Sexuality amongst Bogazici University Students." Unpublished master's thesis (Istanbul: Bogazici University).

Ezekiel, Judith. 2006. "French Dressing: Race, Gender, and the Hijab Story." *Feminist Studies* 32.2: 256–78.

Farrer, James. 2002. *Opening Up: Youth Sex Culture and Market Reform in Shanghai* (Chicago: University of Chicago Press).

Fine, Michelle. 1988. "Sexuality, Schooling, and Adolescent Females: The Missing Dis-course of Desire." *Harvard Educational Review* 58.1: 29–53.

Firestone, Shulamith. 1972. *The Dialectic of Sex* (London: Paladin).

Freeman, Carla. 2007a. "The 'Reputation' of Neo-liberalism." *American Ethnologist* 34.2: 252–67.

———. 2007b. "Neoliberalism and the Marriage of Reputation and Respectability: Entrepreneurship and the Barbadian Middle Class," in *Love and Globalization*, eds. Mark B. Padilla et al. (Nashville, TN: Vanderbilt University Press), 3–38.

———. 2010. "Analyzing Culture through Globalization," in *Handbook of Cultural Sociology*, eds. John R. Hall, Laura Grindstaff, and Ming-cheng Lo (London: Rout-ledge), 577–87.

———. 2014. *Entrepreneurial Selves: Neoliberal Respectability and the Making of a Carib-bean Middle Class* (Durham, NC: Duke University Press).

Gelbal, Sellahatin, and Veli Duyan. 2006. "Attitudes of University Students toward Lesbians and Gay Men in Turkey." *Sex Roles* 55.7–8: 573–79.

Gellner, Ernest. 1989. *Muslim Society* (Cambridge: Cambridge University Press).

Genel, Sema, and Kerem Karaosmanoglu. 2006. "A New Islamic Individualism in Tur-key: Headscarved Women in the City." *Turkish Studies* 7.3: 473–88.

Gerhards, Jürgen. 2010. "Non-Discrimination towards Homosexuality: The European Union's Policy and Citizens' Attitudes towards Homosexuality in 27 European Countries." *International Sociology* 25.5: 5–28.

Gerson, Kathleen. 2009. "Changing Lives, Resistant Institutions: A New Generation Negotiates Gender, Work, and Family Change." *Sociological Forum* 24.4: 735–53.

Giddens, Anthony. 1990. *The Consequences of Modernity* (Stanford, CA: Stanford University Press).

———. 1991. *Modernity and Self-Identity: Self and Society in the Late Modern Age* (Stan-ford, CA: Stanford University Press).

———. 1992. *The Transformation of Intimacy: Sexuality, Love, and Eroticism in Modern Societies* (Stanford, CA: Stanford University Press).

Ginsburg, Faye. 1989. "Dissonance and Harmony: The Symbolic Function of Abortion in Activists' Life Stories," in *Interpreting Women's Lives: Feminist Theory and Per-sonal Narratives*, eds. Personal Narratives Group (Bloomington: Indiana University Press), 59–85.

Gocek, Muge. 2000. "To Veil or Not to Veil: The Contested Location of Gender in Contemporary Turkey." *Interventions* 1.4: 521–31.

Goddard, Victoria. 1987. "Honour and Shame: The Control of Women's Sexuality and Group Identity in Naples," in *The Cultural Constructions of Sexuality*, ed. Pat Caplan (London: Tavistock), 166–92.

Gökarıksel, B., and A. J. Secor. 2010. "Between Fashion and *Tesettür*: Marketing and Consuming Women's Islamic Dress." *Journal of Middle East Women's Studies* 6.3: 118–48

———. 2012. "'You Can't Know How They Are Inside': The Ambivalence of Veiling and Discourses of the Other in Turkey," in *Religion and Place: Landscape, Politics, and Piety*, eds. Lily Kong, Peter Hopkins, and Betsy Olson (Berlin: Springer), 95–114.

Goksel, Iklim. 2006. "Virginity and Masculinity," in *Men of the Global South: A Reader*, ed. Adam Jones (London: Zed), 55–57.

Göle, Nilüfer. 1996. *The Forbidden Modern: Civilization and Veiling* (Ann Arbor: University of Michigan Press).

———. 1997a. "The Gendered Nature of the Public Sphere." *Public Culture* 10.1: 61–81.

———. 1997b. "The Quest for the Islamic Self within the Context of Modernity," in *Rethinking Modernity and National Identity in Turkey*, ed. Sibel Bozdogan and Resit Kasaba (Seattle: University of Washington Press), 81–94.

———. 2000. "Snapshots of Islamic Modernity." *Daedalus* 129.1: 91–117.

———. 2002. "Islam in Public: New Visibilities and New Imaginaries." *Public Culture* 14.1: 173–90.

———. 2003. "The Voluntary Adoption of Islamic Stigma Symbols." *Social Research* 70.3: 809–28.

Gonzalez-Lopez, Gloria. 2005. *Erotic Journeys: Mexican Immigrants and Their Sex Lives* (Berkeley: University of California Press).

Greer, Germaine. 1970. *The Female Eunuch* (New York: HarperCollins).

Griffin, J. Larry. 2004. "Generations and Collective Memory Revisited: Race, Region, and Memory of Civil Rights." *American Sociological Review* 69.4: 544–57.

Gross, Neil, and Solon Simmons. 2002. "Intimacy as a Double-Edged Phenomenon? An Empirical Test of Giddens." *Social Forces* 81.2: 531–55.

Gurin, Patricia. 1985. "Women's Gender Conciousness," *Public Opinion Quarterly* 49.2: 143–163.

———. 1987. "The Political Implications of Women's Statues," in *Spouse, Parent, Worker: On Gender and Multiple Roles*, ed. Faye J. Crosby. (New Haven, CT: Yale University Press).

Harvey, David. 1991. "Flexibility: Threat or Opportunity?" *Socialist Review* 21.1: 65–78.

———. 2005. *A Brief History of Neoliberalism* (Oxford: Oxford University Press).

Hasso, S. Frances. 2001. "Feminist Generations? The Long-Term Impact of Social Movement Involvement on Palestinian Women's Lives." *AJS* 107.3: 586–611.

Hearn, Jeff. 2004. "From Hegemonic Masculinity to the Hegemony of Men." *Feminist Theory* 5.1: 49–72.

Hegna, Kristinn. 2007. "Coming Out, Coming into What? Identification and Risks in the 'Coming Out' Story of a Norwegian Late Adolescent Gay Man." *Sexualities* 10.5: 582–602.

Heper, Metin, and Sule Toktas. 2003. "Islam, Modernity, and Democracy in Contemporary Turkey: The Case of Recept Tayyip Erdogan." *Muslim World* 93.2: 157–85.

Hirsch, Jennifer. 2007. "Love Makes a Family: Globalization, Companionate Marriage, and the Modernization of Gender Inequality," in *Love and Globalization*, eds. Mark B. Padilla et al. (Nashville, TN: Vanderbilt University Press), 93–107.

Hocaoğlu, Murat. 2002. *Eşcinsel erkekler: Yirmi beş tanıklık* [Homosexual Men: Twenty-Five Witnesses] (Istanbul: Metis).

Hoodfar, Homa. 1997. "The Veil in Their Minds and on Our Heads: Veiling Practices and Muslim Women," in *The Politics of Culture in the Shadow of Capital*, eds. David Lloyd and Lisa Lowe (Durham, NC: Duke University Press), 248–80.

Houston, Christopher. 2002. "Legislating Virtue; or, Fear and Loathing in Istanbul?" *Critique of Anthropology* 22.4: 425–44.

Illouz, Eva. 1997. *Consuming the Romantic Utopia: Love and the Cultural Contradictions of Capitalism* (Berkeley: University of California Press).

Ilyasoglu, Aynur. 1998. "Islamist Women in Turkey: Their Identity and Self-Image," in *Deconstructing Images of "The Turkish Woman,"* ed. Zehra F. Arat (New York: St. Martin's), 241–63.

Jackson, Peter A. 1997. "Kahhoey >< Gay >< Man: The Historical Emergence of Gay Male Identity in Thailand," in *Sites of Desire and Economies of Pleasure: Sexualities in Asia and the Pacific*, eds. Lenore Manderson and Margaret Jolly (Chicago: University of Chicago Press), 166–90.

———. 2007. "An Explosion of Thai Identities: Global Queering and Re-Imagining Queer Theory," in *Culture, Society, and Sexuality: A Reader*, eds. Richard Parker and Peter Aggleton (London: Routledge), 341–57.

Jamieson, Lynn. 1999. "Intimacy Transformed? A Critical Look at the 'Pure Relationship.'" *Sociology* 33.3: 477–94.

Joseph, Gloria I. 1986. "Black Mothers and Daughters: Their Roles and Function in American Society," in *Common Differences: Conflicts in Black and White Feminist Perspectives*, by Gloria I. Joseph and Jill Lewis (Boston: South End Press), 75–126.

Joseph, Suad. 1993. "Gender and Relationality among Arab Families in Lebanon." *Feminist Studies* 19.3: 465–86.

———. 1994. "Brother/Sister Relationships: Connectivity, Love, and Power in the Reproduction of Arab Patriarchy in Lebanon." *American Ethnologist* 21.1: 50–73.

———. 1999. "Intimate Selving: Theories and Dynamics of Self, Gender, and Identity in Arab Families," in *Intimate Selving in Arab Families: Gender, Self, and Identity*, ed. Suad Joseph (Syracuse, NY: Syracuse University Press), 1–17.

Jouili, S. Jeanette, and Schirin Amir-Moazami. 2006. "Knowledge, Empowerment, and Religious Authority among Pious Muslim Women in France and Germany." *Muslim World* 96.4: 617–42.

Kadioglu, Ayse. 1998. "Republican Epistemology and Islamic Discourses in Turkey in the 1990s." *Muslim World* 88.1: 1–21.

Kandiyoti, Deniz. 1987. "Emancipated but Not Liberated." *Feminist Studies* 13.2: 317–37.

———. 1988. "Bargaining with Patriarchy." Gender and Society 12.3: 274–90.

———. 1991. "Identity and Its Discontents." *Millennium: Journal of International Studies* 20.3: 429–43.

———. 1995. "Ataerkil Örüntüler: Türk Toplumunda Erkek Eğemenliğinin Çözümlenmesine Yönelik Notlar" (Patriarchal Patterns: Notes towards Dissolution of Male Dominance in Turkish Society), in 1980'ler Türkiyesinde Kadın Bakış Açısından Kadınlar (Women in 1980s Turkey from Women's Perspective), ed. S. Tekeli (Istanbul: İletişim).

———. 1998. "Some Awkward Questions on Women and Modernity in Turkey," in *Remaking Women*, ed. Lila Abu-Lughod (Princeton, NJ: Princeton University Press), 270–88.

———. 2002. "Introduction: Reading the Fragments," in *Fragments of Culture: The Everyday of Modern Turkey*, eds. Deniz Kandiyoti and Ayse Saktanber (London: Tauris), 1–21.

———. 2011. "A Tangled Web: The Politics of Gender in Turkey." *OpenDemocracy*, January 5, available at https://www.opendemocracy.net/author/deniz-kandiyoti (accessed on October 12, 2014).

Kandiyoti, Deniz, and Ayse Saktanber. 2002. *Fragments of Culture: The Everyday of Modern Turkey* (London: Tauris).

Kasaba, Reşat. 1997. "Kemalist Certainties and Modern Ambiguities," in *Rethinking Modernity and National Identity in Turkey*, eds. Sibel Bozdogan and Resit Kasaba (Seattle: University of Washington Press), 15–36.

Kasaba, Reşat, and Sibel Bozdogan. 2000. "Turkey at a Crossroad," *Journal of International Affairs* 54.1: 1–7.

Kaye, Howard L. 1994. "Theory on Steroids: Anthony Giddens on Modernity." *Qualitative Sociology* 17.4: 433–37.

Keskin, Burcak. 2002. "Confronting Double Patriarchy: Islamist Women in Turkey," in *Right-Wing Women*, eds. Paola Bacchetta and Margaret Power (New York: Routledge), 245–59.

Keyman, E. Fuat. 2007. "Modernity, Secularism, and Islam: The Case of Turkey," *Theory, Culture & Society* 24.2: 215–34.

Keyman, E. Fuat, and Ahmet Içduygu. 2003. "Globalization, Civil Society, and Citizenship in Turkey: Actors, Boundaries, and Discourses." *Citizenship Studies* 1.2: 219–34.

Keyman, E. Fuat, and Ziya Oniş. 2007. *Turkish Politics in a Changing World: Global Dynamics and Domestic Transformations* (Istanbul: Bilgi University Press).

Kilicbay, Baris, and Binark Mutlu. 2002. "Consumer Culture, Islam, and the Politics of Lifestyle: Fashion for Veiling in Contemporary Turkey." *European Journal of Communication* 17.4: 495–511.

Kocacioglu, Dicle. 2004. "The Tradition Effect: Framing Honor Crimes in Turkey," *Differences* 15.2: 118–51.

Kollontai, Alexander. 1972. *Sexual Relations and the Class Struggle* (Bristol, England: Falling Wall Press).

Komsuoglu, Aysegul. 2004. "The 'New' Veiled Woman in Turkey: An Unintended Phenomenon." *Pakistan Journal of Women's Studies: Alam-e-Niswan* 11.2 97–113.

Korobov, Neill. 2009. "'He's Got No Game': Young Men's Stories about Failed Romantic and Sexual Experiences." *Journal of Gender Studies* 18.2: 99–114.

Kuru, Ahmet. 2009. *Secularism and State Policies toward Religion: The United States, France, and Turkey* (New York: Cambridge University Press).

Lindisfarne, Nancy. 1994. "Variant Masculinities, Variant Virginities: Rethinking 'Honour and Shame,'" in *Dislocating Masculinity: Comparative Ethnographies*, eds. Andrea Cornwall and Nancy Lindisfarne (London: Routledge), 82–96.

Lucey, Helen, and Valerie Walkerdine. 2003. "Psychosocial Aspects of Becoming Educationally Successful for Working-Class Young Women." *Gender and Education* 15:3: 285–99.

Luhmann, Niklas. 1986. *Love as Passion: The Codification of Intimacy* (Cambridge, MA: Harvard University Press).

Mahmood, Saba. 2005. *The Politics of Piety: The Islamic Revival and the Feminist Subject* (Princeton, NJ: Princeton University Press).

Majid, Anouar. 2002. "The Politics of Feminism in Islam," in *Gender, Politics, and Islam*, eds. Therese Saliba, Carolyn Allen, and Judith A. Howard (Chicago: University of Chicago Press), 53–94.

Mannheim, Karl. 1972. "The Problem of Generations," in *Essays on the Sociology of Knowledge*, ed. Paul Kecskemeti (London: Routledge & Kegan Paul), 276–321.

Mardin, Serif. 2006. *Religion, Society, and Modernity in Turkey* (Syracuse, NY: Syracuse University Press).

Marshall-Aldikacti, Gul. 2005. "Ideology, Progress, and Dialogue: A Comparison of Feminist and Islamist Women's Approaches to the Issues of Head Covering and Work in Turkey." *Gender & Society* 19.1: 104–17.

Massad, Joseph Andoni. 2002. "Re-Orienting Desire: The Gay International and the Arab World." *Public Culture* 14.2: 361–85.

Maxwell, Claire. 2007. "'Alternative' Narratives of Young People's Heterosexual Experiences in the UK," *Sexualities* 10.5: 539–58.

McDowell, Linda. 2003. *Redundant Masculinities* (Oxford: Blackwell).

McLelland, Mark J. 2000. *Male Homosexuality in Modern Japan: Cultural Myths and Social Realities* (Richmond, England: Curzon).

McLeod, Julie. 2002. "Working Out Intimacy: Young People and Friendship in an Age of Reflexivity." *Discourse: Studies in the Cultural Politics of Education* 23.2: 211–26.

McNay, Lois. 2000. *Gender and Agency: Reconfiguring the Subject in Feminist Social Theory* (Cambridge, England: Polity).

Mernissi, Fatima. 1982. "Virginity and Patriarchy," *Women's Studies International Forum* 5.2: 183–91.

Messner, Michael. 2011. *King of the Wild Suburb: A Memoir of Fathers, Sons, and Guns* (Austin, TX: Plain View Press).

Miller, D. A. 1988. *The Novel and the Police* (Berkeley: University of California Press).

Miller, Niel. 1992. *Out in the World: Gay and Lesbian Life from Buenos Aires to Bangkok* (London: Penguin).

Misciagno, Patricia. 1997. *Rethinking Feminist Identification: The Case for De Facto Feminism* (Westport, CT: Praeger).

Moghadam, M. Valentine. 2002. "Islamic Feminism and Its Discontents: Towards a Resolution of the Debate," in *Gender, Politics, and Islam*, eds. Therese Saliba, Carolyn Allen, and Judith A. Howard (Chicago: University of Chicago Press), 1–51.

Mojab, Shahrzad. 2004. "The Particularity of 'Honour' and the Universality of 'Killing,'" in *Violence in the Name of Honour: Theoretical and Political Challenges*, eds. Shahrzad Mojab and Nahl Abdo (Istanbul: Bilgi University Press), 15–39.

Moller, Michael. 2007. "Exploiting Patterns: A Critique of Hegemonic Masculinity." *Journal of Gender Studies* 16:3: 263–76.

Murray, Stephen O., and Will Roscoe, eds. 1997. *Islamic Homosexualities: Culture, History, and Literature* (New York: New York University Press).

Najmabadi, Afsaneh. 2006. "Gender and Secularism of Modernity: How Can a Muslim Woman Be French?" *Feminist Studies* 32.2: 239–55.

Narlı, Nilufer. 1999. "The Rise of the Islamist Movement in Turkey." *Middle East Review of International Affairs* 3.3: 38–48.

Navaro-Yashin, Yael. 2002. "The Market for Identities: Secularism, Islamism, Commodities," in *Fragments of a Culture: The Everyday of Modern Turkey*, eds. Deniz Kandiyoti and Ayse Saktanber (London: Taurus), 221–53.

Neyzi, Leyla. 2001. "Object or Subject? The Paradox of 'Youth' in Turkey." *International Journal of Middle East Studies* 33.3: 411–32.

O'Donnell, Mike, and Sue Sharpe. 2000. *Uncertain Masculinities: Youth, Ethnicity, and Class in Contemporary Britain* (London: Routledge).

Olson, Emelie A. 1985. "Muslim Identity and Secularisms in Contemporary Turkey: 'The Headscarf Dispute.'" *Anthropological Quarterly* 58.4: 161–70.

Öncü, Ayse. 1997. "The Myth of the 'Ideal Home' Travels across Cultural Borders to Istanbul," in *Space, Culture, and Power: New Identities in Globalizing Cities*, eds. Ayse Öncü and Petra Weyland (London: Zed), 59–76.

———. 1999. "Istanbulites and Others: The Cultural Cosmology of Being Middle Class in the Era of Globalism," in *Istanbul: Between the Global and the Local*, ed. Çaglar Keyder (Oxford, England: Rowman & Littlefield), 95–121.

———. 2002. "Global Consumerism, Sexuality as Public Spectacle, and the Cultural Remapping of Istanbul in the 1990s," in *Fragments of Culture: The Everyday of Modern Turkey*, eds. Deniz Kandiyoti and Ayse Saktanber (London: Tauris), 171–90.

O'Neil, Mary. 2008. "Being Seen: Headscarves and the Contestation of Public Space in Turkey." *European Journal of Women's Studies* 15.2: 101–15.

Öniş, Ziya. 1997. "The Political Economy of Islamic Resurgence in Turkey: The Rise of the Welfare Party in Perspective." *Third World Quarterly* 18.4: 743–66.

Ortner, Sherry. 1978. "The Virgin and the State." *Feminist Studies* 4.3: 19–35.

Özbay, Cenk. 2006. "Virilities for Rent: Navigating Sexuality, Masculinity, and Class in Istanbul." Unpublished master's thesis, Bogazici University.

———. 2010. "Nocturnal Queers: Rent Boys' Masculinity in Istanbul." *Sexualities* 13.5: 645–63.

Özbay, Cenk, and Serdar Soydan. 2003. *Eşcinsel kadınlar: Yirmi dört tanıklık* [Homosexual Women: Twenty-Four Witnesses] (Istanbul: Metis).

Ozdalga, Elizabeth. 1998. *The Veiling Issue, Official Secularism, and Popular Islam in Modern Turkey* (Richmond, England: Curzon).

———. 2005. "Redeemer or Outsider? The Gulen Community in the Civilizing Process." *Muslim World* 95.3: 429–46.

Ozyegin, Gul. 2001. *Untidy Gender* (Philadelphia: Temple University Press).

———. 2011. "My Father, an Agent of State Feminism, and Other Unrelatable Conversations," in *Transatlantic Conversations: Feminism as Traveling Theory*, eds. Kathy Davis and Mary Evans (Farnham, England: Ashgate), 33–41.

Özyürek, Esra. 2006. *Nostalgia for the Modern: State Secularism and Everyday Politics* (Durham, NC: Duke University Press).

Parla, Ayse. 2001. "The 'Honor' of the State: Virginity Examinations in Turkey," *Feminist Studies* 27.1: 65–88.

Pascoe, C. J. 2005. "'Dude, You're a Fag': Adolescent Masculinity and the Fag Discourse." *Sexualities* 8.3: 329–46.

Passerini, Luisa. 1989. "Women's Personal Narratives: Myths, Experiences, and Emotions," in *Interpreting Women's Lives: Feminist Theory*, ed. Personal Narratives Group (Bloomington: Indiana University Press), 189–97.

Peter, Frank. 2006. "Individualization and Religious Authority in Western European Islam." *Islam and Christian-Muslim Relations* 17.1: 105–18.

Pew Global Attitudes Project. 2007. *Global Unease with Major World Powers*. Available online.

Pilcher, Jane. 1994. "Mannheim's Sociology of Generations: An Undervalued Legacy." *British Journal of Sociology* 45.3: 481–95.

———. 1998. *Women of Their Time: Generation, Gender Issues, and Feminism* (Farnham, England: Ashgate).

Redman, Peter. 2001. "The Discipline of Love." *Men and Masculinities* 4.2: 186–200.

Rofel, Lisa. 2007. *Desiring China: Experiments in Neoliberalism, Sexuality, and Public Culture* (Durham, NC: Duke University Press).

Rose, Nikolas. 1991. *Governing of the Soul: The Shaping of the Private Self* (London: Routledge).

———. 1996. "Authority and the Genealogy of Subjectivity," in *Detraditionalization: Critical Reflections on Authority and Identity*, eds. Paul Heelas, Scott Lash, and Paul Morris (Oxford: Blackwell), 294–327.

Rutz, Henry J., and Erol M. Balkan. 2009. *Reproducing Class: Education, Neoliberalism, and the Rise of the New Middle Class* (New York: Berghahn).

Saktanber, Ayse. 2002a. *Living Islam: Women, Religion, and the Politicization of Culture in Turkey* (London: Tauris).

———. 2002b. "Whose Virtue Is This? The Virtue Party and Women in Islamist Politics in Turkey," in *Right-Wing Women*, eds. Paola Bacchetta and Margaret Power (New York: Routledge), 71–85.

———. 2002c. "'We Pray Like You Have Fun': New Islamic Youth in Turkey between Intellectualism and Popular Culture," in *Fragments of Culture: The Everyday of Modern Turkey*, eds. Deniz Kandiyoti and Ayse Saktanber (London: Tauris), 254–76.

———. 2006. "Women and the Iconography of Fear: Islamization in Post-Islamist Turkey." *Signs* 32.1: 21–31.

———. 2007. "Cultural Dilemmas of Muslim Youth: Negotiating Muslim Identities and Being Young in Turkey." *Turkish Studies* 8.3: 417–34.

Saktanber, Ayse, and Gul Corbacioglu. 2008. "Veiling and Headscarf-Skepticism in Turkey." *Social Politics* 15.4: 514–38.

Sancar, Serpil. 2011. *Erkeklik: İmkansız İktidar: Ailede, Piyasada ve Sokakta Erkekler* [Masculinity: The Impossible Power] (Istanbul: Metis).

Savci, Evren. 2011. *Queer in Translation: Paradoxes of Westernization and Sexual Others in the Turkish Nation*. Ph.D. diss., University of Southern California.

Schalet, Amy. 2010. "Sexual Subjectivity Revisited." Gender and Society, 24, no.3: 304-329

Scott, Joan. 1996. Foreword to *Autobiography of a Generation: Italy, 1968* (London: Wesleyan University Press).

Seckinelgin, Hakan. 2006. "Civil Society between the State and Society? Turkish Women with Muslim Headscarves." *Critical Social Policy* 26.4: 748–69.

Secor, J. Anna. 2002. "The Veil and Urban Space in Istanbul: Women's Dress, Mobility, and Islamic Knowledge." *Gender, Place, and Culture* 9.1: 5–22.

Sedgwick, Eve Kosofsky. 1990. *Epistemology of the Closet* (Berkeley: University of California Press).

Seidman, Steven, et al. 1999. "Beyond the Closet? The Changing Social Meaning of Homosexuality in the United States." *Sexualities* 2.1: 9–34.

Seral, Gulsah. 2000. "Virginity Testing in Turkey: The Legal Context," in *Women and Sexuality in Muslim Societies*, ed. Pinar Ilkkaracan (Istanbul: Women for Women's Human Rights), 413–16.

Shively, Kim. 2002. *Body and Nation: Religious Radicalism and Nationalist Discourse in Modern Turkey*. Ph.D. diss., Brandeis University.

Sirman, Nukhet. 1989. "Feminism in Turkey: A Short History." *New Perspectives on Turkey* 3.1: 1–34.

———. 2004. "Kinship, Politics, and Love: Honour in Post-Colonial Contexts: The Case of Turkey," in *Violence in the Name of Honour: Theoretical and Political Challenges*, eds. Shahrzad Mojab and Nahla Abdo (Istanbul: Bilgi University Press), 39–57.

Skeggs, Beverley. 1997. *Formations of Class and Gender: Becoming Respectable* (London: Sage).

Sprengnether, Madelon. 1990. *The Spectral Mother: Freud, Feminism, and Psychoanalysis* (Ithaca, NY: Cornell University Press).

Srivastava, Sanjay. 2007. *Passionate Modernity: Sexuality, Class, and Consumption in India* (New Delhi: Routledge India).

Stokes, Martin. 1994. "Turkish Arabesk and the City: Urban Popular Culture as Spatial Practices," in *Islam, Globalization, and Postmodernity*, eds. Ahmed Akbars and Donnan Hastings (London: Routledge), 21.

Talbot, Kirsten, and Michael Quayle. 2010. "The Perils of Being a Nice Guy: Contextual Variation in Five Young Women's Construction of Acceptable Hegemonic and Alternative Masculinities." *Men and Masculinities* 13.2: 255–78.

Tapınç, Huseyin. 1992. "Masculinity, Femininity, and Turkish Male Homosexuality," in *Modern Homosexualities: Fragments of Gay and Lesbian Experience*, ed. Ken Plummer (New York: Routledge), 39–53.

Tekeli, Sirin. 1981. "Women in Turkish Politics," in *Women in Turkish Society*, ed. Nermin Abadan Unat (Leiden: Brill), 293.

———. 1986. "Emergence of the Feminist Movement in Turkey," in *The New Women's Movement: Feminism and Political Power in Europe and the USA*, ed. Drude Dahlerup (London: Sage): 413–39.

Toksöz, Gulay. 2012. "The State of Female Labour in the Impasse of the Neoliberal Market and the Patriarchal Family," in *Gender and Society in Turkey: The Impact of Neoliberal Policies, Political Islam, and EU Accession*, eds. Saniye Dedeoglu and Adem Y. Elveren (London: Tauris), 47–64.

Tolman, Deborah. 1994. "Doing Desire: Adolescent Girls' Struggles for/with Sexuality." *Gender and Society* 8.3: 324–42.

Tsang, A. Ka Tat, and P. Sik Ying Ho. 2007. "Lost in Translation: Sex and Sexuality in Elite Discourse and Everyday Language." *Sexualities* 10.5: 623–44.

Tugal, Cihan. 2009. *Passive Revolution: Absorbing the Islamic Challenge to Capitalism* (Stanford, CA: Stanford University Press).

Turner, S. Bryan. 2002. "Strategic Generations: Historical Change, Literary Expression, and Generational Politics," in *Generational Consciousness, Narrative, and Politics*, eds. June Edmunds and Bryan Turner (New York: Rowman and Littlefield), 13–29.

Walkerdine, Valerie. 2003. "Reclassifying Upward Mobility: Femininity and the Neoliberal Subject." *Gender and Education* 15.3: 237–48.

Wallach Scott, Joan. 2007. "Gender as a Useful Category of Historical Analysis," in *Culture, Society, and Sexuality* (2nd edition), eds. Richard Parker and Peter Aggleton (London: Routledge), 61.

Weeks, Jeffrey. 1985. *Sexuality and Its Discontents: Meanings, Myths, and Modern Sexualities* (London: Routledge).

Weitman, Sasha. 1999. "On the Elementary Forms of the Socioerotic Life," in *Love and Eroticism*, ed. Mike Featherstone (London: Sage), 71–111.

Weston, Kath. 1995. "Forever Is a Long Time: Romancing the Real in Gay Kinship Ideologies," in *Naturalizing Power*, eds. Sylvia Yanagisako and Carol Delaney (New York: Routledge), 87–113.

Whitaker, Brian. 2006. *Unspeakable Love: Gay and Lesbian Life in the Middle East* (London: Dar al-Saqi).

White, Jenny B. 1994. *Money Makes Us Relatives: Women's Labor in Urban Turkey* (Austin: University of Texas Press).

———. 1999. "Islamic Chic," in *Istanbul: Between the Global and the Local*, ed. Caglar Keyder (Oxford: Rowman and Littlefield), 77–95.

———. 2002. "The Islamist Paradox," in *Fragments of Culture: The Everyday of Modern Turkey*, eds. Deniz Kandiyoti and Ayse Saktanber (London: Tauris), 191–218.

Winter, Bronwyn. 2006. "Secularism aboard the Titanic: Feminists and the Debate over the Hijab in France." *Feminist Studies* 32.2: 279–98.

Women for Women's Human Rights (WWHR). 2002. *The New Legal Status of Women in Turkey* (Istanbul: WWHER–New Ways).

———. 2005. *Turkish Civil and Penal Code Reforms from a Gender Perspective: The Success of Two Nationwide Campaigns* (Istanbul: WWHER–New Ways).

Yavuz, M. Hakan, and John L. Esposito. 2003. "Islam in Turkey: Retreat from the Secular Path?" in *Turkish Islam and the Secular State: The Gulen Movement*, eds. M. Hakan Yavuz and John L. Esposito (Syracuse, NY: Syracuse University Press), xiii–xxxiii.

Yerginar, Nur. 2000. *Din, Toplum ve Siyasal Sistem* [Religion, Society, and Political System]. (Istanbul: Baglam).

Young, Iris Marion. 1989. "The Ideal of Community and the Politics of Difference," in *Feminism/ Postmodernism*, ed. Linda Nicholson (London: Routledge), 300–323.

———. 1997. *Intersecting Voices: Dilemmas of Gender, Political Philosophy, and Policy* (Princeton, NJ: Princeton University Press).

Yüzgün, Arslan. 1986. *Türkiye'de eşcinsellik: Dün, bugün* [Homosexuality in Turkey: Yesterday, Today] (Istanbul: Hüryüz).

———. 1993. "Homosexuality and Police Terror in Turkey." *Journal of Homosexuality* 24.3–4: 159–69.

Ze'evi, Dror. 2006. *Producing Desire: Changing Sexual Discourse in the Ottoman Middle East, 1500–1900* (Berkeley: University of California Press).

Zihnioglu, Yaprak. 2003. *Kadınsiz İnkilap* [Revolution without Women] (Istanbul: Metis Yayinlari).

INDEX

Abortion rights, 19

Accumulation by dispossession, 313

Açık ortam (open milieu), 154

Adam, Barry, 253

Adkins, Lisa, 334n8

Agency, 127, 168

AKP. *See* Justice and Development Party

Aktif (inserter), 252, 253, 338n14; masculinity and, 255

Alcohol, 19, 186, 310, 311

Alemdaroglu, Ayca, 57

Allen, Louisa, 108

Altruism, 60, 125, 235

Ambivalence: of gays, 298–300; of mother's religiosity, 229; to passionate love, 218; of pious women, 200–201; upward mobility and, 38, 163–64; toward virginity, 141

Amnesty International, 317

Androgyny, 93, 99–100, 105, 323

Artificial virginity, 52

Aşk. See Passionate love

Assertive secularism, 8

Atatürk, Mustafa Kemal, 306, 310, 337n4

Autonomous self, 148

Autonomy, 1; feminism and, 324; in ideal relationships, 63–64, 65; privatization and, 114; pure love and, 31; upward mobility and, 26; virginity and, 55–57, 90

Bauman, Zygmunt, 38, 164

Bayan (lady), 47, 334n2

BDSM. *See* Bondage, Discipline, Sadism, Masochism

Beauty: headscarf and, 187; of women, 122

Become a Muslim (*hidayete ermek*), 185

Benjamin, Jessica, 26, 27–30, 112, 127, 143, 148

Bereket, Tarik, 253

Birth control, 42

Boğaziçi University, 4–5, 38–43; pious women at, 194–96; upper class at, 234

Bondage, Discipline, Sadism, Masochism (BDSM), 297

Bonds of Love (Benjamin), 29

Bourdieu, Pierre, 33–38, 52–53, 61, 122, 334n8

Bozdogan, Sibel, 6

Breast-feeding, 19, 316

Business: AKP and, 18; class and, 189; gays in, 288–91, 306; men in, 114–15; middle class in, 15; women in, 48, 123–24, 233. *See also* Labor force

Butler, Judith, 253

Capitalism, 1, 19–20, 109, 114, 235–36; gays and, 243; romantic love and, 32

Carpenter, Laura, 52–53

Charisma: femininity and, 121–24; vulnerable masculinity and, 165–66

Charismatic self, 132

China, gays in, 248

Citizenship, of women, 16–17

Civil Code, 250

Clandestinely (*gizli kapaklı*), 209

355

privatization of, 10–11; sexuality and, 75; upper-middle class and, 25, 263; vulnerable masculinity and, 163

Emotionality (*duygusallık*), 53, 89; of fathers, 118; of gays, 258; in long-term relationships, 122; romance and, 108; vulnerable masculinity and, 159, 162

Empathy, 89

Emphasized femininity, 29, 150

Empowerment: of pious women, 224; self-empowerment, 155; virginity and, 92

Energy-giving girls, 125–27, 322

Entrepreneurial freedom, 1, 114

Entrepreneurship of self, 107

Epistemology of the Closet (Sedgwick), 244

Equality, 31, 63, 123–24; AKP and, 312; gays and, 256, 257; gender, 17, 53–54, 156, 238; in ideal relationships, 64

Erbakan, Necmettin, 174

Erdoğan, Tayyip, 18–19, 313, 315, 316, 333n1

Erotic domination, 29–30

Eşcinsel (same sex), 283–84

EU. *See* European Union

Eurocentrism, 245–46

European Human Rights Commission, 174

European Union (EU), 7, 50, 175; feminism and, 17; gays and, 250

Façades: of gays, 5, 282, 299, 305–6; of lesbians, 97–98. *See also* Virginal façades

Faggot. See *İbne*

Family, 25, 103; feminism and, 16; gays and, 282–83, 301–4; selfhood and, 3, 23; tradition and, 19; virginal façades and, 68, 75–77. *See also* Head of family; Kinship; Parents; Patriarchy

Fast-breaking dinner in Ramadan (*iftar* dinner), 195, 311

Fathers: connectivity with, 261–62; domination by, 142, 151; emotionality of, 118; feminism and, 306, 323; gays and, 261–62, 274–78; gender roles of, 118; headscarf and, 178, 231; of pious women, 189,

198–99, 228–29, 231, 236–37; protective masculinity and, 113–20; provider role of, 114, 116, 118, 318, 321; religiosity of, 309–10; risk taking and, 116; self-denial of, 116, 151; women and, 306

Female desire, 27, 123; ideal man and, 214; in ideal relationships, 65–67; of lesbians, 94–95, 101–2, 104; for masculinity, 58–63, 151–52; nonexpression of, 83; parents and, 127; selfhood and, 321; selfishness and, 145; vulnerable masculinity and, 138, 166

Femininity, 23, 120–33; emphasized, 29, 150; equality and, 123–24; feminism and, 87; of gays, 252, 296–97; gender roles and, 124; hegemonic masculinity and, 150; housewifery and, 86; ideal, 122–23, 156; of lesbians, 100; love and, 27; masculinity and, 109–10; maternal selflessness and, 127, 318; new definition of, 322; positive girls and, 125–27, 151; power and, 29, 150; risk taking and, 124; romance and, 108, 151–52; romantic utopia and, 33; selfhood and, 57; selfishness and, 121–24, 151; selfless, 3, 21, 26, 55, 126, 321; sexual guilt and, 80–87; sexuality and, 85; tradition of, 57; virginity and, 80–87

Feminism: AKP and, 91; autonomy and, 324; domestic violence and, 18; empathy and, 89; fathers and, 306, 323; femininity and, 87; gender roles and, 197; head of family and, 320; headscarf ban and, 175–77; honor crimes and, 50–51; honor killings and, 18; Islam and, 18, 170, 176, 196, 336n9; Koran and, 336n9; lesbians and, 93–106; maternal selflessness and, 196; parents and, 84–85; pious women and, 196–98, 228; politics and, 16–17; power from, 78; psychoanalytical, 26, 27–30; secularism and, 18; sexuality and, 78–79; virginity and, 18, 52

103, 296; mothers and, 97–98, 105–6;
passion of, 100; passive resistance and,
93–106; romance of, 100; self-making
of, 105–6; sexual secrecy of, 98; violence against, 305; virginity and, 98, 101
LGBT. *See* Gays; Lesbians; Transgenders
Logic, marriage of, 219–23, 320
Long-term relationships, 122. *See also*
Marriage
"Lost in Translation" (A. Ka Tat Tsang and
P. Sik Ying Ho), 45–46
Love (*sevgi*), 204; femininity and, 27; by
gays, 257–59, 301; gender and, 27–30;
intimacy and, 64; men and, 226; in
patriarchy, 112; pious women and,
236–37; protective masculinity and,
112; submission and, 112; utopia and,
32–33; varieties of, 30–33; virginity and,
53, 71; vulnerable masculinity and,
159–60; women and, 108, 162. *See also*
Passionate love
Lovemaking (*sevişme*), 85

Macroeconomic policies, of neoliberalism, 15
Male ego, 126, 158
Male youth morality (*delikanlı ahlakı*),
287
Mannheim, Karl, 20, 169–70, 226, 230–31
Marriage: adverse feelings toward, 56–57;
AKP and, 315, 316; of compatibility,
219–23, 320; corporeal compatibility
and, 216–23; domesticity and, 75;
equality in, 24; of gays, 291; gender
roles in, 119, 220, 320; gender segregation in, 119; head of family and, 320;
Islam and, 320; of logic, 219–23, 320;
in middle class, 226; of parents, 119,
320; passionate love and, 207, 209–11;
of patriarchy, 219–23; of pious women,
203–4, 219–23; rape and, 50; romantic
love and, 31; selfishness in, 147; sexuality in, 138–39; subjecthood from, 225;

virginity and, 43, 49–50; vulnerable
masculinity and, 138–39
Masculinity, 23, 107–66; *aktif* and, 255;
boundaries of, 61; class and, 61, 140;
dependency and, 126; domination and,
144; female desire for, 58–63, 151–52;
femininity and, 109–10; freedom and,
144; gays and, 252; of ideal man, 58–63,
215; of lesbians, 100, 103, 296; maternal
selflessness and, 143; middle class and,
108–9; in neoliberal capitalism, 114;
neoliberalism and, 107–52; new definition of, 322; nonhegemonic, 59, 135;
paternalism and, 142–50; patriarchy
and, 59, 110–11, 113–20; power and, 29;
premarital sex and, 55; romance and,
108, 151–52; romantic utopia and, 33;
selfhood and, 110; self-making and, 111;
sexuality and, 27; upper class and, 113,
305; upper-middle class and, 113. *See
also* Hegemonic masculinity; Patriarchy; Protective masculinity; Vulnerable masculinity
Massad, Joseph, 245–46
Masturbation, 40–41
Maternal selflessness, 124; femininity and,
318; feminism and, 196; masculinity
and, 143; patriarchy and, 127; pious
women and, 198–201; rejection of, 143
McLeod, Julie, 333n6
Media, 11
Memur kafası (mind of government employee), 114, 115, 116
Men: in business, 114–15; charismatic
women and, 121–24; femininity and,
120–33; *fitrat* and, 19, 238; heterosexual,
6, 107–52; love and, 226; male ego of,
126, 158; neoliberal masculinity and,
107–52; positive girls and, 125–27; selfish
women and, 121–24; self-making of,
107; sexuality and, 108, 162. *See also* Fathers; Gays; Head of family; Ideal man;
Masculinity; Paternalism; Patriarchy

and, 177–88; headscarf ban and, 192;

kissing by, 118; marriage of, 119, 320;

obedience of, 192–93; pious women

and, 188–93; religiosity of, 190–91,

309–10; romantic love and, 31; self-

sacrifice of, 193; sexuality and, 334n7;

upward mobility and, 193; virginal

façades and, 129–30; virginity and,

71–73; vulnerable masculinity and,

132, 135–36, 139–42. See also Fathers;

Mothers

Parla, Ayse, 51–52

Parliament, quota system in, 17–18

Pascoe, C. J., 338n12

Pasha. See Müren, Zeki

Pasif (receiver), 252–53, 338n14

Passion: of lesbians, 100; love and, 30–33;

Passionate love (*aşk*), 137, 203–11; ambiva-

lence to, 218; corporeal compatibility

and, 218; dangers of, 203–11; education

and, 207; marriage and, 207, 209–11;

pious women and, 203–11; sexuality

Passive male "homosexuality" (*ubnah*),

337n11

Passive resistance, lesbians and, 93–106

Passivity, 31; of gays, 252; of mothers,

142–43

Paternalism: declining power of, 7;

hegemonic masculinity and, 150;

masculinity and, 142–50; neoliberal

capitalism and, 109; patriarchy and, 16,

150; privatization and, 319; protective

masculinity in, 151; welfare system and,

Patriarchy: Atatürk and, 306; charismatic

self and, 132; connectivity and, 26;

domination in, 134; fathers and, 116,

306; feminine and, 23; guilt and, 26;

hegemonic masculinity and, 150; ideal

man and, 58–63; of Islam, 168; kin-

ship in, 24; love in, 112; marriage of,

219–23; masculinity and, 23, 59, 110–11,

113–20; maternal selflessness and, 127;

obedience in, 134; paternalism and, 16,

150; protective masculinity and, 112;

psychoanalysis and, 27; romance and,

59; selfishness and, 148; subjecthood

and, 112; unconscious structure of, 26;

upward mobility and, 318; valued self

and, 132; virginity and, 48, 92; vulner-

able masculinity and, 140–42; with

Peer groups: gays and, 279; sexuality and,

68–69, 334n7; virginity and, 68–69;

Physical appearance: androgyny in, 323;

headscarf and, 185; of ideal man, 60;

vulnerable masculinity and, 155–56; of

women, 122. See also Clothing

Pious women, 6, 167–242; agency of, 168;

altruism and, 235; ambivalence of,

200–201; at Boğaziçi University, 194–

96; capitalism and, 235–36; class and,

235; clothing and, 168; consumption

culture and, 168; crafting selves by,

177–88; domesticity and, 227; dressing

cabin for, 167; dressing plainly and,

228–42; empowerment of, 224; fathers

of, 189, 198–99, 228–29, 231, 236–37;

feminism and, 196–98, 228; gender

equality and, 238; gender roles and,

238–39; gender segregation and, 177,

224; generation of actuality and, 169;

habitus and, 225; headscarf and, 177–

88; headscarf ban and, 167, 168, 170,

171–77; hegemonic masculinity and,

201–3; ideal man for, 204, 211–23, 232;

intimacy and, 236–37; Islam and, 201–

3; Koran and, 231; leisure and, 168;

ABOUT THE AUTHOR

Gul Ozyegin is Associate Professor of Sociology and Gender, Sexuality, and Women's Studies at the College of William and Mary. She is the author of *Untidy Gender: Domestic Service in Turkey* and editor of *Gender and Sexuality in Muslim Cultures.*